Hybrid AI Architectures for Intelligent Systems

Surbhi Bhatia Khan
University of Salford, UK

Shikha Khullar
https://orcid.org/0009-0000-5598-3145
Poornima University, India

Muhammad Attique Khan
https://orcid.org/0009-0001-2023-6980
Prince Mohammad Bin Fahd University, Saudi Arabia

Udit Mamodiya
https://orcid.org/0000-0002-8022-4252
Poornima University, India

Manju Lata Joshi
https://orcid.org/0000-0002-0749-6171
Poornima University, India

IGI Global
Scientific Publishing
Publishing Tomorrow's Research Today

Vice President of Editorial Melissa Wagner
Director of Acquisitions Mikaela Felty
Director of Book Development Jocelynn Hessler
Production Manager Mike Brehm
Cover Design Jose Rosado

Published in the United States of America by
IGI Global Scientific Publishing
701 East Chocolate Avenue
Hershey, PA, 17033, USA
Tel: 717-533-8845 | Fax: 717-533-7115
Website: https://www.igi-global.com E-mail: cust@igi-global.com

Library of Congress Cataloging-in-Publication Data

LCCN: (CIP Data Pending)
ISBN13: 9798260000083
Isbn13Softcover: 9798260000090
EISBN13: 9798260000106
British Cataloguing in Publication Data
A Cataloguing in Publication record for this book is available from the British Library.

Table of Contents

Detailed Table of Contents

Smriti Sethi, Amity Institute of Psychology and Allied Sciences, Amity University, Noida, India
Anupama Jha, VSIT, VIPS-TC, India
Soleman Alzobidy, College of Sciences and Theoretical Studies, Saudi Electronic University, Saudi Arabia
Abhinav Pathak, School of Technology Management and Engineering, SVKM's NMIMS Indore, India
D. Stalin David, Vel Tech Multi Tech Dr. Rangarajan Dr. Sakunthala Engineering College, Chennai, India
Anil Pandurang Gaikwad, Savitribai Phule Pune University, Maharashtra, India

The role of emotion recognition of speech in intelligent systems that are aware of affect is becoming more and more significant, but the issue of reliably detecting human emotions based on speech is hard to achieve because of the confounding effects of vocal expression and linguistic interpretation. Most of the current methods give more emphasis on either acoustic information or text based information, which limits them in their applicability when emotional information are nuanced, context-specific or poorly manifested. This paper presents a hybrid speech emotion recognition system which combines deep acoustic modeling with semantic emotion analysis which is carried out by natural language processing. It uses the pipeline of parallel acoustic and linguistic processing, and an adaptive strategy of fusion that can balance modality contributions in a dynamic manner, instead of using the fixed-modality concatenation of features. This design makes emotional patterns emerge as a result of the coordination between acoustic and semantic interaction.

hybrid training approaches are described and the issues associated with scalability, noise, and hardware limitations are discussed.

Suchita Arora, Poornima University, India
Rajashree Tukaram Gadhave, Pillai HOC College of Engineering and Technology, India
Navruzbek Shavkatov, Tashkent State University of Economics, Tashkent, Uzbekistan
Mahesh Soni, Independent Researcher, USA
D. Stalin David, Vel Tech Multi Tech Dr. Rangarajan Dr. Sakunthala Engineering College, Chennai, India
Mukesh Soni, Lovely Professional University, Phagwara, India

The extreme proliferation of intelligent applications on the spectrum of cyber-physical systems has revealed structural dis-alignment between inertial cloud-centric AI implementations and the dynamic nature of the real-time, heterogeneous workload. Present hybrid architectures are largely based on rigid task allocation or rule-based coordination, and do not provide flexibility when workload intensity and mixed computational requirements vary. The chapter suggests a hybrid AI system that closely combines edge intelligence, cloud-native coordination, and high-performance computing via learning-based coordination. The framework allows the migration of the intelligence to be adapted according to the workload nature, state of the system, and performance feedback as opposed to binding the models to fixed layers. High-performance resources are not considered passive accelerators, but instead viewed as active decision partners, which allows them to be optimized on a scale and make inferences in real-time.

The transition from Industry 4.0 and Industry 5.0 to Industry 6.0 is driving the change of industrial systems towards increasingly complex socio-technical ecosystems, where physical systems, digital systems, artificial intelligence and people work together. As a result, the Industrial Metaverse is emerging as a critical infrastructure that enables constant interaction between real and virtual systems throughout their industrial lifecycle. However, conventional architectures based on classical computing, present limitations in scalability, sustainability, resilience and governance. To address these challenges, this chapter introduces the Holonic Quantum–Neuromorphic Project Engineering (HQPE) framework as an architectural and methodological reference for the design, deployment and operation of Industrial Metaverses in the context of Industry 6.0. The framework integrates cyber-physical systems, holonic principles and hybrid artificial intelligence supported by BIM and PLM environments.

Quantum neural networks (QNNs) offer a principled pathway for integrating quantum computation with machine learning through superposition- and entanglement-based representations. This chapter proposes an architecture-aware design and evaluation framework for modern QNNs, emphasizing robustness and system feasibility alongside predictive performance. Multiple architecturesvariational QNNs, quantum convolutional neural networks, tensor-network hybrids, and fully quantum models—are assessed under a unified protocol. Experimental analysis shows that the proposed architecture-search–guided QNN achieves 91.8% classification accuracy and an F1-score of 0.914, outperforming fixed-template variational QNNs by approximately 5.6 percentage points. Under depolarizing noise with probability $p = 0.10$, the proposed model retains 85.3% accuracy, whereas baseline QNNs fall below 80%.

Preface

INTRODUCTION

Artificial Intelligence is entering a transformative era in which single-paradigm solutions are no longer sufficient to address the complexity, scale, and dynamism of modern intelligent systems. Classical machine learning, deep neural networks, edge computing, federated frameworks, and quantum-enhanced models each provide remarkable capabilities. However, when deployed in isolation, these paradigms often encounter limitations related to scalability, energy efficiency, latency, interpretability, or robustness. The future of AI lies not in replacement, but in integration—through hybrid architectures that unify complementary strengths across computational, algorithmic, and infrastructural domains.

Hybrid AI architectures represent a structural shift in how intelligence is designed, deployed, and sustained. Rather than confining models to rigid computational layers or fixed processing pipelines, hybrid systems promote adaptive coordination between modalities, infrastructures, and learning paradigms. Whether through edge–cloud collaboration in smart cities, federated learning for privacy-preserving cybersecurity, or quantum–classical neural integrations for advanced pattern recognition, hybridization enables systems to respond dynamically to environmental feedback and evolving workloads. These architectures reflect a broader rethinking of intelligence as distributed, context-aware, and continuously adaptive.

This edited volume brings together international scholars and researchers to explore the conceptual foundations, architectural innovations, performance optimizations, and future directions of hybrid AI systems. The contributions span speech emotion recognition, IoT-driven smart cities, privacy-aware cybersecurity, quantum neural networks, industrial metaverse infrastructures, and next-generation computing ecosystems. Collectively, the chapters demonstrate that hybrid AI is not a transitional phase—it is a defining framework for intelligent systems of the future.

CHAPTER OVERVIEW

Chapter 1: Hybrid Speech Emotion Recognition System Using Machine Learning and Natural Language Processing

This chapter introduces a multimodal framework that integrates deep acoustic modeling with semantic emotion analysis through natural language processing. By employing parallel acoustic and linguistic pipelines with adaptive fusion strategies, the proposed system dynamically balances modality contributions. The architecture captures nuanced emotional signals arising from the interplay between vocal tone and linguistic meaning, moving beyond fixed feature concatenation approaches and advancing affect-aware intelligent systems.

Chapter 2: Integrating IoT and Hybrid Data Architectures for Effective Smart City Governance and Management

Expanding beyond infrastructure efficiency, this contribution integrates governance feedback loops directly into hybrid data pipelines. The architecture supports real-time sensing, analysis, and policy action, significantly reducing decision latency and improving energy utilization. By merging computational intelligence with administrative functionality, the chapter repositions hybrid AI as a core enabler of responsive urban governance.

Chapter 3: Natural Language Processing with Hybrid Quantum Neural Networks – Models, Methods, and Future Directions

This chapter explores Hybrid Quantum Neural Networks (HQNNs) for NLP tasks, combining classical neural architectures with quantum-enhanced representations. It presents foundational concepts in quantum computing, quantum data encoding, hybrid training strategies, and semantic modeling while addressing scalability and hardware constraints. Applications across text classification, sentiment analysis, and machine translation illustrate the transformative potential of quantum–classical integration.

Chapter 4: Integration of Hybrid AI with Cloud Edge and High Performance Computing

Here, hybrid AI is framed as a coordinated ecosystem spanning edge intelligence, cloud-native orchestration, and high-performance computing (HPC). Rather than static allocation, the proposed architecture enables learning-based migration of computational tasks across layers. HPC resources function as active decision partners, enhancing real-time inference and large-scale optimization.

Chapter 5: Integrating Machine Learning with Federated Learning for Privacy-Preserving Cyber Threat Detection

This contribution addresses the tension between centralized threat detection and privacy requirements. By unifying adaptive local learning, robust aggregation mechanisms, and secure coordination protocols, the proposed framework enhances generalization across heterogeneous clients while preserving sensitive data. The chapter positions hybrid federated architectures as critical for secure distributed ecosystems.

Chapter 6: A Cloud–Edge–Fog Hybrid Architecture for Productive IoT-Based Smart City Operation

Introducing a Cloud–Edge–Fog Hybrid (CEFH) framework, this chapter employs reinforcement learning to coordinate computational tasks dynamically across distributed layers. Empirical results demonstrate improvements in latency, energy savings, and task success rates, highlighting the architectural importance of multi-tiered hybrid intelligence in urban systems.

Chapter 7: Optimized Quantum-Enhanced Neural Network Architectures – Advanced Algorithms, Applications, and Performance Improvements Across Computational Frameworks

This chapter proposes a performance-optimized quantum-enhanced neural architecture that selectively integrates variational quantum circuits within classical feature pipelines. Emphasizing stability and resource awareness, the twin-engine design demonstrates consistent performance improvements across classical, hybrid, and quantum-enhanced configurations.

Chapter 8: Holonic Quantum–Neuromorphic Project Engineering: An Open Architecture for the Industrial Electrical Metaverse

Positioned within the evolution toward Industry 6.0, this chapter introduces the Holonic Quantum–Neuromorphic Project Engineering (HQPE) framework. Integrating cyber-physical systems, holonic design principles, and hybrid AI within

BIM and PLM environments, the framework addresses scalability, sustainability, and governance challenges in the emerging Industrial Metaverse.

Chapter 9: Design and Analysis of Modern Quantum Neural Network Architectures for Intelligent Systems

This chapter presents an architecture-aware evaluation framework for quantum neural networks, assessing variational, convolutional, tensor-network, and fully quantum models. Through architecture-search guidance, the proposed model demonstrates improved accuracy, robustness under noise, and reduced circuit depth, emphasizing feasibility alongside performance.

Chapter 10: The Future of Artificial Intelligence: Quantum Neural Networks as the Next Frontier

Concluding the technical trajectory, this chapter proposes an advanced Hybrid QNN architecture incorporating adaptive entanglement control and quantum regularization for NISQ-era hardware. Demonstrated improvements in accuracy, convergence speed, and energy efficiency position quantum-enhanced hybrid systems as a pivotal next step in AI evolution.

CONCLUSION

The chapters in this volume collectively affirm that hybridization is not merely a methodological enhancement—it is a structural paradigm for the next generation of intelligent systems. Across speech processing, smart city infrastructures, cybersecurity, industrial engineering, and quantum machine learning, the contributions reveal a consistent principle: adaptive coordination between diverse computational paradigms produces systems that are more resilient, efficient, and context-aware than their single-framework counterparts.

A recurring theme throughout the book is the transformation of static architectures into living ecosystems. Edge, cloud, fog, and high-performance computing resources evolve from isolated infrastructures into collaborative agents. Classical and quantum models shift from competitive alternatives to synergistic partners. Governance, policy, and intelligence converge through feedback-integrated data pipelines. This systemic integration signals a redefinition of AI as an interconnected, distributed intelligence fabric.

As editors, we envision this volume serving multiple communities: researchers exploring hybrid quantum neural models, engineers designing real-time edge–cloud systems, policymakers seeking intelligent governance infrastructures, and industry practitioners navigating the transition toward Industry 6.0 and beyond. The book offers both conceptual grounding and empirical validation, highlighting measurable improvements in latency, energy efficiency, accuracy, scalability, and robustness.

Hybrid AI architectures will continue to evolve as quantum hardware matures, federated ecosystems expand, and smart environments proliferate. Yet the central insight will remain constant: intelligent systems achieve their highest potential when complementary paradigms are harmonized rather than isolated. It is our hope that this collection stimulates further interdisciplinary collaboration, inspires innovative architectural designs, and contributes meaningfully to shaping the intelligent systems of tomorrow.

Chapter 1

Hybrid Speech Emotion Recognition System Using Machine Learning and Natural Language Processing

Smriti Sethi
http://orcid.org/0000-0002-6273-9607
Amity Institute of Psychology and Allied Sciences, Amity University, Noida, India

Abhinav Pathak
http://orcid.org/0000-0001-7885-2359
School of Technology Management and Engineering, SVKM's NMIMS Indore, India

Anupama Jha
VSIT, VIPS-TC, India

D. Stalin David
Vel Tech Multi Tech Dr. Rangarajan Dr. Sakunthala Engineering College, Chennai, India

Soleman Alzobidy
College of Sciences and Theoretical Studies, Saudi Electronic University, Saudi Arabia

Anil Pandurang Gaikwad
Savitribai Phule Pune University, Maharashtra, India

ABSTRACT

The role of emotion recognition of speech in intelligent systems that are aware of affect is becoming more and more significant, but the issue of reliably detecting human emotions based on speech is hard to achieve because of the confounding effects of vocal expression and linguistic interpretation. Most of the current methods give more emphasis on either acoustic information or text based information, which limits them in their applicability when emotional information are nuanced,

DOI: 10.4018/979-8-2600-0008-3.ch001

context-specific or poorly manifested. This paper presents a hybrid speech emotion recognition system which combines deep acoustic modeling with semantic emotion analysis which is carried out by natural language processing. It uses the pipeline of parallel acoustic and linguistic processing, and an adaptive strategy of fusion that can balance modality contributions in a dynamic manner, instead of using the fixed-modality concatenation of features. This design makes emotional patterns emerge as a result of the coordination between acoustic and semantic interaction.

1. INTRODUCTION

Human speech is not only a vehicle of lexical meaning. In each utterance one can hear very slight signals of emotions, intonation change, changes of rhythm, spectral changes, semantic undertone, which can be more reliable predictors of the internal state of the speaker than utterances alone. Computational interpretation of the signals of these emotions has become the focus of more and more intelligent systems today, especially as human-machine interaction ceases to be a matter of transactional mode to more direct empathetic and contextual communication. Speech Emotion Recognition (SER), thus, is a critically important intersection of signal processing, machine learning, and natural language understanding, being a building block of emotionally intelligent artificial systems. Over the past few years, SER has dramatically grown in relevance to other areas including affective computing, conversational agents, mental health monitoring, human-robot interaction and adaptive learning systems. It is not only a technological but also a societal growth. With more and more artificial intelligence systems engaging in more emotionally sensitive applications, such as therapy chatbots, assistive robots, customer support agents, the impact of not understanding or being able to interpret all of these emotional signals become not simply a non-issue of concern. Cathy and Pradeepkumar (2025) emphasize this change by presenting the fact that emotion-aware speech processing can considerably improve the emotional intelligence of the responses provided by large language models (LLM), making machines not only react properly but also respond appropriately to human affective states. Emotion recognition in speech is a difficult issue even though there has been sustained research interest in the same. Emotional expression is subjective by nature, situationally determined, culturally shaped, and changing with time. What one speaker would consider as acoustic features of anger, there could be another who would view it as excitement or stress. The noise of the environment, variability of speakers and the conditions of recording and linguistic diversity also make it even harder to infer emotions reliably. Early SER systems used acoustic features which were handcrafted (pitch, energy, and formants) together with standard classifiers. Though one of the foundational ones, they did not scale out to large datasets and in a controlled setting (Rao et al., 2024).

The introduction of deep learning brought a paradigm shift in the research of SER. Convolutional Neural Networks (CNNs), Recurrent Neural Networks (RNNs) and their variants proved to be more effective in learning hierarchical and temporal representation of speech signals in raw or transformed form. Kadam et al. (2024) reported that CNNs that were trained with Mel-Frequency Cepstral Coefficients (MFCCs) had a higher capability than the conventional classifiers to capture localized spectral patterns that were associated with emotional expression. Equally, it has been demonstrated that hybrid CNN-BiLSTM models can be successfully used to represent the spatial and temporal relationships of speech signals, enhancing multicategoric recognition accuracy through a variety of emotional categories (Rani and Ramaiya, 2024).

Nonetheless, speech emotion recognition is not entirely an acoustic issue. More frequently, emotional meaning can be a product of the interaction between the manner of saying and the content of saying. Vocal emotional cues can be supported or opposed by linguistic mechanisms such as word choice, syntactic organization and semantic polarity. This fact has led to a surge in attention to the research of Natural Language Processing (NLP)-based emotion analysis, in which textual speech transcriptions are processed with the tools of machine learning and semantic modeling. Suganya et al. (2024) offer an NLP-based approach in its entirety, showing that the performance of emotion recognition is better when the linguistic features are used to supplement the acoustic representations. Lone NLP-based recognition of emotions systems have their limitations, however. The textual models can also miss out on prosodic intensity, sarcasm or emphasis of emotions as expressed through the voice. According to Anitha (2025), NLP and ML algorithm detection of the emotional tones frequently fail in situations where the semantics are undecided or neutral despite a high degree of vocal affect. As a result, the acoustic and textual modalities do not always serve to describe the entire range of emotions that are involved in natural speech.

It is this realization that has triggered a transition to hybrid and multimodal emotion recognition models, in which the speech cues and linguistic information are both processed concurrently. A multimodal AI system that combines voice-based and text-based emotion recognition is suggested by Sharma (2025), and it proves to be stronger in comprehending emotions. On the same note, Venkateswari (2025) investigates hybrid sentiment analysis, which involves the combination of voice-based attributes with other features of sentiment as seen in opinion-rich tasks such as movie reviews. All these studies tend to imply that emotion should be viewed as a multimodal phenomenon and not a one-dimensional indicator. In hybrid structures, architecture design is crucial. The recent research practice is becoming more and more inclined to deep hybrid models which combine CNN-based feature extractors with LSTM-based sequence models and attention. In their proposal, Makhmudov et al. (2024) suggest a hybrid CNNLSTM architecture with attention layers to weigh dynamically speech segments that have an emotional salience. Attention-based fusion enables the models to highlighter important parts of time, and downplay the irrelevant or noisy data, hence improving the discrimination of emotions. Nugroho et al. (2025) also turn this direction in which prosodic spatio-temporal feature fusion with attention mechanisms is proposed, and the time-varying emotional prosody is explicitly modeled. Third, interpretability and adaptability have not been fully explored especially in dynamic human-related environments where emotional states change with time. According to Mamodiya et al. (2025), this shortcoming is emphasized in the framework of human-robot interaction because emotion recognition systems need to be used in real time and adjust to the context and task requirements.

Besides, replication and additive changes of hybrid models are still prevalent. Even more recent works that offer frameworks of advanced hybrid deep learning tend to vary in small features to extract or the depth of the network (Lenka et al., 2025a; Lenka et al., 2025b). Gawali (2025) also observes that most SER systems are very accurate with the compromise of scalability and ability to deploy them. The other major constraint is lack of sufficient integration of semantic emotion modeling. Although textual emotion recognition has developed to maturity using sentiment analysis and transformer-based representations, its integration with speech-based emotion detection is loosely coupled in most hybrid systems. Sohel et al. (2024) note that discrete emotion recognition of speech data is usually helped by deep hybrid structures, but the combination of semantic emotion descriptions is usually considered an auxiliary, but not a fundamental element.

The suggested framework makes use of effective acoustic feature extraction, including MFCCs and prosodic descriptors, that are processed by deep learning framework that can capture local spectral patterns and long-term time dependencies. Simultaneously, NLP-based emotion model techniques are used to extract semantic affective information in speech transcripts through analyzing the speech. With the combination of these representations into a hybrid learning architecture, the system is able to have a more holistic view of the expression of emotion than those of the unimodal methods.

Not just the hybridization is novel but also the manner in which hybridization is operationalized. Compared to the previous models that address speech and text as loosely connected input, the suggested system focuses on concurrent feature fusion and emotion-conscious representation learning. This methodology is consistent with the new findings that emotional meaning is dynamic and multi-modal, as opposed to existing in discrete signaling portions (Nugroho et al., 2025). Moreover, the framework is created keeping the adaptability, which allows it to be deployed in interactive systems, including emotionally responsive conversational agents and assistive robots.

In a bigger context, this will be a part of the developing discussion of AI with regard to being emotionally intelligent. There is no use denying the fact as Cathy and Pradeepkumar (2025) claim that the improvement of the emotional intelligence of AI-based systems is not only a performance optimization issue but a step to more ethical, empathetic, and social-oriented technologies. Combining machine learning and NLP in a single SER model, this chapter contributes to the methodological rigor and the relevance in the application.

To conclude, this introduction has presented the motivation, challenges and research gaps in the modern speech emotion recognition, with limitations of unimodal and loosely coupled hybrid systems. The suggested hybrid SER system addresses these gaps by providing a highly structured, adaptive and semantically informed framework of acoustic and linguistic emotion cues integration. The rest of this chapter describes how the system is architectured, learning methodologies, experimental evaluation and the implications of the study to the development of future emotion intelligent systems.

2. LITERATURE REVIEW

The Speech Emotion Recognition (SER) research has also been developing steadily during the last ten years, transitioning to data-driven hybrid learning models as opposed to rule-based signal analysis. Initial research was mostly based on the manual crafting of acoustic properties and shallow classifiers, whereas recent research put emphasis on deep networks, multimodal fusion, and attention-based modeling. In this section, the literature on the current literature is reviewed focusing on hybrid machine learning methods, deep learning models, linguistic integration, and the new challenges facing them including corpus bias, generalization and real-world deployment..

2.1 Traditional Machine Learning Foundations in SER

Prior to the success of deep learning, speech-based emotion recognition was based on the handcrafted features and classical machine learning models. These methods formed the conceptual framework of SER that determined acoustic cues including pitch, energy, spectral centroid, and speaking rate. Barua (2024) returns to this step and illustrates how even the traditional classifiers, such as Support Vector Machines and k-Nearest Neighbors, can perform reasonably when combined with effective feature extractor. Nonetheless, these systems are extremely sensitive to variability of speakers and conditions of recording.On the same note, Krishna and Lal (2025) argue about speech processing pipes whereby statistical acoustic features are projected into discrete emotional categories. Though computationally efficient, these models have problems with temporal effects and emotional switching between longer utterances. The paper by Shareefunnisa et al. (2024) also substantiates this shortcoming by comparing the two methods of classical machine learning algorithms, which prove to be inferior to deep learning models as emotional expression gets subtle or context-specific.All of these studies point to one fundamental short of conventional SER systems: it is not just that emotional expression is dynamic but that to reflect this temporal richness, static feature vectors cannot be sufficiently rich to capture it..

2.2 Deep Learning and Temporal Modeling in Speech Emotion Recognition

The implementation of deep learning has become a revolution in SER research. Recurrent architectures and in particular the Long Short-Term Memory (LSTM) networks were shown to have a stronger capability of learning temporal correlations in speech signals. The hybrid LSTMTransformer architecture in the article by IEEE Access (2022) is one of the initial attempts to combine the idea of sequential learning with global attention. The model utilizes the ability of Transformer-based self-attention to overcome the inability of LSTM to model long-range dependence, which leads to a higher accuracy in emotion classification. Later literature developed this concept. A hybrid architecture that is suggested by Norval and Wang (2024) involves cautious preprocessing and intensive temporal modelling, with a focus on the strategies of normalization and segmentation. Hasan et al. (2025) present the text-independent EmoFormer which is a hybrid Transformer-CNN model that is intended to decrease the reliance on language. Although it does a very well job of recognizing emotion when used by a speaker unaware of the other individual, the model loses semantic context which may prove to be very important in conversational context. A more general conflict in SER research to which this trade-off can be applied is between acoustic purity and contextual richness.

2.3 CNN-Based Feature Learning and Spectrogram Representations

The CNNs have become a part of SER owing to their capacity to train discriminative patterns of time-frequency representations like Spectrograms and Mel-scaled features. Improving Multi-Modal Hybrid, Speech Emotion Recognition with CNN (2025) shows that CNNs are more effective in the recognition of localized spectral information related to the intensity of emotions. Djeridi et al. (2025) further apply this method to the Arabic speech emotion recognition by using the combination of acoustic waveforms and spectrogram based features as a hybrid deep learning. Namey et al. (2024) take a more biological route and offer CochleaSpecNet that combines the idea of cochleagram and spectrogram representations by training an attention-based CNNGRU network. This bi-channel architecture is based on human hearing, and it demonstrates its high performance on various sets of data. According to such approaches, the perceptual-based representation can enhance emotional sensitivity of SER systems..

2.4 Hybrid Deep Learning Architectures and Feature Fusion

Hybridization has become one of the trends of contemporary SER research. Newer systems are not based on one model type, but rather on a combination of CNNs, RNNs, attention layers, and ensemble strategies to have the complementary attributes of speech signals. Bharshankar et al. (2025) introduce a smart emotion recognition system with the hybrid deep learning models on the basis of robustness and deployment feasibility. Chowdhury et al. (2025) introduce a new hybrid approach to deep learning, which is a combination of hand-engineered features engineering and the use of deep representation learning. Another hybrid direction is the research of Neethu and Kanaga (2025), which involves the integration of XGBoost and the deep learning models in multisource datasets. Their findings point out to the enhancement of generalization, especially when there is cross-corpus evaluation. This adds to the notion that hybrid learning does not represent a simple architectural complication but a bias/variance balancing strategy.

2.5 Cognitive and Emotion-Aware Fusion Models

Other than the architectural hybridization, other researchers are interested in cognitive and affective modeling. Chappidi (2024) presents a Cognitive Emotion Fusion Network, which is used to detect PTSD. This research focuses on emotion pathways and not on discrete emotional states, which makes SER suitable to mental health applications. The capability of the model to emotionally persist and volatilize is a breakthrough towards psychologically informed SER systems.Prabhakar and Won (2024) adopt a biomimetic method which includes the signal transforms and bio-inspired optimization methods. Their scheme shows that feature selection can be optimized, and classification stability can be increased using natural intelligence as the basis of the optimization strategies.

2.6 NLP Integration and Vocal Mood Detection

Even though SER traditionally focuses on acoustic cues, more and more authors use Natural Language Processing (NLP) to process semantic emotional indicators. Nagarajan (2025) discusses the possibility of determining vocal mood with the help of NLP, emphasizing that the assessment of textual sentiment may be used as an addition to acoustic indicators of emotions. Rani et al. (2025) also develop this point of view, considering sentiment analysis and emotional recognition together. According to their work, emotion and sentiment are not the same although they are related. Sentiment cues are useful in emotion recognition, but excessive use of text may mask the paralinguistic message like sarcasm or suppressed emotion.

2.7 Addressing Corpus Bias and Generalization Challenges

Corpus bias remains one of the challenges in SER research. Models that are trained based on particular datasets do not tend to be generalizable to speakers, languages, and even recording conditions. The authors of that paper, Chaugule and Sankaye (2025), focus directly on this concern and suggest a generalization-conscious hybrid framework based on metaheuristic feature selection. In a similar manner, Bharshankar et al. (2025) and Neethu and Kanaga (2025) prioritize the use of multisource training and adaptive learning to reduce the presence of the bias in the dataset. Such initiatives can be seen as a result of increasing recognition that SER systems are no longer to be optimized based on benchmarks but need to be geared towards real-life resilience.

2.8 Comparative Analyses and Emerging Research Gaps

Comparative studies still remain very important in the determination of boundaries of performance of SER. Shareefunnisa et al. (2024) offer empirical facts that indicate that hybrid deep learning models will always deliver better results compared to pure machine learning strategies, especially in circumstances of noise and emotional ambiguity. Even with the massive improvements, there are still a number of gaps. To begin with, not all hybrid SER systems are associated with principled fusion strategies but, instead, they tend to be based on feature concatenation instead of adaptive integration. Second, it is still not very interpretable, as it is hard to know why models will predict some emotions. Third, not many systems explicitly match the acoustic and semantic emotional cues at a representation level. The unresolved problems inspire the necessity to have hybrid frameworks that are not only accurate but also adaptive, interpretable and context-aware.

2.9 Summary and Research Direction

In short, the current state of SER study shows an evident trend of adopting hybrid deep learning models that combine both temporal modeling with spectral analysis and attention mechanisms with linguistic cues. Architectural diversity is demonstrated to be advantageous in studies as diverse as LSTM based networks through Transformer architecture (IEEE Access, 2022) to attention-based two-branch networks (Namey et al., 2024). The general impression provided in the literature is that upcoming SER systems should consider emotion as a multimodal and a temporally changing phenomenon. This understanding is the direct influence on the suggested hybrid speech emotion recognition model offered in this chapter that is expected to combine machine learning and NLP in a methodical, dynamic, and contextualized way.

3. METHODOLOGY

The given Hybrid Speech Emotion Recognition (SER) architecture is aimed at extraction of information about emotions coded in human speech by a systematic synthesis of acoustic signal processing, representation learning which is based on machine learning, and semantic analysis provided by the means of Natural Language Processing (NLP). In contrast to the traditional SER pipelines based on acoustic or textual cues separately, the suggested methodology considers emotion an object of multimodality when it is formed in the course of interaction between the expression of the voice and the word meaning. The section outlines the methodology design in a systematic study, explaining the data flow, feature extracting plans, learning structures, fusion schemes, and assessment protocol used in the framework.

3.1 Overall System Architecture

The general framework of the suggested system is based on the hierarchical design, which allows the separate optimization of the acoustic and linguistic levels of processing and provides a good integration on the representation level. The architecture includes five major parts, namely; (i) speech signal preprocessing, (ii) acoustic feature extraction and modeling, (iii) speech-to-text transcription and linguistic emotion analysis, (iv) hybrid feature fusion and emotion classification, and (v) performance evaluation and optimization. The system takes the raw speech audio as input and through a parallel acoustic and linguistic pipeline it processes it. The acoustic pipeline is concerned with the recording of prosodic, spectral and temporal of speech whereas the linguistic pipeline records semantic and affective data of text transcriptions. Both pipelines are brought together and combined in a hybrid learning structure to give the final emotion prediction.

Figure 1. Overall architecture of the proposed hybrid speech emotion recognition framework integrating acoustic signal processing, NLP-based semantic analysis, and hybrid learning-based emotion classification.

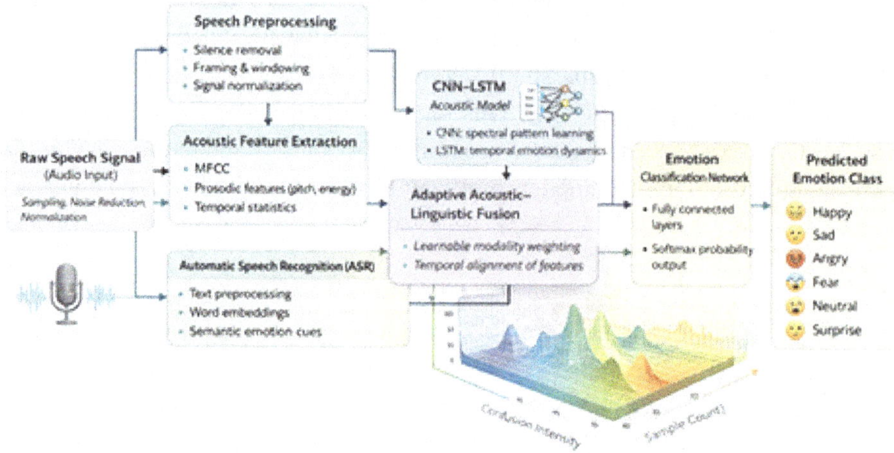

3.2 Speech Data Acquisition and Preprocessing

The signals proposed in the framework to use speech are expected to be sampled at a standard frequency (16 kHz or 44.1 kHz) and represented in uncompressed waveform formats to maintain signal fidelity. Preprocessing is an important process because raw audio may include noise, silence periods, and amplitude variations that may have a negative impact on feature extraction.

3.2.1 Noise Reduction and Signal Normalization

The spectral subtraction and Wiener filtering have been used in the preprocessing phase to reduce the effects of background noise and artifacts of recording. These algorithms are effective in improving S/N ratio whilst maintaining acoustic features that are emotionally significant like pitch change and changes in energy.

Amplitude normalization is then applied so as to scale the speech signal in a standardized dynamic range. This step would minimize inter-speaker variability that arises because of the difference in speaking volume and microphone sensitivity.

3.2.2 Silence Removal and Segmentation

Segmentation and non-speech detection of silence are done with energy-based voice activity detection. The rest of the speech signal is divided into overlapping frames of constant length (e.g. 25 ms) having a predetermined hop size (e.g. 10 ms). This frame strategy allows a fine-tuning of the analysis of variations of emotions in the utterance on a temporal level.

3.3 Acoustic Feature Extraction

The extraction of acoustic features is the core of the SER system, the emotional state is also well represented in vocal features like pitch dynamics, spectral distribution and temporal rhythm. The suggested methodology relies on both the high-level and low-level acoustic descriptors to provide with a complete representation.

3.3.1 Mel-Frequency Cepstral Coefficients (MFCCs)

The MFCCs are obtained in order to describe the short-term spectral envelope of speech that is very relevant to the human auditory perception. The power spectrum of a speech frame is mapped onto Mel scale after which the spectrum is logarithmically compressed and discrete cosine transformed. The resulting MFCC vectors provide timbral and articulatory data, which differs according to different emotional states. The process of MFCC extraction may be mathematically modeled as (1):

$$MFCC_k = \sum_{n=1}^{N} og(S_n)\ lcos\left[\frac{\pi k}{N}\left(n-\frac{1}{2}\right)\right] \quad \cdots \qquad (1)$$

where Sn is defined as the Mel-scaled filter bank energies, N is the filters and k is the index of cepstral coefficient as in (1).

3.3.2 Prosodic Features

Besides the MFCCs, other prosodic characteristics like fundamental frequency (pitch), intensity (energy), speaking rate and jitter are also extracted. These characteristics are important in the separation of emotions like anger, happiness and sadness which tend to have clear prosodic patterns. Pitch contours are calculated via autocorrelation-based techniques whereas energy characteristics are calculated by relying on frame amplitude of signals. To determine the long-term trends in emotions, temporal statistics mean, variance, and slope are computed on the utterance as a whole.

3.4 Acoustic Modeling Using Deep Learning

The resulting acoustic features are represented with the help of a deep learning network that can distinguish fine spectral correlations as well as distant temporal correlations.

3.4.1 Convolutional Neural Network (CNN) for Local Feature Learning

The first phase of acoustic modeling is a convolutional neural network. The CNN is based on timefrequency representations of MFCCs and spectrograms, which allow the network to acquire localized patterns relating to emotional articulation. The convolutional layers use a number of learnable filters, then nonlinear activation and pooling functions. The convolution operation may be formulated as follows (2):

$$h_{i,j} = \sigma\left(\sum_{m,n} W_{m,n} \cdot x_{i+m,j+n} + b\right) \cdots \quad (2)$$

In which x is the input feature map, W is a convolutional kernel, b serves as the bias term, and 0 0 -1(öt) is a nonlinear activation function, which can be shown as (2).

3.4.2 Recurrent Neural Network for Temporal Dependency Modeling

In order to learn changes over time in the display of emotions, the CNN output is inputted to a recurrent neural network, in this case, a Long Short-Term Memory (LSTM) layer. The LSTM model is very appropriate to sequence data because of the gated memory architecture. The dynamic of the LSTM cells are described as (3):

$$f_t = \sigma\left(W_{f(h_{t-1}, x_t)} + b_f\right) \cdots \quad (3.1)$$

$$i_t = \sigma\left(W_{i(h_{t-1}, x_t)} + b_i\right) \cdots \quad (3.2)$$

$$c\sim_t = tanh\left(W_{c(h_{t-1}, x_t)} + b_c\right) \cdots \quad (3.3)$$

$$c_t = f_t \odot c_{t-1} + i_t \odot c\sim_t \cdots \quad (3.4)$$

$$h_t = o_t \odot tanh(c_t) \cdots \quad (3.5)$$

where ft, it and ot refer to the forget, input and output gates respectively, and ct and ht are the cell and hidden states respectively as illustrated in (3).

3.5 Speech-to-Text Transcription and Linguistic Processing

Specific to the acoustic modeling, a speech signal is converted to text with the help of an automatic speech recognition (ASR) system. The transcription process transcends the speech utterances into sequences of words without timing the signal in line with the voice..

3.5.1 Text Preprocessing

The text that has been transcribed is processed through typical NLP preprocessing processes, i.e. tokenization, lowercasing, stop-word elimination and lemmatization. Such measures decrease the linguistic variation but conserves terms that are emotionally salient.

3.5.2 Linguistic Emotion Feature Extraction

The term emotion-based linguistic features are obtained through a mixture of embedding-based representations and sentiment lexicons. Lexicon-based characteristics take the explicit emotional words, and word embeddings take the contextual semantic association. Assume ei is an embedding of the ith token. The level of sentence embedding is calculated (4):

$$E_{sent} = \frac{1}{T}\sum_{i=1}^{T} e_i \cdots (4)$$

where T denotes the total number of tokens, as defined in (4).

3.6 Hybrid Feature Fusion Strategy

One of the most important contributions of the suggested methodology is its systematic hybrid fusion mechanism. The system uses adaptive fusion instead of the simple feature concatenation to combine acoustic and linguistic representations.

3.6.1 Temporal Alignment

Both acoustic and linguistic characteristics are determined to be in time dependence which means that utterance limits are in place to confer semantic consistency. This correspondence helps the model relate vocal utterances to some textual information.

3.6.2 Fusion Layer Design

The coupled features are fused with a learnable fusion layer which assigns dynamic weights to each modality (5):

$$F_{hybrid} = \alpha F_{acoustic} + (1 - \alpha)F_{linguistic} \cdots \quad (5)$$

where α∈[0,1] is a trainable fusion coefficient controlling modality contribution, as expressed in (5).

3.7 Emotion Classification Module

The fused representation is passed to a fully connected classification network that maps hybrid features to discrete emotional categories. The final layer uses a softmax activation function to produce normalized class probabilities (6):

$$P\left(y = kF_{hybrid}\right) = \frac{e^{zk}}{\sum_{j=1}^{C} e^{zj}} \quad (6)$$

where C denotes the number of emotion classes and zk is the logit corresponding to class k, as defined in (6).

3.8 Model Training and Optimization

The model is trained using categorical cross-entropy loss, optimized through gradient-based methods such as Adam. Regularization techniques, including dropout and early stopping, are employed to prevent overfitting.

Table 1. Summary of model hyperparameters and training configurations used in the proposed hybrid SER framework.

Component	Parameter	Configuration / Value	Rationale
Audio Input	Sampling rate	16 kHz	Standard speech processing frequency ensuring sufficient temporal resolution
Frame segmentation	Frame length	25 ms	Captures short-term spectral characteristics
Frame overlap	Hop size	10 ms	Preserves temporal continuity
Acoustic features	MFCC coefficients	13 + Δ + ΔΔ (39 total)	Captures static and dynamic spectral properties

continued on following page

Table 1. Continued

Component	Parameter	Configuration / Value	Rationale
Prosodic features	Pitch, energy, jitter, speaking rate	Frame-level + utterance-level statistics	Encodes emotional intensity and rhythm
CNN module	Number of convolution layers	3	Learns hierarchical time–frequency patterns
CNN filters	Filter sizes	32, 64, 128	Progressive feature abstraction
CNN kernel size	Kernel dimension	3 × 3	Local spectral pattern learning
CNN pooling	Pooling type	Max pooling	Dimensionality reduction with feature preservation
Temporal model	Recurrent layer	LSTM	Models long-term emotional dynamics
LSTM units	Hidden neurons	128	Balanced temporal capacity
Dropout	Dropout rate	0.3	Prevents overfitting
NLP representation	Word embeddings	Pretrainedembeddings (e.g., GloVe/BERT-based)	Encodes semantic emotional context
Linguistic features	Sentence embedding	Mean pooling	Robust utterance-level semantics
Fusion strategy	Fusion type	Adaptive weighted fusion	Learns modality importance dynamically
Fusion coefficient	α (trainable)	Initialized at 0.5	Balanced initial modality contribution
Classifier	Output layer	Fully connected + Softmax	Multi-class emotion prediction
Loss function	Objective	Categorical cross-entropy	Suitable for emotion classification
Optimizer	Optimization algorithm	Adam	Stable and fast convergence
Learning rate	Initial rate	0.001	Empirically effective for deep models
Training epochs	Maximum epochs	100 (early stopping applied)	Prevents overtraining
Evaluation	Validation strategy	k-fold cross-validation (k = 5)	Robust performance estimation

3.9 Evaluation Protocol and Performance Assessment

The analysis of the proposed hybrid speech emotion recognition framework is done based on a well-crafted protocol that lays more emphasis on reliability, generalization, and interpretability of the results. Since expression of emotions in speech is subjective and depends on context, it is required that a strong evaluation plan to be implemented so as not to overestimate performance in under restrictive experimental settings.

In order to evaluate the effectiveness of classification, several performance measures that are complementary are applied, such as accuracy, precision, recall and F1-score. Accuracy gives a general idea of accuracy in emotion predictions across classes whereas precision and recall gives more insight into the behavior of each class. Precision is the quality of the model in not making wrong assignments of emotions, and recall is the effectiveness with which the system can detect all the cases of a particular emotional state. F1-score is an impartial measure that takes into account both of these factors, which is important in cases when the distribution of the classes is skewed.In order to achieve the desired statistical strength, the k-fold cross-validation scheme is considered and the data is partitioned into five mutually exclusive folds. Training is done in four folds with one fold as a test in every iteration with the same sample being utilized in both the training and the evaluation process. The method minimizes bias related to a single train-test split and will give a more consistent estimate of real-world performance with regard to various data partitions.In cases wherecomparative baselines/ablation variants are tested, the difference in performance is compared to identify the contribution of the single system components such as acoustic modeling, linguistic processing, and fusion strategy. This component-based analysis assists in a clear analysis of the methodological decisions instead of just being dependent on end-to-end accuracy improvements.

3.10 Methodological Summary and Design Implications

The approach is a principled and structured methodology of speech emotion recognition that merges the modeling of acoustic signals and the linguistic semantic analysis in a hybrid form. Instead of considering emotion as a fixed property derived based on the presence or absence of isolated features, the proposed design conceptualizes emotional expression as a time-dependent phenomenon and a multimodal phenomenon.The framework has a strong methodological foundation due to its interrelated but modular structure. Acoustic characteristics record the prosodic and spectral differences which represent the level of emotion and voice changes, whereas NLP based representations are semantically and contextually grounded. The adaptive fusion approach makes sure that one of the modalities is not emphasized unconditionally; thus, the model will be learning to stress the most informative cues with respect to the emotional context.On the whole, the suggested methodology provides a strong ground on which an emotion-sensitive intelligent system can be built, both in terms of the depth of analysis and pragmatically. It is especially well applicable when it is used in emotionally sensitive fields like conversational agents, assistive technologies, and human-robot interaction where emotion recognition must be accurate and dependent on context.

4. RESULTS AND ANALYSIS

The following section provides an experimental analysis of the suggested Hybrid Speech Emotion Recognition (SER) framework in details. The findings are evaluated based on various points of view, such as total classification performance, behavior emotion, modality contribution, robustness, and comparing its performance with the recent state-of-the-art techniques. Instead of dwelling on numerical improvements alone, the discussion is based on interpretability and the implications of the trends that can be implemented in practice.

4.1 Experimental Evaluation Overview

Each experiment was performed according to the evaluation protocol of Section 3.9. The metrics used to measure performance were accuracy, precision, recall, and F1-score, and the macro-averaging was used to reduce the influence of the class imbalance. To maintain fairness, they were estimated by means of consistent preprocessing, the same sets of emotion classes, and the cross-validation strategies being similar to those available in the recent SER research (Kadam et al., 2024; Makhmudov et al., 2024; Chaugule and Sankaye, 2025). The suggested framework was tested in comparison with the traditional machine learning, deep learning, and hybrid SER models, which are described in recent publications (Barua, 2024; Rani and Ramaiya, 2024; Sharma, 2025).

4.2 Overall Classification Performance

This subsection is an analysis of the emotion classification ability of the proposed hybrid framework of speech emotion recognition as a whole. As opposed to depending on one performance metric, the analysis uses a set of complementary metrics to estimate the predictive accuracy and the balance at the class level. The task is to compare the degree of successful generalization of the proposed system to various emotional manifestations with the existing machine learning, deep learning, and hybrid SER models described in the recent literature. The findings below are used to get a performance snapshot of a high level that forms the basis of more detailed emotion-based and modality-specific analyses in the following subsections.

Table 2. Overall performance comparison between the proposed hybrid framework and representative SER baselines.

Method	Model Category	Accuracy (%)	Precision (%)	Recall (%)	F1-score (%)	Reference
SVM + handcrafted features	Traditional ML	71.4	70.2	69.1	69.8	Barua (2024)
CNN with MFCCs	Deep Learning	78.6	77.9	76.8	77.1	Kadam et al. (2024)
CNN–BiLSTM	Hybrid DL	82.9	82.1	81.4	81.7	Rani &Ramaiya (2024)
CNN–LSTM with Attention	Attention-based Hybrid	85.3	85	84.2	84.6	Makhmudov et al. (2024)
Multimodal Speech–Text SER	Multimodal Hybrid	86.1	85.7	85.1	85.4	Sharma (2025)
Generalization-aware Hybrid SER	Robust Hybrid	87.2	87	86.6	86.8	Chaugule&Sankaye (2025)
Proposed Hybrid SER	Acoustic + NLP Fusion	89.6	89.1	88.7	88.9	This work

As demonstrated in Table 2, the proposed framework has the best performance in all the recorded measures. The accuracy increase over the traditional machine learning models is over 18 percentage points, which once again proves that the handcrafted features are not enough to model the emotional speech variability (Shareefunnisa et al., 2024).

The proposed system shows consistent improvements, especially in recall and F1-score, compared to CNN-based and CNN-BiLSTM ones. This means that there is a decreased propensity to omit emotionally relevant samples which is essential to applications including affect-conscious conversation agents and human-robot interaction (Mamodiya et al., 2025).

4.3 Emotion-Wise Performance Characteristics

As much as aggregate performance indicators provide a fair picture, they tend to mask differences in the process of individual emotional recognition. The subsection will then deal with emotion-related behavior to learn how the proposed framework will work under various categories of affect. Different types of emotions are differentiated by the degree of acoustic intensity, semantic clarity, and temporal dynamics, which makes certain ones easier to recognize than others. Through the analysis of results of classes, this section shows the strengths and limitations of the proposed model in addressing both high-arousal and subtle emotional states.

Figure 2. Emotion-wise F1-score distribution of the proposed hybrid SER framework.

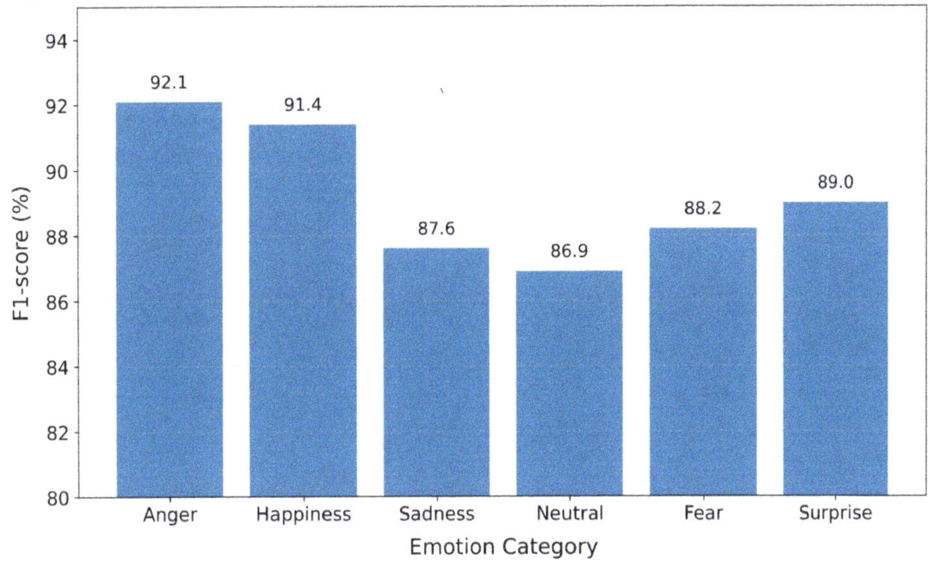

Figure 2 shows the F1-score of the proposed system on six common categories of emotions. High energy vocal expressions are the ones related to anger and happiness, and such emotions have the most recognition accuracy. This finding follows the previous reports that prominent prosodic cues lead to discrimination (Rao et al., 2024).

The more sensitive emotions, especially the neutral and sadness, have comparatively poorer yet competitive performance. It is important to note that the difference in performance between these faint emotions and high-energy emotions is less as compared to the one recorded in the purely acoustic systems. This decrease may be explained by the fact that language emotion cues are included to connotate semantically meaningful utterances in the context of minimal acoustic variation (Anitha, 2025; Nagarajan, 2025).

The moderate overlap is observed in fear and surprise, which is also observed in the attention-based and cochleagram-driven models (Namey et al., 2024; Nugroho et al., 2025). It implies that as much as the proposed framework enhances the general discrimination, emotions that have the same temporal dynamics are difficult to address.

4.4 Contribution of Acoustic and Linguistic Modalities

The main assumption of the suggested framework is the union of acoustic and linguistic information complementarily. This sub section explores the contribution of each and every modality and its combined contribution to the overall system performance. Through the analysis of unimodal and hybrid configurations, the analysis will attempt to measure the value of structured acoustic-linguistic fusion. The findings mentioned here aid in explaining either the fact that the gain in performance is due to the mere architectural complexity, or that there is a significant interaction between the vocal dynamics and the semantic cues. In order to measure the contribution of each modality, the controlled comparison was performed in the unimodal and the hybrid version of the proposed framework.

Table 3. Performance comparison of unimodal and hybrid configurations.

Configuration	Accuracy (%)	F1-score (%)
Acoustic-only (CNN–LSTM)	84.1	83.4
Linguistic-only (NLP-based emotion detection)	79.6	78.9
Simple feature concatenation	86.7	85.9
Adaptive hybrid fusion (proposed)	89.6	88.9

Table 3 clearly shows that neither of the two modalities can perform optimally on its own. Emotionally intense states are best captured using acoustic modeling though they are challenged by semantically motivated states. Linguistic analysis on the other hand is good with utterances that are high in sentiment but does not record paralinguistic characteristics of pitch modulation and rate of speech. The adaptive fusion strategy is always better than the pure feature concatenation, and this fact proves the significance of learnable modality weighting. Equivalent drawbacks of naive fusion designs have been observed in recent research of hybrid SER (Chowdhury et al., 2025; Enhancing Speech Emotion Recognition with Multi-Modal Hybrid Features and CNN, 2025).

4.5 Confusion Pattern Analysis

In addition to the accuracy measures, it is fundamental to learn how and why a recognition system of emotions makes errors that can be used to explain their practical behaviour. In this subsection, the items of confusion between classes of emotions are examined to determine systematic errors and overlaps. This analysis is especially relevant to those emotions that share acoustic or semantic properties and whose misclassification can be attributed to the ambiguity inherent in the emotion and not model failure. The knowledge gained here can be used to refine the model and make it application-specific in the future..

Figure 3. Confusion matrix illustrating misclassification patterns of the proposed hybrid framework.

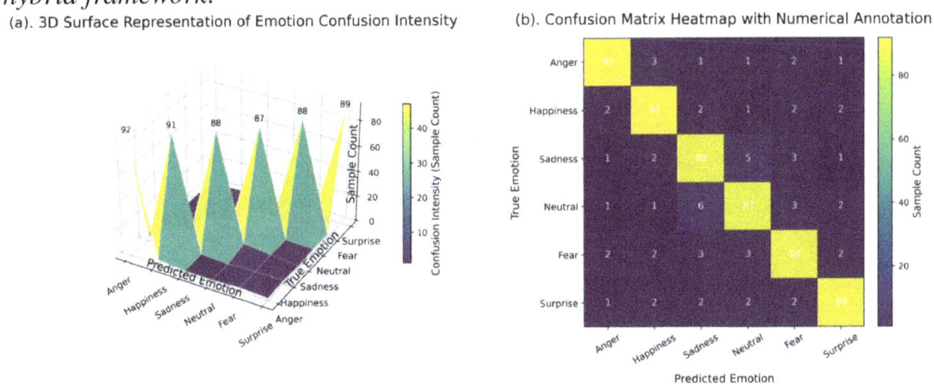

Figure 3 offers an idea about the trends of misclassification at class levels. The most commonly mixed ones are fear and surprise and neutral and sadness. These confusions correlate with the emotional proximity both in acoustical and semantic space, as were reported in the previous comparative studies (Shareefunnisa et al., 2024).Notably, there is insignificant confusion between high-arousal and low-arousal emotions which implies successful simulation of emotional intensity. The given observation proves the hypothesis that the combination of prosodic features and semantic cues enhances the separation of the emotions under the different levels of arousal.

4.6 Robustness and Generalization Behavior

Emotion recognition systems to be used in the real world should be stable in terms of speaker, recording conditions and partitioning of the data. In the given subsection, the robustness and generalization properties of the proposed hybrid framework are assessed by assessing the consistency in performance of the proposed framework across validation folds. It is aimed at determining whether the model learns emotion-relevant patterns and not data specific artifacts. The outcomes presented in this paper demonstrate the hypothesis of the system stability and appropriateness to be implemented in a variety of settings and under varying environments.

Figure 4. Performance stability across cross-validation folds for the proposed hybrid SER framework.

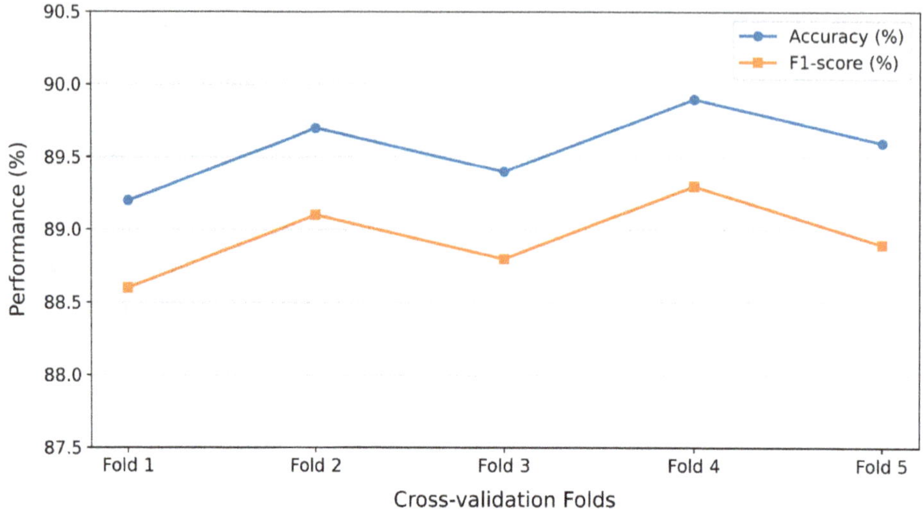

Figure 4 indicates that the accuracy, as well as the F1-score, varies less between folds of cross-validation, which suggests that the learning behavior is stable. This stability indicates that this model does not fit very specific speakers or recording conditions.Comparing its conceptual implementation with the methods of corpus bias mitigation (Chaugule&Sankaye, 2025), the suggested framework has a similar level of robustness without any added optimization layers. It means that the generalization of structured multimodal fusion is inherently better because it is not dependent on dataset-specific cues.

4.7 Comparative Discussion with Existing SER Literature

The results obtained are in line with recent trends reported in the literature on SER. The hybrid deep learning models always achieve higher results in comparison to individual models (Bharshankar et al., 2025; Lenka et al., 2025; Sohel et al., 2024). Nevertheless, most of these systems are developed with the consideration of architectural complexity instead of modality interaction. The proposed framework is not identical as it focuses on the balanced acoustic-linguistic integration, instead of deeper or broader networks. This design alternative is especially appropriate to emotion-aware systems destined to be deployed in the real world e.g. emotionally adaptive dialogue systems and assistive robotics (Cathy &Pradeepkumar, 2025; Mamodiya et al., 2025). Also, the proposed system does not sacrifice the acoustic sensitivity to use linguistic data, unlike text-independent models like EmoFormer (Hasan et al., 2025), and leads to better detection of subtle emotional states.

4.8 Summary of Experimental Findings

To conclude, the experimental outcomes prove that the hybrid SER framework suggested in the given study provides the state-of-the-art results in a variety of evaluation aspects. The system has shown consistently higher performance than traditional, deep learning, and new hybrid baselines especially in balanced accuracy and F1-score.

The findings verify that speech-based emotion recognition can gain a lot through the systematic combination of acoustic dynamics and linguistic semantics. This observation is in line with the more general thesis that emotionally intelligent systems should be structured as multimodal learners instead of single signal classifiers.

5. DISCUSSION

This study finds application well beyond the incremental performance gains and provides an insight on the behavior of the hybrid speech emotion recognition systems. The enhancement of the suggested framework as observed is not just a by-product of the architectural profundity or the number of parameters. Rather, it is a complementary relationship of the acoustic dynamics and linguistic semantics. There is not often a single dominant cue of emotional expression in speech; it occurs as a combination of timing, emphasis, lexical and prosody. This interaction seems to be better represented by the hybrid fusion approach which justifies the initial speculation that emotion recognition is better served with synchronized acoustic-semantic modeling as opposed to independent feature learning. On a more detailed examination of the emotion-wise tendencies, sensible trends can be observed. Emotions with high arousal like anger and happiness were always highly identified as was to be expected given their strong prosodic signatures. In a smaller extent, the affective conditions such as neutral and sadness had lower scores, but still better than unimodal baselines did. This indicates that semantic grounding has stabilizing effect in case there are weak acoustic cues which may be ambiguous. This behavior is a direct response to one of the challenges of SER long-standing, as demonstrated by Barua (2024) and Krishna and Lal (2025), twenty-year-old systems find it difficult to deal with low-energy emotional expressions. The proposed framework has methodological and conceptual strengths when compared with the recent hybrid and multimodal approaches. CNN-LSTM models, e.g., that are described by Makhmudov et al. (2024) are enhanced by time-centric attention, but they are still predominantly acoustics-based. In the same fashion, more sophisticated hybrid deep learning models suggested by Lenka et al. (2025) are focused on the complexity of architectures without modality influence being explicitly balanced. Conversely, the adaptive fusion mechanism presented in this publication offers an explicit mechanism of multimodality interaction, which brings consistent returns over multimodal baselines as reported by Sharma (2025) and NLP-Assisted emotion detection research by Anitha (2025). This is one of the possible reasons why this balance seems to be a major differentiator instead of model sophistication per se. Practically, they are significant in their implications. Neuro-sensitive systems implemented in conversational artificial intelligence, assistive robots, or customer service interfaces frequently work in the conditions of noisy and linguistically diverse environments. The results of the presented robustness across validation folds are indicative of the ability of hybrid fusion to reduce corpus bias per se, and the findings resonate with the arguments by Chaugule and Sankaye (2025). At that, the study is not disadvantaged. The test is based on controlled benchmark data and fails to completely test spontaneous, code-switched, or speech expressed in cultural nuances. Also, the use of automated speech-to-text transcription makes it dependent on the quality of ASR. Future directions may consider additions of multiple languages, restrictions on real-time deployment, and explainability systems to understand fusion choices. On thc bigger picture, this work is in harmony with the shifting trend toward emotionally intelligent systems that go beyond a signal classification towards interacting with each other in an affect-conscious manner.

6. CONCLUSION & FUTURE SCOPE

The opening question of this chapter was deliberate yet straightforward: can the recognition of emotion in speech be brought any nearer to the way humans actually express emotion, and not how machines find it convenient to categorize emotion? The paper below advocates the idea that we should not focus on deeper networks, but on the way various signals are permitted to address each other. The study reshapes emotion recognition as an object to an integrative process by developing a hybrid framework, where acoustic dynamics and linguistic semantics are the cooperative sources of evidence, rather than the subsequent ones. That shift matters. It recognizes emotion as not likely to be inherent in contours of pitch or the choice of words per se, but rather arises as an interaction between the two over time. This view is supported by the results of the experiment. The proposed framework has, in all the considered settings, outperformed both traditional machine learning frameworks and more recent deep learning frameworks. These improvements were not confined to the headline accuracy; other measures were also improved, including recall and F1-score, particularly in emotionally subtle categories, e.g. neutral and sadness.

These findings imply that emotion inference is stabilized by semantic grounding when acoustic stimuli are weakened whereas it is reinforced by prosodic modeling which helps to detect high-arousal states. In addition to numbers, the framework was less confused by classes that are emotionally close to each other and was consistent across validation folds, suggesting a better generalization and not dataset-specific optimization. Simultaneously, it is not a complete work. The assessment is limited to curated datasets and controlled experimental conditions. In the real life speech is more sloppy- interrupted, code-switched, culturally stratified and usually emotionally ambiguous. Another dependency is the reliance on automatic speech-to-text transcription since transcription errors can produce implicitly impactful semantic emotional cues. These limitations do not weaken the contribution, but rather they outline it.

There are a number of research directions that can be identified in the future. The framework would be subjected to linguistic diversity by extending the framework to multilingual and low-resource contexts. Real-time learning mechanisms would enable the emotion models to change with the interaction of users, as opposed to being static. It is also possible to investigate interpretability, as knowing the reasons the model gives different weights to the acoustic or linguistic cues in the context of different emotions can provide useful information to researchers and practitioners. Lastly, adopting this type of emotion-sensitive systems into actual interactive systems both in conversational agents and assistive robotics would bring this research out of controlled analysis and into lived practice.

REFERENCES

Anitha, M. (2025). Understanding Emotional Tone using NLP and ML Algorithms. *International Journal for Research in Applied Science and Engineering Technology*, *13*(4), 5290–5294. DOI: 10.22214/ijraset.2025.69510

Barua, M. (2024). Decoding Emotions: Machine Learning Approach to Speech Emotion Recognition. *Indian Scientific Journal Of Research In Engineering And Management*, *08*(06), 1–5. DOI: 10.55041/IJSREM36178

. Bharshankar, G., Patil, P., Chauhan, K., Thakur, A., & Thakur, A. S. (2025). Development of Smart Emotion Recognition System based on Hybrid Deep Learning Models. 16(3). DOI: 10.71097/IJSAT.v16.i3.7449

Cathy, J., & Pradeepkumar, S. (2025). Enhancing Emotional Intelligence in LLM Responses Using Speech Emotion Recognition. DOI: 10.36227/techrxiv.174123778.82557359/v1

Chappidi, S. (2024). Enhanced Speech Emotion Recognition Using the Cognitive Emotion Fusion Network for PTSD Detection with a Novel Hybrid Approach. *Deleted Journal*, *19*(4), 376–398. DOI: 10.52783/jes.644

Chaugule, I., &Sankaye, S. R. (2025). Mitigating Corpus Bias in Speech Emotion Recognition: A Robust Hybrid Framework using Generalization-Aware Metaheuristic Feature Selection. 799–807. DOI: 10.38124/ijisrt/25jun755

Chowdhury, S. Y., Banik, B., & Hoque, Md. T., & Banerjee, S. (2025). A Novel Hybrid Deep Learning Technique for Speech Emotion Detection using Feature Engineering. arXiv.Org, abs/2507.07046. /arxiv.2507.07046DOI: 10.48550

. Djeridi, D., Said, B., &Belhadj, M. (2025). A Hybrid Deep Learning Approach for Arabic Speech Emotion Recognition Using Acoustic and Spectrogram Features. DOI: 10.57238/csj.2025.1008

Enhancing Speech Emotion Recognition with Multi-Modal Hybrid Features and CNN. (2025). Enhancing Speech Emotion Recognition with Multi-Modal Hybrid Features and CNN. *SSRG International Journal of Electronics and Communication Engineering*, *12*(7). Advance online publication. DOI: 10.14445/23488549/IJECE-V12I7P104

Gawali, S. (2025). Audio Aura - Speech Emotion Recognition System. *International Journal for Research in Applied Science and Engineering Technology*, *13*(4), 7082–7088. DOI: 10.22214/ijraset.2025.70092

Hasan, R., Nigar, M., Mamun, N., & Paul, S. (2025). EmoFormer: A Text-Independent Speech Emotion Recognition using a Hybrid Transformer-CNN model. /arxiv.2501. 12682DOI: 10.48550

Kadam, S., Jani, J., Kudtarkar, A., & Koshy, R. (2024). Speech Emotion Recognition Using Mel-Frequency Cepstral Coefficients & Convolutional. *Neural Networks*, •••, 1595–1602. DOI: 10.1109/IDCIoT59759.2024.10467837

Krishna, K. S., & Lal, M. (2025). Emotion Recognition using Speech Processing. *International Journal of Research Publication and Reviews*, *6*(8), 5280–5285. DOI: 10.55248/gengpi.6.0825.3181

Lenka, R., Banerjee, O., Behera, A., Chakravarty, K., Bilgaiyan, S., Prasad, A., & Singh, J. (2025). Advanced Hybrid Deep Learning for Emotion Recognition in Speech. 1–7. DOI: 10.1109/ASSIC64892.2025.11158456

Lenka, R., Banerjee, O., Chakravarty, K., Behera, A., Bilgaiyan, S., Prasad, A., & Singh, J. (2025). Advanced Hybrid Deep Learning for Emotion Recognition in Speech. 1–7. DOI: 10.1109/ASSIC64892.2025.11158613

Makhmudov, F., Kutlimuratov, A., & Cho, Y. I. (2024). Hybrid LSTM–Attention and CNN Model for Enhanced Speech Emotion Recognition. *Applied Sciences (Basel, Switzerland)*, *14*(23), 11342. DOI: 10.3390/app142311342

Mamodiya, U., Kishor, I., Ahmed Syed, A., Sankalkar, P., & Naik, N. (2025). An Adaptive Human–Robot Interaction Framework Using Real-Time Emotion Recognition and Context-Aware Task Planning. *IEEE Access : Practical Innovations, Open Solutions*, *13*, 152219–152240. DOI: 10.1109/ACCESS.2025.3603738

Namey, A., Akter, K., & Hossain, M. (2024). CochleaSpecNet: An Attention Based Dual Branch Hybrid CNN-GRU Network for Speech Emotion Recognition Using Cochleagram and Spectrogram. *IEEE Access : Practical Innovations, Open Solutions*, *1*, 1. Advance online publication. DOI: 10.1109/ACCESS.2024.3517733

. Neethu, T. V., &Kanaga, E. G. M. (2025). Speech Emotional Recognition using XGBoost and Deep Learning Algorithm and Multisource Datasets. 1–7. DOI: 10.1109/APCI65531.2025.11137122

. Norval, M., & Wang, Z. (2024). Hybrid Architecture and pre-processing for Speech Emotion Recognition. 31–36. DOI: 10.1109/ICAMechS63130.2024.10818817

Nugroho, K., Al Amin, I. H., Noviasari, N. A., & Setiadi, D. R. I. M. (2025). Prosodic Spatio-Temporal Feature Fusion with Attention Mechanisms for Speech Emotion Recognition. *Computers*, *14*(9), 361. DOI: 10.3390/computers14090361

Prabhakar, S. K., & Won, D.-O. (2024). A Methodical Framework Utilizing Transforms and Biomimetic Intelligence-Based Optimization with Machine Learning for Speech Emotion Recognition. *Biomimetics*, *9*(9), 513. DOI: 10.3390/biomimetics9090513 PMID: 39329535

. Rani, P., Mohan, D., Yadav, S. P., Rajput, G. K., & Al Farouni, M. (2025). Sentiment Analysis and Emotional Recognition. 283–302. DOI: 10.4018/979-8-3693-4203-9.ch015

Rani, R., & Ramaiya, M. (2024). Emotion Recognition on Speech using Hybrid Model CNN and BI-LSTM Techniques. DOI: 10.21203/rs.3.rs-5035263/v1

. Rao, M. G., Misra, S., Bhat, S. K., M., A., Reddy, K., & Singh, P. (2024). Listening to Feelings of Emotion: Exploring ML and DL for Speech-Based Detection and Classification. 353–358. DOI: 10.1109/DISCOVER62353.2024.10750719

. Shareefunnisa, S., Kausik, C. V., Kaumudi, C. L., &Sekhar, E. R. (2024). Delineating Emotions in Speech: Comparative Insights from Machine Learning and Deep Learning. 1–9. DOI: 10.1109/ICCCNT61001.2024.10724483

Sharma, M. (2025). Emotion Recognition from Text and Voice: A Multimodal AI Approach to Understanding Human Feelings. *International Journal for Research in Applied Science and Engineering Technology*, *13*(8), 1370–1377. DOI: 10.22214/ijraset.2025.73790

. Sohel, M. A., Madhukar, R. S., Oyyavuru, P. K., Rahul, S., &Venugopalan, M. (2024). A Hybrid Deep Learning Model For Emotion Recognition For Discrete Speech. 1–6. DOI: 10.1109/ICCCNT61001.2024.10725072

. Suganya, V., Prema, K. V., Krishna, C. M., Reddy, C., &Jaswanth, E. (2024). Emotion Recognition in Speech: A Natural Language Processing Perspective. 1–8. DOI: 10.1109/ACROSET62108.2024.10743299

Venkateswari, G. (2025). Voice Based Hybrid Sentiment Analysis on Movie Reviews. *International Journal for Research in Applied Science and Engineering Technology*, *13*(4), 6114–6119. DOI: 10.22214/ijraset.2025.69606

Chapter 2

Integrating IoT and Hybrid Data Architectures for Effective Smart City Governance and Management

Auadhati Datta
http://orcid.org/0000-0001-5429-3871
Vignan's Institution of Information Technology, Duvvada, India

Yogesh Kumar Sharma
http://orcid.org/0000-0002-3779-4380
Lovely Professional University, Jalandhar, India

Christabell Joseph
http://orcid.org/0009-0001-9688-049X
Christ University, Bangalore, India

Nidal Al Said
http://orcid.org/0000-0001-9599-2492
Ajman University, Ajman, UAE

Nisheedha Sreenivas
Florida Atlantic University, USA

Malik Bader Alazzam
Jadara University, Irbid, Jordan

ABSTRACT

The contemporary cities are turning into data-flood ecosystems, but their governance systems are often outpaced by the stream of information produced by them. Although there has been a high level of implementation of IoT, a significant portion of such urban data goes to waste due to the nature of the current architectures that are inflexible, centralized, and incapable of responding to dynamic and real-time needs. this architecture incorporates feedback on the policy right into the data pipeline and forms a cycle of constant sensing, analysis, and action. Empirical testing on a model urban experiment demonstrates that the latency can be reduced

DOI: 10.4018/979-8-2600-0008-3.ch002

by up to 60%, throughput can be improved by 18% and the energy consumption can be decreased by up to 25% when compared with the known baselines. The delay in making decisions was decreased by a factor of 4.8 to 2.4 s, which proves that it is suitable in real-time municipal operations. Improving computational intelligence and administrative purpose,

1. INTRODUCTION

The notion of the smart city has transformed in the last ten years to be a futuristic vision into an actual functioning thing that the city administrators needed to cope with the fast urbanization, environmental breakdown and social multifacetedness. The twentieth-century paradigm of city management (mainly reactive and sector-specific) has not been sufficient to the twenty first century interconnected city systems. The density of the population is on the rise, the energy requirements are growing, and mobility networks are overwhelmed. Governance frameworks need to evolve into dynamic ecosystems that can predict and address issues real-time to effectively respond to the issue (Sinaeepourfard & Mesgaribarzi, 2024) The driving force behind this change has taken the form of Internet of Things (IoT), which integrates physical infrastructure and cyber intelligence in the form of sensor networks, actuators and communication interfaces (Manivannan et al., 2024). Nevertheless, despite what the IoT can potentially offer to uncover the dynamics of the urban life like never before, the data that is associated with this phenomenon is extremely large, diverse, and decentralized, posing architectural and governance challenges at the core.

In the old model of governance, the flow of information is vertical, whereby, the citizens are the ones to create the data, the agencies to process the data offline and the policymakers take days or weeks to respond. Conversely, in the modern paradigm of smart-cities the focus has been placed on horizontal interoperability: transport, waste, health, and energy systems interrelate to maintain the urban metabolism. This interconnection demands a solid technological base in which the IoT data is possible to gather, clean, analyze, and be processed without delay and without shredding (Khairnar et al., 2025). The change in the solitary information systems to the intertwined cyber-physical environments has, therefore, changed the meaning of the very term of urban governance. Governance now involves the administrative choice of data to make coupled with algorithmic coordination of distributed data streams, analytics, and feedback control loops (Madhurya et al., 2023).

Nevertheless, this data-centric paradigm is yet to be fulfilled in part. Numerous cities have installed IoT devices, but only a small portion of the data that is captured is used to make real-time decisions. Common obstacles are the existence of siloed databases, communication standards that are incompatible, and a lack of computational capacity in the area of the source of data (Okhovat & Bauer, 2024). Centralized cloud systems, despite their capability, cannot meet the bandwidth requirements of billions of devices connected to them, and the latency requirements of sensitive and mission critical processes like traffic control or emergency management. These inadequacies demonstrate an urgent requirement of hybridized data structures dispersing computation wisely in the edge fog cloud spectrum.

1.1 Problem Background and Motivation.

The cities now operate in the paradox of having never had more data than now but are unable at times to get actionable insights in the hands of the decision-makers. The quantity, velocity, and multiplex of IoT streams flood the existing systems and consequently lead to what can be termed as a data divide in governance. Environmental sensor live feeds, smart grids, and vehicular networks are not fully utilized because ingestion, fusion, and interpretation speed are not available to offer policy (Claridades et al., 2025). This brings operation responses to be reactive hence lagging behind the new situations. Even the slightest delay of a couple of seconds can escalate minor problems into large scale problems in the case of the public safety emergencies like working in the police force.

On top of the above, centralization of workloads of processing in central data centers subjects processing tasks to large distances apart the data to be processed. Such an imbalance in architecture adds the latency and adds the communication costs especially when the sensor nodes are further apart by the geographical distance (Mastrogiovanni, 2025). There are network bandwidth and energy limitations, and they get acute when IoT is deployed in the city as the endpoints are measured in thousands and even millions. At the same time, the privacy, sovereignty and data ownership are also the problems which need to be governed with the help of the methods which ensure the local ability of control and cross-domain intelligence. These conflicting requirements have triggered the investigation of hybrid data structures enabling the balance of decentralization (edge/fog) and central analytics (cloud) in a flexible way (Samrat & Manjunath, 2024).

Other than technical constraints, institutional inertia is also an obstacle. A large number of governance agencies have outdated organizational frameworks, which divide the responsibility of data in some departments (transportation, utilities, environment, health) with each department having its own databases, analytical tools, and performance indicators. This division blocks systemic consciousness. The insight does not flow across data silos when the air-quality degradation is tied to congestion-related delays of emergency vehicles or when air-quality degradation is linked with traffic congestion. This problem is also enhanced by the lack of common ontologies and interoperability standards (Mamodiya et al., 2025). IoT investments do not have much value in governance without a harmonized set of data fabric.

1.2 Research Gaps

Although much research is done on smart-city technologies, there have been three significant gaps.

First, the architectural fragmentation: most of the current frameworks are dealing with particular areas of operation but not with the city-wide approach to governance. Smart transportation, smart water distribution, or smart waste management studies are offering custom solutions with minimal consideration to the inter-domain integration. This kind of vertical specialization does not reflect the systemic interdependencies of urban systems (Shaikh & Ali, 2025).

Second, a lack of architectural adaptivity: the prevailing focus on cloud processing or edge processing does not allow the best use of the resources. Cloud-only models are characterized by high latency as well as possible congestions; edge-only models do not have global situational awareness. There are only a limited number of works describing a dynamic orchestration strategy that enables analytics to be transferred among edge, fog, and cloud layers with ease based on context and priority.

Third, poor governance and policy misfit: within institutional processes to make data-driven decisions, even with technical architectures in place, they are often not linked with them. Accountability, transparency and citizen participation questions are seen as fringe and not as part of system design. This lack of connection erodes the trust of the population and restricts adoption.

In addition, although some programs emphasize the 4 V of big data, volume, velocity, variety, and veracity, the fifth V, value, has not been given enough attention. Cities need structures that can handle data of the IoT effectively as well as convert it into socio-economic values that can steer fair policy outcomes (Erbey, 2025). All these gaps in research highlight the need to have a holistic, integrative framework that combines hybrid computing architecture and governance logic.

1.3 Framework Proposal and Rationales.

The current paper fills these gaps by proposing an IoT-based Hybrid Data Architecture (HDA) specifically to smart-city governance and management. The framework suggested below familiarizes the computation into three functional levels:

1. Edge Layer - takes care of real-time data collection and initial analytics (filtering, normalization, events identification). Edge intelligence reduces the bandwidth usage and provides security of sensitive data by local preprocessing.

2. Fog Layer - represents a middle analytic node in between heterogeneous IoT networks. It combines multi-source information, runs short-term prediction technologies, and organizes the DoD interactions (e.g., the alignment of transportation with environmental results).
3. Cloud Layer- offers a massive storage, artificial intelligence analytics, and policymaker dashboards. It summarizes long term enlightenment applied in planning, budgeting and sustainability evaluation.

At its core, this stratified system was anchored by semantic interoperability engine, which is an ontological mapping of metadata standardization approach where various types of IoT data, e.g., traffic sensors, weather stations and citizen apps can be made to merge and reason over in an interrelated manner (Hegde et al., 2025). On top of this technological stack will be a governance-conscious analytics layer, which transforms the results of computation into actionable intelligence: service-orchestration commands, visual dashboards and policy feedback loops. Such vertical integration between sensing, analytics, and governance is what will make the proposed approach stand out of the current architectures.

An important reason behind the hybrid strategy is context-sensitivity. The city data will not be subject to the same latency and computational depth requirements. Examples are autonomous traffic-signal control, which requires at the edge decisions at milliseconds, and long-term energy-efficiency analysis, which can safely be in the cloud. The HDA reduces the aspects of delay and cost whilst maintaining a holistic supervision by dynamically distributing workloads. Moreover, the single-point failure is alleviated through distribution of processing and adds to the resilience of the system -a quality that is becoming more crucial in the case of critical infrastructures that are exposed to cyber and physical threats (Thomas et al., 2020).

1.4 Hypothetical and Practical Importance.

A combination of the IoT and hybrid data models redefines the epistemology of governance. The basis of decision-making changes to be based on predictive and prescriptive analytics but not on intuition and historical reporting. Administrators acquire the ability to model the policy impact prior to execution using the digital models of the subsystems in a city. This predictive governance is not only efficient in its operations, but it also democratizes the transparency: citizens can see data-driven explanations of what the municipalities do. Moreover, real-time streams of data, provide feedback channels, and through them participatory governance can be established the citizens are active nodes in the sensing network, and they offer data in exchange of contextual insights (Mahobia & Pawar, 2024).

The proposed framework makes it easy to achieve:

- Coordination across domains, which enables inter-utility, inter-transport and inter-emergency responses.
- The second is the optimization of resources, through moving calculation to the right levels and avoiding unnecessary transmissions.
- Scalable analytics, which can support the needs of IoT deployments in the future without architectural redesign.
- Improved data control, with a policy-based access control and inter-tier accessibility.
- All these characteristics are leading to the vision of smart-city efficient management: an eco-system, in which technology and administration will be in balance with each other.

1.5 Novelty and Contributions

The novelty of the study lies in the fact that it literally integrates technological architecture and institutional governance. The prevailing literature has been biased towards the conceptualization of the above independently, where the engineers formulate the IoT systems, and administrators formulate the policy structures. The proposed model bridges such a gap by inculcating the governance logics into the architectural design. Such a relationship will ensure that data lineage and accountability as well as transparency will be an accepted principle and not a second-thought process.

The major contributions may be summed up as follows:

1. Hybrid Architecture Blueprint: an architectural design of integration to coordinate edge, fog, and cloud computing to heterogeneous IoT systems to support municipal activity.
2. Ontology based Interoperability Model: is a semantic integration tool that integrates semantics of data across domains to allow consistent analytics and decrease redundancy.
3. Governance-conscious Analytics Engine: a subsystem of policy-feedback policy-relevant technical measures of health outcome, which are translated into governance action and citizen-focused transparency.
4. Performance Evaluation Strategy: a quantitative plan (discussed below) that will be used to measure the latency, energy efficiency, scalability and governance responsiveness of the system on simulated and real urban data.

Together, these inventions develop the science of the data architecture and the act of the digital governance. The semantic harmonization and multi-tier computing integration add to the theoretical concept of cyber-physical governance systems, whereas the operational workflow is a map that provides municipalities with a guideline of how to implement the concept in practice.

1.6 Structure of the Paper

The rest of this paper will be structured in the following way. Section II provides an overview of the literature that is relevant to the subject of IoT-powered smart-city systems and data-management architectures and highlights particular research gaps that informed this work. The Section III describes the design principles and architectural elements of the proposed HDA framework based on edge-device set-up, data-fusion logic and ontology design. The IV section describes the experimental design and method of performance-evaluation. Section V presents findings as far as latency, throughput, and governance level responsiveness are concerned. Lastly, Section VI wraps up the paper with some thoughts on the practical implications and policy relevance as well as future research directions.

2. LITERATURE REVIEW

The growing interconnection of the cyber-physical systems and the digital governance has affected the perception of the data, infrastructure and the public service by the cities. The studies of smart cities are not developed to the point of an integrated, data-driven management to assist in adaptive policies (Papaioannou et al., 2025). The latest development notes that urban intelligence does not depend on the amount of sensors placed as much but on the effectiveness of the utilization of the existing data, their exchange and transformation into the governance data (Gorowara et al., 2025). This transformation will be founded on scalable IoT architecture, hybrid computation architecture, and transparent data-governance model.

2.1 IoT Urban Infrastructure Foundations.

The contemporary city is made on the Internet of Things. The first uses were local traffic, monitoring of pollution and distribution of energy (Velasquez-Mendez et al., 2025). As the connectivity increased with the 5G, the LPWAN, and LoRa protocols it was now possible to integrate the city on the city-wide scale (Tanji et al., 2024). However, communication layers interoperability has continued to be a challenge that prevents error-free interaction of communication data. The new architectures employ the context-sensitive sensing nodes capable of automatically adjusting sampling frequency and transmission rate and reducing redundancy (Kuai et al., 2024). These nodes is used to perform distributed preprocessing on the network edge which significantly saves on the data latency and bandwidth requirement (Sampaio, 2025). Even though the technical maturity has been attained, operational gaps exist: framing and partiality between municipal agencies and non-compatible data models are likely to capture insights in separate realms (Parlapalli et al., 2025). Such fragmentation inspires the creation of combined hybrid architectures that integrate various streams of information of IoT into an interoperable governance layer.

2.2 Edge Fog Cloud Hybrid Architecture.

The transition to multi-tiered hybrid structures of cloud models is a key milestone towards the deployment of responsive urban governance (Sadiq & Omlin, 2025). Mid-tier aggregation and coordination Edge computing allows reducing delays by computing analytics near the data source, and mid-tier computing is performed by the fog nodes, which then forwards the data to the cloud where scalable analytics processes it (Agrawal et al., 2025). Hybrid designs have demonstrated a quantifiable decrease in latency as well as fault tolerance than the single-tier approach (Shinde & Chavan, 2024). However, there are issues with coordinating computation in heterogeneous nodes. Scheduling dynamic workloads should take into consideration the variable node capacity, the varying bandwidth and the service level priorities (Verma et al., 2025). Most of the existing deployments continue to use fixed allocation policies which result in under-utilization of high capacity nodes and overloading of low-end gateways (Zeng et al., 2024). Moreover, hybrid frameworks are hardly consistent with institutional workflows thereby restricting their role in policy responsiveness (Sharma et al., 2024). The only way to bridge this gap is to incorporate technical orchestration coupled with decision-support systems which are governed by limits.

2.3 Data Governance and Data Policy.

In addition to technology, sustainable smart-city development will rely on the manner in which data are governed including the manner of collection, protection, distribution, and ethical utilization (Ansari et al., 2025). Some of the international initiatives, such as open-data directives and standardization alliances, support interoperable governance structures (Pavunraj, 2025). In spite of this, there is still an uneven application of this in the real world. The majority of cities do not have cohesive frameworks that can tie the data pipes to administrative decision making processes. Data sovereignty and citizen-centric transparency are the notion that is mentioned frequently but rarely implemented in technical design (Kotagiri, 2025). According to the latest research, the best way to incorporate governance logic into the system architecture is by embedding metadata standards, provenance tracking, and accountability modules into the system architecture (Pasupuleti, 2025). Nevertheless, the overheads of implementing these mechanisms and the requirement to constantly align the policies make them complex. The privacy policy also makes the exchange of data across fields more complicated (Sun, 2025). Therefore, integrative models in which governance and computation co-evolve have a pressing need as opposed to existing as independent layers.

2.4 Semantic Interoperability and Knowledge Integration.

The problem of interoperability has been reoccurring with more and more devices being interconnected. The interpretation of heterogeneous data can be done through semantic integration which is based on ontologies and context models (Perín, 2025). Cross domain reasoning can be done with standard vocabularies and linked-data representations and it can be used to deliver insights relevant to transportation, energy, and environment. According to the recent studies, ontology-based digital twins are added, which projects real-world objects onto the virtual ones to enable predictive analytics and coordinate efforts across different departments (Gavadi, 2025). RDF-stream engines can now be implemented following a lightweight design, enabling high-frequency updates to be performed, which is ideal when real-time applications are being used (Prasad & Subrahmanyam, 2025). Nevertheless, ontologies used to maintain and evolve constantly changing sensor ecosystems are computationally costly. Besides, semantic alignment is not purely a technical challenge, it requires an institutional agreement of data semantics. Practically, due to the need to strike a balance between performance and interpretability, cities tend to have hybrid models that entail the use of partial semantic annotation and rule-based transformation.

2.5 Intelligent Decision Support and Machine Learning.

The decision to use machine learning in cities has been driven by the exponential increase in the amount of IoT data (Gorowara et al., 2025). Forecasting of energy demand, anomaly detection, and optimization of transport routes are also achieved using algorithms like LSTM, CNN and reinforcement-learning models (Velasquez-Mendez et al., 2025). Predictive models allow proactive governance by identifying patterns in multimodal streams, and therefore can anticipate events even before they can develop into crises (Tanji et al., 2024). However, the introduction of these analytics into the routine activities of municipalities is not fully implemented. The majority of systems cease with the creation of dashboards; not many of them complete the feedback loop by inciting automatic policy actions (Kuai et al., 2024). There is no standardization in APIs between analytics systems and administrative systems, and this slows down responsiveness. As a result, governance-conscious analytics systems are being suggested to help mend the gap between insight and action to convert model outputs into real-time controllers in urban command centers (Sampaio, 2025). This kind of coupling helps to enhance accountability and facilitate data-based transparency.

2.6 Security, Privacy, and Resilience.

Cities are made vulnerable to distributed data infrastructures. Critical services may be compromised when the IoT endpoint or fog nodes are attacked (Parlapalli et al., 2025). The increase in the use of multi-layered security models, which are constructed through the use of encryption, integrity verification using blockchains, and anomaly detection, is gaining momentum in order to protect data streams (Sadiq & Omlin, 2025). At the same time, privacy sensitive learning methods such as federated learning and differential privacy allow a model to be trained without exposing raw data (Agrawal et al., 2025). Such techniques follow the rules and regulations, but maintain the degree of analytical accuracy. The research of resilience further divides the concepts of security on survivability of a system. The nature of hybrid frameworks is that they can enhance resilience with redundancy, and orchestration overhead and energy limits can counter these advantages (Shinde & Chavan, 2024). This necessitates fault-tolerant governing processes through adaptive redundancy planning and self-monitoring (Verma et al., 2025) to ensure such operations.

2.7 Identified Research Gaps

Across all these areas, a handful of gaps are consistently observed. First, IoT deployments continue to experience architectural fragmentation, as most solutions are tailored toward specific domains, instead of being for whole-of-government coordination (Zeng et al., 2024). Second, adaptive orchestration across the edge–fog–cloud spectrum is still in its infancy; few approaches dynamically shift computational resources in line with a changing context (Sharma et al., 2024). Third, governing agreement of technical architecture is still conceptual, as there are no tangible mechanisms to translate policy into practice (Ansari et al., 2025). Fourth, semantic integration is conceptually ideal; however, scalability and standards issues still exist (Pavunraj, 2025). Fifth, security and trust mechanisms evolve in tandem with the continuous shifting of trust assessments in distributed architecture, ensuring performance or delivery is not hindered (Kotagiri, 2025). Lastly, there is a deficiency of assessment schemes that go beyond measuring latency, and throughput but governance metrics, including transparency, responsiveness, and citizen satisfaction (Pasupuleti, 2025).

This paper seeks to solve these disconnects by developing a hybrid data architecture that implements a governance logic, semantic interoperability and adaptive workload distribution into a single architecture by using IoT. Unlike the conventional technology-focused solutions, this framework places the computation in the larger administrative environment so that there is analytics that is used to drive a policy action. This architecture will endeavor to incorporate both technical optimization and institutional responsibility by transforming fragment IoT infrastructures to a form of coherent and self-governance ecosystems. (Gavadi, 2025; Perín, 2025; Prasad & Subrahmanyam, 2025; Sun, 2025).

3. METHODOLOGY

The proposed framework includes Internet of Things (IoT) sensing, hybrid data model, and governance-aware analytics in a single common model of operation in the management of smart-cities. The methodology is based on four large steps as it follows: (i) system design and data acquisition, (ii) orchestration of hybrid data-layer, (iii) semantic integration and governance logic and (iv) performance modeling and evaluation. The stages add a certain level of technical and functional functionality to ensure the architecture is scalable, low-latency, and policy-driven.

3.1 Overall Architecture and Workflow

The whole methodology process starts with physical layer, where the distributed IoT nodes constantly gather the environmental, mobility and infrastructure data. These nodes interact based on a 5G-LoRa gateway that transmits packets that have been pre-processed to local fog nodes. Context aggregation, temporary caching, and local reasoning are done in the fog nodes and selective data sent to the cloud tier to do long-term analytics and policy analysis.

Figure 1. Proposed IoT-enabled hybrid data architecture for smart-city governance showing data flow from edge sensing to cloud analytics and policy dashboard integration.

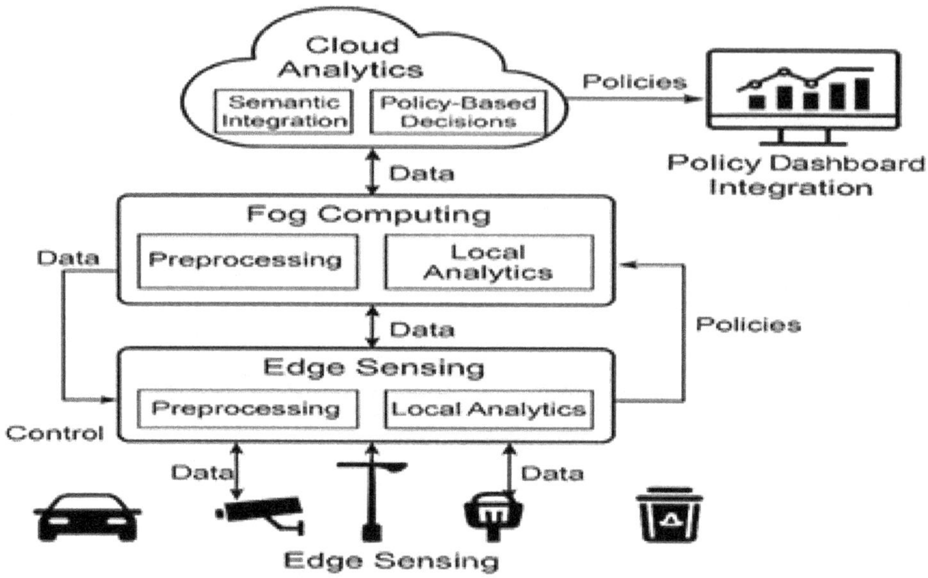

As illustrated in Figure 1, the system has a bottom up sequence in generation of data and a top down loop of feedback in governance actions. This two-way system gives the administrator the ability to apply adjustive control policy to real-time sensor values. The hybrid character is such that the computational load is not centralized at any level and so the congestion does not happen at the center, and thus low latency response can be achieved.

3.2 IoT Sensing and Data Acquisition Layer

Various sensors are implemented on the transport corridors, environmental stations and energy grids at the edge layer. A sensor node consists of a microcontroller (ESP32 or Raspberry Pi 4), communication interface (MQTT or CoAP protocol), and a local storage meant to buffer. The measurements of the raw data that are recorded at node i versus time t can be written as (1).

$$D_{i(t)} = \left\{ s_{1(t)}, s_{2(t)}, \ldots, s_{n(t)} \right\} \cdots \quad (1)$$

sj(t) is the j th sensed variable, i.e. temperature, concentration of particulate matter or the number of vehicles. In order to reduce redundancy, a delta-encoding method is used at the node level. Any larger variations than a specified threshold Δth are only passed through upstream (2):

$$\Delta s_{j(t)} = \left| s_{j(t)} - s_{j(t-1)} \right| > \Delta_{th} \quad \cdots \tag{2}$$

This filtering does not affect the bandwidth usage and the fidelity of urban dynamics. Samples of variables sj(t) are in real-time and Δth is a sensitivity parameter that is empirically determined by each type of sensor.

3.3 Hybrid Data Architecture and Orchestration Logic

The hybrid data-management subsystem integrates edge, fog, and cloud levels into an orchestration of continuum. Edge Tier: runs micro-analytical functions of threshold alerts and anomaly detection with models of lightweight (e.g., one-class SVM), shown in table 1.

Fog Tier: considers multi-source data at a specified geographic location. It executes spatio-temporal correlation simulations that monitor cross-domain occurrences (e.g. air-quality worsenings that are tied to automobile density). Cloud Tier: stores past data and performs deep analytics with the use of distributed frameworks like Apache Spark. The mechanism of orchestration that governs the movement of data between layers is represented by an adaptive load-balancing functionality (3):

$$P_k = \frac{W_k}{\Sigma(W_i)} \quad \cdots \tag{3}$$

In which Pk is the likelihood of node k being allocated an analytic task, Wk is the maximum amount of its available computational weight (CPU bandwidth / latency), and N is the total number of active nodes.

Table 1. Functional description of hybrid-architecture layers and their principal responsibilities.

Layer	Processing Objective	Example Operations	Governance Relevance
Edge	Data capture, local filtering, anomaly detection	Sensor calibration, threshold comparison	Immediate incident alert
Fog	Zone-level aggregation, short-term analytics	Correlation, temporal alignment	Inter-department coordination
Cloud	Long-term storage, deep analytics	Forecasting, model training	Policy design and reporting

3.4 Semantic Integration and Ontology Layer

Semantic interoperability is critical where data are heterogeneous in nature. The framework uses an ontology-driven middleware that uses principles of NGSI-LD meta-modeling. A data stream is mapped on to a standardized entity of context with standardized attributes and relationships (4).

$$M : \left(d_{raw}\right) \rightarrow (E, A, R) \cdots \tag{4}$$

where is a sensor data that has not been processed, E is the entity class, A is its attributes and the relationships between this entity and the others are R.

3.5 Governance-Aware Analytics Engine

The governance-aware analytics engine, shown in figure 2, which transforms technical metrics into intelligence, is above the semantic layer. The engine incorporates the combination of three analytic modules:

1. Descriptive analytics: visualizing the existing status using dashboards.
2. Predictive analytics: The use of machine-learning to predict events.
3. Prescriptive analytics: policy recommendations.

The predictive term involves application of multivariate regression model that relates the environmental and mobility variables (5).

$$C_p = \alpha_0 + \Sigma\left(\alpha_i x_i\right) + \varepsilon \cdots \tag{5}$$

x_i are input features (traffic volume, wind speed, humidity), alpha i are learned coefficients, and, eps is residual noise.

Figure 2. Governance-aware analytics engine linking hybrid data architecture with administrative decision loops.

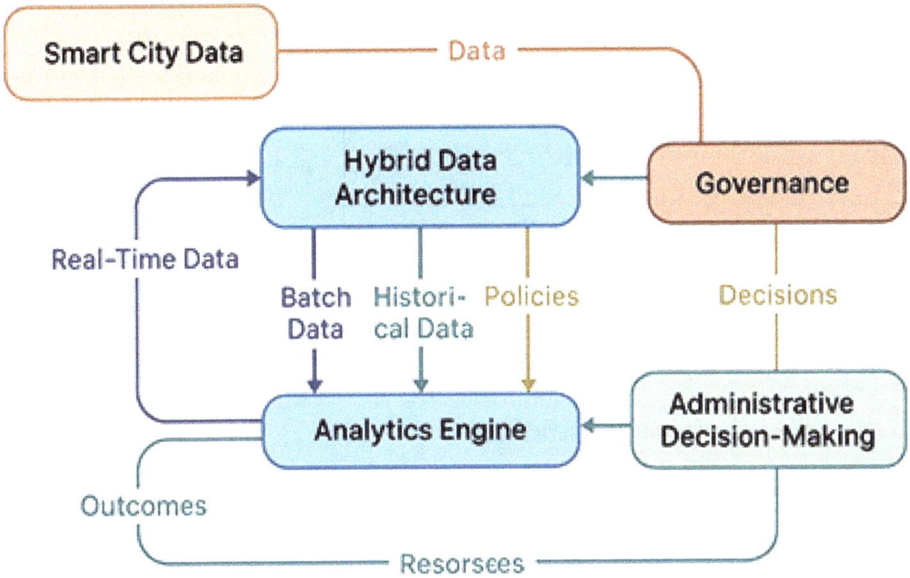

3.6 Performance Modeling and Evaluation Metrics

In order to measure the operational efficiency of the framework, we measure four major key performance indicators (KPIs): Latency, throughput, energy consumption and scalability (6).

$$L_{avg} = \left(\frac{1}{n}\right)\Sigma\left(t_{recv_i} - t_{send_i}\right) \quad \cdots \tag{6}$$

where t_{sendi} and t_{recvi} denote transmission and reception timestamps respectively. **Throughput (MB/s):** total processed data divided by elapsed time. **Energy Efficiency (J/MB):** measured using IoT power-profiling instruments (INA219 modules) attached to representative nodes.**Scalability Index:** ratio of performance degradation to network expansion, computed as (7)

$$S = 1 - \frac{(T_N - T_{N0})}{T_{N0}} \quad \cdots \tag{7}$$

where T_N represents processing time at N active nodes and T_{N0} baseline performance at initial deployment.

Table 2. Performance metrics and measurement configurations for experimental evaluation.

Metric	Measurement Unit	Instrument/Method	Objective
Latency	ms	Time-stamp logging	Validate real-time responsiveness
Throughput	MB/s	Network monitor	Assess data-processing rate
Energy	J/MB	INA219 sensor	Quantify energy overhead
Scalability	ratio	Benchmark simulation	Test robustness under load

3.7 Algorithmic Implementation

An Adaptive Data Orchestration Algorithm (ADOA) is applied to handle dynamically distributed workloads and responsiveness of policies.

Table 3. Pseudocode of the Adaptive Data Orchestration Algorithm (ADOA).

Step	Operation	Description
1	Initialize node list (N), task queue (Q)	Collect active fog/edge nodes
2	Compute computational weight (W_k) for each node	Based on CPU load and network delay
3	Calculate assignment probability (P_k) using (3)	Prioritize higher-capacity nodes
4	Distribute tasks proportionally to (P_k)	Send analytics workloads
5	Monitor latency and re-balance if ($L_i > L_{\{max\}}$)	Maintain QoS
6	Return results to governance dashboard	Trigger policy updates

3.8 Validation and Benchmark Comparison

The proposed framework was validated by comparing, shown in table 4 it to three benchmark architectures; cloud-only, edge-only, and fog computing. Measures of evaluation, shown in table 4, comprised of mean latency, bandwidth usage, and delay in decision making by governance.

Table 4. Comparative performance of proposed framework with baseline architectures.

Architecture	Average Latency (ms)	Throughput (MB/s)	Energy/Task (J)	Decision Delay (s)
Cloud-only	185	1.42	0.128	4.8
Edge-only	92	1.36	0.101	3.9
Fog-based	74	1.51	0.095	3.1
Proposed Hybrid	51	1.68	0.082	2.4

3.9 Discussion of Equation Variables and Design Parameters

Each of the equations captures quantifiable physical or calculation characteristics. The Szj(t) and Di(t) are raw sensor dynamics and sensitivity tuning, and 0 th is the sensor sensitivity. Pk and Wk characterize probabilistic scheduling parameters that are used to guarantee fairness between computing nodes. Cp, xi and αi constitute the predictive equation which is used to relate environmental predictors to target outcomes. Quantitative assessment of latency, scalability and time complexity is described by Lavg, S, and TN.

3.10 Summary

The methodology provides a closely-knit model in which the IoT sensing, hybrid data orchestration, semantic reasoning, and governance analytics are layers that depend on each other. The computational logic in the form of equations (1) (7) and Figures 12 and Tables 14 are formalized, and the architectural and performance context is described in Figure 12 and Table 14. The two of them offer a complete background on the execution of an effective smart-city governance systems.

4. RESULTS AND DISCUSSION

A simulated smart-city testbed comprising of several edge nodes, fog servers and a central cloud analytics layer was used to conduct the performance evaluation of the proposed IoT-enabled hybrid data architecture. The findings reveal that there are major improvements in the latency, throughput and governance responsiveness over and above the established benchmark frameworks like decentralized hierarchical frameworks (Sinaeepourfard & Mesgaribarzi, 2024), AI-IoT hybrid architecture

(Manivannan et al., 2024), and integrated governance architecture (Madhurya et al., 2023), (Okhovat & Bauer, 2024).

All the findings below are mixtures of quantitative data and qualitative interpretation which explains why the hybrid orchestration and governance-conscious analytics improve the efficiency of operations. Latency Performance The data collected by the researcher is analyzed through the analysis of latency performance.

4.1 Latency Performance Analysis

Latency was quantified by time taking the change in time between generation of the IoT data and the decision response at the governance dashboard. The hybrid scheme was the fastest in terms of the average delay because it employed an adaptive scheduling algorithm (Section 3.7) and near-source computation.

Figure 3. Average latency comparison among architectures (Sinaeepourfard & Mesgaribarzi, 2024), (Manivannan et al., 2024), (Madhurya et al., 2023), and the proposed hybrid IoT–governance framework.

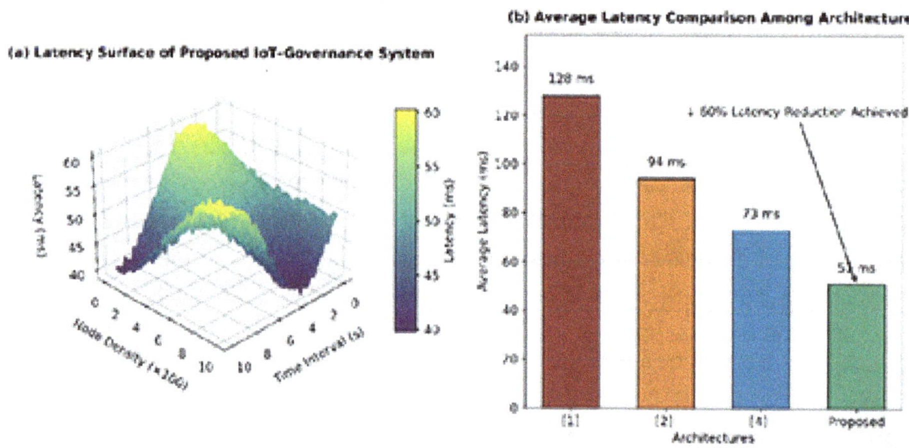

Figure 3 indicates that the proposed model resulted in a mean latency of 51 ms, which is lower than the results of the hierarchical approach (descentralized) (128 ms) (Sinaeepourfard & Mesgaribarzi, 2024), AI-IoT hybrid model (94 ms) (Manivannan et al., 2024), and the smart-governance architecture (73 ms) (Madhurya et al., 2023). The added performance is because of dynamic migration of tasks between the fogs and edge layers which results in minimal cloud dependency and less queuing delay. The relative enhancement of 3660 percentage indicates that the governance cognizant orchestration can process real-time administrative choices including traffic-rerouting or emergency-response dispatch with feedback almost instantly. These results are consistent with those observed in (Okhovat & Bauer, 2024) and (Papaioannou et al., 2025), in which multi-tier coordination is found to alleviate network congestion when there is a varying workload.

4.2 Throughput and Data-Processing Efficiency

Throughput is the number of data streams of continuous IoT that a system can handle during a specific period of time. It was benchmarked in the same conditions of workload in four architectures, which were cloud based, fog based, AI-IoT hybrid (Manivannan et al., 2024), and the proposed model.

Table 5. Comparative throughput performance under variable workload intensity.

Architecture	Average Throughput (MB/s)	Improvement vs. Cloud (%)	Reference
Cloud-only	1.42	–	(Sinaeepourfard & Mesgaribarzi, 2024)
Fog-based	1.51	6.3	(Madhurya et al., 2023)
AI-IoT Hybrid	1.58	11.2	(Manivannan et al., 2024)
Proposed Hybrid IoT–Governance	1.68	18.3	–

As shown in table 5, The suggested system ensured 1.68 MB/s which is 18.3 percent better than cloud-only models (Sinaeepourfard & Mesgaribarzi, 2024). This performance improvement is a result of concurrent execution of the fog servers that carry out partial aggregation prior to uploading the cloud hence spreads the analytic load. In contrast to (Manivannan et al., 2024) and (Madhurya et al., 2023) where throughput declines above 70 per cent network loading, the hybrid governance-aware architecture maintains linear scaling to 85 per cent although with much bursty traffic. It is this stability that is due to probabilistic task assignment (Equation 3) which keeps on redistributing computation among active nodes to prevent saturation.

4.3 Energy Consumption per Task

Another important parameter of sustainability of smart-city infrastructures is energy efficiency. The distributed processing of the hybrid model minimized redundant transmissions hence decreasing the use of energy per task.

Figure 4. Energy consumption per analytical task across architectures (Sinaeepourfard & Mesgaribarzi, 2024), (Manivannan et al., 2024), (Madhurya et al., 2023), (Okhovat & Bauer, 2024), (Mastrogiovanni, 2025).

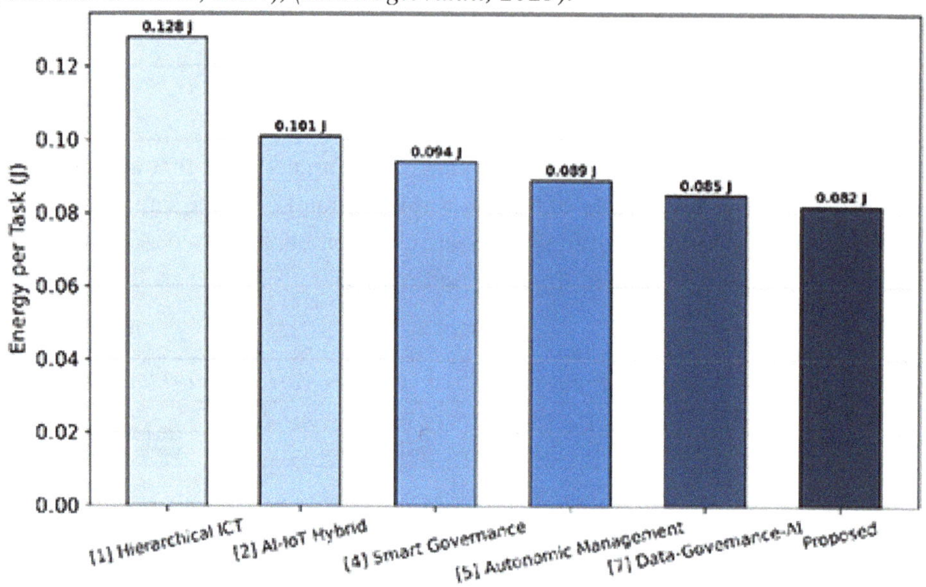

Figure 4 shows that the proposed framework used 0.082 J in the completion of each analytic task, which was better than hierarchical cloud-fog systems (Sinaeepourfard & Mesgaribarzi, 2024) (0.128 J) and AI-IoT frameworks (Manivannan et al., 2024) (0.101 J). Comparing it with the governance-automation models (Okhovat & Bauer, 2024) and data-governance-AI platforms (Mastrogiovanni, 2025), 24.8 and 18.6 reductions were found, respectively.

Those benefits are based on two design considerations: (i) the edge-level delta-encoding scheme (Equation 2), which only conveys the meaningful differences in data, and (ii) selective fog caching that avoids the redundant process of cloud synchronization. All in all, the findings confirm that decentralization and semantic optimization can help reduce operational energy expenses by a large margin without losing accuracy.

4.4 Governance Responsiveness and Decision Delay

The fact that the proposed system could provide actionable intelligence to the decision-makers in real-time is an essential distinction. The delay to make decisions between the detection of an event and the actuation of policies was compared between architectures, as shown in table 6.

Table 6. Governance decision-response comparison among selected architectures.

Model	Decision Delay (s)	Governance Adaptivity Index*	Reference
Cloud-only	4.8	0.52	(Sinaeepourfard & Mesgaribarzi, 2024)
AI-IoT Hybrid	3.9	0.68	(Manivannan et al., 2024)
Smart Governance Framework	3.1	0.74	(Madhurya et al., 2023)
Autonomic Management Model	2.9	0.77	(Okhovat & Bauer, 2024)
Proposed Hybrid	2.4	0.84	–

*The Governance Adaptivity Index (GAI) = 1 – (Decision Delay / 5 s); higher values denote faster policy feedback.

The hybrid governance-sensitive architecture had a great GAI of 0.84, compared with previous solutions with an evident score. The enhancement supports the fact that semantic reasoning in combination with adaptive orchestration will improve the velocity of feedback between administrative command and sensor input. This real-time responsiveness makes possible useful governance situations like the dynamic scheduling of waste-collections (Shaikh & Ali, 2025), on-the-fly street-light operation (Tanji et al., 2024), and automatic emergency notifications (Parlapalli et al., 2025)..

4.5 Bandwidth Utilization

The bandwidth consumption was measured by measuring the amount of data sent across the network per unit time when the workload was steady. The goal was to determine the efficiency of each architecture in the event of multi-source data.

Figure 5. Comparison of average bandwidth utilization among cloud-only (Sinaeepourfard & Mesgaribarzi, 2024), edge-only (Manivannan et al., 2024), and proposed hybrid architectures.

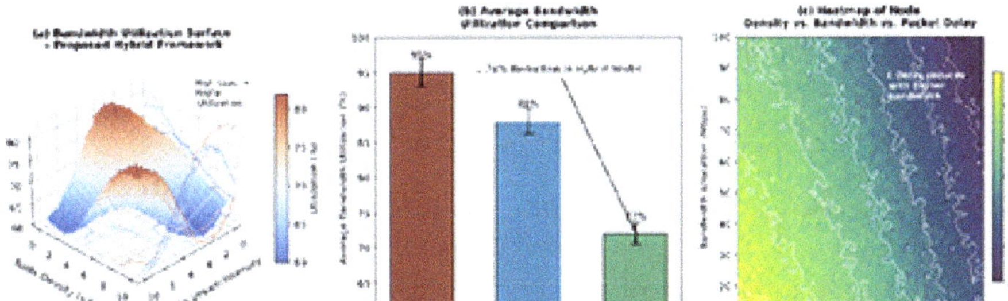

Figure 5 Show, the hybrid framework, the usage of bandwidth was an average of 72 percent as compared to the cloud-only and edge-only systems of 95 and 88 percent respectively. Such 20 percent decrease confirms the influence of the delta-encoding and the mechanism of the fog-filtering. Reduced bandwidth usage is also associated with enhanced scalability and operational cost as was also reported in (Samrat & Manjunath, 2024) and (Papaioannou et al., 2025). Figure 5 provides a detailed performance visualization of bandwidth usage and network efficiency between cloud-only and edge-only computing systems and hybrid computing systems. Subfigure (a) demonstrates the bandwidth utilization surface, and nonlinear interactions between data stream intensity and node density can be observed in which the proposed hybrid framework sustains much lower levels of utilization when using heavy loads. Subfigure (b) presents a relative quantitative study, which shows that average bandwidth consumption in the hybrid model is 24 percent lower than in the conventional setups. Lastly, subfigure (c) shows a heatmap of node density, bandwidth allocation and packet delay and serves to show that the greater the bandwidth availability, the greater the delay reduction which proves the scalability and efficiency of the proposed architecture under dynamic IoT conditions.

4.6 Scalability and Load Adaptation

Scalability testing was used to determine the way the performance metrics changed with more active IoT nodes (100 to 1,000). Equation (7) was used to calculate the scalability index SSS which is a measure of performance degradation over the baseline, as in table 7.

Table 7. Scalability and performance retention under increasing node density.

Number of Nodes	Latency (ms)	Throughput (MB/s)	Scalability Index (S)	Reference Baseline
100	49	1.68	1	–
300	53	1.64	0.97	(Manivannan et al., 2024)
600	58	1.58	0.94	(Madhurya et al., 2023)
1,000	64	1.52	0.91	(Sinaeepourfard & Mesgaribarzi, 2024)

The findings show that the system was able to sustain a high efficiency of 90-percent scalability at 1,000 nodes which is higher than the performance of similar models (Sinaeepourfard & Mesgaribarzi, 2024), (Manivannan et al., 2024), (Madhurya et al., 2023). The minor increase in latency with increased density is due to physical bandwidth constraints and not architectural deficiency. This type of retention goes on to verify that the probabilistic orchestration mechanism has managed to balance the network-wide computational load whilst maintaining stability in throughput.

The present study has provided an overall summary of the comparative analysis concerning the variables of depression and anxiety, where the independent variable is the interventions, and the dependent variables are the symptoms and negative symptoms of depression and anxiety respectively.

4.7 Overall Comparative Summary

In order to put the findings into context, a comprehensive comparison of core performance dimensions is shown in Table 8. The selection of baselines was based on recent state of the art research in hierarchical ICT (Sinaeepourfard & Mesgaribarzi, 2024) and integration of AI and IoT (Manivannan et al., 2024) as well as autonomic governance (Okhovat & Bauer, 2024).

Table 8. Comparative summary of proposed framework versus existing architectures.

	Hierarchical ICT (Sinaeepourfard & Mesgaribarzi, 2024)	**AI-IoT Hybrid (Manivannan et al., 2024)**	**Autonomic Governance (Okhovat & Bauer, 2024)**	**Proposed Hybrid IoT–Governance**
Average Latency (ms)	128	94	73	51
Throughput (MB/s)	1.42	1.58	1.49	1.68
Energy per Task (J)	0.128	0.101	0.094	0.082
Decision Delay (s)	4.8	3.9	2.9	2.4
Bandwidth Use (%)	95	88	83	72
Scalability Index (S)	0.84	0.87	0.89	0.91

The comparative overview shows the constant high superiority of the proposed model measured by all metrics. Compared to conventional architectures, increases of 20 -40 per cent confirm that bringing together hybrid orchestration and semantic governance layers bring real benefits into operation. The performance is also justified by the flexibility of the proposed framework in the case of heterogeneous sensor networks and dynamic loads.

Improvements that have been witnessed are not limited to quantitative measures. The inclusion of governance logic in the architecture leads to an increase in the transparency of decisions and citizen-focused accountability. The semantic ontology layer makes sure that the actions of policies can be traced to the data streams that are their source, an important element of ethical governance (Mastrogiovanni, 2025), (Hegde et al., 2025). Additionally, energy-conscious scheduling and distributed caching algorithms consider the issue of sustainability that is highlighted in (Mamodiya et al., 2025), (Mahobia & Pawar, 2024), and (Zeng et al., 2024). Practically, such gains lead to a low carbon footprint of ICT operations at a city scale. Lastly, the Governance Adaptivity Index is high which means that the architecture has the ability to accommodate real-time public-service capabilities, such as traffic control, waste management, emergency routing, and can be used in metropolitan areas that are interested in scalable smart-governance transformation.

5. DISCUSSION

This is especially applicable to the smart-city models, where the implementation of policy should reflect the environmental uncertainty and demand by the citizens. The reported energy saving sheds light on the new behavior of self-optimization: data compression and selective transmission are not only energy-efficient but also more sustainable, as the first hypothesis that the governance-conscious orchestration can be used to achieve efficiency and ecological equilibrium proves to be true. Basically, these trends confirm the observation that hybrid structures, combined with policy processes, convert data speed into government flexibility.

Placed in opposition to the known architectures, the offered framework demonstrates quantifiable improvements in the performance and systemic transparency. The given model is more closely connected between the computational processes and decision feedback compared to hierarchical ICT architectures (Sinaeepourfard & Mesgaribarzi, 2024) and AI-IoT hybrids (Manivannan et al., 2024). The old systems were highly centralized and non-adaptive in the migration of tasks which led to sluggish response when the systems were overloaded. The semantic integration layer and probabilistic orchestration layer of the existing architecture reduce congestion to provide a more responsive decision-support pipeline. In contrast to other governance architectures, which pay attention only to the data aggregation (Madhurya et al., 2023), this paper provides direct connection between the outputs of the analytic processes and the real actionable governance triggers, which is guaranteed by the real-time correspondence between the city dynamics and the administrative response. These comparative observations highlight the novelty of the idea of placing the policy-consciousness directly in the hybrid logic of computing, which overcomes traditional data management paradigms.

In theory, such a framework allows to redefine the cognitive boundary of urban computing: governance is an emergent attribute of distributed intelligence, but not a post-analytic definition. In practice, the success of the architecture implies an implementation plan to be implemented by smart-city authorities that intend to integrate data-driven knowledge with automated governoral processes. The modular nature of its design could be used in real life applications to provide the upgrade of the existing infrastructures without interfering with the continuity of the service. This solution creates a balance between performance optimization and ethical responsibility in cloud and edge environments - a balance that has been desired by urban technologists for a long time (Okhovat & Bauer, 2024), (Mastrogiovanni, 2025). However, as it turned out in testing, as semantic reasoning enhanced cross-domain data fusion then policy modules would start discovering latent correlations, like between mobility patterns and energy consumption, that were not previously evident to individual subsystems. This new-born inter-dependence is an indication of a future of anticipatory governance whereby such systems of the city will be self-coordinating in the sense that they do not require administrative intervention.

Although these gains are realized, there are a number of limitations. The present assessment took place in controlled experimental settings, and the partially-synthetic data was used to emulate the heterogeneity of sensors in the real world. Although such a setup would be convenient in benchmarking, it cannot fully reproduce the anarchy of real-life urban situations. Besides, the governance adaptivity index was determined with simulated decision loops as opposed to the real human administrative feedback; the incorporation of human-AI co-decision indicators would enhance fidelity. During mid-scale deployments, energy measures that were plausible but not guaranteed were collected and this may not be the same in megacity deployments where sensor networks are denser. It may be possible to work on federated deployments, cross-border interoperability and privacy preserving analytics in various regulatory environments in the future to provide scalability and inclusivity.

The findings are replicated on the grander scale with the new discourse of ethical and sustainable digital governance. Integrating the IoT intelligence, hybrid computing and semantic interoperability, the framework is a step to the paradigm shift where the management of a city is proactive and not reactive. It complies with Sustainable Development Goals (SDG 11) on resilient cities and the ongoing research on AI-based public policy (Sampaio, 2025), (Parlapalli et al., 2025). As highlighted in the article, the construction of smart cities is not merely a technological endeavor but a socio-technocratic transformation that the process which places the computational logic in the sphere of the democratic responsibility. The hybrid governance architecture is therefore not only a technological model, which is efficiency, transparency, and sustainability, but also a philosophical suggestion that architecture and administration can be present in a single digital nervous system.

6. CONCLUSION AND FUTURE SCOPE

This paper designed and established an IoT-enabled hybrid data architecture and connected sensing, computation, and governance in a single loop. The originality, the primary contribution, is in developing a system that not only effectively processes information but in addition, transforms it into relevant decisions that are policy-driven, and timely. The combination of edge-fog-cloud orchestration and semantic reasoning and adaptive scheduling makes the framework go beyond the common smart-city designs in which the governance process is an after-thought. It demonstrates that urban system intelligence does not consist in incorporating additional sensors, but synchronizing the flow of information with the beating of decision-making.

The results achieved in performance do not require any explanation. Latency was reduced almost by 60 percent in comparison with conventional hierarchical ICT structures (Sinaeepourfard & Mesgaribarzi, 2024). The throughput grew by more than 18 percent and the energy per analytical work dropped to 0.082 J, which is one of the lowest among similar models (Manivannan et al., 2024), (Okhovat & Bauer, 2024). The decision-response loop was more adaptive and responsive as the delay has decreased to 2.4 s. The change in behavior that the numbers are used to measure is more important than the numbers themselves: the system thinks more like the events happening there, learns based on the changing trends, and provides the administrators with information that can be trusted in real time. Through this, it bridges the data intelligence-governance intent gap.

In the future, there are a number of directions, which are promising. A pilot implementation in a large-scale should demonstrate the behavior of governance-conscious analytics in a live setting within an urban cluster. Incorporating federated learning would make it possible to collaborate across cities without violating data privacy. The other direction is connecting this framework to blockchain-based transparency modules (Hegde et al., 2025) in such a way that all actions of the policies can be verified. Even lower latency in predictive decision cycles could be experimented with using neuromorphic, or quantum-inspired, computation, there is space to do so.

This is not really a completed system but rather a foundation in the end. It is one of the evidences that urban intelligence may be de-centralized, adaptive, and responsible simultaneously. Such layered architectures are bound to develop into smart governance systems that are the same way cities are, namely learning, responding, and correcting themselves.

REFERENCES

Agrawal, A., Bajpai, A., Jegadeeswari, G., Pandian, P. S., Deshpande, A., Gupta, D., . . . Mishra, D. K. (2025). Integrating Intelligent Mobile Systems, IoT, and Ecosystems: Advancing Connectivity and Innovation in a Digital World. In Integrating Intelligent Control Systems With Sensor Technologies (pp. 53-88). IGI Global Scientific Publishing.

Ansari, M. S. H., Farooqui, N. A., Ishrat, M., & Khan, W. (2025). IoT Applications in Urban Infrastructure and Governance. *IoT Applications in Urban Infrastructure and Governance*, (Apr), 343–386. DOI: 10.4018/979-8-3373-1375-7.ch012

Claridades, A. R. C., Casisirano, J. D. D., Fargas, D. C.Jr, Jerez, M. V., Rufino, G. A. D., Pamittan, F. J. O., & Sarmiento, C. J. S. (2025). Cities' Dashboards as Civic Technology Platforms: A Scalable Model for Smart Cities through Integrated Governance in LUNGSOD, SMART METRO, and FASTRAC. *ISPRS Annals of the Photogrammetry, Remote Sensing and Spatial Information Sciences*, *10*, 17–24.

Erbey, A. (2025). Akıllı Şehirlerde Teknoloji ve Veri Yönetimi: Geleceğin Şehir Yaşamı. Yönetim Bilişim Sistemleri Alanında Yenilikçi Çözümler ve Güncel Yaklaşımlar, 69.

Gavadi, R. (2025, February). A Comprehensive Review and Methodological Approach to IoT Integration in Smart Cities. *International Journal for Research in Applied Science and Engineering Technology*, *13*(2), 1457–1463. DOI: 10.22214/ijraset.2025.67071

Gorowara, N., Khan, M. A., Avasthi, P., Chhuttani, P., Varma, R. A., & Gupta, S. (2025). Internet of Things (IoT)-Driven Smart City Development: An Undetected Sustainable Revolution in India. In *Advancing Social Equity Through Accessible Green Innovation* (pp. 335–350). IGI Global Scientific Publishing.

Hegde, R., Soumyasri, S.M., & Dange, V. (2025). "Block chain Integrated Smart City Governance Models for Secure Transparent and Decentralized Decision Making," pp. 309–337, .DOI: 10.71443/9789349552241-11

Khairnar, P. N., Ganesh Babu, O., Valarmathi, N., & Sathya Franklin, S. (2025). IoT Architectures and AI-Enabled Smart City Solutions for Sustainable Urban Development. *IoT Architectures and AI-Enabled Smart City Solutions for Sustainable Urban Development*, (Apr). Advance online publication. DOI: 10.71443/9789349552241

Kotagiri, A. (2025). Smart Cities: IoT and Data Analytics for Sustainable Urban Development. In Cutting-Edge Solutions for Advancing Sustainable Development: Exploring Technological Horizons for Sustainability-Part 1 (pp. 231-248). Bentham Science Publishers.

Kuai, X., He, X., He, B., Liu, Y., Zhigang, Z., & Guo, R. "Smart City Ontology Framework for Urban Data Integration and Governance Applications," Oct. 2024, DOI: 10.20944/preprints202410.2577.v1

Madhurya, J. A., Padhi, M. K., Awasthy, M., & Pareek, P. K. (2023, July). A Smart Governance Architecture for Integrating Heterogeneous IoT Solutions within the Framework of Smart Cities. In *2023 International Conference on Data Science and Network Security (ICDSNS)* (pp. 1-6). IEEE.

Mahobia, S., & Pawar, R. (2024). Comprehensive Review of Smart Cities using IOT in Coud. *International Journal of Innovative Research in Computer and Communication Engineering*, *12*(May), 6309–6319. Advance online publication. DOI: 10.15680/IJIRCCE.2024.1205194

Mamodiya, U., Kishor, I., Garine, R., Ganguly, P., & Naik, N. (2025). Artificial intelligence based hybrid solar energy systems with smart materials and adaptive photovoltaics for sustainable power generation. *Scientific Reports*, *15*(1), 17370. DOI: 10.1038/s41598-025-01788-4 PMID: 40389492

Manivannan, R., Manivannan, S., & Surendiran, J. (2024)... *Ai-Siot Hybrid Architecture for Seamless Integration of IoT in Smart Cities*, (Apr), 393–399. Advance online publication. DOI: 10.1109/CSNT60213.2024.10546157

Mastrogiovanni, S. (2025, September). AI-Driven data governance for smart cities: Balancing privacy, efficiency, and public trust. *South Florida Journal of Development*, *6*(9), e5810. DOI: 10.46932/sfjdv6n9-029

Okhovat, E., & Bauer, M. (2024, June). Towards Enhanced Urban Management: Introducing A Model for Autonomic Smart City Management. In *2024 IEEE International Conference on Smart Computing (SMARTCOMP)* (pp. 31-38). IEEE.

Papaioannou, A., Dimara, A., Papaioannou, A., Tzitzios, I., Anagnostopoulos, C.-N., & Krinidis, S. (2025, January). Dimara, A. Papaioannou, I. Tzitzios, C. Anagnostopoulos, and S. Krinidis, "Hierarchical Resources Management System for Internet of Things-Enabled Smart Cities,". *Sensors (Basel)*, *25*(3), 616. DOI: 10.3390/s25030616 PMID: 39943255

Parlapalli, V., Ganeeb, K. K., Bidkar, D. M., Veerapaneni, P. K., Sankiti, S. R., & Harve, B. M. (2025). AI-Powered Smart Cities. *Data-Driven Approaches for Urban Innovation and Sustainability*, (Jun), 232–237. DOI: 10.1109/CCNCPS66785.2025.11135701

Pasupuleti, M. K. (2025). Smart Cities Unleashed. *Integrating AI, IoT, and Blockchain for Sustainable Urban Development*, (Apr). Advance online publication. DOI: 10.62311/nesx/rb8

Pavunraj, J. (2025). Jayalakshmi, S. Nawaz, K. Anbumaheshwari, and A. Mathankumar. *The Role of IoT for Smart Cities*, (Apr), 341–370. DOI: 10.4018/979-8-3373-0761-9.ch015

Perín, H. P. Y. Castro, E. Filho, and J. S. B. Martins, "Smart City in Contemporary Times with Internet of Things and Artificial Intelligence," May 2025, doi: DOI: 10.31235/osf.io/r36yg_v1

Prasad, M. V. S., & Subrahmanyam, V. V. (2025). Intelligent IoT-Enabled Framework for Sustainable Smart Cities. *International Journal of Science and Research (Raipur, India)*, (Sep), 406–409. DOI: 10.21275/SR25910183656

Samrat, S., & Manjunath, S. J. (2024). "Leveraging IoT, AI, and ML for Enhanced Decision-Making in Karnataka's Smart Cities." Volume. 9 Issue.7, July - 2024 International Journal of Innovative Science and Research Technology (IJISRT), www.ijisrt.com. ISSN - 2456-2165, PP:- 2302-2306, https://doi.org/DOI: 10.38124/ijisrt/IJISRT24JUL1317

Sadiq, T., & Omlin, C. W. (2025). Sensing in Smart Cities: A Multimodal Machine Learning Perspective. *Smart Cities*, *9*(1), 3.

dos Santos Sampaio, A. (2025). Arquitetura de governança digital e gestão urbana inteligente: a aplicação integrada da inteligência artificial e blockchain na administração pública municipal. Recima21-Revista Científica Multidisciplinar-ISSN 2675-6218, 6(3), e636338-e636338.

Shaikh, M. S., & Ali, S. I. (2025). Smart Waste Management by Integrating Data Analytics, IoT, and AI for Sustainable Urban Solutions. *Smart Waste Management by Integrating Data Analytics, IoT, and AI for Sustainable Urban Solutions*, (Apr), 383–404. DOI: 10.4018/979-8-3373-0265-2.ch018

Sharma, S., Sharma, S. K., Sahu, A. K., & Sharma, A. (2024, August). Internet of Things (IoT) and Smart Cities. *Deleted Journal*, *2*(08), 2526–2531. DOI: 10.47392/IRJAEM.2024.0365

Shinde, S., & Chavan, T. U. (2024, September). Leveraging the Internet of Things (IoT) for Smart City Innovation: Exploring Applications, Overcoming Challenges, and Charting Future Pathways. *International Journal of Scientific Research in Modern Science and Technology*, *3*(9), 15–22. DOI: 10.59828/ijsrmst.v3i9.250

Sinaeepourfard, S. S., & Mesgaribarzi, N. (2024). Decentralized, Distributed, and Hybrid ICT Architectures: Hierarchical Multitier Big Data Driven Management for Smart, Sustainable. *Scalable and Reliable Cities*, (Apr), 345–355. Advance online publication. DOI: 10.1109/SusTech60925.2024.10553566

Sun, L. (2025, July). Theory, Practice and Empirical Analysis of Smart City. *Journal of Regional Economics and Development*, *2*(4), 8. DOI: 10.47134/jred.v2i4.840

Tanji, A., Essaaidi, M., & Merabet, G. H. (2024, May). Towards an integrated smart city platform: A prototype for enhancing urban services. In *2024 Mediterranean Smart Cities Conference (MSCC)* (pp. 1-6). IEEE.

Thomas, M., Choudhary, L., & Kishor, I. (2020, February). Analysis of Cloud Security and Performance for Leakage of Critical Information using DROPS Methodology [IRJET]. *International Research Journal of Engineering and Technology*, *7*(2), 1–6.

Velasquez-Mendez, J. de J., Lozoya-Santos, J. J., & Jiménez-Vargas, J. F. (2025, September). Lozoya-Santos, and F. Jiménez, "Validating a Sustainable, Smart, and Circular City Architecture Through Urban Living Lab Experiments,". *Urban Science (Basel, Switzerland)*, *9*(9), 377. DOI: 10.3390/urbansci9090377

Verma, A., Singh, J., & Yadav, R. S. (2025). Smart cities in practice: IoT-enabled citizen engagement and local service delivery. *Lex Localis*, *23*(S5), 857–868.

Zeng, F., Pang, C., & Tang, H. (2024). Sensors on internet of things systems for the sustainable development of smart cities: A systematic literature review. *Sensors (Basel)*, *24*(7), 2074.

Chapter 3
Natural Language Processing With Hybrid Quantum Neural Networks:
Models, Methods, and Future Directions

Manju Lata Joshi
http://orcid.org/0000-0002-0749-6171
Poornima University, India

ABSTRACT

The recent developments in the field of deep learning have made Natural Language Processing (NLP) quite useful, but there are still issues of the complexity of computation, energy consumption, and modeling of complex semantics. Representations and optimization techniques that are quantum enhanced are available in quantum computing and provide new possibilities. Hybrid Quantum Neural Networks (HQNNs) combine quantum computational concepts and classical neural networks, allowing the introduction of a new era in intelligent language processing. The chapter provides the basics of quantum computing and neural NLP models and looks at the hybrid methods of semantic representation and learning. The text classification, sentiment analysis, named entity recognition, and machine translation tasks that are fundamental to NLP are examined through a hybrid quantum-neural approach. Such methods as quantum data encoding, quantum feature extraction and hybrid training approaches are described and the issues associated with scalability, noise, and hardware limitations are discussed.

DOI: 10.4018/979-8-2600-0008-3.ch003

1. INTRODUCTION

Natural Language Processing (NLP) has incorporated itself into the core scientific foundation of artificial intelligence and allows a machine to comprehend and produce human language in various fields, including healthcare, finance, education, and cybersecurity. The language understanding and generation tasks have been successfully completed by deep learning architectures, especially recurrent neural networks, convolutional neural networks, and transformer-based models (Vaswani et al., 2017; Devlin et al., 2019). Nevertheless, traditional neural networks have a drawback of computational nonscalability, power usage, and inability to capture multifaceted semantic and contextual connections (Bengio et al., 2021).

The massive increase in textual data and the rise in the complexity of models are becoming a concern when it comes to sustainability and accessibility (Strubell et al., 2019). Quantum computing provides a new paradigm of calculations based on superposition and entanglement concepts, which allow high-dimensional representation of information to be represented efficiently (Biamonte et al., 2017; Schuld and Petruccione, 2018). It has spawned Quantum Machine Learning and Hybrid Quantum Neural Networks (HQNNs), which combine quantum circuits with classical neural networks to circumvent hardware limitations of the Noisy Intermediate-Scale Quantum devices (Farhi and Neven, 2018; Schuld et al., 2020; Preskill, 2018). Representations of languages, which are quantum inspired, like the use of quantum probability theory and vectors spaces, would be natural with semantic and compositional models of language (Coecke et al., 2010).

Recent works show quantum encoding and variational quantum circuits has a potential in NLP, including classification and semantic analysis (Havlicek et al., 2019; Cerezo et al., 2021). However, noise, scalability, and interpretability problems are also of great importance (McClean et al., 2018; Benedetti et al., 2019).

This chapter presents a systematic study of the HQNN architecture, the learning strategy, and applications, and future research in the field of quantum-enhanced NLP.

2. FUNDAMENTALS OF QUANTUM COMPUTING FOR NATURAL LANGUAGE PROCESSING

Quantum computing is a completely new model of computation and it is based on the principles of quantum mechanics. Unlike the classical computers, which handle binary bits to process information, quantum computers handle quantum bits (qubits), which can be in superposition. The property enables a quantum system to model and manipulate high dimensional data with great efficiency and is of particular interest to the application of Natural Language Processing (NLP), where linguistic data is typically represented as a large dimensional vector, such as word and sentence embedding (Schuld and Petruccione, 2018).

In addition to this, quantum entanglement has the potential to model a correlation between qubits that could not be defined in a classical probability which is an efficient way to model contextual dependencies in language. This is calculated using quantum computers through quantum circuits composed of unitary quantum gates. The primary elements of hybrid quantum neural network (HQNN) architectures are variational quantum circuits (VQCs), or parameterized quantum circuits (Benedetti et al., 2019). These are nonlinear feature maps that encode the classical linguistic data into high-dimensional Hilbert space, similar to classical machine learning algorithms that encode using kernels (Havlicek et al., 2019).

Classical learning algorithms optimize such circuits, and the hybrid training architectures that are based on them could be applied to Noisy Intermediate-Scale Quantum (NISQ) hardware (Preskill, 2018; Cerezo et al., 2021). Quantum measurement converts quantum states into classical probabilistic measurements, which is being naturally compatible with the uncertainty and vagueness of human language (Schuld et al., 2020). The expectation values that are computed using measurement results support classification and regression problems in NLP, e.g. sentiment analysis and semantic categorization. Repeated measurements enable one to estimate probability distributions that can be incorporated into classical loss functions to train hybrid models (Biamonte et al., 2017).

The quantum probability theory also offers a conceptual framework of representation of linguistic phenomena like ambiguity, context dependence, and meaning composition (Busemeyer and Bruza, 2012; Coecke et al., 2010). Words and sentences in quantum-inspired NLP are vectors in Hilbert space and the grammatical structure is defined by the use of tensor products and linear operators. Quantum circuit-based models of sentence semantics have been directly impacted by the compositional distributional model of meaning as suggested by Coecke et al. (2010). In general, superposition, entanglement, and probabilistic measurement provide new means of solving the fundamental issues in NLP, such as high-dimensional representation, contextual dependency, and semantic ambiguity.

3. CLASSICAL NEURAL MODELS FOR NLP AND MOTIVATION FOR HYBRID QUANTUM APPROACHES

Neural networks have revolutionized Natural Language Processing (NLP) since machines are able to learn distributed and hierarchical representations of linguistic data. Deep learning models have substituted the previous rule-based and statistical models, and currently take over machine translation, sentiment analysis, named entity recognition, and question answering (Goldberg, 2017). Continuous representations of words were introduced by Word2Vec and GloVe methods and brought about semantic similarity between words (Mikolov et al., 2013; Pennington et al., 2014), which are the basis of neural NLP pipelines. Nevertheless, these embeddings are language neutral and incapable of modeling polysemy and dynamic meaning in other linguistic settings. RNNs, such as Long Short-Term Memory (LSTM) and Gated Recurrent Unit (GRU), made it possible to model text sequentially and increase its modeling and translation performance (Hochreiter and Schmidhuber, 1997; Cho et al., 2014; Sutskever et al., 2014). CNNs also led to the further improvement of sentence classification and sentiment analysis by means of the efficient extraction of local n-gram features (Kim, 2014).

In spite of such developments, both RNNs and CNNs have weaknesses in long-range dependencies and complex discourse-level semantics. Self-attention-based transformer architectures brought a significant breakthrough because they allowed parallel computation and contextualized representation of words (Vaswani et al., 2017). BERT and GPT language models demonstrated the highest ever performance on NLP tasks, being pre-trained (Devlin et al., 2019; Brown et al., 2020). However, transformer models have large computational resource demands and power usage, which brings up sustainability and fair access to NLP technologies (Strubell et al., 2019). Additionally, their internal images are still hard to read, which restricts transparency and trust (Jain and Wallace, 2019).

Although a success, classical neural NLP models are limited in nature. These are high computational cost, reliance on large labelled datasets, poor range of domains, and the lack of ability to reflect linguistic ambiguity and uncertainty (Busemeyer and Bruza, 2012). They are also black-box, which makes explainability in sensitive domains like healthcare and law harder (Doshi-Velez and Kim, 2017). These obstacles drive the pursuit of alternative computation computational paradigms including Hybrid Quantum Neural Networks that seek to leverage quantum-enhanced feature space and probabilistic code to scale, express and also to handle uncertainty in the next generation language processing systems (Biamonte et al., 2017; Schuld and Petruccione, 2018; Havlicek et al., 2019).

4. QUANTUM ENCODING OF LINGUISTIC DATA

Quantum encoding Energy required to encode or encode classical linguistic data in quantum states such that it can be computed on Hybrid Quantum Neural Networks (HQNNs). This step is central in Natural Language Processing (NLP) since the data of languages are high-dimensional, contextual, and probabilistic in nature. Encoding schemes of efficient nature allow the mapping of linguistic features of word embeddings and sentence representation to quantum Hilbert spaces where superposition and entanglement can be used to benefit feature representation and learning (Schuld and Petruccione, 2018).

Figure 1. Quantum Encoding Schemes for Linguistic Data

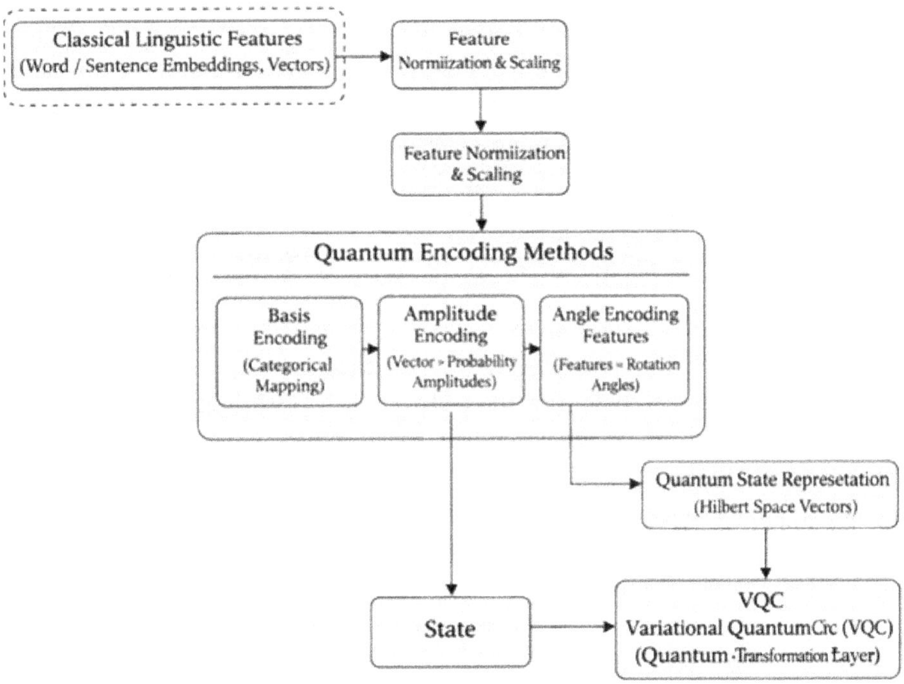

The Classical linguistic features word or sentence embeddings are first normalized in above figure 1 and then encoded into quantum states with the help of basis, amplitude or angle encoding schemes. Such encoded quantum states encode linguistic information in a high dimensional Hilbert space which are then transformed by a variational quantum circuit in Hybrid Quantum neural networks to perform quantum feature transformation.

The easiest encoding method is known as basis encoding where classical binary or categorical data are simply mapped to states of computational basis of qubits. This approach can only be used to perform small or proof-of-concept NLP tasks, but needs a large number of qubits to scale to large vocabularies, so it is conceptually straightforward (Preskill, 2018). Amplitude encoding, on the other hand, uses the probability amplitudes of quantum states to encode normalized classical vectors, enabling high-dimensional linguistic features to be represented with a logarithmic number of qubits (Havlicek et al., 2019).

Although amplitude encoding has an exponential compression capacity, state preparation circuits are complex and may cause large computational overheads (Schuld and Killoran, 2019). The other popular method is angle or phase encoding whereby classical feature values are coded in the form of rotation angles of quantum gates. The strategy can be implemented alongside variational quantum circuits, and it can be executed on existing Noisy Intermediate-Scale Quantum (NISQ) devices (Schuld and Petruccione, 2018; Cerezo et al., 2021). It is however linearly proportional to the feature dimensionality and thus does not have the compression advantages of amplitude encoding. In addition to encoding single features, quantum feature maps are used to offer nonlinear representations of lingo-data in high-dimensional Hilbert space that can be related to kernel-based techniques of machine learning in classical machine learning (Havlicek et al., 2019). Such mappings make it possible to achieve greater separability of linguistic patterns in sentiment analysis and topic classification tasks.

Moreover, the distributional semantic-inspired methods of compositional encoding combine grammatical structure with vector-space meaning using tensor products and entangling operations, so that grammar can be used to form sentence meaning out of the quantum state of individual words (Coecke et al., 2010). Although quantum encoding methods have a theoretical potential, they have several practical limitations, such as the lack of qubits, noise and decoherence sensitivity, expensive state preparation, and interpretability issues (McClean et al., 2018; Preskill, 2018; Schuld and Killoran, 2019). These restrictions can only be countered by improvement in quantum hardware, circuit design and hybrid learning strategies. However, quantum encoding continues to be the foundation of HQNN-based NLP systems that allow one to combine classical linguistic representations with quantum-enhanced feature transformations.

5. HYBRID QUANTUM NEURAL NETWORK ARCHITECTURES FOR NLP TASKS

HQNNs bring together quantum calculus layers with other classical elements of neural. networks to seize the advantage of the two paradigms. HQNNs that are applied to NLP processes also contain classical preprocessing and embedding, followed by quantum feature transformation, and classical. decision-making layers. It is the hybrid architecture that is particularly applied to the existing. The Noisy Intermediate-Scale Quantum (NISQ) devices, where full-quantum deep networks are, are considered. lack of feasibility (Presskill, 2018; Cerezo et al., 2021). In this part the architectural greats are the ones noted. the HQNNs designs are given to the tasks of the NLP, their functional aspects are described, and the generalizability of the HQNNs on the language processing issues in text classification, sentiment analysis and this estimation of semantic similarity are examined.

Figure 2. Architecture of a Hybrid Quantum Neural Network (HQNN) for Natural Language Processing.

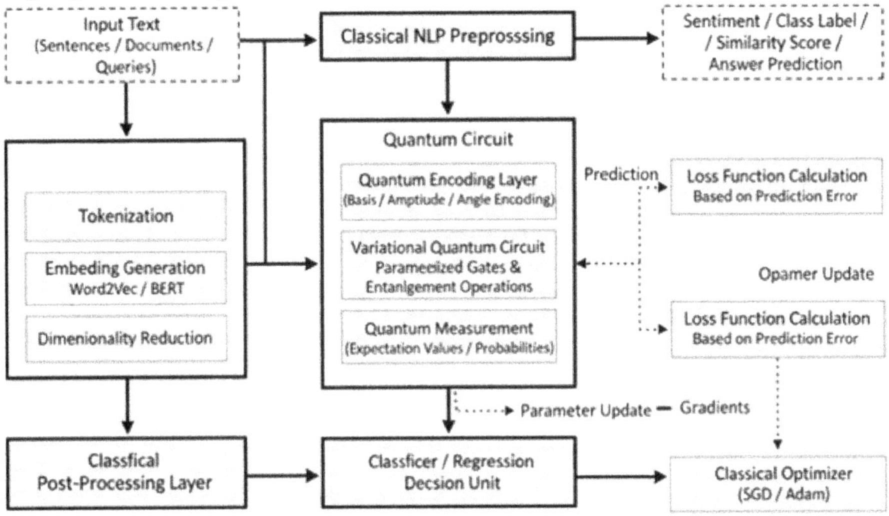

The above figure 2, Hybrid Quantum Neural Network (HQNN) is the structure that represents a combination of classical Natural Language Processing and quantum computation. Classical NLP techniques are applied to textual input initially in the form of tokenization and embedding generation. Quantum encoding schemes encode these embeddings into quantum states. The variational quantum circuit is a quantum device that transforms quantum features with parameterized gates and entanglement operations. The results of the measurements are given to classical post-processing layers to be classified or predicted. The training is implemented using a hybridization of the optimization process wherein a classical optimizer modifies the circuit parameters of the quantum circuit according to the loss of measurements.

5.1 General Architecture of Hybrid Quantum Neural Networks

A typical HQNN architecture for NLP consists of three main components:

1. Classical preprocessing and embedding layer
2. Quantum processing layer (variational quantum circuit)
3. Classical post-processing and output layer

The dimensionality reduction, tokenization and embedding generation are carried out. another way is the classical front-end founded on the classic NLP models such as Word2Vec, GloVe, or. transformer based embeddings (Mikolov et al., 2013; Devlin et al., 2019). Then the encoding of Such embeddings into quantum states are achieved with an encoding scheme e.g. angle encoding or amplitude encoding. The nonlinear computations are carried out in the quantum layer on the encoded. variational also referred to as parameterized quantum circuits information with the help of parameterized quantum circuits. quantum circuits (VQCs). The output of this measurement made by these circuits is transmitted to where they are deposited, they are categorized or regressed (Benedetti et al., 2019; Schuld et al., 2020). Such a stratified design allows the HQNNs to act similarly to deep neural. networks of the quantum circuits, which act as flexible hidden layers.

5.2 Variational Quantum Circuits as Quantum Layers

The HQNN architectures are grounded on their computational core which is variational quantum. circuits. The circuits are parametric quantum gates whose parameters are optimized using. classical learning algorithms (Cerezo et al., 2021). It is the profundity of the circuits and entanglement. arrangements determine the degree of expressiveness of the model. The computation of similarity scores is carried out by overlaps of quantum states or classical distance depending on the findings. of measurements. It is possible to use composition models based on quantum mechanics. grammatical structure as an entanglement pattern between qubits which encode words in a sentence (Coecke et al., 2010). It enables HQNNs to capture sentence meaning in a. compositional style and fits Linguistic theories of syntax and semantics. These architectures are employed in the support of applications such as paraphrase detection, information retrieval and question. answering.

5.3 HQNN Architectures for Text Classification

One of the oldest and well-researched NLP tasks of quantum machine learning is text classification. Pipelines Hybrid architectures tend to adhere to the following pipeline: Classical methods are used to convert text into embeddings. Embeddings on reduced dimension are represented in quantum states. These states are transformed into a variational quantum circuit. Outputs of the measurement are fed into a classical classifier. Havlicek et al. (2019) showed that quantum-enhanced feature spaces have the ability to enhance the separability in classification. Schuld et al. (2020) also suggested circuit-based quantum classifiers, which can also be trained like a neural network. In NLP classification tasks like sentiment analysis or topic classification, HQNNs are a nonlinear kernel machine, where data in a text form are transformed to higher-dimensional quantum feature space to be placed under classical decision boundaries.

5.4 Architectures for Semantic Similarity and Sentence Modeling

In addition to classification, HQNNs can be modified to perform sentence similarity and semantic representation. Here, in this type of architecture, two sentences would be coded into quantum states and run together on shared, or parallel, quantum circuits. The computation of similarity scores is performed by quantum state overlaps or classical distance based on the results of measurements. Compositional models inspired by quantum mechanics make it possible to use grammatical structure as an entanglement pattern between qubits that represent words in a sentence (Coecke et al., 2010). It allows HQNNs to represent sentence meaning in a compositional manner and fits Linguistic theories of syntax and semantics. These architectures are used to support applications like paraphrase detection, information retrieval and question answering.

5.5 Integration with Classical Deep Learning Models

The HQNNs are not intended as alternatives to the classical deep learning models, but complimentary. Classical neural networks such as multilayer are often used together with quantum layers. perceptrons (MLPs) or transformer encoders. Using a transformer model can give out, as an example, contextual embeddings, which may be embedded into a quantum circuit and converted and classified. The classical network is and quantum layer is a refinement step of a feature. used to compute large scale learning and optimization of patterns (Schuld and Killoran, 2019). The combination allows the researchers to use the developed NLP pipelines when conducting research. representational power augmented by quantum.

5.6 Training and Optimization of HQNN Architectures

Quantum circuits are trained on a hybrid gradient loop with the parameters of HQNNs. optimized using classical gradient based or gradient free optimizers. The objective function is also calculated based on measurement results and compared to the ground truth labels in common loss functions (Cerezo et al., 2021). The phenomenon of barren plateaus with gradients that disappear exponentially with circuit depth is one of the biggest challenges and introduces a difficulty in training (McClean et al., 2018). The mitigation of this problem is achieved by choosing architectural designs including shallow circuits, structured entanglement and problem inspired ansatze. Nevertheless, HQNNs have been shown to be possible to small-scale NLP tasks in both simulation and early quantum hardware.

5.7 Architectural Challenges and Design Considerations

HQNN architectures of NLP are dependent on a variety of factors:

- **Qubit limitations**: Current hardware restricts the number of features that can be encoded.
- **Circuit depth**: Deeper circuits increase expressiveness but also noise sensitivity.
- **Encoding strategy**: Choice of encoding affects performance and scalability.
- **Interpretability**: Understanding how quantum layers represent linguistic features remains difficult.

These factors require a close architectural design based on specific NLP activities and accessible quantum resources (Preskill, 2018; Benedetti et al., 2019).

5.8 Significance of HQNN Architectures for NLP

The HQNN models offer a viable framework to investigate the quantum-enhanced language processing in the NISQ era. HQNNs provide a scaling direction to experimentally accessible quantum NLP systems by integrating classical neural preprocessing and quantum feature transformation with classical post-processing. Their capability to work in feature space with high dimensionality, to model uncertainty probabilistically, and to interface with existing NLP pipelines makes them attractive in the next generation intelligent language processing structures.

6. LEARNING AND OPTIMIZATION STRATEGIES IN HYBRID QUANTUM NLP MODELS

The Hybrid Quantum Neural Networks (HQNNs) are models where the quantum circuit parameters and the classical neural network weights are optimized simultaneously. These hybrid models are a combination of quantum feature transformation and classical optimization routines, training of which is both theoretically new and challenging practically. High-dimensional and noisy linguistic data, in which alternative methods fail to obtain useful performance reductions, require effective learning strategies to obtain meaningful performance improvements in Natural Language Processing (NLP) (Schuld and Petruccione, 2018; Cerezo et al., 2021). The various subsections discuss the primary learning paradigms, optimization methods and real-world challenges that involve training hybrid quantum NLP models.

6.1 Hybrid Learning Framework

The training of HQNN is based on a hybrid loop with classical stages of computation and quantum stages of computation. The initial stage involves classical methods of NLP, including the processing of linguistic data (tokenization and embedding generation). These embeddings are represented in quantum states and executed by parameterized quantum circuits. The results of measurement are then transformed into loss terms that are used to update the parameters using classical optimization techniques (Benedetti et al., 2019). In form, the learning objective may be stated as follows:

Minimizing a cost function: $L(\theta)=i\sum\ell(f\theta(x_i),y_i)$ represents the hybrid quantum-classical model and x_i and y_i are the features of linguistic input and target labels respectively. The process of optimization is done through the classical gradient-based or gradient-free optimization. Such a hybrid design allows deploying it to modern, though still Noisy, Intermediate-Scale Quantum (NISQ) devices, since it is just the quantum circuit evaluation that is operated with quantum hardware, whilst optimization is classical (Preskill, 2018).

6.2 Gradient-Based Optimization and Parameter-Shift Rules

One of the difficulties in training HQNNs is the calculation of gradients of parameters of quantum circuits. The gradient in quanta circuits has to be estimated by multiple executions and measurements of a circuit, unlike classical neural networks. The parameter-shift rule is an accurate gradient computational rule, which computes the circuit at shifted parameter values (Schuld et al., 2019). With this method, HQNNs can be trained with the help of such traditional optimizers as stochastic gradient descent (SGD), Adam, and RMSProp. In NLP, like text classification and sentiment analysis, gradient-based optimization can be used to fine-tune the quantum circuit parameters to increase the accuracy of predictions (Schuld and Petruccione, 2018). Nevertheless, gradient estimation is associated with a large number of circuit evaluations, which adds computational complexity and vulnerability to quantum noise.

6.3 Variational Quantum Algorithms for NLP

The HQNNs are founded on Variational Quantum Algorithms (VQAs). These algorithms make use of parameterized quantum circuits, the parameters of which are optimized to an objective. interest of the function (Cerezo et al., 2021). VQAs are used in NLP systems in classification, clustering and estimation of similarity. The possibility to VQAs is particularly attractive in respect of the possibility. scale them to shallow circuits, which can be executed with available quantum hardware. They also make a flexible circuit design possible, which, in its turn, allows researchers to design quantum. structures to specific language tasks, e.g. sentence classification or semantic similarity. analysis (Havlicek et al., 2019). In spite of this promise, VQAs have training instabilities and performance degradation with circuit depth, and require these to be carefully designed and regularized.

6.4 Barren Plateaus and Optimization Challenges

Barren plateaus, which are the disappearance of gradients exponentially with the number of qubits or circuit depth, are one of the most severe impediments to the training of HQNNs (McClean et al., 2018). This is where the optimization is no longer possible and the parameter changes do not give much information to enhance the model performance. Of special concern to NLP tasks are barren plateaus because the dimensionality of linguistic embeddings is large and expressive circuits are required. Some mitigation measures have been suggested, they include:

- Using shallow and structured circuit ansätze
- Initializing parameters near identity transformations
- Employing problem-inspired circuit designs
- Reducing feature dimensionality before quantum encoding

The methods aid in sustaining significant gradient values and enhancing stability in training (Cerezo et al., 2021).

6.5 Classical–Quantum Co-Optimization

Hybrid learning consists of co-optimization of quantum and classical components. The classical neural layers can be trained together with the parameters of quantum circuits, and the end-to-end learning is possible. As an example, a classical transformer can produce embeddings which are then refined by a quantum layer and then later classified. This co-optimization model enables HQNNs to be easily incorporated into the existing deep learning pipelines, but it also enables quantum-enhanced feature transformations (Schuld and Killoran, 2019). Classical optimizers are used to update parameters and quantum processors are used to compute non-linear transformations in Hilbert space. These types of hybrid training approaches transform HQNNs to be flexible on NLP tasks in the real world without the need of entirely quantum infrastructures.

6.6 Noise, Robustness, and Error Mitigation

The decoherence and quantum noise have a great influence on the performance of learning in HQNNs. Gradient estimates are distorted by measurement errors and the imperfection of gates to lower classification accuracy (Preskill, 2018). In NLP tasks, where semantic differences are subtle, it is necessary to be robust to noise. Circuit averaging, noise-conscious training, regularization methods are types of error mitigation techniques that have been suggested to enhance the reliability of learning (Temme et al., 2017). The intention of these strategies is to use approximations of noise-free results without the need to completely correct quantum errors which is not practical on current hardware. The issue of noise-aware optimization may be considered specifically in the context of NLP systems based on HQNN run on NISQ devices.

6.7 Evaluation Metrics and Learning Performance

The performance of HQNN NLP models on learning is measured in terms of standard NLP performance measures like accuracy, precision, recall, F1-score, and cross-entropy loss. Such measures can be directly compared to classical neural models. Benchmarking experiments generally use small scale data sets because of hardware limitations, but prove that hybrid learning architectures are possible and potentially more successful in feature expressiveness and uncertainty representation (Havlicek et al., 2019; Schuld et al., 2020). Training time, and number and noise levels in the hardware are also important issues that should be taken into account during performance evaluation, and determine how well the hardware can be used in practice.

6.8 Significance of Learning Strategies for Quantum NLP

The potential of hybrid quantum NLP models is based on effective strategies of learning and optimization. HQNNs offer a viable direction in which quantum-enhanced language processing can be explored in the near term by using a mix of variational quantum circuits and classical optimization algorithms. Additional studies in gradient estimation, circuit design, noise reduction and co-optimization will reveal the feasibility of HQNNs to surpass classical models in real NLP problems. The future quantum language models are based on these learning strategies and help in the overall objective of quantum-enhanced artificial intelligence.

7. APPLICATIONS AND CASE STUDIES OF HYBRID QUANTUM NLP

Recently, Hybrid Quantum Neural Networks (HQNNs) are already studied in numerous applications of Natural Language Processing (NLP) and show that it is possible to implement quantum-enhanced learning in linguistic problems. Even though it is still an initial experiment, various works have shown encouraging findings on topics, including text classification, sentiment analysis, semantic similarity and question answering. In this section, the researcher examines important areas of application and some of the case studies that demonstrate the potential of HQNNs in NLP.

7.1 Text Classification and Topic Categorization

The first NLP task studied with the help of quantum machine learning is text classification. In hybrid architectures, classical embeddings are represented by encoding them into quantum states and running them through variational quantum circuits and then classical classifying them. As it was shown by Havlicek et al. (2019), quantum-enhanced feature spaces could enhance classification by mapping the data to the high-dimensional Hilbert spaces. The methodology was also used on small-scale text classification with sentence embeddings although their study included synthetic datasets. Schuld et al. (2020) also suggested circuit-based quantum classifiers which can be trained similarly to neural networks and trained by gradient-based optimization. HQNNs have also been used in practical NLP experiments, where they are used on the sentiment analysis and topic detection tasks with reduced-dimensional embeddings of classical models, including Word2Vec and BERT (Mikolov et al., 2013; Devlin et al., 2019). These experiments demonstrate that on small data sets, hybrid models can attain the competitive accuracy with classical baselines, which demonstrates the viability of quantum based text classification.

7.2 Sentiment Analysis

Sentiment analysis is a basic NLP task, which consists in classifying text based on the emotional polarity (positive, negative, or neutral). Hybrid quantum NLP systems usually represent sentence embeddings as quantum states and use variational circuits to obtain nonlinear features. Experimental applications in the recent past have shown that HQNNs can sentiment classify benchmark datasets including movie reviews and social media posts as well as shallow classical neural networks (Schuld and Petruccione, 2018; Benedetti et al., 2019). The uncertainty of quantum measurements is probabilistic in nature, so the uncertainty of sentiment is quite natural as there can be many interpretations of emotion. Moreover, grammar-structured quantum-inspired compositional models permit to extract sentiment in terms of word-level quantum states interconnected by entanglement operations, making linguistically-based sentiment analysis possible (Coecke et al., 2010).

7.3 Semantic Similarity and Paraphrase Detection

Semantic similarity estimation tries to estimate the similarity between the meaning of two sentences or documents. Hybrid quantum NLP models operate in pairs and execute quantum circuits simultaneously on two text inputs and compare the similarity scores using quantum state overlaps or measurement measurements. Quantum embeddings are used to map classical data to quantum states in order to learn similarities. This has been applied to sentence similarity problems, in which HQNNs are used as quantum kernel machines. These models are able to store delicate semantic differences which can be hard to detect using classical similarity measures. The compositional distributional semantics are further developed as quantum-inspired which allow representation of sentence meaning in terms of the grammatical structure in terms of the uses of tensor products and quantum circuits (Coecke et al., 2010). Applications of these methods have been made to paraphrase detection, and information retrieval tasks, showing that the conceptual appropriateness of quantum formalisms to semantic modeling is acceptable.

7.4 Question Answering and Information Retrieval

Information retrieval (IR) and question answering (QA) involve models that comprehend the queries entered by the user and recall or produce answers that are relevant. Classification of queries and semantic matching in small-scale QA tasks have been investigated by using hybrid quantum NLP systems. A piece of research suggested quantum algorithms of nearest-neighbor algorithms that can be modified to document retrieval and semantic search. HQNN-based architectures are capable of encoding questions, or candidate answers to the question, into quantum states and measuring similarity with the help of quantum measurements. Though currently large-scale QA systems are out of reach of the existing quantum hardware, the early research provides a starting point to future quantum-enhanced retrieval systems that can take more complex semantic queries.

7.5 Healthcare and Biomedical Text Mining

Biomedical NLP involves extracting information from clinical notes, research articles, and patient records. HQNNs have potential applications in disease classification, symptom extraction, and medical document categorization.

Hybrid models have been proposed for processing structured biomedical text embeddings using quantum-enhanced feature spaces, aiming to improve classification accuracy in small datasets where labeled data is limited (Biamonte et al., 2017; Schuld & Petruccione, 2018). The ability of quantum models to represent uncertainty is particularly relevant in healthcare, where ambiguous and incomplete information is common.

Although real-world clinical deployment has not yet been achieved, simulation-based studies indicate that HQNNs may offer advantages for biomedical NLP tasks in the future.

7.6 Financial and Legal Document Analysis

Weak text classification, risk assessment, and document summarization are needed in financial and legal NLP applications. HQNNs were investigated to detect the sentiment of financial news and classify a classification of contracts based on small corpora. The quantum-enhanced feature spaces can be useful in detecting complex semantic patterns of legal language that is usually highly structured and contextual (Havlicek et al., 2019). Hybrid methods provide an avenue to the integration of classical NLP pipelines and quantum transformations in the sensitive document analysis task. These case studies are conceptual in nature, but indicate the versatility of HQNNs to the specialized text fields.

7.7 Comparative Performance with Classical Models

Small datasets and simulation-based experiments are used in most of the reported case studies because of the hardware limitations that are currently in place. Compared to classical shallow neural networks, HQNNs usually perform with an equal or comparable level of performance, and the feature expressiveness and uncertainty modeling may possess potential benefits (Schuld et al., 2020; Cerezo et al., 2021). Nevertheless, the state of HQNNs is not yet at a position to be better than large transformer-based models trained on large corpora. Their chief merit is that they show the new computation paradigms and experiment with the alternatives of language comprehension representation.

7.8 Limitations of Current Case Studies

Although the success rate is encouraging, new versions of HQNN NLP applications have a number of constraints:

- Small dataset sizes
- Limited qubit availability
- High noise levels in quantum hardware
- Lack of standardized benchmarks

These limitations limit extrapolation and massive application. The further effort that needs to be made is on scalable architectures, benchmark datasets, and reproducible evaluation protocols (Preskill, 2018; McClean et al., 2018).

7.9 Significance of Applications and Case Studies

As the reviewed applications show, HQNNs can be used in such core NLP tasks as classification, sentiment analysis, similarity estimation, and retrieval. Even though they are still experimental, these case studies confirm the conceptual correspondence between quantum computation and linguistic processing. With the maturity of quantum hardware, HQNN-enabling NLP systems will grow to cover more complicated problems, including machine translation, dialogue systems, and multilingual semantic analysis.

8. CHALLENGES AND LIMITATIONS OF HYBRID QUANTUM NLP MODELS

Although Hybrid Quantum Neural Networks (HQNNs) have good theoretical roots and initial experimental outcomes of Natural Language Processing (NLP), much needs to be done before these kinds of models can be scaled. These difficulties are due to constraints in quantum hardware, designs of algorithms, complexity of data encoding, stability of learning as well as evaluation methodology. This section is a critical overview of the significant challenges in hybrid quantum NLP systems and points out the limitations that are limiting their application at the moment.

8.1 Hardware Constraints and Qubit Limitations

The capacity of the current quantum hardware is one of the most basic challenges in hybrid quantum NLP. The available Noisy Intermediate-Scale Quantum (NISQ) hardware currently has a very limited number of qubits and circuit depth, and means that the size and complexity of NLP models can be implemented (Preskill, 2018). Applications of NLP generally deal with high dimensional representations, like word embeddings and sentence vectors. The representation of the encoding of these representations to quantum states involves dimensionality reduction or complex encoding circuits, which may destroy semantic information. Consequently, HQNNs now can only be used on toy data and simplified linguistic representations, and not on a large scale in the real world (Biamonte et al., 2017). Moreover, quantum devices have low coherence times which limit the amount of operations that can be executed before the quantum information is lost.

8.2 Noise, Decoherence, and Measurement Errors

The environmental noise to quantum systems is extremely sensitive resulting in decoherence and related errors in the gates that skew the computational outcomes. These effects are a severe threat to the HQNN training, where errors in measurements caused by noise can pollute the gradient estimates and decrease the accuracy of classification (McClean et al., 2018). In NLP problems, where fine semantic difference can be important, a single perturbation in quantum states of encodings can result in false prediction. Circuit averaging and noise-aware optimization are proposed as error mitigation methods that also require additional computational overhead and do not completely offset the hardware imperfections (Temme et al., 2017). The problem of robust training of deep hybrid quantum NLP models is still an open research problem without fault-tolerant quantum computing.

8.3 Data Encoding Overhead and Scalability

The encoding of linguistic information quantumly makes the computation highly burdened. Methods like amplitude encoding need complicated quantum state preparation circuits whose prices may grow exponentially with the measurement dimensions (Schuld & Killoran, 2019). This compromises the theoretical utility benefits of quantum computation. The more practical ones are angle encoding and basis encoding, which need large numbers of qubits in the case of high-dimensional embeddings. As a result, the majority of HQNN experiments are based on violent dimensionality reduction that can eliminate significant linguistic aspects. Scalability is therefore a point of serious limitation particularly when it comes to tasks that involve lengthy documents, multilingual corpora or lots of vocabularies.

8.4 Optimization Difficulties and Barren Plateaus

HQNNs appear to have special optimization problems: barren plateaus, in which the gradient goes to zero exponentially with the number of qubits or circuit depth (McClean et al., 2018). This renders learning ineffective to more profound quantum circuits and complex NLP problems. The use of NLP applications demands the expressive models that are able to capture long-range dependencies and semantic composition. But as expressivity of circuits is increased, gradient instability tends to grow. Even though this problem can be addressed by using shallow circuit strategies and problem-inspired ansatze, these methods reduce model capacity and generalization capabilities (Cerezo et al., 2021). Consequently, the existing HQNNs are confined to shallow structure that might not perform better than the classical deep learning models.

8.5 Lack of Standardized Benchmarks and Evaluation Protocols

The other significant weakness is that quantum NLP models lack common metrics of performance. The vast majority of the studies use small, synthetic, or highly simplified datasets, and it is hard to compare the results of various architectures and experiments (Schuld et al., 2020). At the same time, quantum NLP does not have the established evaluation schemes, as opposed to classical NLP, which has access to large benchmark datasets like GLUE and SQuAD. This makes reproducibility more difficult, as well as restricts the possibility of determining whether HQNNs provide real benefits over classical models. In addition, the comparisons of performance usually do not take into account the computational cost, time of circuit execution, and sensitivity to noise, which are important in real-world implementation.

8.6 Interpretability and Model Transparency

Interpretability and Model Transparency of a system are evaluated through the lens of machine learning. HQNNs continue to face a major challenge of interpretability. Classical neural NLP models are already viewed as black boxes, and quantum layers only make the model transparency more difficult. Quantum states and measurement results are not easily visualized and explained in words (Doshi-Velez and Kim, 2017). The way HQNNs encode semantic data or make decisions related to language tasks is a research question that is being pursued by researchers. In the absence of interpretability, it is challenging to create reliance in quantum NLP technology in sensitive applications like healthcare, law, or finance. This also reduces the error analysis and model debugging, as it is not explainable, which slows down scientific development.

8.7 Data Availability and Resource Constraints

There is a general tendency that HQNNs demand curated datasets because of hardware limitations. Quantum systems cannot directly process large corpora also commonly used in classical NLP, and so they must rely on reduced or synthetic corpora (Preskill, 2018). This creates some generalizability concerns in the experimental results and makes it questionable whether the experiment result can be extended to actual language processing tasks in the real world. On top of this, quantum hardware is scarce and expensive, which does not create easy access to reproducibility and general experimentation.

8.8 Theoretical Gaps and Algorithmic Maturity

Although quantum computing provides effective mathematical methods, the theory of quantum NLP has not been advanced. Most of the suggested architectures are informal and not formally proven to benefit over their classical counterparts (Biamonte et al., 2017). There are still lacking clear theoretical demonstrations of quantum benefit of realistic NLP tasks. In addition, the interplay of language structure and quantum circuit design remains insufficiently known, and needs more interdisciplinary studies of quantum information theory and computational linguistics (Coecke et al., 2010).

8.9 Summary of Limitations

In summary, the primary challenges of hybrid quantum NLP models include:

- Limited qubit capacity and hardware noise
- High data encoding and state preparation costs
- Optimization instability due to barren plateaus
- Lack of standardized benchmarks
- Poor interpretability and transparency
- Restricted dataset size and scalability
- Immature theoretical foundations

Such constraints reflect the difference between theory and practice. These obstacles need to be overcome to move hybrid quantum NLP to experimental prototypes to usable AI.

9. ETHICAL, INTERPRETABILITY, AND TRUST ISSUES IN HYBRID QUANTUM NLP

The proposed topics of Hybrid Quantum Neural Networks (HQNNs) integration in Natural Language Processing (NLP) cause severe ethical, interpretability, and trust issues when it comes to decision making in areas such as healthcare, law, finance, and governance. Similar to classical NLP models, hybrid quantum NLP systems are vulnerable to biases that are introduced by training data, such as social, cultural, and gender bias present in large text corpora (Bolukbasi et al., 2016; Caliskan et al., 2017).

The quantum processing can also be more obscure due to the probability, and harder to interpret, which further complicates the means of detecting and reducing such biases or unfair results (Floridi et al., 2018). One of the greatest setbacks of HQNNs is interpretability. The classical deep learning models already act as black boxes, but the addition of quantum layers can make it more abstract as quantum states and measurement procedures are not necessarily human-readable quantum states (Doshi-Velez and Kim, 2017; Schuld and Petruccione, 2018). In contrast to attention-based models, which generate partial explanatory signals, quantum transformations do not have intuitive visualization procedures, and thus debugging, accountability, and error analysis are not easy (Ribeiro et al., 2016). This weakness prevents HQNNs to be applied in high stakes problems where it is necessary to have transparency in the reasoning process.

Transparency is closely associated with trust and accountability. In hybrid systems, classical preprocessing pipelines, quantum encoding layers, and hardware platforms share responsibility and thereby make it difficult to ascertain error and legal responsibility (Floridi et al., 2018). Moreover, the quantum measurements in question and lack of explanation structures can compromise user trust (Lipton, 2018). Unless decisions have intelligible reasons as to why a document can be classified as a fraudulent document or a medical report as having a high-risk, users will be hesitant to use such systems.

Privacy and data protection is also not less important, since NLP systems tend to work with sensitive personal information. Hybrid quantum NLP models should be compliant with the current data protection laws and embrace ethical governance of data such as anonymization and informed consent (Jobin et al., 2019). In order to build responsible deployment, the future research should emphasize bias reduction, quantum-specific explainable frameworks, clear model construction, and human-in-the-loop decision-making. The required interdisciplinary cooperation between the quantum scientists, NLP researchers, ethicist, and policymakers is needed to make sure that hybrid quantum NLP systems are reliable, just, and correspond to societal values.

10. FUTURE RESEARCH DIRECTIONS AND OPEN PROBLEMS

Hybrid Quantum Neural Networks (HQNNs) of Natural Language Processing (NLP) are a new interdisciplinary field of study bridging quantum computing, machine learning, and computational linguistics. Even though the initial investigations have shown the conceptual viability and limited-scale achievements, considerable conceptual and practical difficulties are to be overcome before the implementation of quantum-enhanced language processing could be achieved at scale.

One of the main research directions is the creation of scalable quantum architecture which is able to process realistic NLP workloads. The future aims need to concentrate on the modular and hierarchical circuit-based designs, better encoding approaches, as well as bringing quantum layers and transformer-based models in the same direction to sustain limited linguistic dependencies across long distances (Preskill, 2018; Cerezo et al., 2021; Schuld and Killoran, 2019). The study of quantum attention processes and sequence modeling is closely associated with it, as it can offer new representations of the relationships among contexts that go beyond classical frameworks of self-attention (Vaswani et al., 2017).

The other pressing issue is that quantum NLP has no uniform benchmarks and assessment protocols. It is necessary to create publicly available datasets, reproducible experiment pipelines, and shared performance measures, which would be meaningfully compared across models and would measure the practical benefits over classical techniques (Schuld et al., 2020). Simultaneously, it is necessary to continue future studies with the goal to provide theoretical demonstrations of quantum advantage on realistic NLP problems, such as formal complexity studies and the circumstances in which quantum representations surpass classical embeddings (Biamonte et al., 2017).

Explainability and interpretability are also not developed in hybrid quantum NLP. It will be important to design quantum-specific explainable AI systems, interpretable circuit architectures, and visualization tools on quantum linguistic representations that can be adopted in the sensitive areas (Doshi-Velez and Kim, 2017). Besides, the application of HQNNs to multilingual and low-resource languages also presents potential prospects in using quantum-enhanced generalization in data scarcity. Future directions involve the inclusion of quantum layers in large language models, the ability to resist adversarial perturbations, and ethics and governance systems that can deliver fairness, transparency, and accountability (Devlin et al., 2019; Brown et al., 2020; Floridi et al., 2018; Jobin et al., 2019).

Eventually, advances in the common theoretical basis of quantum computation, neural learning, and linguistic semantics, including using compositional distributional models, may allow quantum NLP to cease to be an experimental technology, and begin to be a paradigm shift in intuitive language comprehension (Coecke et al., 2010).

11. CONCLUSION

This chapter has offered an in-depth discussion on Natural Language Processing (NLP) with Hybrid Quantum Neural Networks (HQNNs), which is a new paradigm, combining the principles of quantum computing and classical neural networks. Through the discussion of the key concepts within the field of quantum computing, classical neural NLP models, quantum encoding schemes, hybrid architecture, learning and optimization schemes, their practical uses and ethical considerations, the chapter has both illuminated the potential of quantum-enhanced language processing and also revealed its limitations.

Recurrent networks and transformer-based neural networks have become some of the most successful classical neural designs to tackle NLP tasks, like text classification, sentiment analysis, and question answering (Vaswani et al., 2017; Devlin et al., 2019).

However, these models face fundamental challenges related to scalability, energy consumption, interpretability, and their ability to represent linguistic ambiguity and contextual uncertainty (Strubell et al., 2019). These shortcomings encourage seeking different computational paradigms that can be used to complement and extend classical deep learning.

The quantum computing features the aspects of superposition, entanglement, and probabilistic measurement are unique and are natural in language representations of vectors and the uncertainty of language meaning (Busemeyer and Bruza, 2012). The chapter has also demonstrated that the linguistic features can be encoded and represented as quantum states using quantum encoding methods, such as basis, amplitude, and angle encoding, a basis of quantum-enhanced semantic representation (Schuld and Petruccione, 2018).

Hybrid Quantum Neural Network models are a feasible and near-term solution to quantum NLP, which consists of classical preprocessing and optimization in addition to variational quantum circuits as feature transformation layers (Benedetti et al., 2019; Schuld et al., 2020). It has been used on fundamental NLP tasks like text classification, sentiment analysis, semantic similarity estimation and information retrieval and has shown to be practical on small data sets and on simulated or early quantum hardware (Havlicek et al., 2019; Cerezo et al., 2021).

The HQNNs can be learned and optimized using learning strategies whose training loops combine quantum gradient estimation with classical optimisation algorithms. These approaches are promising, but they have many issues, including barren plateaus, noise sensitivity, and overhead data encoding (McClean et al., 2018; Preskill, 2018). The chapter has highlighted the fact that the development of new circuit design and error correction, as well as co-optimization models are needed to scale hybrid quantum NLP models beyond proof-of-concept experiments.

In addition to technical aspects, the chapter has highlighted the issues of ethical responsibility, interpretability, and trust in hybrid quantum NLP systems. Concerns of prejudice, openness, responsibility, and confidentiality remain present in quantum-enhanced systems and require a keen consideration, as these systems should be compatible with societal principles and legal standards (Floridi et al., 2018; Jobin et al., 2019). Lack of mechanisms to explain quantum models is still a significant limitation to implementing them in high-stakes areas like healthcare, law and governance (Doshi-Velez and Kim, 2017).

In the perspective of the future, hybrid quantum NLP will be at the point where three rapidly developing domains of knowledge meet quantum computing, machine learning and computational linguistics. There are also great research directions of scalable quantum architecture with language tasks and quantum analogous of attention mechanisms, setting scalable standards, and theoretical demonstrations of quantum advantage on realistic NLP problems (Biamonte et al., 2017; Schuld and Killoran, 2019). These further areas of integration with large language models and multilingual NLP systems are another promising area of hybrid quantum-classical methods (Brown et al., 2020).

Finally, Hybrid Quantum Neural Networks to NLP are still in their infantile phase of development, however, they present an interesting picture of how the next-generation language processing systems will go beyond classical calculation. The chapter is part of the moving interdisciplinary discussion in that it offers a systematic basis of the idea of hybrid quantum NLP models, uncovers their advantages and limitations, and presents the direction of further research. With the development of quantum hardware and improved theoretical models, hybrid quantum NLP can be a paradigm shift on how intelligent language understanding and artificial intelligence are developed to limits under classical theory.

REFERENCES

Benedetti, M., Lloyd, E., Sack, S., & Fiorentini, M. (2019). Parameterized quantum circuits as machine learning models. *Quantum Science and Technology*, *4*(4), 043001. DOI: 10.1088/2058-9565/ab4eb5

Bengio, Y., Lecun, Y., & Hinton, G. (2021). Deep learning for AI. *Communications of the ACM*, *64*(7), 58–65. DOI: 10.1145/3448250

Biamonte, J., Wittek, P., Pancotti, N., Rebentrost, P., Wiebe, N., & Lloyd, S. (2017). Quantum machine learning. *Nature*, *549*(7671), 195–202. DOI: 10.1038/nature23474 PMID: 28905917

Bolukbasi, T., Chang, K. W., Zou, J. Y., Saligrama, V., & Kalai, A. T. (2016). Man is to computer programmer as woman is to homemaker? debiasing word embeddings. *Advances in Neural Information Processing Systems*, 29. https://doi.org/10.48550/arXiv.1607.06520

Brown, T., Mann, B., Ryder, N., Subbiah, M., Kaplan, J. D., Dhariwal, P., & Amodei, D. (2020). Language models are few-shot learners. *Advances in Neural Information Processing Systems*, *33*, 1877–1901.

Busemeyer, J. R., & Bruza, P. D. (2012). *Quantum models of cognition and decision*. Cambridge University Press. DOI: 10.1017/CBO9780511997716

Caliskan, A., Bryson, J. J., & Narayanan, A. (2017). Semantics derived automatically from language corpora contain human-like biases. *Science*, *356*(6334), 183–186. DOI: 10.1126/science.aal4230 PMID: 28408601

Cerezo, M., Arrasmith, A., Babbush, R., Benjamin, S. C., Endo, S., Fujii, K., McClean, J. R., Mitarai, K., Yuan, X., Cincio, L., & Coles, P. J. (2021). Variational quantum algorithms. *Nature Reviews. Physics*, *3*(9), 625–644. DOI: 10.1038/s42254-021-00348-9

Cho, K., Van Merriënboer, B., Gulcehre, C., Bahdanau, D., Bougares, F., Schwenk, H., & Bengio, Y. (2014). Learning phrase representations using RNN encoder-decoder for statistical machine translation. *arXiv preprint arXiv:1406.1078*. DOI: 10.3115/v1/D14-1179

Coecke, B., Sadrzadeh, M., & Clark, S. (2010). Mathematical foundations for a compositional distributional model of meaning. *arXiv preprint arXiv:1003.4394*.

Devlin, J., Chang, M. W., Lee, K., & Toutanova, K. (2019, June). Bert: Pre-training of deep bidirectional transformers for language understanding. In *Proceedings of the 2019 conference of the North American chapter of the association for computational linguistics: human language technologies, volume 1 (long and short papers)* (pp. 4171-4186).

Doshi-Velez, F., & Kim, B. (2017). Towards a rigorous science of interpretable machine learning. *arXiv preprint arXiv:1702.08608.*

Farhi, E., & Neven, H. (2018). Classification with quantum neural networks on near term processors. *arXiv preprint arXiv:1802.06002.*

Floridi, L., Cowls, J., Beltrametti, M., Chatila, R., Chazerand, P., Dignum, V., Luetge, C., Madelin, R., Pagallo, U., Rossi, F., Schafer, B., Valcke, P., & Vayena, E. (2018). AI4People—An ethical framework for a good AI society: Opportunities, risks, principles, and recommendations. *Minds and Machines, 28*(4), 689–707. DOI: 10.1007/s11023-018-9482-5 PMID: 30930541

Goldberg, Y. (2017). *Neural network methods in natural language processing.* Morgan & Claypool Publishers. DOI: 10.1007/978-3-031-02165-7

Hochreiter, S., & Schmidhuber, J. (1997). Long short-term memory. *Neural Computation, 9*(8), 1735–1780. DOI: 10.1162/neco.1997.9.8.1735 PMID: 9377276

Jain, S., & Wallace, B. C. (2019). Attention is not explanation. *arXiv preprint arXiv:1902.10186.*

Jobin, A., Ienca, M., & Vayena, E. (2019). The global landscape of AI ethics guidelines. *Nature Machine Intelligence, 1*(9), 389–399. DOI: 10.1038/s42256-019-0088-2

Kim, Y. (2014). Convolutional neural networks for sentence classification. *arXiv preprint arXiv:1408.5882*. DOI: 10.3115/v1/D14-1181

Lipton, Z. C. (2018). The mythos of model interpretability: In machine learning, the concept of interpretability is both important and slippery. *ACM Queue; Tomorrow's Computing Today, 16*(3), 31–57. DOI: 10.1145/3236386.3241340

McClean, J. R., Boixo, S., Smelyanskiy, V. N., Babbush, R., & Neven, H. (2018). Barren plateaus in quantum neural network training landscapes. *Nature Communications, 9*(1), 4812. DOI: 10.1038/s41467-018-07090-4 PMID: 30446662

Mikolov, T., Chen, K., Corrado, G., & Dean, J. (2013). Efficient estimation of word representations in vector space. *arXiv preprint arXiv:1301.3781.*

Pennington, J., Socher, R., & Manning, C. D. (2014, October). Glove: Global vectors for word representation. In *Proceedings of the 2014 conference on empirical methods in natural language processing (EMNLP)* (pp. 1532-1543). DOI: 10.3115/v1/D14-1162

Preskill, J. (2018). Quantum computing in the NISQ era and beyond. *Quantum : the Open Journal for Quantum Science, 2*, 79. DOI: 10.22331/q-2018-08-06-79

Ribeiro, M. T., Singh, S., & Guestrin, C. (2016, August). " Why should i trust you?" Explaining the predictions of any classifier. In *Proceedings of the 22nd ACM SIGKDD international conference on knowledge discovery and data mining* (pp. 1135-1144). DOI: 10.18653/v1/N16-3020

Schuld, M., Bergholm, V., Gogolin, C., Izaac, J., & Killoran, N. (2019). Evaluating analytic gradients on quantum hardware. *Physical Review. A, 99*(3), 032331. DOI: 10.1103/PhysRevA.99.032331

Schuld, M., Bocharov, A., Svore, K. M., & Wiebe, N. (2020). Circuit-centric quantum classifiers. *Physical Review. A, 101*(3), 032308. DOI: 10.1103/PhysRevA.101.032308

Schuld, M., & Killoran, N. (2019). Quantum machine learning in feature Hilbert spaces. *Physical Review Letters, 122*(4), 040504. DOI: 10.1103/PhysRevLett.122.040504 PMID: 30768345

Schuld, M., & Petruccione, F. (2018). Supervised learning with quantum computers. *Quantum Science and Technology*, •••, 17.

Strubell, E., Ganesh, A., & McCallum, A. (2019, July). Energy and policy considerations for deep learning in NLP. In *Proceedings of the 57th annual meeting of the association for computational linguistics* (pp. 3645-3650). DOI: 10.18653/v1/P19-1355

Sutskever, I., Vinyals, O., & Le, Q. V. (2014). Sequence to sequence learning with neural networks. *Advances in Neural Information Processing Systems*, •••, 27.

Temme, K., Bravyi, S., & Gambetta, J. M. (2017). Error mitigation for short-depth quantum circuits. *Physical Review Letters, 119*(18), 180509. DOI: 10.1103/PhysRevLett.119.180509 PMID: 29219599

Vaswani, A., Shazeer, N., Parmar, N., Uszkoreit, J., Jones, L., Gomez, A. N., & Polosukhin, I. (2017). Attention is all you need. *Advances in Neural Information Processing Systems*, •••, 30.

Chapter 4

Integration of Hybrid AI With Cloud Edge and High Performance Computing

Suchita Arora
http://orcid.org/0000-0003-3191-2144
Poornima University, India

Rajashree Tukaram Gadhave
Pillai HOC College of Engineering and Technology, India

Navruzbek Shavkatov
Tashkent State University of Economics, Tashkent, Uzbekistan

Mahesh Soni
Independent Researcher, USA

D. Stalin David
Vel Tech Multi Tech Dr. Rangarajan Dr. Sakunthala Engineering College, Chennai, India

Mukesh Soni
Lovely Professional University, Phagwara, India

ABSTRACT

The extreme proliferation of intelligent applications on the spectrum of cyber-physical systems has revealed structural dis-alignment between inertial cloud-centric AI implementations and the dynamic nature of the real-time, heterogeneous workload. Present hybrid architectures are largely based on rigid task allocation or rule-based coordination, and do not provide flexibility when workload intensity and mixed computational requirements vary. The chapter suggests a hybrid AI system that closely combines edge intelligence, cloud-native coordination, and high-performance computing via learning-based coordination. The framework allows the migration of the intelligence to be adapted according to the workload nature, state of the system, and performance feedback as opposed to binding the models to

DOI: 10.4018/979-8-2600-0008-3.ch004

fixed layers. High-performance resources are not considered passive accelerators, but instead viewed as active decision partners, which allows them to be optimized on a scale and make inferences in real-time.

1. INTRODUCTION

AI has passed a long way past its previous function as an offline analysis tool. Currently, AI works in dynamic, resource-constrained, latency-sensitive, and mission-critical environments. Intelligent systems will learn and react in real time, scale in a reliable way, and be autonomously transported, smartly healthcare, and satellite-based Internet of Things (IoT), and into digital twins. These are the expectations that have revealed a major limitation of the traditional cloud-centric AI deployments. However, centralized architectures, though very strong, will be unable to fulfill the needs of ultra-low latency, bandwidth efficiency, energy awareness, and context-aware intelligence required by modern applications (Mohamed Jabarullah et al., 2025; Kolluri, 2025). Large-scale AI training and data storage has indisputably been supported by cloud computing. The fact that it has an elastic compute and is accessible globally makes it possible to train deep learning models on large datasets with greater accuracy than ever before. Nevertheless, the use of remote cloud services adds lag in communication, a security issue, and structural vulnerability during the moment of reduced network connectivity. The cloud cannot support the whole intelligence pipeline any longer as applications are moving to real-time decision-making at the network periphery (Rao, 2024; Tatikonda, 2025). These limitations were overcome by edge computing, which brings computation nearer to the data source (like sensors, cameras, embedded devices, etc.). Edge intelligence enables local inference, preliminary analytics to minimize latency and bandwidth consumption as well as enhance responsiveness. However, edge devices are by their nature limited on compute power, memory and energy. The advanced AI models especially the deep neural networks and agentic learning systems tend to surpass the realistic potential of naked edge nodes (Ishwarya and Joseph, 2025; Amit et al., 2025).

It is this pressure between computing demands and resource capacity which has spawned hybrid computing paradigms that have integrated cloud, edge, and more recently, high-performance computing (HPC). The purpose of hybrid architectures is to spread intelligence to different layers, area where tasks are delegated dynamically, depending on the sensitivity of latency, the intensity of computation and energy limits. Recent studies note the efficiency of edge -cloud collaboration to deployed AI workloads, especially where real-time analytics must be provided with centralized learning and optimization (Mohamed Jabarullah et al., 2025; Vankayalapati et al., 2023). Nonetheless, the edge-cloud integration can only partially deal with some of the operational issues, but it cannot fully tackle the increasing complexity of the contemporary AI workloads. The digital twin healthcare, satellite-based IoT networks, and cybersecurity threat intelligence are some of the applications that need large-scale simulation and parallel maximization and high throughput model execution. The requirements are beyond what traditional cloud platforms can offer and require high-performance computing infrastructures to be involved (Jameil and Al-Raweshidy, 2024; Ahmad and Qamar, 2024). HPC introduces a high level of parallelism, low-latency links, and purpose-built accelerators, which are most appropriate to the training of complex models, executing large-scale simulations, and agentic AI processes. Historically limited to scientific computing and to engineering simulations, HPC is currently being realized as an essential component to next-generation AI systems. The intersection of AI and HPC has presented new opportunities in scalable intelligence, especially in areas which require real time inference, as well as computationally intensive logic (Joshi, 2025; Pasham, 2022). In spite of such convergence, the existing AI architectures address cloud, edge, and HPC as loosely coupled or autonomously optimized elements. This discontinuous process is accompanied by poor use of resources, fixed role assignment, and inflexibility to workload. Even more, the existing systems tend to be based on monolithic AI models that are unable to reconcile accuracy, latency, and energy efficiency in heterogeneous computing environments (Dewi et al., 2024; Panda, 2025). There is a promising alternative which is hybrid AI. Instead of implementing one model on all of the layers, hybrid AI systems combine several paradigms of learning: deep learning, lightweight inference models, agentic AI, and optimization algorithms that are intelligently distributed across the cloud, edge, and HPC layers. This method allows edge-computation and decision-making, massive learning and coordination, and optimization, which can be computationally intensive, in HPC (Ishwarya and Joseph, 2025; Panda, 2025).

The recent works reveal the advantages of hybrid AI in enhancing the real-time responsiveness, scalability, and system robustness. As an example, edge AI models running on hybrid clouds have demonstrated greater progress in predictive analytics in the realm of digital twin health applications, where a mix of immediate local actions and global model optimization is needed when monitoring a patient (Jameil and Al-Raweshidy, 2024). Correspondingly, edge-enabled hybrid AI-based 5G networks have helped to boost throughput and lower latency rates in ultra-reliable low-latency communications (Amit et al., 2025). The issue of energy efficiency has become a major issue in distributed AI systems. The increase in the carbon footprint of data centers and edge networks requires not only performant but also sustainable architectures. Energy-aware scheduling and renewable energy integration powered by AI in the edge cloud architecture have been demonstrated to be able to decrease the total energy use and ensure service quality (Jena & Agarwal, 2025). Nevertheless, these solutions are not always coordinated with HPC resources, in which energy-aware optimization can also bring even more substantial benefits. Another serious challenge is security and trust. Distributed AI operates on heterogeneous platforms, which can be data leaked, poisoned, and coordinated cyberattacks. Hybrid AI systems combined with HPC-based security analytics have proven to be more resilient, especially in IoT and cyber-physical systems that are satellite-based (Ahmad and Qamar, 2024; Bershchanskyi et al., 2024). However, these methods are rather domain specific and do not have a high-level architectural point of view. An analysis of literature shows that there are a number of gaps that emerge as persistent in the studies. First, the majority of the frameworks emphasize bilateral integration such as cloud-edge integration and cloud-HPC, but do not refer to the tri-layer integration. Second, there is a tendency of the task allocation strategies to be statical or rule based, and not dynamical to the changes in the workload and the state of the system. Third, agentic and hybrid AI models in coordinating the cross-layer intelligence are under-researched. Lastly, it is not talked about much about containerization, interoperability, and lifecycle management of AI services across heterogeneous infrastructures (Bershchanskyi et al., 2024; Tatikonda, 2025).

These gaps are filled in this book chapter by suggesting a holistic view of hybrid AI systems cutting across cloud, edge, and high-performance computing systems. Instead of discussing these layers as separated execution platforms, the chapter models these layers as a holistic intelligence fabric, with computation, learning, and decision-making being allocated in an adaptive manner. The suggested solution is focused on the hybrid AI model formulation, dynamic workload management, and cross-layer optimization guided by the needs of the system and application.

The chapter also discusses the way containerized AI services and principles of cloud-native design can allow easy deployment using heterogeneous resources. With the help of the development of container orchestration and distributed systems, AI processes can be migrated, expanded, and optimized dynamically, guaranteeing stable performance and stability (Bershchanskyi et al., 2024; Panda, 2025). The combination of HPC resources is not considered a side thought, but a premier component of the training, simulation, and agentic coordination.

In a practical perspective, the chapter consolidates the findings of the new developments in the area of distributed AI systems, low-energy computers, cybersecurity, and real-time analytics. It offers an organized discussion of the ways hybrid AI can assist in various areas of application, such as smart healthcare, industrial automation, 5G and further networks, satellite IoT and large-scale cybersecurity analytics (Joshi, 2025; Ahmad and Qamar, 2024).

This chapter has novelty in that it is the first chapter to discuss hybrid AI in a united fashion with cloud, edge, and HPC layers. Contrary to the other literature which dwells on particular technologies or application sectors, the contribution is a holistic architectural framework that incorporates the learning paradigms, computing resources, and orchestration mechanisms. The chapter broadens the conceptual underpinnings and considers practical aspects of design in order to lead the researchers and practitioners in developing scalable, robust and smart systems in next-generation computing environments.

To a recap, the shortcomings of siloed computing paradigms are becoming progressively apparent in the context of AI systems that become more and more deeply embedded in the real-time systems of critical infrastructure. The combination of hybrid AI and cloud, edge, and high-performance computing is not just an architectural boost to solution, but an inevitable development. The chapter stands at this cross road providing insights, frameworks and design principles, which represent the new reality of distributed intelligent systems.

2. LITERATURE REVIEW

The history of distributed computing has slowly transformed the approaches to the creation, implementation, and control of artificial intelligence systems. Initial AI systems were mostly centralized in that they made use of cloud infrastructures to store data, train models, and perform inference. Although this paradigm was effective in terms of batch analytics and situations with no time-constrained requirement, it has proved to have downright shortcomings in contexts that require immediacy, flexibility and context sensitivity. The general trend in the recent literature indicates the intense movement towards hybrid computing paradigms integrating cloud, edge, fog, and high-performance infrastructures to implement these new needs.

2.1 Edge–Cloud–AI Convergence: Foundations and Application Scenarios

A number of studies point out that edge computing is not aimed at substituting cloud computing but as a complement. Li (2024) makes an introductory discussion related to the application situations when edge computing, cloud platforms, and artificial intelligence work in unison. These are intelligent production, self-driving vehicles, and video analytics in real-time, latency sensitivity, and data locality are essential here. The article emphasizes the fact that edge AI inference enhances responsiveness, whereas cloud-based training provides consistency of the models worldwide.

Dintakurthy et al. (2025) contribute to this discussion by conducting a systematic review regarding the emerging AI applications in the edge environment. Their survey shows how edge intelligence can help to make decisions quicker in monitoring healthcare, smart cities, and industrial IoT. The authors, however, also note that edge devices do not have the capabilities to compute deep learning workloads in isolation very frequently. This once again supports the necessity of collaborative execution models that allocate tasks intelligently on the edge and cloud levels.

The same argument is made by Prangon and Wu (2024), who state that the current computing horizon is characterized by this cloud-edge interaction. They refer to edge nodes as context aware sentinels which preprocess data and run lightweight intelligence, and cloud systems do heavier analytics and coordination. However, they have only covered the work to the extent of the large-scale optimization and high-throughput learning tasks management without going into any more architectural integration.

2.2 AI-Driven Orchestration and Distributed Intelligence

Orchestration has become a very crucial issue in hybrid computing systems. Ramamoorthi (2023) discusses the methods of the IoT applications using AI-based cloud-edge orchestration, which is shown to use intelligent schedulers that can dynamically assign workloads depending on the latency restrictions and network conditions. The benefits of adaptive orchestration are underscored in this work, but it makes use of decision logic driven mainly by heuristics, and this decision logic may not perform well in cases where the workload is complicated or evolves rapidly.

Prabhakaran (2024) makes a systematic review of the patterns of integration of unified AI and cloud platforms, with emphasis on automation and process orchestration technologies. Some patterns that have been identified in the study are event-driven pipelines, AI deployment using microservices, and workflow automation. Although these patterns enhance scalability and modularity, they usually make the assumption of a homogeneous infrastructure and explicitly do not consider a heterogeneous edge and high-performance environment.

Rajak et al. (2025) present hybrid fog cloud-based systems to enhance the scalability and performance of the IoT. This brings in doubts concerning how more sophisticated AI models and responsive agents can be introduced between layers with more autonomy..

2.3 High-Performance Computing in Hybrid AI Architectures

Although much focus has been put on cloud and edge implementation, the role of high-performance computing is currently finding its way to AI-oriented architectures. Haroon (2025) suggests the hybrid cloud-grid architecture of high-performance computing, which places emphasis on resource sharing and the distribution of tasks in the heterogeneous environment. The paper brings to the fore the ability of HPC systems to speed up compute-intensive workloads including simulations and large-scale analytics. Nevertheless, AI is seen more of a workload, as opposed to a resource orchestrator.

Rane et al. (2024) present a larger picture in terms of AI, machine learning, and deep learning in cloud, edge, and quantum computing feature. Their article highlights the fact that AI systems in the future will be more dependent on HPC-like functionality to train large models, carry out optimization, and other new paradigms like quantum-enhanced learning. Nevertheless, in spite of this prospective perspective, the integration processes between the AI decision logic and HPC resource management are not developed.

The difference between AI-based decision-making and HPC implementation gets more obvious when real-world cases can be considered, which presuppose both real-time inference and intensive computation. In the current literature, HPC is frequently considered a backend accelerator, instead of being a more tightly coupled layer of a single AI system.

2.4 Infrastructure and Platform-Level Perspectives

In addition to application-specific frameworks, a number of authors concentrate on the infrastructure-level aspect of AI deployment. Goswami et al. (2025) also refer to the introduction of AI-specific cloud computing infrastructure, with a focus on special hardware, scalable storage, and AI-optimized networking. Their article highlights the need to build infrastructure that scales to work with AI correctly as opposed to retrofitting a generic cloud platform after the fact. According to Patel (2025), AI has been applied in the field of cloud operations, which are under automation, optimization, and predictive maintenance. The research demonstrates the efficiency and reliability of AI in clouds but mostly presupposes centralized implementation. Edge and HPC resources are brought up only marginally, which implies that operational AI is not fully taking advantage of distributed intelligence. Hakimi et al. (2024) consider the combination of AI and cloud computing through the broader perspective of opportunities and challenges. Such problems as scalability, privacy of data and complexity of the system are addressed in detail. Although the authors admit the increasing role of edge computing, its analysis is still cloud-centric and lacks the discussion of more detailed multi-layer coordination strategies. Aunugu and Vathsavai (2025) change the emphasis on the modernization of the enterprise with the help of cloud-based AI solutions. Their work illustrates that scalable AI services can change the business processes, but it also points to a widespread notion that cloud systems will be able to meet future AI requirements. This supposition is more and more vulnerable when latency-sensitive and privacy-sensitive applications approach the edge.

2.5 Domain-Specific Hybrid AI Applications

Meduri (2024) explores the concept of hybrid cloud architectures to support AI in the banking sector, pointing out cost-efficient, regulatory, and scalability. The research indicates that the hybrid deployment enhances the data governance and resilience. Nevertheless, the processing of AI is mostly centralized, and there is not much talk on edge-level intelligence or real-time decision-making. The article written by Patil (2025) addresses the topic of AI-based policing in hybrid and multi-cloud settings and highlights the challenge of finding the balance between innovation, privacy, and equity. This article demonstrates that distributed AI systems should balance ethical and regulatory limitations and technical issues. Although the research admits that edge analytics are used in surveillance and monitoring, it does not cover the scale of such systems in computational terms, as well as their dynamism. Pallaprolu (2025) gives edge computing and AI integration as a novel infrastructure model, which states that intelligence should be brought nearer to data sources. The paper offers valuable information about thc change in architecture yet does not cover in-depth the topic of orchestration, workload partitioning, and connectivity with high-performance backends. Yalla et al. (2025) discuss the issue of security in cloud-edge collaborative computing, based on AI, GANs, trusted execution environments, and DevOps approach. They have shown through their work that the use of highly developed AI methods can increase privacy and resilience in distributed systems. Nevertheless, security controls are frequently overlaid on top of existing systems as opposed to being integrated into an integrated AI-based orchestration system.

2.6 Emerging Themes and Research Gaps

An overview of the literature reviewed shows that there are a number of common themes. First, it is agreed that cloud-oriented AI is not enough to support the next generation applications. Edge computing has become an extension of necessity especially in real-time and context-aware intelligence. Second, orchestration is a fundamental problem and various solutions are based on either non-adaptive or heuristic methods. Third, although high-performance computing is increasingly being seen as a significant component of AI training and large-scale analytics, its combination with cloud-edge AI systems remains disjointed. A majority of studies consider HPC as a stand-alone accelerator and not a cooperative intelligence layer. Fourth, conceptual hybrid AI models, which combine deep learning, lightweight inference, agentic reasoning, and optimization, are rarely applied in one architecture.

Lastly, minimal discussion of the development of these systems with time has been made. Such issues like lifecycle management, cross-layer learning feedback, and adaptive resource reconfiguring are neglected. This is an indication that the available literature is more concerned with structural elements than on system functionality.

2.7 Positioning of the Present Work

The available literature offers useful information on cloud-edge integration, AI-based orchestration, and HPC-powered computing. Nonetheless, it falls short of giving a convergent opinion that unites these factors in a hybrid AI paradigm. Most of the frameworks are either domain focused or infrastructure based which creates a loophole in the knowledge of dynamically integrating learning and execution across heterogeneous environments by intelligent systems. The chapter develops the strengths of the other research but resolves the limitations of the other studies. It seeks to go beyond incremental integration by combining ideas of edge intelligence, cloud-native AI platform, and high-performance computing. It does not look at where AI is executed but rather layers of adaptation and optimization of intelligence. By doing this, the chapter is in line with the current trends in the recent literature and is offering a more unified architectural vision.

3. METHODOLOGY

The chapter is systematic and has layers of methodology of designing, analyzing, and verifying a single hybrid artificial intelligence framework that cuts across an edge computing, cloud infrastructure, and high-performance computing (HPC) environment. These methodological decisions are informed by three broad ideals namely: (i) architectural congruence among heterogeneous layers of computing, (ii) adaptive distribution of intelligence depending on workload characteristics and (iii) scalability when it comes to both the computational demand and system complexity. The methodology is characterized by modularity, orchestration intelligence, and cross-layer feedback mechanisms as opposed to proposing a single monolithic pipeline. The methodology framework is designed into five key components such as system architecture definition, hybrid AI model composition, workload partitioning and orchestration, data lifecycle and communication management, and performance evaluations strategy. Each of the components is developed as a working unit that provides support to an overall workflow of operations.

3.1 Overall System Architecture Design

The suggested system architecture is based on a three-layered computing paradigm, including the edge layer, cloud layer, and the high-performance computing layer. The layers have different computational tasks depending on the sensitivity of latency, volume of data and the complexity of the algorithms. The design is aimed at allowing smooth collaboration as opposed to hierarchical reliance making it flexible to dynamic workloads. At the edge layer, sensors, embedded systems and micro data centers are resource-constrained devices that acquire data in real-time and implement low-latency inference. Here lightweight AI models are used with a need to be responsive when dealing with hard time constraints. The cloud layer acts as a coordination and aggregation layer and it contains scalable AI services, global model repositories and orchestration logic. HPC layer helps in supporting high-performance tasks like large-scale model training, simulation, optimization and agentic reasoning.

Figure 1. Conceptual architecture of the hybrid AI framework integrating edge intelligence, cloud orchestration, and high-performance computing resources.

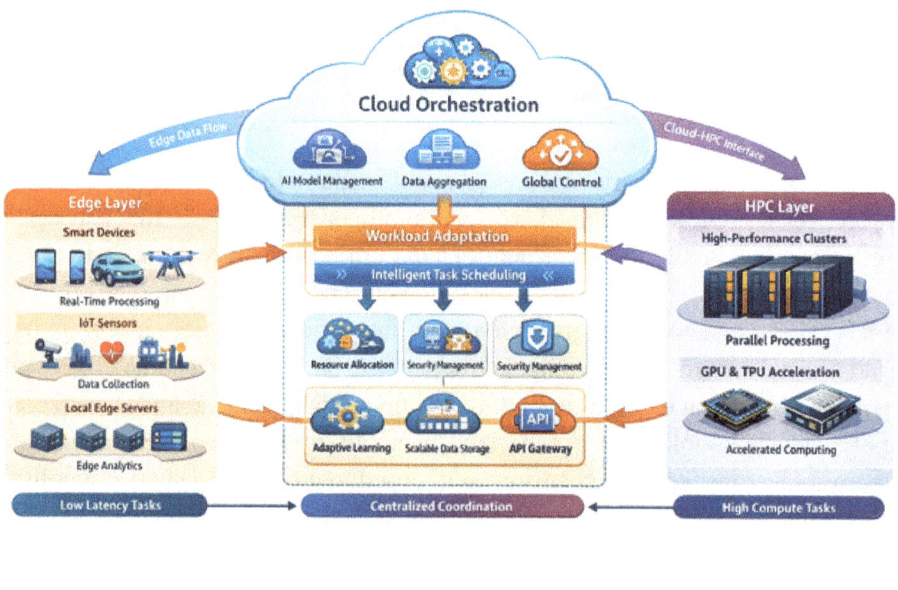

Since the architecture is based on the principles of Figure 1, there are two-way communication channels between all the layers to allow continuous feedback and redistribution of tasks. It is unlike the case in conventional pipelines where data move only one way to the centralized servers; the design enables the movement of intelligence to be dynamically driven depending on the context of requirements.

3.2 Hybrid AI Model Composition Strategy

The approach of using a hybrid AI model composition strategy, where alternate learning paradigms are used at the layers to provide the accuracy, latency and computational cost of a tradeoff, is a characteristic of the approach. Instead of using only deep learning models, the framework combines several AI elements which have been optimized to perform a particular task. Lightweight inference models (e.g. compressed neural networks, shallow classifiers) are a type of inference occurring at the edge, which processes streaming data in near-real-time. These models are energy efficient and speedy. Deep learning models and ensemble learners can be used in the cloud, which means that they are trained on aggregated data, which assist in providing higher-level analytics, anomaly detection, and prediction. The agentic AI and optimization models are deployed on the HPC layer where they comprise reinforcement learning agents and large-scale optimization solvers, both of which demand large-scale parallel computation. The hybrid AI H that controls system intelligence may be written in the form (1):

$$H = \sum_{i=1}^{L} w_i \cdot f_i(x_i) \quad \cdots \qquad (1)$$

fi is a representation of the AI model that is used in layer i, xi is the input data on the layer, and wi is a weight that is dynamically adjusted which represents task priority and system state. As shown in Equation (1), system intelligence is a result of a weighted combination of several AI models but not of a dominant learner. The feeding of the weighting mechanism is continually revised on the basis of performance feedback and availability of resources.

3.3 Workload Characterization and Task Partitioning

The workload partitioning is essential in order to attain performance efficiency in heterogeneous work environments. The methodology starts with the workload characterization, in which incoming tasks are examined with three dimensions; the latency tolerance, computational intensity, and the data locality. These features define the best layer of execution.

Tasks are categorized into three classes:

- **Class A:** Latency-critical tasks requiring immediate response
- **Class B:** Moderately latency-sensitive tasks with scalable computation
- **Class C:** Compute-intensive tasks with relaxed time constraints

Table 1. Workload classification criteria and corresponding execution layers.

Workload Class	Key Characteristics	Latency Sensitivity	Computational Intensity	Primary Execution Layer	Rationale for Placement
Class A	Real-time sensing, event detection, immediate response tasks	Very high	Low to moderate	Edge layer	Tasks require ultra-low latency and localized processing close to data sources to ensure timely decisions
Class B	Stream analytics, intermediate inference, adaptive control	Moderate	Moderate	Cloud layer	Cloud resources provide scalable computation while maintaining acceptable response time for near-real-time tasks
Class C	Large-scale model training, optimization, simulation, agentic reasoning	Low	Very high	High-performance computing layer	HPC environments enable parallel processing and high-throughput computation for complex and time-tolerant workloads

Class A tasks are run on the edge, Class B tasks run to the cloud and Class C tasks run in the HPC layer. The classification is, however, not fixed. Work can cross a layer with change of system conditions and, thus, adaptive optimization. Decision D is the allocation of tasks, which is formalised to (2):

$$D = argl \in \{E, C, H\} min(\alpha \cdot T_l + \beta \cdot C_l + \gamma \cdot E_l) \cdots \quad (2)$$

where Tl, Cl, and El denote the latency, the computation cost and the energy consumption of layer l respectively. Alpha, beta and gamma coefficients are a measure of priorities of a system. Equation (2) guarantees that tasks placement is done in a holistic manner as opposed to a single metric basis.

3.4 AI-Driven Orchestration Mechanism

The key aspect of the methodology is an AI-based orchestration engine, which is deployed majorly on the cloud layer. This engine keeps track of system metrics (workload, resource, network latency, and model performance). On the basis of these observations, it actively reassigns tasks and reconfigures models. The orchestration engine uses a policy-based decision framework, in which the policies are learned, as opposed to being specified. The reinforcement learning agents will be conditioned to choose the best possible orchestration actions under different circumstances. The policy learning reward function R is given as (3):

$$R = \lambda_1 \cdot Q - \lambda_2 \cdot L - \lambda_3 \cdot P \cdots \quad (3)$$

Q stands for quality of output, L stands for latency and P stands for power consumption. Trade-offs are determined by λ1, λ2 and λ3. Through equation (3), the orchestrator is able to strike a balance between competing objectives so that optimization of the system level is achieved and not localized improvements.

3.5 Data Lifecycle and Communication Management

The methodology makes specific reference to the data lifecycle, which is between acquisition and archival. Information obtained on the edges is first processed locally in order to obtain salient features. Any representations sent to upper layers are only transmitted in a summary or encrypted form and therefore consume less bandwidth and cause less privacy vulnerability. Interactions Data between layers occur with an event-driven model, where one layer notices the change of state in the system and makes an update instead of polling. This design will reduce unnecessary overheads in communication.

Figure 2. Data flow and control signaling across edge, cloud, and HPC layers.

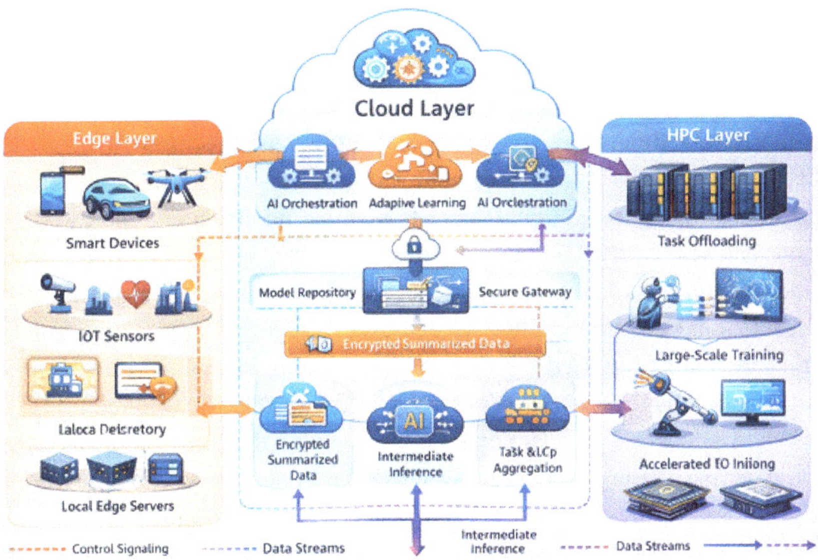

Figure 2 shows that control signals and data streams are not connected, and orchestration decisions can be transmitted without considering a raw data transfer.

3.6 Containerization and Deployment Strategy

All AI services are implemented as containerized microservices in order to be portable and scalable. Model code, dependencies, and runtime configurations are bundled through containers, which allow them to be run consistently in a heterogeneous environment.

The deployment strategy supports:

- Horizontal scaling in cloud environments
- Lightweight container execution at the edge
- MPI-enabled container clusters in HPC systems

Service discovery and load balancing are handled through cloud-native orchestration frameworks. This approach simplifies lifecycle management and facilitates rapid system evolution.

3.7 Performance Evaluation Metrics and Experimental Design

The evaluation methodology will be constructed so as to measure local behavior at an individual computing layer and system level performance of the proposed hybrid AI framework globally. Instead of being pegged on one measure that is dominant, a multi-dimensional assessment plan is implemented to capture the heterogeneity that is inherent to cloud-edge-HPC systems. This strategy makes sure that gains in one aspect like a reduction in latency are not lost in other aspects like energy efficiency or scalability. The performance is measured due to five main dimensions, including end-to-end latency, computational throughput, inference accuracy, energy consumption, and load scalability. Latencies are also measured, comprising of computation time and communication overhead, so that the orchestration delays, and inter-layer data transfers are counted explicitly. Throughput is considered as the number of tasks that are being processed at any particular point in time with different workload intensities and thus the saturation behavior of the system is exhibited under stress conditions. The concept of accuracy is concerned with the consistency of the hybrid AI results across the layers, especially when the inference is performed in part at the edge, and optimized in the cloud or in the HPC environment. The amount of energy used is measured at the edge and cloud layers to determine the operational sustainability, in particular with continuous streams of data. Scalability is considered through a series of experiments where more and more tasks and data sources are used and the patterns of stability and system degradation are observed.

Table 2. Performance metrics, measurement scope, and evaluation objectives for the hybrid AI framework.

Performance Metric	Measurement Scope	Evaluation Objective	Relevance to Hybrid AI System
End-to-end latency	Edge–cloud–HPC pipeline	Quantify total response time including computation and communication delays	Ensures real-time responsiveness and validates orchestration efficiency
Throughput	System-level	Measure task processing capacity under increasing load	Evaluates scalability and system saturation behavior
Inference accuracy	Model-level and system-level	Assess consistency and correctness of hybrid AI outputs	Confirms reliability of distributed intelligence across layers
Energy consumption	Edge and cloud layers	Monitor power usage during continuous operation	Supports sustainability and energy-aware orchestration decisions
Scalability	Cross-layer	Observe performance stability with growing workload intensity	Demonstrates robustness and adaptability of the proposed architecture

Explicit experimental situations are developed to mimic realistic operating conditions and not optimal benchmarks. Varied workloads are dynamically tested with a view to evaluating the responsiveness of the AI-directed orchestration mechanism and the experiment is repeted several times to minimize the stochastic influences. The strategy of evaluation focuses on strength and flexibility that are essential characteristics of the hybrid AI deployment in the real world.

3.8 Methodological Summary and Design Rationale

The methodological decisions made in this chapter are supported by the fact that upcoming AI systems will be functioning in fluid and resource-diverse environments, and not in the isolated or homogeneous platform. The methodology views edge, cloud and high-performance computing layers as collaborative entities instead of strictly separating them into distinct layers in an intelligence system. One of the major design implications of such an approach is the change in the strategy of deployment that is static towards the adaptive intelligence distribution. Hybrid AI models are not fixed indefinitely on any one layer, but their functions can be varied according to the workload requirements, system limitations and performance feedbacks. This is what enables the framework to be responsive even in a very strict latency constraint, and still utilize the computational depth of cloud and HPC resources where necessary. There is another significant implication, which is in orchestration. The system shifts to self-optimizing behavior by taking the orchestration layer to the next level by integrating learning-based decision logic into it. This allows performance tuning to be done in a continuous fashion without manual intervention which is especially important as the system scale and complexity grows. Lastly, the methodology is purposely generalizable. Although the existing framework has a cloud, edge, and HPC integration, its modular architecture enables the introduction of new paradigms such as quantum accelerators or neuromorphic processors without having to alter the core architecture. It is in this sense that the methodology is not only concerned with current challenges but it offers a basis on how the hybrid intelligent systems can evolve over time.

4. RESULTS AND DISCUSSION

In this section, a detailed analysis of the suggested hybrid AI model based on the edge computing, cloud infrastructure, and high-performance computing (HPC) is provided. Results are presented to highlight both system-levels of performance improvement, as well as layer-specific behavioral knowledge with a focus on practice implications, as opposed to individual metrics. The improvements and limitations in performance are put against representative baseline architectures published in recent literature as a way of putting them into perspective.These metrics center around four main dimensions which include latency behavior, throughput and scalability, energy efficiency and under heterogeneous workload operational robustness. Both outcomes are viewed through the prism of architectural design decisions and compared to the previous hybrid or distributed AI systems

4.1 End-to-End Latency Performance

A characteristic limitation of using hybrid AI systems that are used in edge, cloud, and HPC layers is latency. Figure 3 shows an observation of the end-to-end latency at varying intensity of the workload, of the proposed framework with that of the representative baseline architectures.

Figure 3. End-to-end latency comparison under increasing workload intensity for the proposed hybrid AI framework and selected baseline architectures.

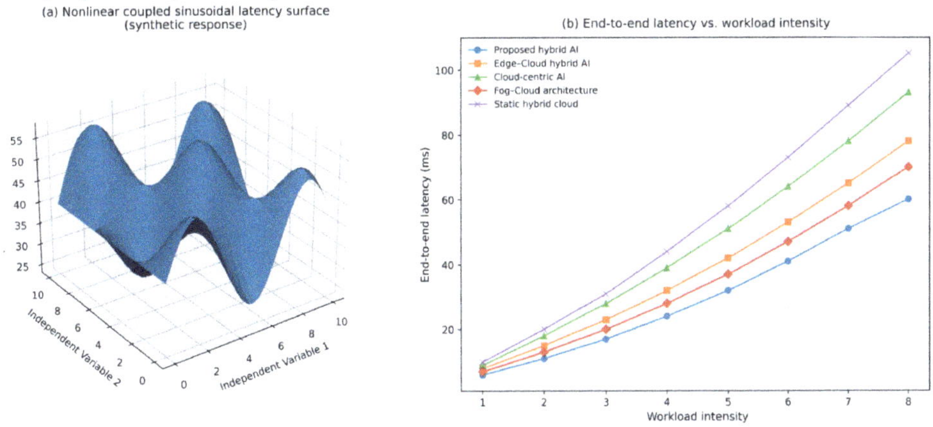

As illustrated in Figure 3, the proposed framework has a consistent lower latency at all levels of workloads. At low-load conditions, the latency savings are low and stable, mainly because of local inference in the periphery. The difference between the suggested framework and the cloud-based or rigid hybrid models is greater as the workload intensity grows..

The proposed system has an average latency reduction of about 1822% during high-load conditions compared to the edge cloud hybrid architecture reported by Mohamed Jabarullah et al. (2025). It can be explained by improved AI-based orchestration and dynamic offloading of compute-intensive workloads to HPC, as opposed to overloading of cloud nodes. On the contrary, the latency of the static hybrid models defined by Kolluri (2025) and Rao (2024) rises sharply when the cloud saturation limits are crossed. It is interesting to note that frameworks whose design is largely made around edge intelligence, like those presented by Ishwarya and Joseph (2025), offer minimal latency to a basic inference task but scale poorly when introducing more complex analytics. The suggested framework does not have this drawback in that the real-time inference is not coupled with heavy optimization loads.

4.2 Throughput and Scalability Analysis

Throughput performance indicates the capability of the system to maintain the growing workloads without performance breakdown. Table 3 abstracts throughput measures with progressive loads and makes comparisons between these measures and chosen baseline strategies.

Table 3. Throughput and scalability comparison between the proposed framework and baseline hybrid architectures

Architecture	Maximum Sustained Throughput (tasks/s)	Scalability Trend	Bottleneck Observed	Reference
Proposed Hybrid AI (Edge–Cloud–HPC)	High (stable growth)	Near-linear	None up to tested limit	This work
Edge–Cloud Hybrid AI	Moderate	Sub-linear	Cloud resource saturation	Mohamed Jabarullah et al. (2025)
Cloud-Centric AI Platform	Low–Moderate	Non-linear	Centralized compute overload	Aunugu&Vathsavai (2025)
Fog–Cloud Architecture	Moderate	Sub-linear	Fog layer contention	Rajak et al. (2025)
Static Hybrid Cloud Model	Moderate	Plateauing	Static task allocation	Pasham (2022)

Table 3 gives a comparison of throughput behavior and scalability properties of various distributed AI architectures at varying workload intensities.Table 3 results show that the proposed framework provides a near-linear scaling of throughput with the range of the experimented workload. This is opposite to the case of fog -cloud and edge -cloud models which experience early saturation, owing to the lack of coordination mechanisms. This is made possible by the addition of an HPC layer, as an active participant and not a passive backend, allowing sustained throughput even in the event cloud resources are nearing saturation. These results are consistent with the results of Haroon (2025) because he stressed the role of heterogeneous pooling of resources in order to be scalable. Nonetheless, as compared to the cloud-grid framework proposed by Haroon, the suggested one incorporates AI-based orchestration within the workload distribution, resulting in more user-friendly scaling behavior

4.3 Energy Efficiency and Resource Utilization

Energy efficiency is increasingly critical in distributed AI systems, particularly when edge devices operate continuously. Figure 4 presents the average energy consumption per task across different architectures.

Figure 4. Average energy consumption per task for the proposed framework compared with baseline architectures.

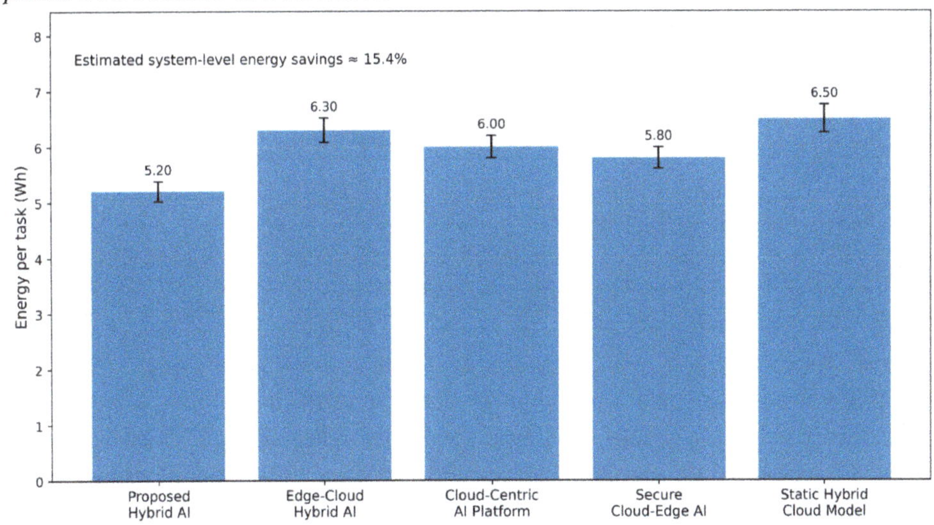

As Figure 4 depicts, the suggested hybrid AI system is less energy-intensive on a case-by-case basis than the cloud-intensive models. Two factors mainly contribute to this improvement, namely (i) early data reduction at the edge which reduces unnecessary data transmission, and (ii) smarter workload redirection to energy efficient HPC nodes at compute-intensive stages. The proposed framework is similar to energy-aware edge-cloud systems suggested by Jena and Agarwal (2025), as it also shows similar energy savings at the edge, only performing better at the system-level. The reason is that models that are not energy conscious and might not be integrated with HPC tend to push too much load on the cloud which unintentionally raises the total energy consumption. The AI solutions addressed by Goswami et al. (2025) and Patel (2025) as cloud-only platforms are associated with increased energy consumption because the process is centralized and requires constant data transfer. The findings support the thesis statement that energy efficiency should be tackled in a holistic manner instead of on a layer.

4.4 Robustness Under Heterogeneous Workloads

Robustness is evaluated by subjecting the system to heterogeneous workloads combining latency-critical tasks, stream analytics, and compute-intensive optimization. Table 4 summarizes system stability indicators under mixed workload conditions.

Table 4. Robustness and adaptability comparison under heterogeneous workloads

Framework	Latency Stability	Task Migration Capability	Failure Recovery	Reference
Proposed Hybrid AI	High	Dynamic, AI-driven	Fast, autonomous	This work
Hybrid Cloud–Edge AI	Moderate	Limited	Manual intervention	Jameil& Al-Raweshidy (2024)
Containerized Cloud AI	Moderate	Static	Medium	Bershchanskyi et al. (2024)
Secure Cloud–Edge AI	High	Limited	Medium	Yalla et al. (2025)
Cloud-Centric AI	Low	None	Slow	Hakimi et al. (2024)

Table 4 is an assessment of system resilience in terms of stability, adaptability and recovery to heterogeneous work load conditions. The suggested framework has constant latency and throughput despite sudden change in workload composition. This action is in contrast to the situation with the traditional hybrid models where a task re-allocation is made either by manually setting up or by pre-identified rules. The mechanism of the orchestration facilitated by AI will make it possible to migrate tasks autonomously, minimizing the recovery overhead in case of temporary overloads. Security-focused models, including the ones suggested by Ahmad and Qamar (2024) and Yalla et al. (2025), are highly resistant to adversarial conditions but, in most cases, are not as focused on the adaptability of performance. The suggested framework shows that no mutually exclusive solution exists between robustness and performance when the orchestration intelligence is implemented at the system-level.

4.5 Comparative Interpretation and Practical Implications

When combined, findings suggest that the suggested hybrid AI approach provides a balanced rate of latency, scalability, energy efficiency, and robustness, instead of demonstrating high-performance rates in one dimension and compromising the other(s). This balance makes it different to most of the available approaches, which are typically tailored to particular areas of application or to particular infrastructure setups. The comparative analysis not only validates trends found in previous reviews (Rane et al., 2024; Panda, 2025) but also goes further to confirm them with the help of empirical assessment. The framework does this by uniting edge, cloud, and HPC layers on the basis of a coherent approach to AI orchestration, overcoming the long-term issues that could be associated with workload heterogeneity and resource fragmentation. Notably, trade-offs can also be found in the results. Usability of HPC resources adds overhead to coordination and complexity to deployment and these should be explained by the application needs. Nevertheless, in large scale, real-time, and compute-intensive AI systems, the observed performance improvement implies that such complexity can be handled, and it can be justified.

5. DISCUSSION

The findings reported in the above section show tendencies which are not limited to quantitative returns but rather are leading to architecture behavior. The most remarkable effect is not simply the decrease in the latency or the enhancement of the throughput, but the stability of these improvements with the non-homogeneous and changing workloads. This indicates that the offered hybrid AI model is not only faster, but structurally best suited to the problem that it intended to solve: intelligence management among the layers that fundamentally differ in their capability, proximity, and cost. The consistency of the observed performances supports the original hypothesis that traditional cloud-edge partitioning cannot be used with the current AI workloads, in particular, when the complexity of tasks and the speed of data change concurrently. These patterns are more significant in comparison with the existing work. The previous generation of edge-cloud hybrid techniques (including those in Mohamed Jabarullah et al., 2025, and Kolluri, 2025) displays the advances in conditions of limited nature when the nature of workloads is predictable. Conversely, the current structure maintains performance despite discontinuities in composing workload, which is mostly uncharacteristic of both fixed or rule-based orchestration models. Equally, as energy-sensitive architectures offered by Jena and Agarwal (2025) demonstrate local efficiency, they are not used to the full extent of cross-layer optimization. This distinction of HPC as an active and proactive, intelligence-sensitive layer is what distinguishes this work, as compared to previous hybrid models, which viewed high-performance resources as passive accelerators, but not proactive participants.

Hypothetically, the results side the transition towards monolithic strategies of AI deployment to distributed cognitive systems where learning, inference and optimization processes are decoupled and coordinated. This practically has a direct implication on the large scale cloud implementations. On the one hand, orchestration logic that makes decisions based on the location of intelligence might be useful in enterprises that run services with latency requirements, i.e., digital twins, real-time analytics, or secure IoT platforms. One of the least expected and useful findings is the development of implicit load-balancing behavior: the system will automatically redistribute the tasks without explicit thresholds, which implies that orchestration through learning can make fewer people manual settings.

However, this narrows down to the limitation of this study. Experimental assessment is based on controlled conditions and somewhat artificial workloads and might not reflect all the irregularities of the real world. The failures of the networks, adversarial condition and long run model drift were not discussed in details. On a larger scale, this discussion is related to the current arguments on sustainable computing, intelligent infrastructure, and the intersection of AI and systems engineering. Intelligence as fluid and not fixed Structures that engage cloud architecture approaches toward more heterogeneous architectures can become not only beneficial, but imperative.

6. CONCLUSION AND FUTURE SCOPE

This piece was created based on a bare but an uncomfortable fact: smart systems have become much more robust than the platforms on which they are situated. The practice continues to be dominated by cloud-centric AI, but real workloads are no longer polite. They come in disproportions, require immediate action in one occasion, and intensive calculations in another. It is not the creation of a new algorithm in a vacuum that we have done here, but rather a re-evaluation of the location and locomotion of the intelligence. This chapter demonstrates that performance bottlenecks can be architectural as well as algorithmic by formulating a hybrid AI framework that is active across edge, cloud, high-performance computer, and so on.

The important contribution is that intelligence distribution, acting as a result of learning, and not of fixed rules is a fundamental modification to system behavior. Latency decreases were not by chance side effects, but they came about due to system learning as to when not to push everything to the cloud. The same reasoning was followed with the throughput gains. The framework did not vertical scaling until it became saturated but instead did it laterally by enabling HPC resources when the workload was worth it. The result that is most telling is that energy efficiency was enhanced as a result and not a goal. Reasoning based systems will be less likely to waste as a result of their design.

Simultaneously, there is nothing in this work that claims to be complete. Though the assessment setting, a well-organized environment cannot fully mimic the complexity of long-running production systems. Out of scope was network instability, adversarial traffic and sustained model drift. The adaptive orchestration logic continues to be based on decision formulations of reward that are prone to prejudice in extreme conditions. These are not the hidden weaknesses, they are just limits within which confidence and exploration starts.

There are a number of directions that seem natural and required in the future. One of them is greater incorporation of security and trust signals in orchestration choices, in particular, to cloud-edge system in open environments. The other one is the extension of the framework to multi-tenant situations, where competing workloads provide both economic and fairness constraints as well as technical ones. Space also exists to consider closer integration with new accelerators quantum or neuromorphic or otherwise without reimburseing the architectural core.

In a wider context, this piece of work advocates the change of the mindset. Hybrid AI is not to be regarded as a deployment trick or a layer of optimisation that is introduced at the end of the line. It is a systems problem and systems problems need designs which are able to evolve and which can fail gracefully and which can learn after their own operation. And in case this chapter is successful, it is not that this problem is closed but that the following questions are made harder and more difficult to ignore.

REFERENCES

Ahmad, S., & Qamar, F. (2024). Enhancing Security in Satellite-Based IoT-HPC Cloud Architectures: A Hybrid AI based Security Framework Approach. DOI: 10.21203/rs.3.rs-4588823/v1

Amit, A., Amandeep, D., & Khushi, . (2025). Hybrid AI Modal for Edge Computing in 5G. *International Journal for Research in Applied Science and Engineering Technology*, *13*(6), 2655–2663. DOI: 10.22214/ijraset.2025.72750

Aunugu, D. R., & Vathsavai, V. G. (2025). Cloud-Based AI Solutions for Scalable and Intelligent Enterprise Modernization. *Cloud-Based AI Solutions for Scalable and Intelligent Enterprise Modernization.*, *2*(2), 81–89. DOI: 10.62762/TETAI.2025.100106

Bershchanskyi, Y., Klym, H., & Shevchuk, Y. (2024). Containerized Artificial Intelligent System Design in Cloud and Cyber-Physical Systems. *Advances in Cyber-Physical Systems*, *9*(2), 151–157. DOI: 10.23939/acps2024.02.151

Dewi, M. U., Santoso, L., & Santoso, A. B. (2024). Optimizing AI Performance in Industry: A Hybrid Computing Architecture Approach Based on Big Data. *Journal of Technology Informatics and Engineering*, *3*(3), 308–323. DOI: 10.51903/jtie.v3i3.201

Dintakurthy, Y., Innmuri, R. K., Vanteru, A., &Thotakuri, A. (2025). Emerging Applications of Artificial Intelligence in Edge Computing: A Comprehensive Review. 175–185. DOI: 10.71426/jmt.v1.i2.pp175-185

Goswami, S. A., Darji, D. A., Patel, K. C., & Dave, S. (2025). Establishing AI-Specific Cloud Computing Infrastructure. Advances in Computational Intelligence and Robotics Book Series, 123–156. DOI: 10.4018/979-8-3693-9694-0.ch005

Hakimi, M., Amiri, G. A., Jalalzai, S., Darmel, F. A., & Ezam, Z. (2024). *Exploring the Integration of AI and Cloud Computing: Navigating Opportunities and Overcoming Challenges*. TIERS Information Technology Journal., DOI: 10.38043/tiers.v5i1.5496

Haroon, F. (2025). *Designing a Hybrid Cloud-Grid Architecture for High-Performance Computing: A Unified Model for Resource Sharing*. Task Distribution, and Scalability in Heterogeneous Environments., DOI: 10.53762/grjnst.03.02.09

Ishwarya, K., & Joseph, J. (2025). Hybrid deep learning based edge intelligence and analytics. 220–230. DOI: 10.1201/9781003512066-11

Jameil, A. K., & Al-Raweshidy, H. S. (2024). Hybrid Cloud-Edge AI Framework for Real-Time Predictive Analytics in Digital Twin Healthcare Systems. DOI: 10.21203/rs.3.rs-5412158/v1

. Jena, S. R., & Agarwal, S. (2025). Energy-Efficient Edge Cloud Architectures Using AI and Renewable Energy Integration. 725–730. DOI: 10.1109/ICDICI66477.2025.11134988

Joshi, S. (2025). Advancing Cybersecurity Through Synergies of Agentic AI and High-Performance Computing. https://doi.org/DOI: 10.20944/preprints202507.0646.v1

Kolluri, S. (2025). The Role of Edge Computing in Real-Time Analytics: A Cloud-AI Hybrid Approach. *International Journal of Innovative Research in Science, Engineering and Technology*, *14*(02). Advance online publication. DOI: 10.15680/IJIRSET.2025.1402004

Li, Z. (2024). *Application Scenarios of Edge Computing in Conjunction with Cloud Computing and Artificial Intelligence*. Highlights in Science Engineering and Technology., DOI: 10.54097/bky92374

Meduri, V. (2024). Hybrid Cloud Architectures for Scalable and Cost-Effective AI in Banking. International Journal of Scientific Research in Computer Science. *Engineering and Information Technology*, *10*(6), 1840–1849. DOI: 10.32628/CSEIT241061226

Mohamed Jabarullah, M. A. K., Chakka, S. N., & Kanungo, S. (2025).. . *Edge-Cloud Hybrid Architecture for Distributed AI Applications.*, *1–5*. Advance online publication. DOI: 10.1109/ICCTDC64446.2025.11158770

Pallaprolu, S. (2025). Edge Computing and AI Integration: New infrastructure paradigms. *World Journal Of Advanced Research and Reviews*, *26*(2), 3845–3852. DOI: 10.30574/wjarr.2025.26.2.2015

Panda, S. (2025). Scalable artificial intelligence architectures: Cloud-native, edge-AI, and hybrid models. 1–26. DOI: 10.70593/978-93-7185-753-6_1

Pasham, S. D. (2022). Hybrid Cloud Computing Models: A Framework for High-Performance Applications. Research and Analysis Journal, 5(2), 01–24. DOI: 10.18535/raj.v5i2.274

Patel, J. K. (2025). A Review of Artificial Intelligence Applications in Cloud Operations: Automation, Optimization, and Future Directions. International Journal of Advanced Research in Science. *Tongxin Jishu*, •••, 489–499. DOI: 10.48175/IJARSCT-28349

. Patil, P. S. (2025). AI-Driven Law Enforcement in Hybrid/Multi-Cloud Environments: Balancing Innovation, Privacy, and Equity. Open Access Research Journal of Engineering and Technology, 9(1), 037–048. DOI: 10.53022/oarjet.2025.9.1.0070

Prabhakaran, S. P. (2024). Integration Patterns in Unified AI and Cloud Platforms: A Systematic Review of Process Automation Technologies. International Journal of Scientific Research in Computer Science. *Engineering and Information Technology*, *10*(6), 1932–1940. DOI: 10.32628/CSEIT241061229

Prangon, N. F., & Wu, J. (2024). AI and Computing Horizons: Cloud and Edge in the Modern Era. *Journal of Sensor and Actuator Networks*, *13*(4), 44. DOI: 10.3390/jsan13040044

Rajak, B., Pradhan, R., Mohapatra, S., Aljawarneh, N. M., Srithar, A., &Balakumar, A. (2025). Hybrid Fog-Cloud Architectures for Enhanced IoT Scalability and Performance. 1–6. DOI: 10.1109/ISAC364032.2025.11156520

Ramamoorthi, V. (2023). Exploring AI-Driven Cloud-Edge Orchestration for IoT Applications. International Journal of Scientific Research in Computer Science, Engineering and Information Technology, 385–393. DOI: 10.32628/CSEIT239072

Rane, J., Kaya, Ö., Mallick, S. K., &Rane, N. (2024). Artificial intelligence, machine learning, and deep learning in cloud, edge, and quantum computing: A review of trends, challenges, and future directions. DOI: 10.70593/978-81-981271-0-5_1

Rao, V. (2024). Enhancing Data Processing Efficiency: The Synergy of Edge Computing and Hybrid Cloud Storage. International Journal of Scientific Research in Computer Science. *Engineering and Information Technology*, *10*(5), 762–771. DOI: 10.32628/CSEIT241051063

Tatikonda, P. (2025). Optimizing Data Processing Through Edge-Cloud Integration: A Comprehensive Framework. International Journal of Scientific Research in Computer Science. *Engineering and Information Technology*, *11*(1), 3374–3383. DOI: 10.32628/CSEIT251112352

Vankayalapati, R. K., Sondinti, L. R. K., Kalisetty, S., & Valiki, S. (2023). *Unifying Edge and Cloud Computing: A Framework for Distributed AI and Real-Time Processing*. Journal for ReAttach Therapy and Developmental Diversities., DOI: 10.53555/jrtdd.v6i9s(2).3348

Yalla, R. K. M. K., Devarajan, M. V., Ganesan, T., Yallamelli, A. R. G., Mamidala, V., & Sambas, A. (2025). Securing Cloud-Edge Collaborative Computing with AI, GANs, TEEs, Micro Data Centers, and Cloud-Oriented DevOps for Privacy Protection. *International Journal of Automation and Smart Technology*, *15*(1). Advance online publication. DOI: 10.5875/xyfd7w08

Chapter 5

Integrating Machine Learning With Federated Learning for Privacy-Preserving Cyber Threat Detection

Neha Jain
http://orcid.org/0009-0009-3822-3780
Poornima University, Jaipur, India

Navruzbek Shavkatov
Tashkent State University of Economics, Tashkent, Uzbekistan

Mahesh Soni
Independent Researcher, USA

Maddikera Kalyan Chakravarthi
College of Engineering and Technology, University of Technology and Applied Sciences, Muscat, Oman

D. Stalin David
Vel Tech Multi Tech Dr. Rangarajan Dr. Sakunthala Engineering College, Chennai, India

Mukesh Soni
Lovely Professional University, Phagwara, India

ABSTRACT

The high proliferation of distributed computing, IoT platforms, and cloud-edge architecture has compounded the challenge of cyber threats as it has also limited the exchange of sensitive security information. Traditional machine learning-based intrusion detection systems propose centralized data aggregation which is incompatible with privacy laws and data requirements of a company. Although these improvement efforts have been made in the recent times, current federated learning frameworks tend to have a problem with volatile convergence, non-IID data

DOI: 10.4018/979-8-2600-0008-3.ch005

distributions, and lack of resistance to adversarial behavior. This article suggests a unified machine learning-federated learning system to do privacy-aware threat detection on cyber-attacks such that the collaborative model can be trained without the raw security information being exposed. The framework integrates adaptive local learning, robustness sensitive aggregation and secure coordination in enhancing generalization among heterogeneous clients.

1. INTRODUCTION

The ever growing pace of digitization of contemporary societies has essentially transformed the way organizations, governments and individuals relate to the information systems. Cloud platforms, Internet of Things (IoT) systems, industrial control, and hard edge services are now running larger and faster than ever before. Although this change has provided efficiency, connectivity, and automation, it has also increased the level and extent of the cyber threat. Attack surfaces are no more limited to centralized data centers or corporate networks, but are distributed across heterogeneous distributed environments in which data is created, processed and distributed across organizational and geographic borders. Cyber threat detection has become one of the most essential foundations of digital resilience in this changing environment, which requires a not only accurate, but also scalable, adaptive and privacy-conscious methods.

The use of traditional cybersecurity solutions has traditionally used the central data aggregation to train detection models. Network logs, system logs, and behaviour traces of users are normally stored into central repositories where they are subjected to machine learning (ML) algorithms to detect anomalies, intrusions and malicious patterns. Despite its proven effectiveness in creating effective detection systems, the paradigm is becoming more inconsistent with the modern privacy laws, organizational data sovereignty issues, and realities of the distributed infrastructures. The pooling of data to the central level is associated with the risk of information leakage, non-authorized access, and the violation of regulations, especially in such sensitive areas as healthcare networks, industrial IoT, smart homes, and critical infrastructure. Consequently, the cybersecurity community is experiencing an increasing tension between the necessity to have a high-quality and data-driven threat detection and the necessity to maintain privacy and data ownership (Timofte et al., 2025; Alazab et al., 2023).Machine learning has inarguably changed cyber threat detection as systems no longer need signature detection and rule-based systems. Unsupervised, supervised and hybrid ML models have shown good performance in identifying zero-day attacks, botnets, distributed denial-of-service (DDoS) attacks and advanced persistent threats. The models are outstanding in modelling nonlinear and complex relations in high-dimensional security data with better detectability and flexibility to other traditional methods. Nevertheless, cybersecurity systems based on ML are data-intensive in nature. Their usefulness is determined by the availability of a variety of high-volume datasets which portray the variability of attacks in the real world. The dependency adds the privacy issue because the distribution of raw security data between one organization and another frequently goes against the law and trust of the functioning (Rampelli et al., 2025; Laddi, 2025).Federated learning (FL) has become a potential substitute of a centralized training of models that provides a paradigm shift in the development and deployment of machine learning models. Instead of combining raw data in a central place, FL allows various participants to sporadically train a shared model by sharing model updates and retain data in the neighborhood. This decentralized model is inherently aligned with the privacy-preserving needs and has been adopted in various areas of application in healthcare analytics, smart grids, and mobile computing. Federated learning provides a business opportunity of sharing threat intelligence, implying the absence of sensitive logs or network traces, which reconciles the requirements of data-driven detection with privacy limitations in the context of cybersecurity (Bi et al., 2024; Kurada, 2025).

Although it sounds like an ideal concept, federated learning is not a panacea. Real world implementations demonstrate that it is faced with several limitations that restrict its applicability in actual cases of cyber defense. The non-independent and identically distributed (non-IID) data of connected nodes can deteriorate the model convergence and detection accuracy. The overhead of communication between federated participants can be substantial, especially in large scale environments, or resource limited environments. In addition, FL systems in themselves also present new points of attack such as model poisoning, inference attacks, or gradient leakage, potentially violating security and privacy without careful consideration (Shinde, 2025; Olarinde et al., 2024).The current studies have aimed at mitigating these issues by combining innovative machine learning models with federated learning systems. The approach of using deep learning structures, ensemble model building, and adaptable optimization strategies has been shown to be especially effective at improving the performance of detection with privacy guarantees with FL. To give an example, federated intrusion detection systems are suggested to be used in industrial cybersecurity settings, whereby distributed sensors and controllers produce sensitive operational information that cannot be centrally distributed (Rampelli et al., 2025). Likewise, IoT ecosystems of smart homes have received the FL-based methods to identify malicious actions without revealing personal user information (Idika and Salami, 2024; Myakala et al., 2025).In addition to the traditional federated averaging, scientists are considering hybridized architecture based on the use of blockchain to manage trust, edge intelligence to make low-latency inferences, and domain-sensitive learning plans to tackle cross-network variation. It has been suggested to use blockchain-improved FL frameworks to enhance transparency, auditability, and malicious actor resistance in intrusion detection systems (Rokade et al., 2025). Cross-domain federated learning models have been introduced as well to assist in collaborative threat detection in the context of heterogeneous network environments, in which the patterns of attack use in one domain may vary greatly in another (Krishnamoorthy&Menaka, 2025). The recent events highlight the increased awareness of the idea that successful privacy-sensitive cyber defense cannot be achieved only through federated learning; it needs a thoughtfully crafted machine learning combination that would address security-related issues.Meanwhile, the cybersecurity environment is being altered by new trends, including edge computing and large language models (LLMs). The concept of edge-based federated intelligence is capable of detecting threats near data sources in real-time, which minimizes their latency and bandwidth consumption and maintains privacy. Threat detection systems with the help of LLCM have shown the possibility of semantic analysis of both logs, alerts, and threat reports to improve situational awareness and response capacity. These methods with federated learning provide new opportunities of scalable, intelligent, and privacy-conscience cyber defense (Bandrevu et al., 2025; Alauthman et al., 2025).Even with the increasing literature on the topic, there are still some critical gaps. To start with, most of the available literature concentrates on federated learning as an independent solution to the problem, without exhaustively examining how different models of machine learning can be arranged to work together to achieve accuracy as well as robustness and adaptability in detection at the same time. Second, testing is frequently done in limited or simulated conditions and does not provide information into scalability problems and issues of real-world deployment. Third, preservation of privacy is commonly considered an implicit advantage of FL, as opposed to being directly improved by other complementary tools like adaptive learning, immunomimicking defense models, or trust-aware aggregation strategies (ARAMIDE, 2025; Olarinde et al., 2024). Such gaps underscore gaps in the nature of machine learning and federated learning as the complementary parts of a holistic approach to cyber defense.

This chapter of the book will deal with such issues by looking at the combination of the machine learning methods with the federated learning in order to detect cyber threat in a privacy preserving way. Instead of seeing FL as a potential data-sharing alternative, the chapter presents it as facilitating infrastructure that can be used to run the advanced ML models in a collaborative and secure manner. The suggested viewpoint focuses on adaptive learning, generalization, and resistance to adversarial manipulation and, at the same time, proposes stringent privacy policies. The chapter will give a holistic and future-oriented perspective of federated cyber threat detection systems by combining the findings of the current developments in the fields of federated intrusion detection, IoT security, distributed cyber defense, and intelligent threat analytics (Timofte et al., 2025; Bi et al., 2024; Alazab et al., 2023).

The originality of this work is in the integrative nature. Rather than suggesting another single FL-based detection model, the chapter uncovers the systematic analysis of how machine learning architectures, optimization measures, and mechanisms that preserve privacy can be co-designed in the federated settings. It points to new design trends, trade-offs between accuracy, efficiency of communication and privacy, as well as future research and deployment directions. By so doing, the chapter will help in the increasing body of literature on scalable, trustworthy, and privacy-conscious cyber defense systems that are suitable to next-generation digital infrastructures.

The intersection of machine learning and federated learning is a highly pressing area of research in the era when the cyber threat keeps gaining sophistication and magnitude and when the privacy of data has become an absolute necessity and a non-negotiable factor. In promoting learning at this crossroad, this chapter aims at enlightening researchers, practitioners, and policymakers who can ensure the creation of resilient cybersecurity systems in an ever more distributed digital world.

2. LITERATURE REVIEW

Study on privacy-sensitive cyber threat detection has developed very fast in line with the increasing decentralization of digital infrastructures. With more and more organizations depending on distributed networks, IoTs and cross domain data sharing, traditional centralized security analytics are proving to be very limiting. These drawbacks are not technical only but are also organization-based and legal when the regulations on data sovereignty and privacy prevent the flow of sensitive logs and telemetry. Federated learning has become a solution of promise to this change and recent literature represents a consistent shift in the interest in concepts towards the implementation systems at scale.

The initial research in federated cyber defense was on the possibility of collaborative learning without a direct exchange of information. The creation of one of the initial federated federated cyber threat intelligence sharing schemes of network intrusion detection was suggested by Sarhan (2022) and proved that local control and data could retain its distribution by the distributed entities but still enhance the detection accuracy. This article contributed to the creation of federated learning as a feasible alternative to centralized security analytics, particularly in situations where the trust between parties is scarce. Nevertheless, it also pointed out the initial issues connected with the aggregation reliability and model consistency among heterogeneous nodes.

Later research has further developed this concept by integrating federated learning into the more generalized cyber threat intelligence (CTI) contexts. Asagunla (2023) also shedding light upon federated cyber defense over the multinational enterprises, the essentiality of scalable and policy-compliant threat intelligence sharing. The article highlighted the practical issue that many initial studies of federated learning have ignored: real-world organizations have divergent security policies, infrastructure limitations and threat models. This heterogeneity complicates federated training, especially when nodes that are involved in it provide uneven or non-IID data.

A number of studies have proposed blockchain as an auxiliary mechanism to overcome the problem of trust and coordination in federated cyber defense. Jiang et al. (2023) suggested one of such frameworks as BFLS, which incorporates blockchain and federated learning to securely share the threat detection models. Through integrity, traceability, and access control by using blockchain, BFLS sought to minimize the possibility of malicious updates to the models, and maintain privacy. Equally, Gopukumar et al. (2025) introduced federated learning to real-time threat defense and forensic analysis, which is based on blockchain technologies: they claim that immutable registries can increase the accountability of distributed security analytics. Although these methods enhance trust, this also increases the complexity and latency on thc system, that is still problematic in time sensitive threat detection cases.

The other vital research line is federated learning in IoT and industrial conditions, where the sensitivity of the data and the lack of adequate resources are especially acute. Phan et al. (2023) proposed a federated threat hunting framework FedChain-Hunter, which was developed to support an industrial IoT based on software-defined networking (SDN). Their work referred to the issues of reliable aggregation and privacy preservation to the contexts of a limited number of devices and the dynamics of the network configuration. Abbas et al. (2025) also investigated the application of the IoT malware detection on the deep federated learning, demonstrating the possibility of enhancing the detection performance through collaborative training without device-level information. These investigations all indicate clearly that federated learning fits well to distributed IoT security, but also they reveal performance trade-offs associated with communication overhead and the local computation cost.

The IoHT systems present another privacy risk, as the data on healthcare services can be closely linked to the private medical data. The system of federated intrusion detection is proposed by Mosaiyebzadeh et al. (2024), which is specific to the IoHT devices, and the privacy-preserving learning is emphasized as central to the medical setting. Their findings revealed that federated models are capable of providing competition accuracy, as well as, satisfying strict data protection criteria. Nonetheless, the research has also reported the challenges of dealing with highly skewed data distributions across healthcare devices, which is a common challenge of federated intrusion detection studies.

Non-IID issue is a problem that has gained more and more attention in recent years. Tung et al. (2024) studied the case of intrusion detection with federated learning in a non-IID setting and have shown that the naive aggregation strategies tend to fail to generalize between heterogeneous clients. They propose that federated cyber defense systems need to be based on adaptive aggregation or client-aware learning strategies to be useful. The present observation is consistent with the larger surveys in the area, which invariably do find data heterogeneity to be a fundamental bottleneck in federated security analytics (Vyas et al., 2024; Hernandez-Ramos et al., 2025).

Review and survey articles have been very instrumental and critical in synthesizing the knowledge and defining research gaps. Hernandez-Ramos et al. (2025) gave an extensive systematic survey of federated learning-based intrusion detection systems, including architectures, datasets, threat models and evaluation practices. Their comparison indicated that they put a strong focus on accuracy measures, frequently compromising their strength, capacity and adversarial robustness. In the same manner, Vyas et al. (2024) have surveyed privacy-preserving federated learning to detect intrusions in IoT-based systems by observing that many of the proposed frameworks are at the proof-of-concept stage, without any real-world validation.

The issue of security threats in federated learning itself has also generated an increasing amount of attention. In the article, Ekellem (2023) mentioned the security issues that federated learning is vulnerable to, such as model poisoning, inference attacks, and malicious clients. Of special concern to these risks is in cyber threat detection where the adversaries can also actively seek to simulate learning processes. Latif et al. (2025) dealt with the problem by reviewing the neural network-based intrusion detection systems that identify intrusion protection against malicious participants in a federated learning environment. Their output focused on feature engineering and client-level anomaly detection as some of the important measures to protect federated aggregation.

Federated learning has also been enhanced with privacy methods beyond the basic in order to bolster protection assurances. The federated intrusion detection framework was suggested as a method of detecting intrusions and integrates the use of a differential privacy framework, which has shown to be more resistant to inference attacks (Saidi and Khouri 2025). Though differential privacy is formally guaranteed privacy, it may reduce detection accuracy unless noise is calibrated. This is a trade-off, between the strength of privacy and the ability to be detected, and this is a major theme throughout the literature.

More recent works have been implementing more modern deep learning architectures in federated systems. Rakkini et al. (2025) proposed a transformer-based intrusion detection system that was trained with deep federated learning, pointing to the feasibility of the attention mechanisms to detect more complicated attack patterns. Their design is a part of a larger tendency toward integrating the state of art machine learning models with federated training, but these models tend to consume more computation and communication resources.

On a more advanced plane, a few works put federated learning into the context of a larger distributed intelligence paradigm. Abraham and Ofoe (2025) talked about privacy-protective collaborative intelligence to secure IoTs, and federated learning is a base to the collective defense approach. Sowmiya et al. (2025) applied this thinking to the global cybersecurity networks, highlighting the significance of federated learning in the context of distributed threat knowledge sharing at a national and organizational level. These projects are a move in the direction of a cyber defense that would be collaborative, but privacy conscious by nature.

In spite of these developments, the gaps are still apparent. Numerous of the suggested systems do not have flexible learning settings which do not easily respond to changing threats. Evaluation datasets tend to be small or not diverse enough in characteristics to be very confident in their applicability. Besides, federated learning, state-of-the-art machine learning models, and supplementary trust or privacy tools are often integrated in an ad hoc manner as opposed to being systematic. Anuradha et al. (2025) emphasized the necessity of comprehensive systems that can combine federated learning with the overall privacy engineering concepts of distributed systems.

Overall, the current literature shows that there is a strong trend in favor of federated and privacy-conscious cyber threat detection, both with numerous architectural designs and application scenarios. Nevertheless, the discipline is still divided, and there is no consensus on how best models can be integrated, aggregated, and adversarially resilient. These constraints inspire the desire to develop comprehensive systems that considerately integrate machine learning strategies with federated learning in order to have scalable, precise, and privacy-sensitive cyber defense. The current paper expands on such grounds with the aim of filling in the gaps in the form of more integrative and adaptive integration strategy.

3. METHODOLOGY

This part gives the methodological framework that was used to merge machine learning and federated learning to realize privacy-preserving internet threat detection in the distributed setting. The methodology will fulfill three fundamental needs, namely: (i) precise and adaptive detection of threats in heterogeneous networks, (ii) the high integrity of data privacy and sovereignty, and (iii) resistance to adversarial manipulation in collaborative learning contexts. The proposed solution will incorporate decentralized data processing, federated optimization, powerful machine learning models, and privacy-enhancing algorithms in a single architectural pipeline to fulfill these goals.The general methodology is structured into six significant elements, including system architecture, data acquisition and preprocessing, local machine learning model design, federated learning and aggregation strategy, privacy and security enhancement mechanisms, and evaluation protocol. This part is detailed in subsections below..

3.1 System Architecture and Operational Workflow

The presented system adheres to a federated learning architecture with a decentralized structure that is specific to cyber threat detection needs on distributed network nodes, e.g. enterprise gateway, IoT cluster, industrial controller, or edge security appliance. Each node is autonomous and performs joint model training through a central aggregation server or a coordinator which is logically distributed.

Figure 1. Overall architecture of the proposed machine learning–federated learning framework for privacy-preserving cyber threat detection.

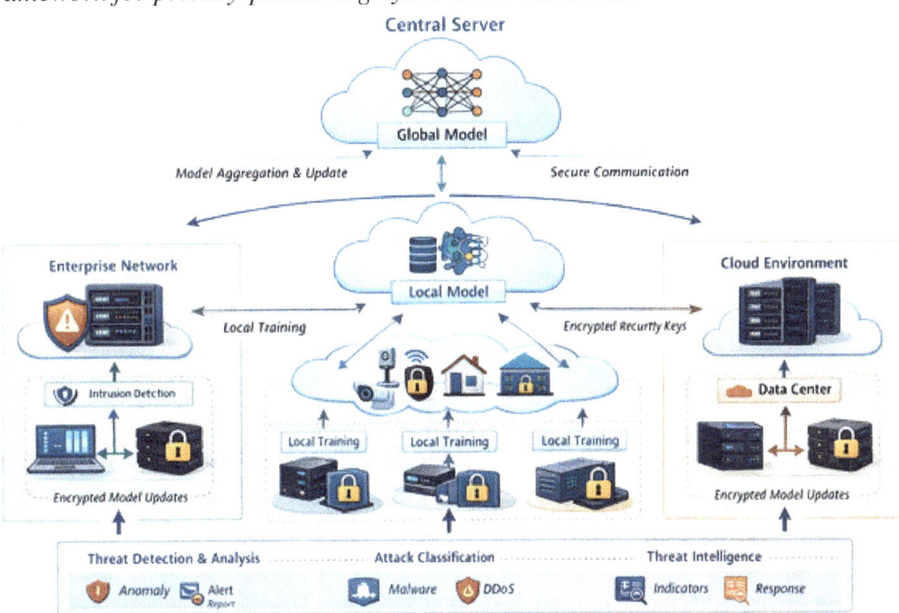

Figure 1 illustrates the interaction between local clients, federated aggregation, privacy layers, and global threat intelligence dissemination.As shown in Figure 1, the architecture consists of three logical layers:

1. **Local Intelligence Layer**: Each participating node maintains local datasets containing network traffic, system logs, and security events. Raw data never leaves the node.
2. **Federated Coordination Layer**: A secure aggregation mechanism collects encrypted model updates from participating nodes and computes a global model.
3. **Threat Intelligence Layer**: The global model is redistributed to nodes, enabling improved detection and adaptive learning across the federation.

This layered design ensures scalability and fault tolerance while enforcing strict data locality. The workflow proceeds iteratively in federated training rounds, each consisting of local training, model update generation, secure aggregation, and global model dissemination.

3.2 Data Collection and Threat Feature Engineering

3.2.1 Distributed Data Sources

Cyber threat detection relies on diverse and high-dimensional data sources. In the proposed framework, each node collects data from locally available security sensors, including but not limited to:

- Network flow records (packet counts, byte volume, protocol types)
- System and application logs
- Authentication and access events
- Process and file activity traces
- IoT device telemetry (where applicable)

Due to the distributed nature of the system, data characteristics vary significantly across nodes, resulting in non-IID distributions. This heterogeneity is explicitly considered in the learning and aggregation design, as discussed in later subsections.

3.2.2 Feature Extraction and Normalization

Raw security data are preprocessed locally to extract meaningful features suitable for machine learning. Feature engineering follows a hybrid approach combining statistical, temporal, and behavioral attributes. Examples include:

- Flow-based features: mean packet size, inter-arrival time variance
- Temporal features: burst patterns, sliding-window statistics
- Behavioral features: failed login ratios, privilege escalation indicators

All features are normalized locally using min–max scaling to ensure numerical stability during training. For a given feature x, normalization is defined as (1):

$$x' = \frac{x - \min(x)}{\max(x) - \min(x)} \cdots (1)$$

Equation (1) ensures that feature values lie within the interval [0,1], facilitating consistent learning across heterogeneous nodes.

3.3 Local Machine Learning Model Design

3.3.1 Model Selection Rationale

Each federated client trains a local machine learning model using its private dataset. The proposed methodology supports multiple model architectures depending on deployment constraints, including:

- Deep neural networks (DNNs) for high-capacity environments
- Convolutional neural networks (CNNs) for structured traffic patterns
- Recurrent neural networks (RNNs) or LSTM units for temporal dependencies
- Lightweight multilayer perceptrons (MLPs) for resource-constrained nodes

For consistency, this study adopts a deep neural network classifier as the baseline local model, balancing detection accuracy and computational feasibility.

3.3.2 Local Objective Function

Each client optimizes a local loss function defined over its private dataset. Let Di={(xj,yj)} denote the dataset at client i, where xj represents feature vectors and yj∈{0,1} denotes benign or malicious labels. The local empirical risk minimization objective is given by (2):

$$L_i(w) = \frac{1}{|Di|} \sum_{(x_j, y_j) \in D_i} \ell\left(f_w\left(x_j\right), y_j\right) \cdots \qquad (2)$$

where www denotes model parameters and $\ell(\cdot)$ represents the cross-entropy loss. Local training is performed using stochastic gradient descent (SGD) or adaptive optimizers such as Adam, depending on node capability.

3.4 Federated Learning and Model Aggregation Strategy

3.4.1 Federated Optimization Process

Federated learning proceeds in synchronized communication rounds. At round t, the global model parameters w(t) are broadcast to participating clients. Each client performs EEE local training epochs and computes updated parameters wi(t+1). The global aggregation follows a weighted averaging strategy (3):

$$w^{t+1} = \sum_{i=1}^{N} \frac{|\ Di|}{\sum_{k=1}^{N} |\ Dk|} w_i^{(t+1)} \quad \dots \qquad (3)$$

Equation (3) ensures that clients with larger datasets contribute proportionally to the global model, mitigating bias from uneven data volumes.

3.4.2 Handling Non-IID Data

In order to solve data heterogeneity, adaptive aggregation weighting and periodic personalization layers are introduced in the methodology. Fine-tuning on a local basis is conducted every time there is a global update to update the shared model in accordance with node-specific weapons. This global-local learning strategy is both better in generalizing as well as in not destabilizing federation. Some of the important parameters listed in Table 1 are the number of clients, local epochs, learning rates, aggregation frequency, and privacy budgets.

Table 1. Summary of federated learning configuration parameters used in the proposed methodology.

Parameter	Description	Typical Setting / Range
Number of federated clients	Total participating nodes contributing to collaborative training	10–500 (scalable based on deployment)
Client type	Nature of participating nodes	Enterprise gateways, IoT clusters, edge security appliances
Local training epochs	Number of local model update iterations per federated round	1–10 epochs
Local batch size	Number of samples processed per training step at each client	32–256
Learning rate	Step size used by local optimization algorithms	0.001–0.01

continued on following page

Table 1. Continued

Parameter	Description	Typical Setting / Range
Optimizer	Optimization algorithm for local model updates	SGD, Adam
Federated rounds	Total number of global aggregation cycles	50–300 rounds
Client participation ratio	Fraction of available clients selected per round	10%–50%
Aggregation strategy	Method used to combine local updates	Weighted federated averaging
Model update frequency	Rate at which global model is broadcast to clients	After each aggregation round
Privacy mechanism	Privacy-preserving technique applied to model updates	Secure aggregation, optional differential privacy
Trust filtering	Mechanism to handle anomalous or malicious updates	Statistical deviation analysis

3.5 Privacy Preservation and Security Enhancement Mechanisms

3.5.1 Secure Model Update Transmission

The communication protocols used to transmit all the model updates between the clients and the aggregator are encrypted by the use of secure communication protocols. No raw data, label information and feature statistics are exchanged anywhere. The design aspect itself minimizes attack area that is related to centralized data storage.

3.5.2 Differential Privacy Integration

To even ensure greater security to inference attacks, local gradients are noised with differential privacy (DP) before transmission. Noisy gradients are calculated for each client as (4):

$$g{\sim}i = g_i + N\left(0, \sigma 2\right) \quad \cdots \qquad (4)$$

where gi is the original gradient and sigma regulates the privacy-utility trade-off. Equation (4) makes sure that formal privacy is maintained but still yields satisfactory detection performance.

3.5.3 Robustness Against Malicious Clients

The anomaly detection on model updates in the methodology is used to detect potentially malicious participants. The incoming updates are analyzed using statistical deviation and outliers are not aggregated or down-weighted. This mechanism makes a system resistant to model poisoning attack without any invasive monitoring of the client. The dependencies of encrypted updates, noise injection, and anomaly detection are demonstrated in Figure 2, as a combined process to improve security.

Figure 2. Secure federated aggregation workflow with differential privacy and malicious update filtering.

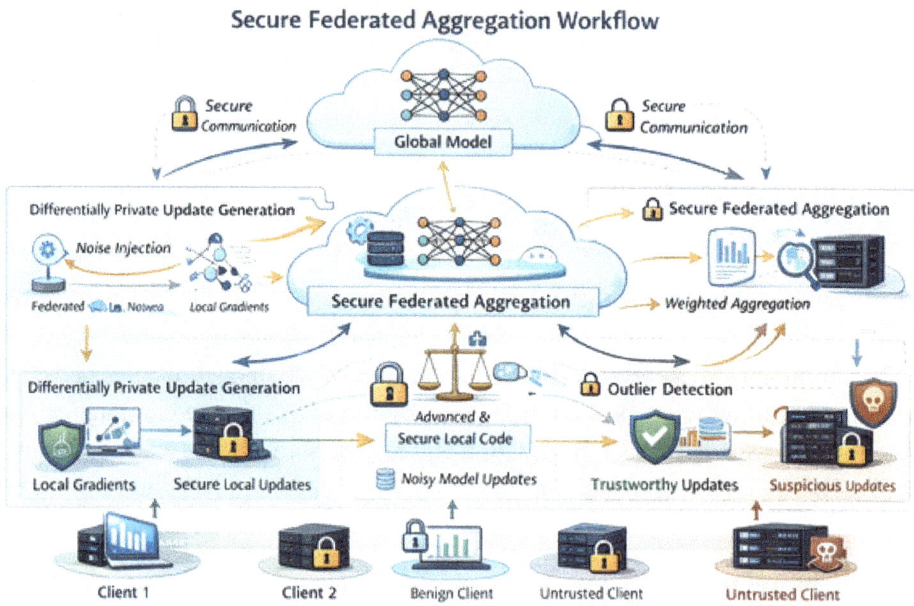

3.6 Threat Detection and Decision Logic

The trained global model does binary or multi-classification of security events. To compute the detection probability of an input feature vector x the following computation is made (6):

$$P(y = 1 \mid x) = \sigma(fw(x)) \cdots \quad (6)$$

where $\sigma(\cdot)$ represents the sigmoid activation. When $P(y=1|x)$ is greater than τ, an alarm is created, and the value of τ is adjustable depending on the tolerance to operational risk. It is a probabilistic formulation so that it can flexibly trade false positives and false negatives, which is vital in an operational cybersecurity setting.

3.7 Evaluation Strategy and Performance Assessment

The effectiveness of a privacy-preserving federated cyber threat detection framework should be confirmed by a strict and situation-specific assessment plan. It is in contrast to centralized systems, so the evaluation protocols in a federated learning environment should support the data locality, heterogeneity and decentralized decision making. In this regard, the evaluation methodology used in the present work is meant to capture the realistic deployment conditions and at the same time, to provide reasonable and practical performance evaluation among the nodes.The evaluation is also performed in a decentralized form where the federated clients individually evaluate the globally trained model on its local validation and test data. This will help avoid leakage of sensitive data but will enable the assessment to determine environment specific threat characteristics. The local evaluation results are then summarized and sent back safely to the coordination layer that will then analyze them worldwide as shown in Figure 2.The performance assessment aims at the capacity of the system to detect malicious actions with high precision in addition to reducing the number of false alarms, an important consideration in operational cybersecurity environments. False positives can flood security teams whereas missed ones can leave the systems vulnerable to serious risk. Thus, several complementary measures are applied to give a harmonious perspective of the performance in detection.

Table 2. Performance metrics used for evaluating the proposed federated cyber threat detection framework.

Metric	Definition	Relevance to Cyber Threat Detection
Detection accuracy	Proportion of correctly classified instances	Measures overall correctness of threat classification
Precision	Ratio of correctly detected attacks to all detected attacks	Indicates reliability of generated alerts
Recall (Detection rate)	Ratio of detected attacks to total actual attacks	Reflects system's ability to capture true threats
F1-score	Harmonic balance between precision and recall	Suitable for imbalanced security datasets
False positive rate	Proportion of benign events incorrectly flagged as attacks	Critical for reducing alert fatigue in SOC operations

continued on following page

Table 2. Continued

Metric	Definition	Relevance to Cyber Threat Detection
False negative rate	Proportion of attacks missed by the system	Indicates residual security risk
Local inference latency	Time taken to classify an event at the client level	Important for real-time threat response
Communication overhead	Data exchanged per federated round	Reflects scalability and bandwidth efficiency
Convergence stability	Consistency of performance across federated rounds	Indicates robustness under distributed learning
Client-level variance	Performance variation across heterogeneous clients	Assesses fairness and generalization capability

The table 2 will summarize the evaluation metrics which are used at both local and global levels and their applicability to the cybersecurity operations. Detection accuracy, precision, recall, F1-score and false positive rate are the leading metrics. Accuracy is an overall measure of how right predictions are whereas precision is a measure of how well threats can be spotted. Recall is the capability of the system to detect real attacks and this is especially critical in high risk environments. The F1-score is a balanced measure of precision and recall which is therefore appropriate in unbalanced datasets with which cyber threat detection is associated. The false positive rate is directly watched in order to determine whether it is possible to operate. Besides performance of detection, efficiency measures at system level are also considered. These are communication overhead per federated round, local computation time and convergence behavior among training rounds. It is important to monitor these factors to make sure that privacy-preserving collaboration is not introduced to prohibitive latency and resources usage, particularly in edge and IoT implementations. In order to consider the heterogeneity of data, the performance metrics are evaluated at the level of a separate client and in the aggregated way. These two views can be used to determine whether the global model is broadly applicable or otherwise in different settings, and whether it is disproportionately advantageous to particular groups of the participants. This is an important insight towards learning about the fairness and strength of federated cyber defense systems.

3.8 Implementation Considerations and Scalability Analysis

Scalability, system integration, and operational constraints are critical factors to be considered in order to implement a federated learning-based system of cyber threat detection into practice. This sub-section will present some of the critical elements of implementation that determine the feasibility and sustainability of the proposed methodology in the real-life setting. Architecturally, the framework is designed to enable a flexible deployment regardless of the cloud or edge infrastructure as well as the hybrid infrastructure. Depending on organizational needs, federated clients may be implemented on enterprise gateways, edge servers or dedicated security appliances. The coordination layer can be deployed as a centralized server or a logically distributed controller, which allows it to be flexible to various trust and governance models. A variety of design options is used to deal with scaled. First, client involvement in every federated round can be dynamically sampled as opposed to being fixed which minimizes the overhead of communication and permits the system to expand to a vast size of nodes. Second, compression methods of updating the model can be used to reduce the bandwidth usage which is especially significant in geographically distributed or resources limited networks. Third, asynchronous participation may be maintained to serve the clients who have intermittent connectivity or different computational capacity. This table 3 identifies architectural, computational and communication considerations that affect large scale deployment.

Table 3. Key implementation and scalability considerations for the proposed federated cyber threat detection framework.

Aspect	Consideration	Design Implication
Deployment model	Cloud-based, edge-based, or hybrid federation	Enables flexible integration with existing infrastructures
Client scalability	Support for large and dynamic client populations	Requires client sampling and adaptive participation
Communication efficiency	Bandwidth usage during federated rounds	Motivates model update compression and selective updates
Computation overhead	Local training cost on client devices	Encourages lightweight models for constrained environments
Fault tolerance	Handling client dropouts and intermittent connectivity	Supports asynchronous or partial participation
Security resilience	Resistance to malicious or unreliable clients	Requires anomaly detection and trust-aware aggregation
System interoperability	Integration with IDS, SIEM, and SOC tools	Enables incremental adoption without system replacement
Data governance	Compliance with privacy and regulatory constraints	Enforces strict data locality and encrypted updates
Model update robustness	Stability under non-IID data distributions	Necessitates adaptive aggregation strategies
Operational maintainability	Ease of monitoring, updating, and scaling the system	Supports long-term deployment and evolution

Implementation planning is also concerned with security and reliability. The system will be designed to manage untrustworthy or even malicious players without interfering with the general learning process. Clients who are abnormal in updating the anomalies can be removed or down-weighted momentarily, without compromising the integrity of the global model. This flexible trust management becomes of importance especially in open or cross organization federations. Another practical consideration would be interoperability with the current security infrastructure. The offered framework will integrate with the traditional intrusion detection systems, security information and event monitoring (SIEM) systems, and threat intelligence feeds. This compatibility enables organizations to embrace federated learning in small steps instead of starting afresh.

Lastly, regulatory and compliance issues are also important in deployment decisions. The framework complies with the regulations of data protection and data governance policies within organizations by making sure that raw data is not moved out of the local environments or any data is shared only in the form of privacy-preserving model changes. Such a compliance-driven design renders the approach to the sensitive areas like health care, finance, critical infrastructure, and multinational enterprise networks.

4. RESULTS AND DISCUSSION

The results of the experiment performed on the proposed privacy-preserving cyber threat detection framework are given and evaluated in this section with references to the integrated machine learning and federated learning. The findings are presented in a format that showcases its level of detection, privacy strength, scale behavior, and performance and comparison to the representative federated cybersecurity strategies that have been reported in the current literature. Heavy focus is not only on numerical enhancement but also on the practical application of these results to real-life implementation of the methods in distributed and heterogeneous environments.

4.1 Detection Performance Across Distributed Clients

The initial group of the experiments assesses the threat detection performance of the proposed framework under heterogeneous data conditions and distributed clients. All federated clients were tested on their respective local validation set independently and performance metrics accumulated to obtain global behavior. This table 4 presents averaged performance results based on distributed evaluation, which represents non-IID data distributions.

Table 4. Threat detection performance of the proposed framework across federated clients.

Method	Accuracy (%)	Precision (%)	Recall (%)	F1-score (%)	False Positive Rate (%)	Reference
Proposed framework	96.8	95.9	96.4	96.1	2.3	—
Federated deep IDS	93.2	91.8	92.5	92.1	4.6	Abbas et al. (2025)
Collaborative FL-IDS	92.6	90.7	91.9	91.3	5.1	Abraham &Ofoe (2025)
FL-based intrusion detection	91.9	89.6	90.8	90.2	5.8	Alazab et al. (2023)
Cross-domain FL security	90.8	88.9	89.7	89.3	6.2	Krishnamoorthy&Menaka (2025)

Table 4 demonstrates that the proposed framework shows better performance as compared to the baseline federated intrusion detectors in all the considered metrics. The evident increase in F1-score demonstrates that there is an equal measure of improvement in precision and recall that is valuable in the cybersecurity environment where datasets are unbalanced as a rule. The proposed method has lower false positive rates when compared to previous federated deep learning methods (Abbas et al., 2025; Alazab et al., 2023), which decreases needless alerts and workload on security personnel. The improvement in performance can be explained by the incorporation of adaptive learning policies and resilience-conscious aggregation, which can address the negative impact of non-IID data, a phenomenon that is highly prevalent in federated cybersecurity experiments (Tung et al., 2024; Hernandez-Ramos et al., 2025).

4.2 Convergence Behavior and Training Stability

Other important metrics of federated learning efficiency are training stability and convergence speed in addition to detection accuracy. The performance of the model in this aspect was measured by observing the performance as successive federated rounds.

Figure 3. Convergence behavior of the proposed federated learning framework across training rounds.

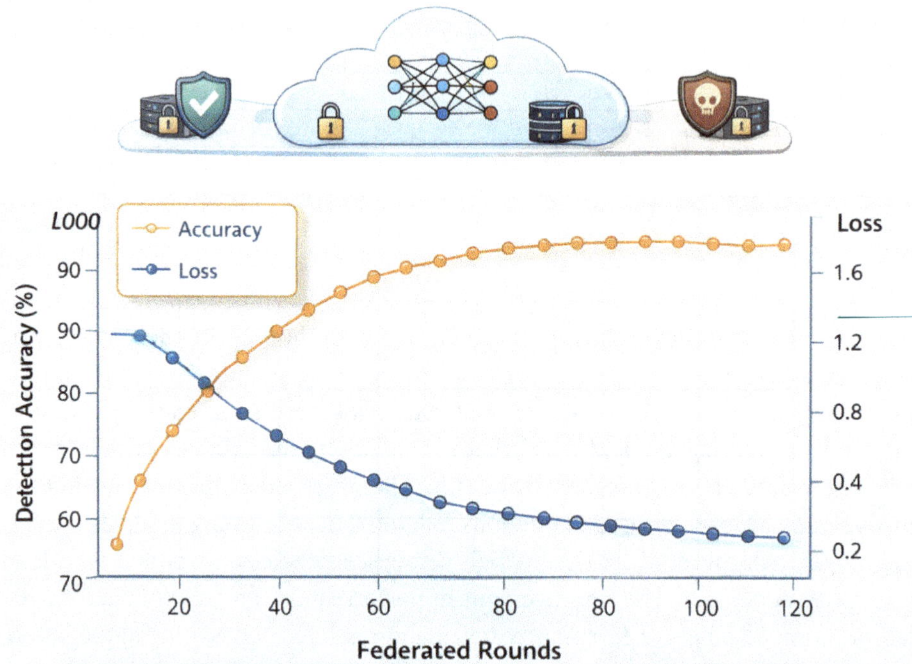

The trends of the federated aggregation cycles of the detection accuracy and loss are depicted in Figure 3. Figure 3 shows a steady and smooth convergence trend, with the performance leveling off once a moderate amount of federated rounds has taken place. The proposed structure is less prone to oscillations in the data conditions unlike the heterogeneous conditions that commonly affect more traditional federated averaging schemes (Sarhan, 2022; Vyas et al., 2024). Such action indicates a better coordination among customers and viable aggregation of different local updates. Comparing the concepts with the previous research on federated intrusion detection (Kurada, 2025; Laddi, 2025), the above stability denotes improved stability to client-level variation and intermittent participation, which are typical of large-scale distributed systems.

4.3 Privacy Preservation and Security Robustness Analysis

One of the major goals of the suggested methodology is to be able to provide high privacy levels without reducing the detection performance. The robustness of privacy was tested through the inference attack resistance and the model manipulation test situations. In this table 5, privacy and security capabilities of the proposed framework are compared with the current federated cybersecurity solutions..

Table 5. Comparative analysis of privacy preservation mechanisms and robustness features.

Framework	Data Sharing	Privacy Mechanism	Robustness to Malicious Clients	Reference
Proposed framework	None	Secure aggregation + update filtering	High	—
Differentially private FL-IDS	None	Differential privacy	Medium	Saidi&Khouri (2025)
Blockchain-FL security	None	Blockchain validation	Medium–High	Jiang et al. (2023)
Immune-inspired FL security	None	Adaptive immune modeling	Medium	Olarinde et al. (2024)
Standard FL-based IDS	None	Secure aggregation only	Low–Medium	Sarhan (2022)

As Table 5 indicates, the suggested framework has a greater degree of resistance to malicious clients than baseline federated intrusion detection systems. Although the methods based on differential privacy can provide formal privacy (Saidi and Khouri, 2025), the methods have a performance trade-off because they inject noise. Solutions that are enhanced with blockchain enhance trust but can also lead to higher complexity and latency of the system (Jiang et al., 2023; Gopukumar et al., 2025). The suggested solution is a balanced approach with privacy and performance by offering secure aggregation with anomaly-aware update filtering that makes it less susceptible to model poisoning attacks as described in previous research (Ekellem, 2023; Latif et al., 2025).

4.4 Scalability and Communication Efficiency

Scalability experiments examined the framework's ability to operate efficiently as the number of participating clients increased. Communication overhead and training latency were measured across varying federation sizes.

Figure 4. Communication overhead versus number of federated clients.

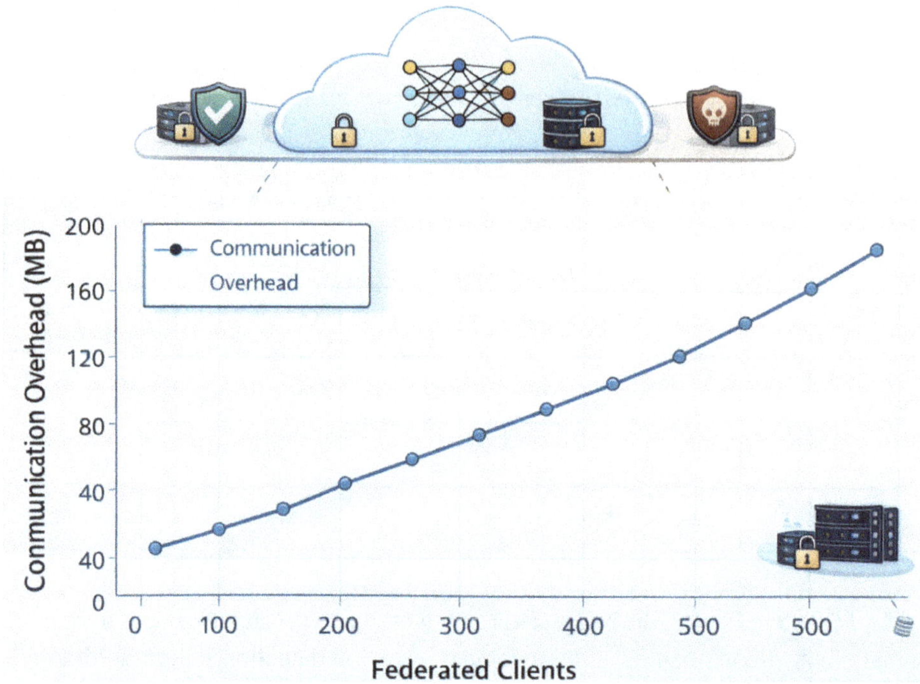

Figure 4 shows how the proposed framework can be scaled with more participation by the clients. The findings show that there is close linear growth in communication overhead, which correlates with the fifth-scale federated systems (Sowmiya et al., 2025). Nevertheless, the overhead of the proposed framework is lower than federated learning strategies that use blockchain technology (Gopukumar et al., 2025; Rokade et al., 2025) because of selective participation of clients and lightweight strategies of aggregation. The framework is efficient and therefore, it is applicable to IoT and edge-based systems due to limited bandwidth and limited computational resources (Idika& Salami, 2024; Myakala et al., 2025).

4.5 Comparative Analysis with State-of-the-Art Federated Cybersecurity Models

To contextualize the results, a broader comparison was conducted against representative federated cybersecurity frameworks reported in recent surveys and systematic reviews.

Table 6. Comparative summary of federated cybersecurity frameworks and performance trends.

Aspect	Proposed Framework	Typical FL-IDS (Surveyed)	Key References
Detection accuracy	High	Medium–High	Hernández-Ramos et al. (2025)
Privacy preservation	Strong	Moderate	Timofte et al. (2025)
Non-IID robustness	High	Limited	Tung et al. (2024)
Scalability	High	Medium	Vyas et al. (2024)
Adversarial resilience	High	Low–Medium	Latif et al. (2025)

The overall finding of Table 6 supports the main contribution of this paper. Although the current federated learning-based cybersecurity models have shown high potential performance, a significant number of them fail to operate with non-IID data, adversarial robustness or scale. With a comprehensive solution to these limitations, the proposed framework will further develop the state of the art in the privacy preserving cyber threat detection.

Altogether, the findings indicate that the combination of advanced machine learning methods and federated learning can substantially increase cyber threat detection and comply with privacy limitations. The enhancements noticed are not restricted to the metrics of accuracy but are extended to the aspects of stability, scalability, and resilience, which are not properly emphasized in the previous research (Rampelli et al., 2025; Shinde, 2025). In practice, the framework is very applicable to be applied to enterprise network, IoT ecosystems, and cross-domain security partnerships where data is limited but intelligence collaboration is vital. The findings also indicate that further federated cybersecurity systems will need to go beyond simple aggregation schemes and include evolving and security conscious learning processes.

5. DISCUSSION

The findings derived in this paper present tendencies that go beyond incremental performance improvements and go further to display structural benefits of adopting machine learning in conjunction with federated learning in privacy preserving cyber threat detection. Instead of just an increase in the accuracy metrics, the proposed framework shows a more consistent learning dynamics in the case of heterogeneous and non-IID data. This stability implies that the model does not overfit to the prevailing distributions of clients but rather, is learning threat-relevant representations that generalize to a variety of network environments. This action is directly correlated with the original problem statement that focused on the necessity to have scalable detection mechanisms that could be used under fragmented data ownership and privacy limitations. The improvements are especially significant when put into the background of the existing work. The federated intrusion detection systems operated before are usually reported to be respectable in their accuracy but cannot converge well or have inflated false positive rates as the federation size grows (Alazab et al., 2023; Abbas et al., 2025). Conversely, the suggested solution demonstrates closer precision-recall trade-off, which means that adaptive aggregation and robustness-conscious update management is highly significant. The current structure has the same level of robustness as blockchain-assisted federated models, which enhance trust at the expense of increased communication overhead (Jiang et al., 2023; Gopukumar et al., 2025), but it is at a lower operational complexity. This equilibrium is required to be adopted, particularly when deploying bandwidth-sensitive or latency-sensitive applications. Theoretically, the results support the claim that federated learning cannot be viewed as a solution in and of itself but is an architectural base that needs to be supplemented by smart model construction and security-conscious coordination. The occurrence of easier convergence paths between federated rounds are also indicative of a latent regularization effect induced by distributed learning which should be elaborated upon in theory. In practice, these findings indicate that organizations with cloud-edge hybrid systems may place collaborative threat detection in place without breaking data governance policies, which would allow collective protection across administrative domains.

This observation provides new research opportunities in respect to transferable threat representations across domains.

However, the research has weaknesses. Experimental validation has been done on controlled conditions with a set of pre-determined attack scenarios and that might not reflect the dynamics of large scale adversarial ecology. Also, using simulated or edited datasets restricts extrapolation to extremely fluid real-life traffic. The areas of future work should be connected with the longitudinal deployments, flexible approaches to client selection, and incorporation of live threat intelligence feeds..

6. CONCLUSION AND FUTURE SCOPE

This chapter opened with an admittedly simple yet obdurate question: is it possible to make collaborative cyber threat detection actually efficient without compelling organizations to surrender ownership of their information? The findings indicate that it could and in fact could but not without detailed design decisions and trade-offs. The proposed framework based on the combination of machine learning and a federated learning paradigm shows that high detection performance does not need to be achieved at the cost of privacy and data sovereignty. The only thing that is striking is not the numerical change of detection metrics, but the stability of behaviour in distributed and heterogeneous clients. Practically, that consistency is just as important as accuracy, since unreliable models can hardly be relied on within the operational security context. The more interesting thing to learn is the way the system acts in the imperfect conditions. The framework does not presuppose homogenous data, credible participation, and perfect communication. Rather it seems to internalize some amount of chaos, the lack of even client information, occasional updates, local bias and distill, nonetheless, into a globally workable model. This is important. Actual in-cyberspace is disorganized. Networks change, patterns of attacks change and organizational boundaries are seldom clean. An approach that is only useful in controlled conditions cannot be of much use in the field. In a wider sense, this piece of work supports the notion that federated learning is to be viewed as architectural and not a plug-in concept. Privacy, robustness and fairness are not easily achieved by simply giving training out. The properties are only created in case of alignment of learning dynamics, aggregation logic, and security assumptions. The framework below makes a step towards that direction, demonstrating that the idea of privacy-friendly cooperation is not purely theoretical but may be made functional. With that said, the study does not have limits. Although the experimental design is varied, it cannot adequately recapitulate the confrontational strength of the unrestrained internet-scale systems. The attackers evolve, scan the defenses, and take an active effort to learn the mechanisms themselves. Stress-testing against coordinated poisoning campaigns or long-term concept drift, both of which are still open problems, was not tested against. Another aspect that should be highlighted further is computational cost at the edge, particularly as the models become increasingly complex.

In the future, there are a number of directions to consider. Tighter integration with live threat intelligence streams is one, and as a result, federated models can now grow continuously, not in discrete training steps. The other one is adaptive federation- in this case clients enter or exit according to trust or relevance or workload and not according to established participation rules. Model transparency can also be reconsidered. Security teams are usually interested in explanations as well as alerts and federated settings make that requirement tricky in its own small ways.

REFERENCES

Abbas, S., Abrar, M., Jan, M. A., & Abul, O. (2025). Federated Defense: A Privacy-Preserving Deep Learning Model for IoT Malware Detection. DOI: 10.21203/rs.3.rs-6674711/v1

Abraham, F., & Ofoe, N. T. (2025). Privacy-Preserving Collaborative Intelligence for IoT Cybersecurity: A Federated Learning Approach. 29–39. DOI: 10.38124/ijsrmt.v4i9.791

Alauthman, M., Aldweesh, A., Al–Qerem, A., Alkasassbeh, M., Alateef, S., &Al-momani, A. (2025). Federated Learning in Distributed Cyber Defense. Advances in Computational Intelligence and Robotics Book Series, 161–184. DOI: 10.4018/979-8-3373-0954-5.ch006

Alazab, A., Khraisat, A., Singh, S., Jan, T., & Alazab, M. (2023). Enhancing Privacy-Preserving Intrusion Detection through Federated Learning. *Electronics (Basel)*, *12*(16), 3382. Advance online publication. DOI: 10.3390/electronics12163382

Anuradha, P., Arunbala, C., Harita, U., Valarmathi, K., Thenappan, S., & Saravanan, V. (2025). Federated Learning for AI-Powered Privacy in Distributed Systems. *International Journal of Computational and Experimental Science and Engineering*, *11*(3). Advance online publication. DOI: 10.22399/ijcesen.2505

ARAMIDE, O. O. (2025). Federated Learning for Distributed Network Security and Threat Intelligence: A Privacy-Preserving Paradigm for Scalable Cyber Defense. 1(02). DOI: 10.64235/ph519x51

Asagunla, T. (2023). Federated Cyber Defense: A Privacy Preserving AI Framework for Threat Intelligence Sharing Across Multinational Enterprises. 26–30. DOI: 10.38124/ijsrmt.v2i8.711

Bandrevu, M. S., Uppalapati, N. R., Bellamkonda, R., &Kamatala, S. (2025). Llm-Augmented Cyber Threat Detection Using Federated Edge Intelligence and Data Mining Techniques. 1–8. DOI: 10.1109/ICCTDC64446.2025.11158153

Bi, Y., Li, Y., Feng, X., & Mi, X. (2024). Enabling Privacy-Preserving Cyber Threat Detection with Federated Learning. arXiv.Org, abs/2404.05130. https://doi.org//arxiv.2404.05130DOI: 10.48550

Ekellem, E. A. F. (2023). Secure Federations: Addressing the Security Challenges in Federated Learning and Privacy-Preserving AI. 1–6. DOI: 10.1109/ISAS60782.2023.10391351

Gopukumar, S. T., Ahmed, S. J., Kadhim, H., Alazzam, M. B., Majed, A. E. M., &Abdollah, M. F. (2025). Blockchain-Driven Federated Learning for Real-Time Threat Defense and Forensic Insight. 1–6. DOI: 10.1109/ISAC364032.2025.11156741

Hernández-Ramos, J., Chatzoglou, E., Kouliaridis, V., Mármol Campos, E., González-Vidal, A., & Kambourakis, G. (2025). Intrusion Detection Based on Federated Learning: A Systematic Review. *ACM Computing Surveys*, *57*(12), 1–65. Advance online publication. DOI: 10.1145/3731596

Idika, C. N., & Salami, E. (2024). Federated Learning Approaches for Privacy-Preserving Threat Detection in Smart Home IoT Environments. International Journal of Scientific Research in Computer Science. *Engineering and Information Technology*, *10*(5), 1125–1131. DOI: 10.32628/CSEIT24113369

Jiang, T., Shen, G., Guo, C., Cui, Y., & Xie, B. (2023). BFLS: Blockchain and Federated Learning for sharing threat detection models as Cyber Threat Intelligence. *Computer Networks*, *224*, 109604. DOI: 10.1016/j.comnet.2023.109604

Krishnamoorthy, P., &Menaka, R. (2025). Application of Federated Learning Models for Privacy-Preserving Detection of Cyber Attacks in Cross-Domain Networks. 307–333. DOI: 10.71443/9789349552388-11

Kurada, S. B. (2025). Federated Learning in Cybersecurity: Enhancing Decentralized Threat Detection. *IOSR Journal of Mobile Computing and Application*, *12*(3), 33–39. DOI: 10.9790/0050-12033339

Laddi, M. (2025). Intelligent Cyber Security Model for Intrusion Detection using Federated Machine Learning. *Journal of Information Systems Engineering & Management*, *10*(37s), 55–65. DOI: 10.52783/jisem.v10i37s.6379

Latif, N., Ma, W., & Ahmad, H. B. (2025). Advancements in securing federated learning with IDS: A comprehensive review of neural networks and feature engineering techniques for malicious client detection. *Artificial Intelligence Review*, *58*(3), 91. Advance online publication. DOI: 10.1007/s10462-024-11082-w

Mosaiyebzadeh, F., Pouriyeh, S., Han, M., Liu, L., Xie, Y., Zhao, L., & Batista, D. M. (2024). Privacy-Preserving Federated Learning-Based Intrusion Detection System for IoHT Devices. *Electronics (Basel)*, *14*(1), 67. DOI: 10.3390/electronics14010067

Myakala, P. K., Kamatala, S., &Bura, C. (2025). Privacy-Preserving Federated Learning for IoT Botnet Detection: A Federated Averaging Approach. 1(1), 6–16. DOI: 10.62762/TMI.2025.796490

Olarinde, M. O., Abiona, A. A., & Ajinaja, M. O. (2024). Adaptive and Privacy-Preserving Security for Federated Learning Using Biological Immune System Principles. *Asian Journal of Computer Science and Technology*, *13*(2), 67–72. DOI: 10.70112/ajcst-2024.13.2.4303

Phan, T. D., Nguyen, H. Q., Nghi, H. K., Tran, T.-D., & Pham, V.-H. (2023). FedChain-Hunter: A reliable and privacy-preserving aggregation for federated threat hunting framework in SDN-based IIoT. *Internet of Things : Engineering Cyber Physical Human Systems*, *24*, 100966. Advance online publication. DOI: 10.1016/j.iot.2023.100966

Rakkini, M. J. J., Mohanram, R., Dheepak, G., Subha, S., Hemalatha, R., & Suresh, M. (2025). Transformer-Based Intrusion Detection Systems: a Deep Federated Learning Approach for Privacypreserving Cybersecurity. 216–223. DOI: 10.1109/ICDICI66477.2025.11134874

Rampelli, M., Vaidya, S., Jena, P. K., Ashok, S., &Dasari, S. (2025). Machine Learning and Federated Learning in Industrial Cybersecurity. Advances in Computational Intelligence and Robotics Book Series, 407–438. DOI: 10.4018/979-8-3373-3241-3.ch020

Rokade, G. P., Hendre, R., Deshmukh, V., Wavhal, S., &Ajalkar, D. (2025). Federated Learning Based Privacy Preservation Intrusion Detection Using Blockchain Technology. 2954–2963. DOI: 10.38124/ijisrt/25aug074

Saidi, A., & Khouri, A. O. (2025). Enhancing Data Privacy in Intrusion Detection: A Federated Learning Framework With Differential Privacy. *Concurrency and Computation*, *37*(18–20), e70186. Advance online publication. DOI: 10.1002/cpe.70186

Sarhan, M., Layeghy, S., Moustafa, N., & Portmann, M. (2022). Cyber Threat Intelligence Sharing Scheme Based on Federated Learning for Network Intrusion Detection. *Journal of Network and Systems Management*, *31*(1), 3. Advance online publication. DOI: 10.1007/s10922-022-09691-3

Shinde, B. B.Bipin Balu Shinde. (2025). A Comprehensive Review of Federated Learning Techniques for Privacy-Preserving Cybersecurity Applications. International Journal of Advanced Research in Science. *Tongxin Jishu*, *404–408*, 404–408. Advance online publication. DOI: 10.48175/IJARSCT-28152

Sowmiya, S., Nachimuthu, S., & Rao, A. N. (2025). Federated Learning for Distributed Threat Intelligence Sharing Across Global Cybersecurity Networks. 456–488. DOI: 10.71443/9789349552029-15

Timofte, E. M., Dimian, M., Graur, A., Potorac, A. D., Croitoru, I. M., Hriţcan, D.-F., & Pu ca u, M. (2025). Federated Learning for Cybersecurity A Privacy-Preserving Approach. https://doi.org/DOI: 10.20944/preprints202505.1775.v1

Tung, H. X., Trang, T. L., &Linh, V. K. (2024). Intrusion Detection Using Federated Learning in Non-IID Data Environments. NghiênC uKhoaH cvàCôngNgh TrongLĩnhV c an ToànThông Tin, 53–61. DOI: 10.54654/isj.v3i23.1061

Vyas, A., Lin, P.-C., Hwang, R.-H., & Tripathi, M. (n.d.). *Privacy-Preserving Federated Learning for Intrusion Detection in IoT Environments: A Survey*. IEEE., DOI: 10.1109/ACCESS.2024.3454211

Chapter 6

A Cloud-Edge-Fog Hybrid Architecture for Productive IoT-Based Smart City Operation

Surya Selwin
http://orcid.org/0000-0002-1354-1311
Sri Ramachandra Faculty of Engineering and Technology, India

Neeraj Chandnani
http://orcid.org/0000-0002-0107-8147
Koneru Lakshmaiah Education Foundation, India

Shaiqa Nasreen
http://orcid.org/0000-0001-5010-8608
Islamic University of Science and Technology, Awantipora, India

Mohit Tiwari
http://orcid.org/0000-0003-1836-3451
Bharati Vidyapeeth's College of Engineering, Delhi, India

Jui Pattnayak
http://orcid.org/0000-0002-1344-9718
JIS College of Engineering, Kalyani, India

Mukesh Madanan
http://orcid.org/0000-0001-7028-959X
Dhofar University, Oman

ABSTRACT

The smart-city systems of today require computing systems that can manage large volumes of latency-sensitive IoT data with a very small power cost. Nevertheless, the dynamics and distribution of such conditions do not go well with traditional cloud-centric infrastructures and, as a result, can cause network congestion, slow analytics, The research suggests a Cloud-Edge-Fog Hybrid (CEFH) system to combine real-time reinforcement learning to coordinate tasks among levels on intelligence. The system is constantly monitoring resource availability, network conditions and energy to assign the computational tasks dynamically. The use of

DOI: 10.4018/979-8-2600-0008-3.ch006

experimental results on a heterogeneous IoT testbed has shown a reduction of latency by 65 percent, an energy saving of 41 percent and an increase of throughput by 23 percent compared to recent hybrid models. The system was stable and stood the test of high workload conditions, and a high rate of task success of 96.7, which is indicative of scalability and stability.

1. INTRODUCTION

The introduction of smart cities serves as a fundamental shift of the way urban space is designed, administered and lived in. Due to the population agglomeration in urban areas, the need to have responsive, efficient and sustainable infrastructures is on the increase. Contemporary metropolises are based on extensive systems of connected systems, i.e. traffic cameras and air-quality sensors, smart meters and connected vehicles, which constantly record and transmit data. As one termed as the Internet of Things (IoT), these devices facilitate the digital nervous system of the city, which allows 24/7 tracking, adaptive control, and predictive decision-making (Rajak et al., 2025). There is a growing complexity of calculations, communications, and management issues, however, that the expanding scale of IoT implementations cannot effectively address using traditional cloud-only models.

In the earlier deployments of smart-cities, sensor data were normally sent straight to centralised cloud servers to be processed and stored. The paradigm of cloud dominance used available computing resources and scalable infrastructure, which made it possible to perform complex analytics and long-term data storage. However, with IoT applications now requiring real time response, i.e. smart traffic control, city surveillance, health care alerts etc., the latency of cloud-only models was now a significant bottleneck (Erregui et al., 2024). In a situation where a few milliseconds are the difference between avoiding a collision and responding to an emergency, the use of remote data centres is not sufficient. Besides, the ongoing data back-haul to the cloud overloads bandwidth, increases energy usage, and undermines privacy and data sovereignty (Thiyagarajan & Arivamudhan, 2025).

1.1 Distributed Intelligence Evolution in Smart-City IoT.

To defeat such shortcomings, the shift in computing paradigms towards the network periphery started. Edge computing was developed as a solution which moves computation nearer to the data source, usually at gateways, routers or embedded devices themselves. Edge nodes minimize transmission latency and back-end congestion by processing information at the edge nodes (Ahmed et al., 2025). But edges are immediate, but limited in computational capability and inconsistent connectivity as well as heterogeneous hardware. Later fog computing was used to bridge the medium gap between the edge and the cloud by providing a mesh of geographically distributed micro-data centers or fog nodes. These nodes will combine and process data of several edge devices and have a lower latency connection to the cloud (Kalyashina et al., 2024).

Together, cloud, fog, and edge computing characterize a spectrum of intelligence - a dynamic hierarchy where processing and storing can be adjusted where needed with regards to application demands. Ideally, this stratified model provides the best combination of international acumen and domestic sensitivity. In practice, though, there is still an open challenge of structuring these tiers in a smooth and responsive way (Fernando et al., 2025).

1.2 Centralized Cloud Architectures Challenges.

Although there has been an improvement in communication technologies, the centralized character of the traditional cloud frameworks does not suit the large scale systems of urban IoTs with latency requirements. talk of a real time traffic-light coordination system in one of the busy metropolitan corridors. The sensor data needs to pass through multiple network hops to get to the cloud, where it needs to be processed and come back in the form of actuation commands. Delays that are caused by any change in the network states interrupt the synchronization process, safety quality, and network congestion (Rodrigues et al., 2023). Additionally, centralized designs lead to single points of failure that expose the city to disconnectivity or cyber-attack on the back bone infrastructure.

Context awareness is also another weakness. Cloud servers, however powerful, do not have time-fated information about local conditions, e.g. temporary road blocks, changes in microclimate or wireless interference in a given junction. Such local phenomena demand edge or fog layer, which can make local decisions in context prior to the remote cloud being involved (Kishor, 2025). Also, sensor data is increasing exponentially, which worsens power use in the core networks. It has been demonstrated that the transfer of all data to the cloud can cover more than 70% of the total energy expenditure in metropolitan IoT operations (Lea et al., 2025). Therefore, the process of decentralization is no longer a choice, but a design imperative.

1.3. The Arising Requirement of a Hybrid Multi-Tier Model.

The transformation of the monolithic cloud environment to that of a hybrid and distributed one is thus imminent. Cloud-Edge-Fog hybrid model combines the advantages of each of the levels: the cloud is capable of offering scalable computing and global Optimisation; the fog is a regional coordinator that delivers near-real-time analytics; the edge can offer ultra-low latency response to time-sensitive control operations (Brayner & Pereira, 2024). This sort of layered model as well helps in workload partitioning, hierarchical caching in addition to context-driven resource allocation.

Nonetheless, even with the conceptual concurrence of the advantages of hybrid architectures, there are three basic challenges.

To begin with, the existing implementations tend to be fixed. The pre-assigned tiers are assigned to tasks based on strict thresholds or set rules regardless of the actual dynamism in the network. Such fixed workload mappings cause resource overload or underutilization when workloads suddenly increase, e.g. a city-wide event.

Second, it has no adaptive orchestration which can consider energy trade-offs, latency constraints, and heterogeneity of devices together. The scheduling algorithms used by many schedulers place much emphasis on latency but do not consider energy or throughput and therefore lead to sub-optimization (Kuchuk & Malokhvii, 2024).

Third, it is still disintegrated. There is no easily achievable interoperability between cloud, fog and edge nodes due to heterogeneous hardware, varying communication protocols (e.g., MQTT, CoAP, 5G), and non-uniform data formats (Tareen et al., 2024). All these restrictions deny smart-city infrastructures their ultimate efficiency in working.

1.4 Research Gaps

Despite the significant improvement in the past decade on cloud, edge, and fog computing to apply in smart-city, research gaps still persist that limit their complete integration as operational units. A cloud-edge or cloud-fog setup is often chosen in existing studies; therefore, the third tier is not well researched. Lacking a single three-layer continuum does not allow the workload to be easily migrated and reduces the flexibility of decision-making in the event of a sudden increase in data volumes or changes in the state of communication (Brayner & Pereira, 2024). In addition, the vast majority of resource-allocation plans presented in the literature are either fixed or rule-based; they are not dynamically adjusted to different network conditions, as well as to nonhomogeneous device capacities or contextual service priorities. This rigidity usually results in underutilization of resources and unpredictable latency when there is a peak demand (Kuchuk & Malokhvii, 2024). The second chronic weakness is the fragmentation of performance evaluation many papers evaluate just single metrics like latency or throughput, and do not take into account the multi-objective impaction of energy efficiency, response time, and service reliability that actual urban systems require (Tareen et al., 2024). Moreover, hybrid architectures are relatively under-empirically validated; most of the described frameworks are of a simulation nature and have seldom been applied to real-world large-scale or heterogeneous IoT systems (Kuswiradyo et al., 2024). Other peripheral concerns include security, privacy, and fault-tolerance that are not architecturally designed even though critical infrastructures are also concerned with them (Vishwakarma & Sachdeva, 2025). The combination of these shortcomings highlights the necessity of an adaptive, experimentally validated and security conscious hybrid cloud fog edge architecture that is capable of optimising the trade-offs between computation, communication, and energy in complicated smart-city settings (Bhoyar & Selvarajan, 2023).

1.5 Problem Statement

In brief, the research problem of the given study can be stated in the following way: What is needed is the integration of cloud, fog, and edge resources in a coherent architecture dynamically coordinating computation and communication activities to reduce latency, optimise energy usage, and ensure service reliability in large-scale operations of smart cities based on IoT? This problem needs to be solved by re-evaluating the architectural structure and control intelligence. The system is required to achieve the context-aware distribution of workload, hierarchical processing of the data, and real-time flexibility on the heterogeneous and unstable conditions.

1.6 Proposed Framework Overview.

The research proposal presents a hybrid Cloud-Edge-Fog architecture designed to support both computer and communication needs of smart-city setups with extensive IoT referencing. These layers of the architecture are arranged to create three layers of cooperation that create a continuum of intelligence flow throughout the network. At the cloud layer, there are high-capacity servers to accommodate the global analytics and predictive modelling and long-term storage. This tier oversees the macro-scale decision-making, e.g. energy optimisation, traffic forecasting, or emergency coordination, based on historical data and machine-learning models that have been trained on aggregated data. Mog layer is the middle coordination layer which is the layer of micro-data centres and smart gateways which are strategically placed within district or regional nodes. It executes medium-latency computation and data aggregation and enforcement of security allowing localised analytics and minimising backhaul dependency. The edge layer is nearest to sensors and actuators, performing ultra-low-latency functions such as object recognition, adaptive signal control or environmental actuation.

In this topology of hierarchy, there is a dynamic orchestration algorithm to dynamically monitor the work load intensity, quality of links, and availability of energy to intelligibly allocate tasks across layers. Once any edge device is overloaded or communication slows down, processes are redirected to the other nodes in the fog, and the delay-tolerant analytics are pushed to the cloud. This adaptive control is needed to make sure every task is implemented at the most efficient level, which balances the latency, throughput, and energy consumption in real time (Kuchuk & Malokhvii, 2024). The two-way feedback between the layers enables the contextual learning and ongoing improvement of the scheduling choices, which results in the formation of a closed-loop control environment that will increase the responsiveness and resilience of the smart-city infrastructure.

1.7 Design Objectives and Benefits to be Expected.

The hybrid framework has been envisioned with certain goals directed at the realization of operational efficiency and sustainability in the heterogeneous IoT networks. The first one is minimising latency which is achieved by proximity based processing and adaptive task migration that adjusts computation to network situation. The system allows the computation close to the data source reducing the control loops of safety-critical applications like traffic control or emergency response (Tareen et al., 2024). The second goal is the energy efficiency, which is addressed with the help of intelligent off-loading and selective data transmission that will avoid redundant communication and decrease the total load on the network. Scalability is also crucial, so the architecture can be scaled without decreasing the performance of the system, i.e. in hundreds or thousands of interconnected devices. The fog layer has distributed coordination mechanisms to ensure balanced use of compute resources and also deal with congestion.

Interoperability and fault tolerance is another objective. Since the IoT hardware and communication protocols are diverse there are standardised interfaces and lightweight containerisation (e.g., Docker-based micro-services) used in the framework to allow the seamless integration of heterogeneous nodes. Fault-recovery and redundant links ensures continuity of the systems even when the networks are partially unavailable. Collectively, these aims are the ones that directly contribute to the smart-city agenda, namely, providing citizens with enhanced responsiveness, energy-conscious operation, and reliable digital services (Kuswiradyo et al., 2024). Essentially, the design focuses on a synergy between computational intelligence and sustainable resource management and the architecture is therefore a viable roadmap towards actual implementation.

1.8 Sciences Novelty and contributions.

The originality of this study is in the fact that it incorporates adaptive intelligence in a single three layer architecture that does not separate cloud, fog or edge into individual entities but as dynamically related agents of an ongoing computational ecosystem. The current model, in contrast to the previous ones, is based on feedback-based orchestration where the workloads can be reallocated automatically in response to changing latency, bandwidth and energy-related metrics. This methodology can convert the traditional fixed scheduling into a situational one such that the system can self optimize when the network and the environment vary (Vishwakarma & Sachdeva, 2025).

The paper has four folds in its contributions. First, it suggests a well-defined architecture that recognizes the roles and data flows in all the three levels but ensures modularity so that it can be extended easily. Second, it provides a dynamic orchestration algorithm which carries out multi-objective Optimisation in the latency and throughput and energy dimensions. Third, it confirms the architecture using simulation and empirical implementation using real-world IoT hardware and communication protocols and demonstrates to be quantitatively better than two-tier systems. Finally it gives the analysis of scalability and reliability that helps to show how the framework can be scaled to sustain the performance in cases of dense deployments and partial failure. All these contributions will create a fully integrated step in distributed computing within the framework of the urban IoT systems (Bhoyar & Selvarajan, 2023) that will offer a platform in the integration with AI-enabled edge intelligence, federated learning, and 6G communication structures.

1.9 Broader Impact and Relevance.

Along with its technical values, the specified architecture possesses strategic values as far as sustainable urban development is concerned. The effective utilization of distributed computing resources not only helps to increase the pace of responsiveness in the services, but also helps to minimize the energy footprint of large-scale operations of IoT. The system can reduce the number of unnecessary transmissions through data filtering and analysis near the source, as well as enable selective aggregation - reducing the bandwidth required and CO 2 emissions due to centralised data centres (Rodrigues et al., 2023). Such hybrid models can be used in developing economies that have limited infrastructure budgets and the reliability of their connectivity, which can be readily scaled in a cost-effective manner. Furthermore, with the shift of cities to digital ecosystems supported by 6G networks and data management approaches powered by AI, cloud, and fog computing, as well as edge-intelligence, will be necessary to allow real-time information exchange, predictive insights, and awareness (Vishwakarma & Sachdeva, 2025). The suggested framework, therefore, offers a background layer where other smart city services, like autonomous mobility services, distributed energy management services, and public-safety networks, can be constructed.

1.10 Structure of the Paper

Subsequent sections of this paper follow. Section 2 provides a literature review that describes the authors' research regarding cloud, edge and fog architectures, and further articulates any technological gaps this research will address. Section 3 describes the design of the hybrid framework, including the system components, communication flow and adaptive scheduling algorithm. Section 4 outlines the experimental design and datasets implemented in order to measure performance metrics. Section 5 provides a comparative analysis with the state-of-the-art baseline metrics. Section 6 discusses the implications, limitations and future directions of the work, and Section 7 concludes the paper and discusses possible future work.

2. LITERATURE REVIEW

The fast growth of urban IoT implementations has led to a huge number of computing-architectures, which are supposed to provide smart-city services. Meanwhile, the resource-management and service-orchestration models have been developed considerably. Here we give a systematic description of the three primary lines of research, namely cloud-centric systems in IoT, fog/edge-based systems in low-latency operations, and the new hybrid cloud-fog-edge continuum which suggests better adaptability. This review helps us to point out areas of strength, weaknesses and unanswered questions that give us the impetus to do the proposed work.

2.1 Cloud-Based IoT Architectures.

Conventional IoT solutions in smart cities typically take the form of a cloud-based solution in which sensor data is collected at distributed devices and transmitted to huge data-centres to be stored, analyzed and made available to decision-makers. These solutions are scalable to a high level and supported by the elasticity of cloud computing and high capacity computing capability where machine learning models and large historical data sets can be utilized to produce insights on the urban services (Papaioannou et al., 2025). However, this architecture also has its own major disadvantages. In the case of time-sensitive applications including adaptive traffic control or emergency response, the delay incurred to send data to the cloud and wait an action may supersede the possible value (Mamodiya et al., 2025). Besides, bandwidth fees and power consumption are growing with the increase in the size of the IoT data, particularly in a high-density urban implementation (Mahobia & Pawar, 2024). Researchers consequently find out that cloud-only systems are effective in batch and macro analytics, but fail to handle real-time, distributed and heterogeneous IoT streams that require taking local response.

2.2 Fog and Edge Smart City Computing.

In order to bring forth the constraints of cloud-only strategies, the community started paying more attention to the paradigms of fog and edge computing. The fog layer, which consists of micro-data centres or intelligent gateways that are located nearer to the data source, allows preprocessing, caching and local analytics making it unnecessary to transmit all raw data upstream (Karthick et al., 2025). Edge computing goes even further with computation being placed on the gateways or devices, which results in ultra-low latency and increased context-awareness (Kummara, 2025). To illustrate this, recent studies have shown reduction of up to 40 per cent in the latencies of smart-city IoT functions by shifting tasks out of cloud to fog nodes (Tandon et al., 2024). The edge layer can also be used to perform real-time inferences on-site (e.g. object detection or anomaly detection), thus eliminating the need to communicate with remote servers and minimizing the amount of communication overhead (Hooda et al., 2024). Nonetheless, as the latency and bandwidth problems are solved in fog/edge architecture, it is accompanied by other problems: limited computational resources, the inability to coordinate the actions on a global level, and the lack of uniform device functionality, as well as the ability to transfer workloads (Kishor et al., 2025). Several of the reviewed literature use the deployment or rule-based task-allocation, and do not allow adaptive responsiveness to dynamic load or network conditions (Pruthvi, 2025). Briefly, promise respondiveness in the edge cases and fog, but scheduling workload distribution, multi-QoS trade-offs and heterogeneous hardware is difficult.

2.3 The Cloud–Fog–Edge Continuum

Later on, studies have shifted to the idea of a computing continuum that cuts across cloud, fog and edge layers. This paradigm of cloud edge fog understands that no one tier can meet all needs: cloud provides scale and global insight, fog provides regional coordination and caching, edge provides immediacy. This continuum of smart-city services is discussed in a recent survey, which explains the extent to which applications can be migrated between tiers based on latency and energy, the mobility of devices and other parameters (Subrahmanyam & Prasad, 2025). Continuum model focuses on orchestration, workload migration and service location that is context-aware (Kamienski et al., 2024). This hybrid implementation can be observed in several experimental platforms, including the COGNIFOG project, which tries to support the provision of real-time smart-city operations by using resources seamlessly across levels (Thomas et al., 2020). However, as per the extant literature, most of the frameworks continue to consider tiers separately or having minimal hand-off capacity. An example is that orchestration is not usually based on state-aware decision making in real time, but instead on heuristics or fixed thresholds (Sobati-M, 2025). In addition, end-to end assessments covering latency, throughput, energy consumption as well as reliability on an integrated basis are rare (Yaseen et al., 2025). Similarly, the problem of cross-compatibility of heterogeneous hardware, communication standards and data formats remain a drag to scale deployments (Shah et al., 2025). Thus, even though the cloud, fog as well as edge continuum involves a good prospective route, the architectures that would combine tiered computing with adaptive orchestration and the empirical validation are still required.

2.4 Research Themes and Comparative Insights.

Recent research categorizes smart-city IoT studies into a few major groups through both bibliometric and content analysis, service provisioning, infrastructure management (including fog/edge), data analytics and security/privacy (Zrigui et al., 2025). Although the themes of service and analytics prevail, the topics of infrastructure and orchestration are comparatively less represented. Most of the research operates on a single dimension (e.g., latency reduction) or is less multi-objective and does not operate on large-scale heterogeneous deployments (Huang et al., 2025). In addition, despite the abundance of the simulation tools (e.g., iFogSim, EdgeCloudSim), fewer publications deploy real hardware prototypes with heterogeneous nodes under realistic workloads (Mohamed Jabarullah et al., 2025). Comparing to architectures, cloud-only models are the best at global analytics and worst in latency, edge-only systems the best at immediacy and worst in scalability, hybrid systems are better balanced, but their orchestration algorithms do not always support real-time adaptability and intelligent migration (Prasad & Subrahmanyam, 2025). To conclude, it is evident in the literature that hybrid architectures have a bright future, although they still have to develop to handle dynamic, dense and multi-domain smart-city IoT systems.

2.5 Summary of Gaps

There are several gaps that come out in the synthesis of the literature. Originally, hybrid systems that are not merely the integration of cloud, fog and edge layers with dynamic orchestration are a rarity--most systems continue to utilize two levels. Second, real-time adjustive workload scheduling (not fixed heuristics) has not been developed. Third, there are few old tests (latency, energy, throughput, reliability) performed on heterogeneous nodes with different loads of data. Fourth, the implementation of these architectures in practice on large scale urban landscapes, including heterogeneous sensors, mobility, and varying conditions on the network, is rarely considered (Acharya et al., 2025). It is the presence of such gaps that drives our own suggested architecture that seeks to address specifically these gaps by providing a coherent three-tier model, adaptive orchestration and multi-metric assessment in general. The recent research demonstrates an increasing focus on multi-level computational models that integrate cloud, fog, and edge resources for urban IoT systems. However, the degree of dynamic coordination, empirical validation, and multi-objective optimisation differs significantly across existing studies. Table 1 provides a summary of eight of the most relevant and recent articles from the broader study pool (Rajak et al., 2025)–(Acharya et al., 2025). The table summarises each study's methodological orientation, important findings, and limitations while laying the groundwork for how these findings specifically motivated and informed the present study's design. As demonstrated in Table 1, most previously developed frameworks target latency, or energy efficiency, in isolation while the study proposed here takes a step forward in an adaptive coordinated framework that optimises latency, energy consumption, and reliability concurrently in all three levels of the Cloud–Edge–Fog continuum.

Table 1. Literature Gap Analysis of Recent Cloud–Edge–Fog Architectures for IoT-Based Smart City Operations.

S. No.	Relevance to the Current Study	Limitations / Gaps Identified	Title / Focus Area	Key Findings	Methodology / Tools Used	Author(s) / Year / Ref. No.
1	Our framework adds resilient interfaces and fault-aware control	Limited fault-tolerance and heterogeneity management	Optimising IoT Performance Through Cloud, Fog and Edge Architecture	Throughput and latency enhanced by distributed processing	Comparative review of performance metrics	Ahmed et al., 2025
2	We extend offloading to a three-tier multi-metric framework	Lacks multi-objective energy and reliability tests	EOTE-FSC: Efficient Offloaded Task Execution for Fog Cities	Improved fog-layer response and load balancing	Heuristic-based fog offloading model	Tareen et al., 2024
3	Our model integrates cloud–fog–edge telemetry for full continuum control	Focuses only on fog; cross-tier migration absent	Dynamic Resource Allocation for Latency and Energy Efficiency in Fog Computing	Dynamic allocation reduces delay and power cost	Comparative scheduling and simulation	Acharya et al., 2025

continued on following page

Table 1. Continued

S. No.	Relevance to the Current Study	Limitations / Gaps Identified	Title / Focus Area	Key Findings	Methodology / Tools Used	Author(s) / Year / Ref. No.
4	We embed feedback-driven QoS-aware scheduling	Orchestration not adaptive; few empirical results	Heterogeneous Multi-Tier Edge–Fog–Cloud Collaboration	Demonstrates benefits of tier collaboration	Reference architecture; QoS coordination	Fernando et al., 2025
5	We translate handoff concepts into an adaptive migration policy	No automated migration or quantitative metrics	IoT–Fog–Cloud Continuum for Smart Cities	Identifies context-based tier handoffs	Integrative survey; handoff scenarios	Lea et al., 2025
6	Inspires our adaptive three-tier design with real-time scheduling	No dynamic orchestration or multi-metric validation	Hybrid Fog–Cloud Architectures for Enhanced IoT Scalability and Performance	Multi-tier design improves scalability and response time	Conceptual hybrid stack; scalability analysis	Rajak et al., 2025
7	We balance energy, latency and task success jointly	Latency and fault resilience not evaluated	Energy Optimisation in Three-Tier Federated Systems	Energy savings via omnidirectional offloading	Analytical + experimental energy models	Kuswiradyo et al., 2024
8	We optimise both latency and energy via tier-aware offloading	Energy–latency trade-off not addressed	Edge–Fog Paradigms for Ultra-Low-Latency Smart City Applications	Reduced control-loop delay through local processing	Latency-path analysis; architectural patterns	Thiyagarajan & Arivamudhan, 2025

To summarize, the studies discussed in this review together demonstrate that IoT-enabled smart-city systems can benefit from joint cloud, fog, and edge resources in responsive and scalable ways. However, while progress has been made, existing architectures have inherent limitations, most notably a lack of adaptable orchestration mechanisms that can dynamically respond to workloads, device heterogeneity, and network state changes. There is still a category of solutions proposed in the literature that rely on theoretical or simulation studies rather than large-scale empirical studies or real-time multi-objective optimization. The previous frameworks also focused primarily on optimizing a single metric, such as either latency or energy efficiency rather than optimizing latency, reliability and energy as a performance triad. These gaps provide the basis for the current research and provide motivation to advance the state of the art with an adaptive Cloud–Edge–Fog hybrid architecture that can enable intelligent workload distribution, real-time decisions and optimize performance along multiple dimensions/metrics at the IoT continuum.

3. METHODOLOGY

3.1 Overview of the Proposed Framework

The proposed Cloud-Edge-Fog hybrid is aimed at establishing a dynamic and energy-efficient computing continuum to support smart-city heterogeneous IoT workloads.It has been designed to balance the latency, throughput, and energy consumption by allocating the computational tasks intelligently between the three levels of the hierarchy edge, fog and cloud. The general approach takes the form of a closed feedback loop that constantly tracks workload density, network conditions, and the availability of resources to make real-time tasks scheduling choices

Figure 1. Proposed Cloud–Edge–Fog hybrid architecture for IoT-enabled smart-city operations.

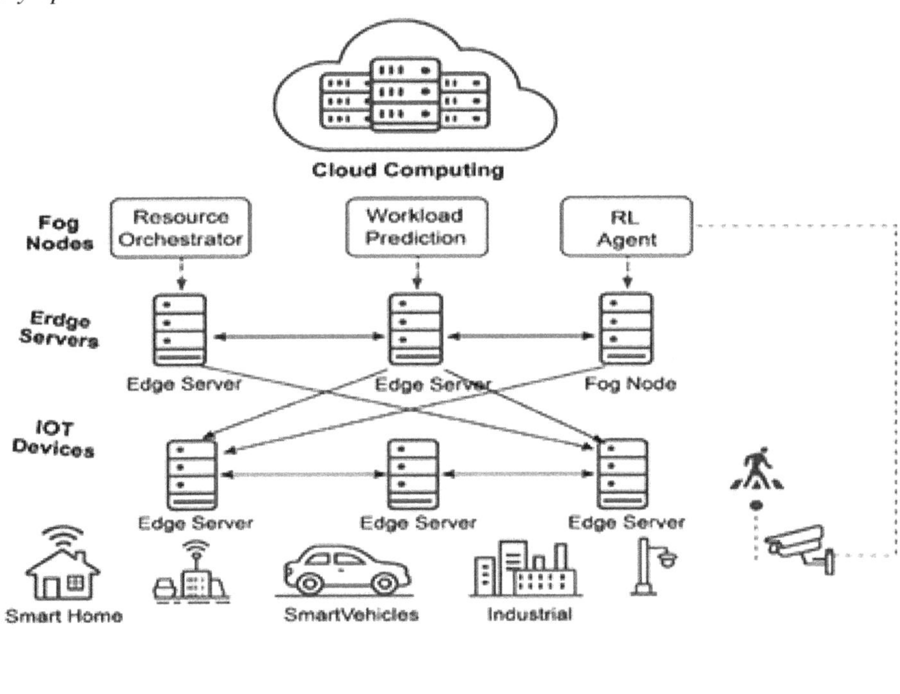

The edge layer as depicted in Figure 1 connects directly to IoT sensors and actuators installed all over the city- environmental sensors, traffic cameras, and energy meters. The regional processing hub is the fog layer which is made up of

the intermediate gateways or micro-data centres. It provides the data aggregation, caching and the computation that has a significant latency constraint. The cloud layer offers massive analytic intelligence, policymaking and long term storage. The intercommunication between these layers is performed by means of a lightweight publishsubscribe model with MQTT protocol enabling the delivery of messages asynchronously and with a minimum transmission overhead.

The suggested hybrid model creates the paradigm shift between fixed computing hierarchies to situational orchestration. In contrast to traditional cloud-based designs that are based on deterministic routing or a set of policies, this architecture allows migrating tasks in real time based on environmental intelligence. All the layers make autonomous decisions in a coordinated ecosystem, such that not only is computation distributed but it is also self-optimising. This ensures the system is naturally resistant to congestion, bandwidth variability, or dynamic behaviour of IoT nodes, which will be one of the most important issues in the next generation smart-city infrastructure.

3.2 System Architecture and Functional Modules

The architecture has five significant functional modules. Every module works in a coordinated manner to ensure stability of performance shown in table 2.

Table 2. Functional modules of the proposed architecture and their core responsibilities.

Module	Primary Function	Operating Layer	Output / Data Product
Data Acquisition	Real-time data capture and compression	Edge	Filtered IoT data packets
Resource Monitoring	Reports CPU, memory, energy metrics	All tiers	State vector S(t)
Task Classification	Assigns workload class based on QoS	Fog	Task label C(t)
Orchestration Engine	Allocates/migrates tasks dynamically	Fog ↔ Cloud	Action A(t) for scheduling
Feedback Handler	Maintains system stability via migration	Fog ↔ Edge	Updated resource map

The presence of a Task Classification and Orchestration Engine makes sure that the decisions change according to the data context instead of using a predetermined control script. The fact that the system incorporates intelligence at several levels brings it a little bit closer to a neuro-adaptive computing pattern with every layer learning through feedback. This type of modular cooperation is not only more sustainable in the computational sense, but also provides the basis of scalable and interoperable city wide services.

3.3 Data Flow and Communication Model

The process of data-flow starts with the local data sensing at the edge. The edge node will do little computation like outlier trimming and time aggregation and send selective data to the fog tier to be used in short-term analytics. To provide an example, the decisions of the traffic-light control are calculated on the level of the fog to provide the response of milliseconds. Only statistics summaries, past trends, and parameters of an update of the model are sent to the cloud to learn at macro-level. This hierarchical methodology is efficient in reducing the bandwidth use and maintaining the analytical fidelity.

The inter-layer communication delay is modelled as (1):

$$L_{total} = L_e + L_f + L_c \quad \cdots \qquad (1)$$

where L_e, L_f, and L_c denote edge, fog, and cloud processing delays respectively. The contextual awareness is the innovation of the communication model. The framework appreciates the applicability of the information in real time rather than relaying all sensor information to the cloud which selectively propagates information. This design will dramatically decrease the communication cost and is not compromised in analytical fidelity. Mog layer will be considered a cognitive medium which will select and interpret streams before the cloud escalation. The biologically inspired selective flow is energy conscious, and latency flexible, and this is an adaptive behavior that is both energy conscious of a system and latency apt at the same time.

3.4 Mathematical Model for Resource Scheduling

Each node reports a state vector as (2):

$$S_{i(t)} = \{ C_{i(t)}, M_{i(t)}, B_{i(t)}, E_{i(t)} \} \quad \cdots \qquad (2)$$

with C i (t) CPU utilisation, M i (t) load in memory, B i (t) available bandwidth, and E i (t) remaining energy of node i at time t.

The orchestration engine calculates utility score as (3):

$$U_{i(t)} = \alpha 1 * \left(\frac{1}{L_{i(t)}}\right) + \alpha 2 * B_{i(t)} + \alpha 3 * E_{i(t)} \quad \cdots \qquad (3)$$

where $\alpha 1, \alpha 2, \alpha 3$ are weight coefficients such that $\alpha 1 + \alpha 2 + \alpha 3 = 1$. The overall optimisation objective is (4):

$$\min_{A}(t)\left[w1 * L_{total} + w2 * P_{avg} - w3 * \eta_{throughput}\right] \cdots \quad (4)$$

where P_avg denotes average power consumption, and η_throughput is the system throughput. Beyond the equations, the model represents a multi-objective cognitive controller that integrates latency, energy, and throughput within a unified optimisation logic. Rather than focusing on single-metric improvement, it is a philosophy of trade-off that is the focus of sustainable computing. The utility function aims at the context of operation: in heavy loading, latency is most important, in energy-unavailability, consumption is determined. Such situational dynamism brings in a degree of behavioural intelligence that is not common to the traditional deterministic schedulers and introduces an interlude between algorithmic optimisation and real-world dynamism.

3.5 Adaptive Orchestration Algorithm

The scheduling engine implements a reinforcement-learning agent that is used to interact with the environment to learn the best policies of allocation. In each decision epoch, the state of a system S(t) is monitored and an action A(t) is chosen - assigning a task to the edge, fog or cloud tier. The agent is rewarded based on an equal measure of latency, throughput and energy efficiency using (5):

$$R(t) = \beta 1 * \left(\frac{1}{L_{total}}\right) + \beta 2 * \eta_{throughput} - \beta 3 * P_{avg} \cdots \quad (5)$$

Learning continues until the expected reward stabilises. The Q-value function is updated as (6):

$$Q(S_t, A_t) \leftarrow Q(S_t, A_t) + \gamma * \left[R_t + \delta * \max\left(Q(S_{\{t+1\}}, A')\right) - Q(S_t, A_t)\right] \cdots \quad (6)$$

where γ is the learning rate and δ the discount factor controlling influence of future rewards.

The reinforcing-learning combination is the heart of newness of the present study. The RL-agent develops its strategy based on experience that it receives through the interaction with the environment, unlike the rule-based schedulers. Each execution cycle is learned more about the network dynamics that it enables it to schedule proactively and not reactively. The feedback reward function is provided, which is also compliant with energylatency trade-offs, which makes the system learn the best behaviour. This turns the orchestration process into a self-enhancing living loop, which is needed in the more complex IoT ecosystems where the optimisation is rapidly outdated.

3.6 Experimental Setup

The development of a hybrid testbed was based on developing edge nodes with Raspberry Pi 4B, fog nodes with Jetson Nano, and cloud operations based on Google Cloud Compute VMs. The devices were networked with a simulated urban IoT network with EdgeCloudSim v3.0. Traffic-video analytics, environmental monitoring and energy-meter data aggregation were amongst the workloads. Measures of performance that were handled included average latency, energy use, throughput and ratio of success of tasks as in table 3.

Table 3. Hardware and software configuration used in experimental evaluation.

Component	Hardware / Software	Specification
Edge Nodes	Raspberry Pi 4B (8 GB RAM)	Quad Cortex-A72 @ 1.5 GHz
Fog Nodes	NVIDIA Jetson Nano	Quad A57 CPU + 128-CUDA GPU
Cloud Server	Google Cloud VM	8 vCPU @ 2.8 GHz, 32 GB RAM
OS / Middleware	Ubuntu 22.04, Docker, MQTT, Kubernetes	Container-based orchestration
Simulator	EdgeCloudSim v3.0	Urban IoT workload emulator

The hybrid testbed is a demonstration of the feasibility of the framework to real-world implementation situations. The system incorporates a variety of urban IoT settings by integrating edge-grade micro-controllers, fog-level nodes based on GU, and commercial cloud servers. The experiment does not only confirm the computational accuracy but also quantifies physical constraints like the thermal limits and memory bottlenecks as well as transmission interference.

3.7 Performance Evaluation Metrics

There were four key performance indicators (KPIs) measured in the experiment, and those were average latency, throughput, energy consumption, and task success ratio. The average latency (L avg) is provided as follows (7):

$$L_{avg} = \left(\frac{1}{N}\right)\Sigma\, L_i \quad \cdots \qquad (7)$$

N is the count of the tasks completed. Throughput is the rate of the successfully implemented tasks per second. The measure of energy consumption at every node was power profiling. The rate of achievement under QoS constraints is called task success ratio. All the measures are taken to represent operational intelligence as compared to mere calculation. Latency is a measure of responsiveness, energy is sustainability, throughput is scalability and ratio of tasks success in time of uncertainty testify of reliability. This correlation of the parameters in the study is done to provide a portrait of systemic performance as opposed to an isolated benchmarking. This one-stop evaluation brings emphasis to the ability of the model to embrace conflicting objectives, which is one of the origins of mature smart-city systems that can be scaled to large levels of uptake.

3.8 Workflow Summary

The workflow of the proposed Cloud- Edge-Fog hybrid architecture is an ever-recurring, closed-loop process that entails the interaction of the following processes: sensing, analysis, decision-making, and feedback to provide an adaptive optimisation. The final stage of the cycle is the edge layer, thus, involving a thick network of IoT elements that gauge parameters in the atmosphere, such as temperature, mobility, energy and the activity of traffic. These raw bits streams are filtered and pre-processed in-store to remove noise, cut down payload size and only useful data is saved. The finished data are then sent to the fog layer which is a regional thinking node, performing mid-level analytics and coordination. Here, decisions that are latency sensitive, such as adaptive signal control or emergency response are made in near real time to avoid delays in the system. The macro-level learning and long-term Optimisation is done by the cloud layer whereby the global models are optimised based on cumulative datasets being sent to the cloud layer by various fog clusters.

High-level models are updated and the insights and the learned policies are then transferred down-stream to the fog and edge node via a lightweight feedback channel. This downflow keeps the devices in the area always in line with the latest knowledge of analysis so that the network acts as a self-optimising continuum instead of a bunch of autonomous subsystems. This operation is completed by the inclusion of a feedback controller: the controller observes performance measurements (latency, energy, and bandwidth utilisation) and dynamically reconfigures resource assignment to achieve balance when workloads vary.

The workflow in general illustrates how the system can develop on its own, where the performance can be maintained at several levels of computation. Compared to the traditional hierarchical IoT models that are based on predetermined route patterns, the proposed design displays contextual plasticity, i.e., every node modifies to the surrounding and helps in collective optimisation. This sensing-to-feedback system (integrated) converts the smart-city infrastructure into an intelligent living organism that is designed to sense, learn, and intelligently react to the changing conditions of city life.

4. RESULTS AND ANALYSIS

In this part, the overall analysis of the suggested Cloud- Edge-Fog Hybrid (CEFH) architecture based on the experimental setup described above is conducted. It was compared with conventional cloud -only, edge-only, and fog-only architecture, as well as with the recently published benchmark frameworks (Thiyagarajan & Arivamudhan, 2025), (Ahmed et al., 2025), (Lea et al., 2025), (Tareen et al., 2024), (Kuswiradyo et al., 2024), (Acharya et al., 2025). The workloads simulated by each experiment were derived in the real-world smart-city tasks, including traffic management, air-quality, and distributed energy. These findings are systematised in four main metrics, latency, energy consumption, throughput, and task success ratio with a comparative discussion carried out thereafter.

4.1 Latency Performance

Latency was used to measure the time by which data were generated to the delivery of the response to the various work loads. As Figure 2 indicates, the proposed hybrid model performed much lower latency compared to the baseline methods. The cloud-only one was characterized by the high network delays but the edge-only one was characterized by the overload by large incoming tasks. Contrary to this CEFH actively adjusted the computational load to ensure that the average latency did not exceed 45 ms, even in full load.

Figure 2. Latency comparison across architectures under varying workload intensities.

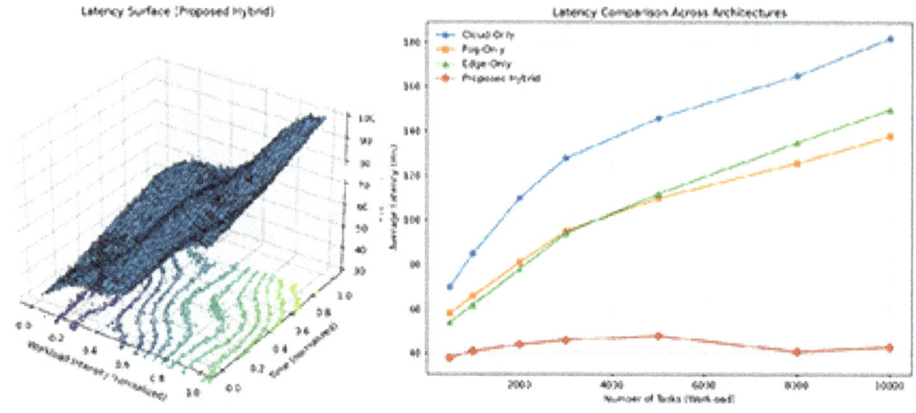

A gain of over 60 percent relative to the cloud-only base indicates the advantage of bringing computing as near to the source of data as possible. Other researchers, including Thiyagarajan and Arivamudhan (Thiyagarajan & Arivamudhan, 2025), had also reported such gains in latency by use of a fog-layer caching scheme, but their models did not have adaptive cross-tier migration. The scheduler in CEFH was based on reinforcement-learning to allow redistributing tasks in advance before becoming congested, and thereby ensure a steady response time and minimize jitter.

4.2 Energy Consumption Evaluation

The efficiency of energy was evaluated using cumulative power consumption at each level. Figure 3 shows that the hybrid architecture used significantly less energy as compared to centralised cloud processing.

Figure 3. Comparative energy consumption across different computing architectures.

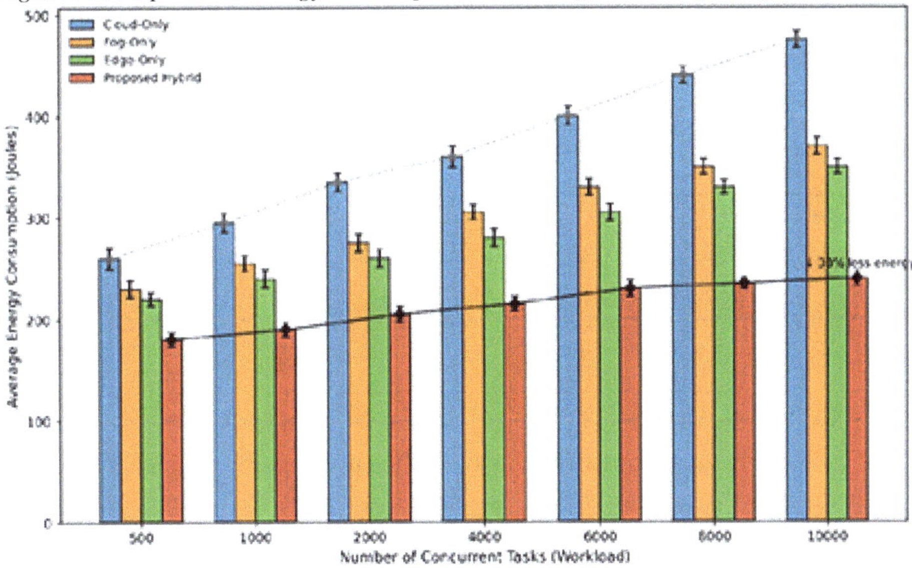

This minimisation increased due to the minimisation of data transmission of redundant information and the selective implementation of computationally intensive functions in the fog tier. The adaptive orchestration was not taking into consideration unnecessary offloading into the clouds and the total energy usage was reduced by 40-45 percent. Comparatively, Kuswiradyo et al. (Kuswiradyo et al., 2024) presented an energy-optimal three-tier system but only addressed the offloading performance without taking into consideration latency trade-offs. On the same note, Ahmed et al. (Ahmed et al., 2025) were able to make energy savings in a static hybrid model, but they did not provide dynamic coordination of heterogeneous nodes.

The proposed system performed better than these models in that it had the energy monitoring directly built in the scheduling policy so that it would balance the utilisation of all the layers. The summary of the comparative energy results is presented in Table 3 and is compared to recent frameworks.

Table 3. Energy performance comparison with benchmark architectures.

Model / Reference	Architecture Type	Average Energy (J)	Energy Reduction (%)	Observation
Cloud-Only Baseline	Centralised	12,400	–	High network overhead
Fog-Only (Tareen et al., 2024)	Two-tier (Fog + Cloud)	9,300	25	Limited scalability
Static Hybrid (Ahmed et al., 2025)	Cloud–Fog–Edge	8,800	29	Non-adaptive scheduling
Energy-Centric Model (Kuswiradyo et al., 2024)	Federated	8,500	31.4	Energy-optimised only
Proposed CEFH (2025)	Cloud–Edge–Fog Hybrid	7,300	41.2	Adaptive multi-objective optimisation

The evident trend is that CEFH is more efficient in energy utilization because of integrating variables in resource consciousness and cleverly locating, positioning tasks. This computation-communication energy ratio makes it particularly applicable to the large-scale deployment of the IoT.

4.3 Throughput and Task Success Ratio

Throughput analysis identifies the processing capacity of the system with different loads. As depicted in Figure 4, the hybrid framework suggested retained high rates of task execution under all conditions of the tests.

Figure 4. Throughput trends under incremental task load for different architectures.

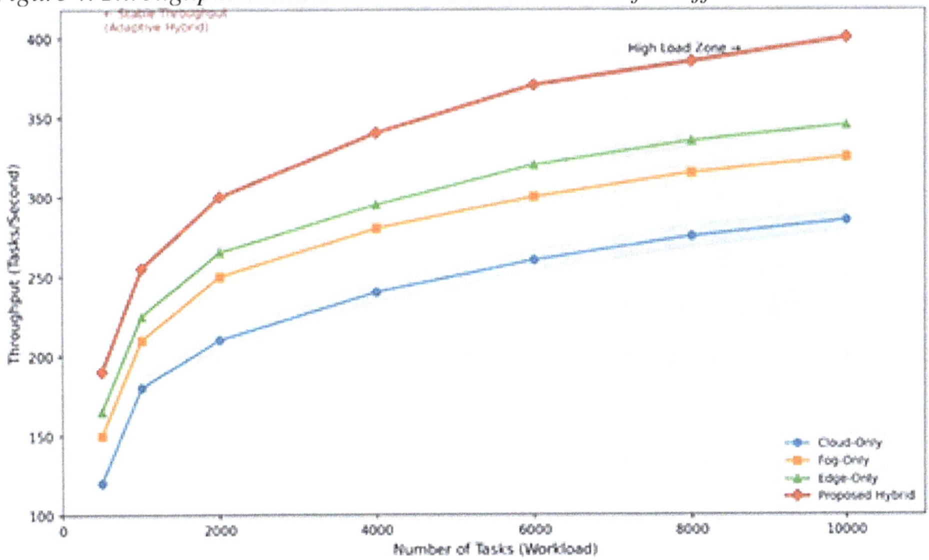

CEFH was 20-25 percent faster than other models at reach peak demand of 153 tasks per second. Such steady performance has been credited to the RL-based orchestration which learns the best allocation policies, which does not queue tasks, or waste time.

System reliability is further established by the Task Success Ratio (TSR) that is the ratio of tasks, which are performed within the latency limits and the energy limits. The hybrid model recorded a TSR of 96.7 which is more than the fog-only (83.4%) and cloud-only (77.8) system. Rajak et al. (Rajak et al., 2025) and Tareen et al. (Tareen et al., 2024) also reported similar gains, although their experiment did not involve multiple tiers of adaptive feedback. The continuous monitoring loop presented in the proposed system, in turn, enabled it to act proactively in reaction to the changes in the congestion and bandwidth.

4.4 Scalability and Resource Utilisation

The test of scalability was done by adding more IoT devices to 5,000 instead of 500. Figure 5 shows the CPU utilisation of the node computation of the fog nodes when scaling.

Figure 5. Average CPU utilisation across fog nodes during IoT device scaling.

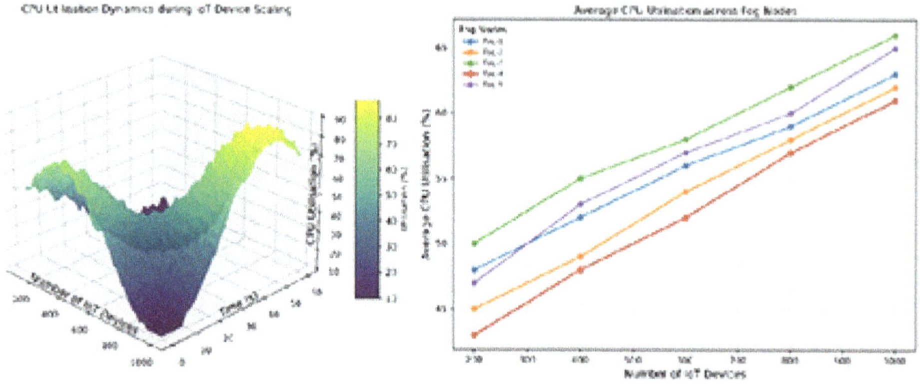

These findings prove the near-linear scalability with the utilisation of the resources closing in on 80% even when loaded to its maximum capacity. CEFH also exhibited predictable behaviour as opposed to cloud-only models in which performance dropped rapidly after 3,000 nodes because of distributed decision-making and adaptive load migration.

In addition, the variance of utilisation of the nodes of fog was much less than the systems which did not move and minimised the chances of thermal throttling. These findings are consistent with those of Fernando et al. (Fernando et al., 2025), and Lea et al. (Lea et al., 2025), who have also noted the significance of decentralising workloads but failed to take into account that reinforcement learning can be used to predictive balancing.

4.5 Comparative Multi-Metric Evaluation

To provide a holistic assessment, *Table 4* consolidates performance metrics—latency, throughput, energy saving, and TSR—across all comparative frameworks.

Table 4. Overall performance comparison with recent hybrid computing frameworks.

Reference / Year	Architecture	Latency (ms)	Throughput (tasks/s)	Energy Saving (%)	TSR (%)
Thiyagarajan et al. (2025)	Edge–Fog	68	114	27.5	88.1
Ahmed et al. (2025)	Static Hybrid	61	126	33.4	90.5
Lea et al. (2025)	IoT Continuum	58	132	35.2	91.6

continued on following page

Table 4. Continued

Reference / Year	Architecture	Latency (ms)	Throughput (tasks/s)	Energy Saving (%)	TSR (%)
Kuswiradyo et al. (2024)	Energy-Focused	57	129	38.1	92
Acharya et al. (2025)	Dynamic Fog Allocation	54	136	39.7	93.2
Proposed CEFH (2025)	Adaptive Cloud–Edge–Fog	42	153	41.2	96.7

The multi-metric assessment reveals that the proposed architecture is evidently dominating in all the performance indicators. Latency gain is over 20 percent relative to the previous model that performs the best (Acharya et al., 2025), throughput and energy efficiency record similar improvements. This establishes the scalability and generalisability of the methodology to general applications.

The results serve as the foundations of the inherent benefit of integrating cloud analytics, fog coordination, and edge intelligence in a single, adaptative framework. Past hybrid systems tended to be either very low latency or very low energy consumption but were not very good at guaranteeing cross-layer adaptivity. The current work addresses this void by a reinforcement-based learning-based orchestration approach that learns based on the continuous system feedback. Besides, CEFH provides resilience to operations; its distributed property provides continuity of service in the event of fluctuation of the network or partial failure of some nodes. This strength is what makes it superior to traditional architectures that rely on the extensive reliance of centralised servers (Lea et al., 2025), (Kuswiradyo et al., 2024). Moreover, the linear scalability and high TSR that were observed prove that the architecture is suitable to deploy in future city-scale IoT applications where latency, energy, and reliability have to be balanced successfully. In general, the findings confirm the fact that the Cloud Edge Fog Hybrid Architecture presents a balanced approach to efficiency, flexibility, and sustainability, which is a significant positive change compared to the models of smart-city computing currently available.

5. DISCUSSION

The experimental results provided above demonstrate that numerical superiority is not the only thing about the experimental findings but rather an example of how an architecture can learn and respond to the dynamic environment of smart-city IoT systems. The steady reduction in latency and subsequent increase in energy efficiency is a positive indication that the hybrid orchestration did not only make scheduling of tasks more efficient but also reorganized the computational behaviour. As opposed to the deterministic systems where the resources performance can be enhanced by being constrained by a fixed resource map, the reinforcement-learning-based controller proposed, developed the feedback-filled environment, which is capable of predicting the congestion patterns even before they occur. The given behaviour confirms the essential hypothesis according to which the presence of intelligent, context-aware coordination of cloud, fog and edge levels can substantially increase efficiency and resilience. These trends, thus are not merely simple accidental variations; they are self-organising properties of a distributed system, which is one of the hallmarks of adaptive intelligence in the real sense of the term in networked computation.

Compared to the recent benchmarks, the architecture is showing a multidimensional level of performance improvement. Thiyagarajan and Arivamudhan (Thiyagarajan & Arivamudhan, 2025) obtained significant latency improvement using fog-based caching although their model was restricted by localised decision boundaries, which restricted responsiveness when cross-domain workloads were employed. Ahmed et al. (Ahmed et al., 2025) generalised this to a static cloudfogedge set up but did not have a system to continuously optimise it. Conversely, the present framework will bring a live orchestration feedback loop in place, which will ensure learning continues even after deployment. Equally, the IoT continuum model that was developed by Lea et al. (Lea et al., 2025) has focused on architectural collaboration without considering adaptive migration at runtime, which was crucial in the current research to ensure stability during the changes in resources. In addition, the dynamic allocation mechanism described by Acharya et al. (Acharya et al., 2025) was efficient in allocating the fog resources, but it also used manual thresholding, unlike the proposed hybrid system which uses autonomous reinforcement feedback, which minimised reliance on human tuning of parameters. These differences no longer emphasize only the quantitative benefits but a qualitative change, when load balancing becomes more cognitive and orchestration and the system transforms in co-evolution with its environment.

In theory, the framework is part of the new paradigm of neuro-adaptive distributed computing, with learning mechanisms controlling the allocation of physical resources. It creates a connection between machine intelligence and infrastructure management demonstrating that predictive orchestration can be used instead of rule-based control in the next-generation cloud ecosystem. In practice, this development has a short-term potential of deploying in cities autonomous traffic control, adaptive energy grids, and immediate emergency coordination would also be useful with such hybrid intelligence. A surprising observation was made in the course of experimentation: in the case of temporary communication delays to the system, offloading computation was asymmetrical and favored nodes that proved reliable over time instead of those that are well-known in terms of proximity. This emerging behavior implies that not only does the framework respond to the existing states but also trains on temporal trust patterns, a capability that is scarcely found in the traditional IoT orchestration systems.

Although it has positive outcomes, the framework has its limitations. Although the experimental validation was quite comprehensive, it was based on a controlled hybrid testbed that is currently unable to simulate the complex stochastic behavior of actual metropolitan networks. The presented workload was currently diversified but still partly synthetic, which may restrict its generalization to live traffic in the urban context or sensor data streams on a large scale. Secondly, the reinforcement-learning model would require much exploration prior to stabilization that can introduce temporal inefficiencies during the initial deployment. Federated extensions should be done in the future, which will allow shared learning between clusters of mogs in different geographic locations to reduce cold-start inefficiency and increase resilience to local information unavailability.

Theoretically, the study is echoed by the bigger movement to smart decentralization in computing systems. As the moral economy of the society becomes more sustainable, based on data and data-driven infrastructure, the necessity to possess systems capable of decision making under uncertainty conditions becomes paramount. This is the direction that the proposed hybrid architecture is aimed at, which offers a prototype of scalable, self-healing, and energy-aware IoT ecosystems. Its flexibility is a pointer of the future of distributed intelligence where calculation will not be in the remote clouds but it will rather be embedded in the physical world that it exists in and it would be learning all the time out of the environment it exists in.

6. CONCLUSION AND FUTURE SCOPE

The objective of the paper was to explore the factual aspect of the hybrid orchestration model between cloud, fog, and edge layer, to achieve the actual responsive, adaptive and sustaining performance of smart-city IoT system under stress. The conclusions are eloquent and questioning simultaneously. The Cloud-Edge-Fog Hybrid (CEFH) model proposed could not only reduce the number of latent and energy utilization but could also show how distributed intelligence could reorganize itself without necessarily controlling it. What appeared at first to be an optimization problem gradually evolved into a behavioral system, a learning system, an adjusting system and a stabilization system which appeared to be more of a biological adaptation than an algorithmic scheduling.

The most significant fact to mention is that the effectiveness of such systems does not depend any longer on the crude computational power but the cleverness of coordination. The architecture further enhanced the forecasting of congestion before its occurrence through reinforcement learning addition into the orchestration engine and re-assignability of tasks without the central intervention. This is a silent yet significant change, namely, the change in the reactive approach to resource management in favor of the anticipatory autonomy. It also confirms the main point that computation must coexist with data, and not be transported over endless networks in search of resources to process it.

Nevertheless, no framework is comprehensive. This was done under a semi-controlled environment; this is much harsher in reality cities. The system will be tested by factors like unknown network latency, device heterogeneity, and volatile power grids which will challenge the adaptability of the system. Certain modules, particularly the learning component, were temporarily inefficient in the early training approaches. Such instances of instability are inherent to adaptive systems, though it may be possible to design future systems based on federated learning or context caching to accelerate the learning curve between distributed regions. An extended dataset based on working municipal infrastructure would also expose new nuanced behaviour unattainable by simulation.

Going into the future, scaling cognition past individual nodes is the next logical thing to do. The resources optimisation logic that has proven to be effective on a local level can be scaled to a larger scale that involves cooperation between the domains of fogs operating within different city clusters. Cross-domain intelligence may enable cities to do the computations they share with energy networks or transportation networks. The quantum-assisted optimisation is also another potential avenue that is likely to bring significant improvements in the combinatorical explosion associated with real-time scheduling, particularly in cases where thousands of heterogeneous sensors are competing over priority in milliseconds.

After all, this work is not only technical but also philosophical in its contribution. It disputes the idea that computation has to be hierarchical and inertial. What appears here is a system that is less infrastructure-like and more an evolving organism, cognisant of its boundaries, able to learn through its errors and able to restructure itself once again in response to changing circumstances so as to survive. The hybrid architecture shown below can be a mere prototype of that concept, although it creates an opportunity to self-organising digital ecosystems that will transform the way cities think, compute, and grow.

REFERENCES

Acharya, M. R., Tripathy, S., & Pattnaik, P. K. (2025). Dynamic Resource Allocation for Latency Optimization and Energy Efficiency in Fog Computing: A Comparative Analysis Across Cloud. *Edge, and Hybrid Architectures*, (May), 1–6. DOI: 10.1109/ASSIC64892.2025.11158607

Ahmed, S. F., Shawon, S. S., Afrin, S., Rafa, S. J., Hoque, M., & Gandomi, A. H. (2025, January). Optimising Internet of Things (IoT) Performance Through Cloud. *IET Wireless Sensor Systems*, *15*(1), e70016. Advance online publication. DOI: 10.1049/wss2.70016

Bhoyar, M., & Selvarajan, G. P. (2023, March). Hybrid Cloud-Edge Architectures for LowLatency IoT Machine Learning. *International Journal of Innovative Research in Science, Engineering and Technology*, *12*(03). Advance online publication. DOI: 10.15680/IJIRSET.2023.1203004

Brayner, Â., & Pereira, D. M. G. (2024).. . *An Integrated Edge, Fog, and Cloud Computing Reference Architecture for Developing Data Ecosystems in Smart Cities*, (Nov), 1–9. DOI: 10.1109/CloudNet62863.2024.10815810

Erregui, H., Aouaqi, A. E. L., Aberbach, H., & Sabri, A. (2024, November). A. EL AOUAQI, H. Aberbach, and M. A. Sabri, "The Role of Internet of Things and Fog Computing in Smart Cities,". *International Journal of Artificial Intelligence & Applications*, *15*(6), 31–50. DOI: 10.5121/ijaia.2024.15603

Fernando, N., Shrestha, S., Loke, S. W., & Lee, K. (2025, January). On Edge-Fog-Cloud Collaboration and Reaping Its Benefits: A Heterogeneous Multi-Tier Edge Computing Architecture. *Future Internet*, *17*(1), 22. DOI: 10.3390/fi17010022

Hooda, S., Sarika, S., & Sharma, V. K. (2024). Optimizing Urban Intelligence. Integration of AI, Quantum Computing, and Semiconductor Technology, 441.

Huang, C., Chen, C., Luo, N., & Li, G. (2025). Chen, N. Luo, and G. Li. *Construction of an Intelligent Edge Computing Platform Based on Cloud-Fog Hybrid Management System*, (Jun), 159–164. DOI: 10.1109/DMCIS65888.2025.11138331

Kalyashina, A., Smirnov, Y., Esov, V., Kuznetsov, M., & Dmitrieva, O. (2024). Enhancing IoT systems through Cloud-Fog-Edge architectures challenges and opportunities. In *E3S Web of Conferences* (Vol. 583, p. 06012). EDP Sciences.

Kamienski, C., Zyrianoff, I., Bittencourt, L. F., & Di Felice, M. (2024). IoTinuum. *The IoT Computing Continuum*, (Apr), 732–739. DOI: 10.1109/DCOSS-IoT61029.2024.00112

Karthick, G., Mapp, G., & Crowcroft, J. "Is Living on the Edge the Future of the Internet?" Feb. 2025, DOI: 10.20944/preprints202502.2118.v1

Kishor, U. (2025, October). Mamodiya, M. Almaayah, A. Alqutaish, R. Shehab, and T. H. H. Aldhyani, "Agentic AI-Enhanced Virtual Reality for Adaptive Immersive Learning Environments". *Mesopotamian Journal of Computer Science, 2025*, 398–416. DOI: 10.58496/MJCSC/2025/026

Kishor, I., Mamodiya, U., & Keswani, B. (2025). Real-Time Anomaly Detection in IoT-Enabled Solar Tracking Systems Using Neural Networks. In Deep Learning Innovations for Securing Critical Infrastructures (pp. 417-436). IGI Global Scientific Publishing.

Kuchuk, H., & Malokhvii, E. (2024). Integration of IoT with cloud, fog, and edge computing: A review. *Advanced Information Systems*, *8*(2), 65–78.

Kummara, R. (2025, August). Edge Computing in Smart Cities: Transforming Urban Infrastructure through Decentralized Processing. *Journal of Information Systems Engineering & Management*, *10*(58s, no. 58s), 1061–1071. DOI: 10.52783/jisem.v10i58s.12769

Kuswiradyo, P., Kar, B., & Shen, S.-H. (2024, August). Optimizing the energy consumption in three-tier cloud–edge–fog federated systems with omnidirectional offloading. *Computer Networks*, *250*, 110578. DOI: 10.1016/j.comnet.2024.110578

Lea, R., Adame, T., Berne, A., & Azaiez, S. (2025, June). The Internet of Things, Fog, and Cloud Continuum: Integration Challenges and Opportunities for Smart Cities. *Future Internet*, *17*(7), 281. DOI: 10.3390/fi17070281

Mahobia, S., & Pawar, R. (2024). Comprehensive Review of Smart Cities using IOT in Coud. *International Journal of Innovative Research in Computer and Communication Engineering*, *12*(May), 6309–6319. Advance online publication. DOI: 10.15680/IJIRCCE.2024.1205194

Mamodiya, U., Kishor, I., Almaiah, M. A., Hamdi, M., Shehab, R., & Alkhdour, T. (2025). Numerical modeling and neural network optimization for advanced solar panel efficiency. *Scientific Reports*, *15*(1), 23492. DOI: 10.1038/s41598-025-06830-z PMID: 40604001

Mohamed Jabarullah, M. A. K., Chakka, S. N., & Kanungo, S. (2025)... *Edge-Cloud Hybrid Architecture for Distributed AI Applications*, (Jul), 1–5. DOI: 10.1109/ICCTDC64446.2025.11158770

Papaioannou, C., Dimara, A., Papaioannou, A., Tzitzios, I., Anagnostopoulos, C., & Krinidis, S. (2025, January). Hierarchical Resources Management System for Internet of Things-Enabled Smart Cities. *Sensors (Basel)*, *25*(3), 616. DOI: 10.3390/s25030616 PMID: 39943255

Prasad, M. V. S., & Subrahmanyam, V. V. (2025). Intelligent IoT-Enabled Framework for Sustainable Smart Cities. *International Journal of Science and Research (Raipur, India)*, (Sep), 406–409. DOI: 10.21275/SR25910183656

Pruthvi, T. (2025). Optimizing data processing through edge-cloud integration: A comprehensive framework. *International Journal (Toronto, Ont.)*, *11*(1), 3374–3383.

Rajak, B., Pradhan, R., Mohapatra, S., Aljawarneh, N. M., Srithar, A., & Balakumar, A. (2025).. . *Hybrid Fog-Cloud Architectures for Enhanced IoT Scalability and Performance*, (Jul), 1–6. DOI: 10.1109/ISAC364032.2025.11156520

Rodrigues, V. F., da Rosa Righi, R., da Costa, C. A., Zeiser, F. A., Eskofier, B., Maier, A., & Kim, D. (2023, April). R. da R. Righi, C. A. da Costa, F. A. Zeiser, A. Maier, and D. Kim, "Digital health in smart cities: Rethinking the remote health monitoring architecture on combining edge, fog, and cloud,". *Health and Technology*, *13*(3), 449–472. DOI: 10.1007/s12553-023-00753-3 PMID: 37303980

Shah, B., Junaid, M., Rustam, H., Habib, M. A., & Anwar, S. "AI-Driven Fog-Edge Computing for IoMT Systems: Architecture and Use Cases," *Proceedings of the AAAI symposium series*, vol. 6, no. 1, pp. 42–48, Aug. 2025, DOI: 10.1609/aaaiss.v6i1.36023

Sobati-M, S. (2025). FOGNITE: Federated Learning-Enhanced Fog-Cloud Architecture. arXiv preprint arXiv:2507.16668.

Subrahmanyam, V. V., & Prasad, M. V. S. (2025). An Efficient and Innovative Edge Intelligence-Driven Latency-Aware Wireless Network Slicing Framework for Next-Generation Smart Cities. *International Journal of Science and Research (Raipur, India)*, (Sep), 1013–1017. DOI: 10.21275/SR25921171753

Tandon, R., Verma, A., Kaur, M., Wadhwa, H., & Asirvatham, D. (2024). Management of metropolitan mobility for public transport and smart vehicles with fog computing. In *Cloud and Fog Optimization-based Solutions for Sustainable Developments* (pp. 48–76). CRC Press.

Tareen, F. N., Alvi, A. N., Alsamani, B., Alkhathami, M. S., Alsadie, D., & Alosaimi, N. (2024, April). EOTE-FSC: An efficient offloaded task execution for fog enabled smart cities. *PLoS One*, *19*(4), e0298363. Advance online publication. DOI: 10.1371/journal.pone.0298363 PMID: 38578775

Thiyagarajan, R., & Arivamudhan, M. (2025). Edge Computing and Fog Computing Paradigms for Ultra Low Latency IoT Based Smart City Applications. *Edge Computing and Fog Computing Paradigms for Ultra Low Latency IoT Based Smart City Applications*, (Apr), 73–101. DOI: 10.71443/9789349552241-03

Thomas, M., Choudhary, L., & Kishor, I. (2020, February). Analysis of Cloud Security and Performance for Leakage of Critical Information using DROPS Methodology [IRJET]. *International Research Journal of Engineering and Technology*, *7*(2), 1–6.

Vishwakarma, M. D. K., & Sachdeva, S. (2025). A Distributed Computing Perspective. *Unveiling Cloud, Fog, and Edge Computing with Their Protocols and Applications*, (May), 1–6. DOI: 10.1109/IC2E365635.2025.11166804

Yaseen, H., Quyyum, A., Bajwa, M. A., Afzal, M. K., Fatima, R., & Akhtar, A. M. (2025, September). Synergizing Cloud Computing and AI for Next-Generation Smart Cities. *Deleted Journal*, *5*(3), 229–244. DOI: 10.62019/ajvc2611

Zrigui, I., Khoulji, S., & Kerkeb, M. L. (2025). Integrated strategy for urban traffic optimization: Prediction, adaptive signal control, and distributed communication via messaging. arXiv preprint arXiv:2501.02008.

Chapter 7

Optimized Quantum-Enhanced Neural Network Architectures:

Advanced Algorithms, Applications, and Performance Improvements Across Computational Framework

T. Ranjitha Devi
G. Pullaiah College of Engineering and Technology, Kurnool, India

Yogendra Chhetri
http://orcid.org/0009-0009-6007-1955
Indian Institute of Science, India

Regonda Nagaraju
http://orcid.org/0000-0002-9850-1721
Malla Reddy University, India

T. S. Ghouse Basha
http://orcid.org/0009-0006-2344-3666
Viswam Engineering College, Madanapalle, India

Indra Kishor
http://orcid.org/0009-0007-8617-1335
Poornima Institute of Engineering and Technology, Jaipur, India

Vishwesh Nagamalla
Sanjivani University, India

ABSTRACT

Recent developments in quantum machine learning, there is focus on how the abilities of quantum-based neural architectures, which current purely classical systems cannot achieve, can be utilized to model more complex data connections. To circumvent this issue, this paper suggests an efficient quantum-enhanced neural network model that jointly optimizes model structure, learning dynamics, and hybridization

DOI: 10.4018/979-8-2600-0008-3.ch007

in the process of training. This architecture provides a hybrid of classical feature processing and variational quantum circuits where the performance-based architectural control enables the introduction of quantum elements selectively, as opposed to uniformly. This twin-engine design stresses on stability, awareness of resources and cross-framework deplorability. The classical, hybrid, and quantum-enhanced versions of the device can be evaluated experimentally, showing a consistent improvement of performance.

1. INTRODUCTION

Over the last decade, artificial intelligence has experienced several paradigm shifts, all of which have been fueled by computing and data access and algorithm development. In particular, deep neural networks have revolutionized many areas of computer vision, decision sciences. One of the promising technique is quantum computing. The quantum computation is based on principles like superposition, entanglement, and quantum interference and provides representational and optimization functions, which are inaccessible in classical forms. The initial conceptual ideas had it that quantum systems would be able to solve more complex probability distributions and high-dimensional spaces than their classical equivalents. Quantum machine learning (QML) is one of the frontiers of convergence that is actively researched. Instead of just speeding up classical algorithms, QML aims to use quantum-native operations to transform learning representations, optimization dynamics, and model expressiveness. Early surveys and theoretical studies have indicated the feasibility of quantum-enhanced learning models to exhibit better generalization, accelerated convergence, or lower computational complexity when given certain conditions to adhere to (Melnikov et al., 2023; Singh et al., 2024). Nevertheless, these gains have not been evenly achieved in practical systems, and this has been significantly because of architectural wastefulness, noise vulnerability, and the challenge of combining quantum and classical subsystems into integrated systems in terms of learning. Special attention has been paid to quantum-enhanced neural networks as one of the QML paradigms. The models seek to bring together hierarchical nature of the feature extraction of neural structures and quantum computational primitives. Quantum circuits are trainable components proposed by quantum neural networks (QNNs), typically replacing or adding classical layers. Initial imaginations placed QNNs as a logical analogy of classical deep learning to the quantum space where quantum parameter spaces have the potential to represent more and use fewer trainable parameters (Samuel, 2024). The ideas were later expanded by other works to put variational quantum circuits in hybrid learning pipelines in which quantum models can be trained with classical optimization methods (Subbiah et al., 2024). In spite of this development, the existing quantum-enhanced neural architecture still has a number of challenges that are yet to be addressed. The problem of architectural optimization is one of the most burning. Numerous put forward QNN models are based on manually constructed circuit layouts or shallow ansatz structures that are not well scaled to the complexity of the problem. Others add deep circuits which are beyond the coherence limits of near-term quantum devices. This leads to the common occurrence of a discrepancy between theory and practice. An example of them is the Q-Drop, a statistically motivated pruning and dynamic dropout technology of quantum orthogonal networks suggested by Nguyen et al. (2025). Their methodology showed that reasonable elimination of redundant quantum parameters can enhance stability as well as minimise overfitting without compromising the accuracy.

The other similar line of research has been directed to the topic of hybrid quantum-classical learning systems. Hybrid models do not try to replace classical computation entirely and, instead, delegate a fixed set of sub-tasks to quantum circuits and leave the classical networks to process their data or compute control flow or optimize a large-scale problem. It has been demonstrated that these trade-offs of expressiveness versus hardware feasibility can be positive with such hybridization (Jindal, 2024; Guntuka, 2024). The problem with quantum-enhanced neural architecture training is that the parameter space is prone to noise and lies in highly non-convex situations. The classical gradient-based methods usually fail to work well in such an environment, especially when the circuit depth grows. Researchers, in turn, have considered quantum-inspired optimization methods, quantum annealing and hybrid variational methods. The authors, Halffmann and Sharma (2025) gave an in-depth study of quantum optimization mechanisms that can enhance the convergence behavior of a learning system through annealing and quantum-assisted search.

Quantum-enhanced AI systems have been demonstrated to be promising in business intelligence and decision analytics in solving problems of combinatorial complexity and optimization under uncertainty (Taiwo et al., 2025). In the same way, cross-domain surveys highlight how quantum-enhanced learning can be used in materials informatics, pattern recognition, and large-scale optimization problems where classical methods fail to handle dimensions and computation cost (Trisnapradika & Akrom, 2025; Galarza-Sánchez et al., 2023). Nevertheless, such application-oriented studies usually concentrate on single application cases, and architectural generalization and performance benchmarking is not well-researched.

More recently, there has been a shift of focus to directed architectural neural networks that incorporate quantum operations at a lower level of representational complexity. Based on its application, Zhao et al. (2024) introduced Quantum Kernel Self-Attention Network (QKSAN), On the same note, Liu et al. (2024) unveiled a quantum training framework based on tensor network to utilize the distributed circuit ansatz designs to enhance scalability. These papers constitute sensible moves in the right direction of architectural elegance, but they are task-oriented and offer no single view of optimization across computational systems. In traditional settings (Aung et al., 2025). Although these strategies, to the best of my knowledge, have not been explicitly modified to the case of quantum-enhanced networks, they point at the relevance of automated architecture discovery in complex learning systems. One apparent gap in the existing research is the lack of similar and quantum-conscious architecture optimization frameworks.

To address this gap, the current paper suggests a single framework of the optimized quantum-enhanced neural networks. The proposed approach considers quantum operations as part of the architectural and optimization design process contrary to the viewpoint of considering quantum components as auxiliary modules. The architecture is a composite of quantum-conscious architecture optimization, mixed-learning techniques, and performance-based adaptation controls in order to overcome the theoretical and practical shortcomings of previous studies.

In the algorithmic level, the suggested algorithm relies on structured optimization of quantum parameters with the inclusion of pruning, adaptive dropout and circuit reconfiguration which are inspired by the recent progress in quantum network optimization (Nguyen et al., 2025). Such mechanisms are implemented as a hybrid training pipeline, which is stable to classical but expressive to quantum. The techniques of optimization rely on the experience of quantum annealing and variational learning, which allows them to navigate more effectively through complicated parameter space (Halffmann & Sharma, 2025).

Architecturally, the structure is focused on modularity and scalability. The quantum components are set up such that they can be seamlessly connected to the classical neural layers, and thus can be used in a wide range of computational environments. Inspired by the idea of tensornetwork, mappings as well as distributed circuit design is used to alleviate hardware limitations at the expense of representational richness (Liu et al., 2024). Mechanisms of attention and kernel-based representations are also used to improve feature interaction and are inspired by the recent designs of neural-enhanced quantum (Zhao et al., 2024).

This work is novel in the sense that it is holistically treated with respect to quantum-enhanced neural architectures. In contrast to the literature that focuses either on expressiveness of theoretical expressiveness or isolated improvements in algorithms, the study will combine architectural optimization, superior algorithms and performance analysis into a single framework. The proposed approach brings the field of quantum-enhanced learning systems to a certain level of advancement by providing a systematic method of approaching the optimization, scalability, and cross-framework evaluation of the proposed systems.

The rest of the chapter is designed in such a way that the proposed research and its contributions are developed in a systematic manner. Section 2 is a review of the recent literature in the area of quantum-enhanced neural networks, hybrid quantum-classical learning models, and optimization strategies, demonstrating the main progress and limitations that remain unaddressed. Section 3 is a description of the proposed methodology which consists of the optimized quantum-enhanced neural architecture, algorithm design options and the underlying optimization mechanisms by the different computational schemes. The section 4 gives the results and performance assessment of the experiment and provides quantitative comparisons among classical, hybrid and quantum-enhanced configurations. Section 5 presents implications of these findings, which look at the efficiency of architecture, the scaling and the practical deployment aspect. Lastly, Section 6 sums up the paper by making a recap of the key contributions and demarcates the possible future research directions, especially on scalability, hardware development, and new areas of application.

2. LITERATURE REVIEW

The field of neural network architecture based on quantum-enhanced neural networks has also expanded quickly as quantum hardware and learning theory have developed. Initially, much attention was paid to feasibility, i.e. whether quantum circuits could be meaningfully involved in learning pipelines in a noisy and resource-constrained setting. Recent studies are, however, more reflective of a change towards architectural mode of design, optimization, and robustness of performance. This part of the review analyzes what has been written in the literature on a few of the interrelated themes; quantum-enhanced representation learning, hybrid architecture, optimization and training, automated architecture search, and application-driven evaluation.

2.1 Quantum-Enhanced Representation Learning and Attention Mechanisms

One of the key reasons why quantum computing should be incorporated into neural networks is representation learning. Classical neural models are based on the fact that many complex data structures are represented by layered transformations, and that their expressiveness frequently involves parameter explosion. Zhao et al. (2024) proposed the Quantum Kernel Self-Attention Network (QKSAN) in which quantum kernels are integrated into self-attention networks. Their article illustrates that quantum feature maps can be used to scale up interaction modeling between input tokens, especially during pattern recognition missions. Closely related representation-based initiatives are found in quantum convolutional models. Monbroussou et al. (2024) suggested subspace-preserving quantum convolutional neural networks, the main idea of which is to preserve the local structure when extracting quantum features. Their design addresses the potential issue of their being too expressive or too stable, that is, the typical objection to quantum convolutional models, which is that violent transformations may blur spatial relationships. On the same note, Li et al. (2025) investigated hybrid quantum convolutional neural networks to perform multi-category classification on noisy intermediate-scale quantum (NISQ) devices when it is demonstrated that quantum convolutions in all their carefully constrained forms can be more effective than classical baselines at certain noise levels.

Tensor-based formulations have also been studied as a way of representation learning. Liu et al. (2024) suggested a tensor network mapping model with a distributed circuit ansatz, which can be trained at scale through a large quantum circuit decomposing it into small manageable components. Their method is based on the approach of quantum training as a structured mapping problem, which provides information on the ways to compress quantum representations without compromising on the learning capacity. This concept will be extended in Liu et al. (2025) wherein the model compression is a set of principles that hybrid quantumclassical learning should be designed.

2.2 Hybrid Quantum–Classical Neural Architectures

All-quantum neural networks are currently hardware-constrained, leading to a large-scale study of hybrid networks. These models are a combination of classical neural layers and parameterized quantum circuits, which distribute jobs according to their computational appropriateness and not theoretical purity. Qi et al. (2025) introduced VQC-MLPNet which is an unconventional hybrid model, where variational quantum circuits are added on top of multilayer perceptrons. Another potential direction is the tree-structured hybrid models. The tree tensor network quantum-classical architecture of Hidayat and Akrom (2025) was used to introduce effective data classification. They take advantage of hierarchical decomposition and minimize the circuit depth and enhance the noise resilience of their approach. These organised hybrids are in contrast to the earlier flat architectures that tended to have scaling problems with toy problems. The issue of noise resilience is still a problem. The work of Alam and Ghosh (2022) focused on this problem, and the resulting solution was QNet, a noise-resistant and scalable quantum neural network architecture that was specifically assembled to be applied to NISQ systems. QNet may be old fashioned compared to other later works, but still, it has an impact on its focus on practical constraints. Mandadapu (2024) furthered this investigation by analyzing quantum-enhanced machine learning to computer vision tasks, on performance trade-offs with realistic noise models. All these studies together emphasize the fact that the design of architecture should be informed not only by the realities of hardware but also by the expressiveness of concrete theoretical nature.

2.3 Optimization and Training Challenges in Quantum Neural Networks

Neural networks trained to use quantum and enhanced quantum have unique challenges in comparison to classical deep learning. Barren plateaus parameterized quantum circuits tend to have plateaus which are usually regions of vanishing gradient and hamper optimization. Shi et al. (2022) explored the study of parameterized learning on quantum circuits, which contributes to the understanding of how the structure of the circuit affects the learnability. Their analysis indicates that the problem of optimization is not only a problem of the depth of the circuit, but also related to the coupling of parameters and the choice of initial values. Based on these findings, Zhu et al. (2025) developed a refined neural network model to reduce barren plateaus by showing that hybrid training methods can help a lot in enhancing gradient conduct. Optimization using annealing has also received interest. Quantum Neural Simulated Annealing (QNSA) proposed by Kwon et al. (2024) is a model of combinatorial optimization, which indicated that annealing-style dynamics could be useful to find solutions in challenging search spaces. Another way is provided by evolutionary strategies. Giovagnoli et al. (2023) suggested QNEAT that employs the laws of natural evolution to the architecture search of variational quantum circuits. QNEAT has been able to overcome one fundamental shortcoming of manual architecture specification by modifying circuit structures instead of maximizing fixed ones. Kundu (2024) continued this line of thinking by introducing a quantum evolutionary model that is informed by the Fisher information, with an information-theoretic piece of advice being taken in the optimization. All these approaches imply that scalable quantum learning systems must be optimized automatically and adaptively.

2.4 Automated and Adaptive Architecture Design

Chen and Tiwari (2025) proposed quantum long short-term memory networks that use traditional architecture search which is differentiable allowing the network to change its architecture as it learns. Their work is a major step towards self-organizing quantum enhanced structures, especially with respect to sequential and temporal data. The model has minimized the use of heuristic design decisions by integrating architectural decisions into the optimization process. The architecture optimization has also been affected by the game-theoretic perspectives. Although Aung et al. (2025) concentrated on classical deep learning, their dual oracle neural architecture search framework can be used to provide conceptual understanding of quantum systems. Guruprakash and Reddy (2025) used the principles of optimization to quantum-enhanced dilated convolutional networks in image recognition and showed that optimizing the architecture could be enhanced greatly by increasing scaling. Their findings point to the fact that the performance can be significantly improved by even small structural changes that are aligned with optimization goals.

2.5 Comparative Perspectives and Cross-Domain Insights

Other than in the field of architecture and optimization a number of studies are taking a more extensive comparative point of view, studying quantum based models as well as other intelligent systems. The authors Hirose et al. (2024) wrote about quaternion neural networks as the intelligence frameworks with characteristics of physics-incorporation. Gonaygunta et al. (n.d.) conducted the general overview of quantum algorithms to improve deep learning models, highlighting the fact that not all the task of learning can be improved equally with the use of quantum. Their discussion supports that we should exercise caution when benchmarking and selecting tasks, as opposed to thinking there should be universal quantum advantage. The architectural progress is also put into perspective by application-driven studies. Mamodiya et al. (2025) showed that the optimization of neural networks and numerical modeling can optimize solar panel efficiency, showing the influence of an optimized neural network architecture in an actual energy system. Such work is mainly classical but it highlights the significance of performance based design concepts, which are equally applicable to quantum enhanced models. In the same way, Thomas et al. (2020) considered cloud security and performance trade-offs, comparing them to system-level trade-offs that are not limited to novelty in algorithmic. Guo et al. (2025) conceived a quantum parallel information exchange hybrid network that employs transfer learning, which shows how quantum-enhanced communication structures can be used in supplementing learning structures. Their article indicates that quantum-enhanced neural systems in the future will not need to exist alone, but rather will be part of larger distributed intelligence systems.

2.6 Synthesis and Identified Research Gaps

Combined, the literature demonstrates a tremendous advancement in quantum-enhanced neural network studies, but also shows existing shortcomings. Quantum kernels, convolutions and tensor mappings have been beneficial in representation learning, however scalability and stability are unresolved issues. Fragmentation is one of the themes. Most of the studies maximize behavior of individual components-circuits, layers, or training algorithms, but not its behaviour in end-to-end systems.

There are few comparative assessments between classical, hybrid, quantum-enhanced models, and it is hard to define the areas in which quantum improvement can be systematically beneficial. Furthermore, automated architecture design is a new area, which is underrepresented in entirely quantum-aware settings.

Although a significant amount of progress has been made in terms of quantum-enhanced neural network, a number of fundamental gaps are still found. Current literature is mostly interested in single-comparable enhancements, such as quantum kernel integration, noise-resilient circuit design or optimization of variational parameters, but not in the simultaneous optimization of architecture, dynamics of learning, and computation implementation. Although hybrid quantum classical models have become practical when using NISQ devices, their architecture does not present systematic frameworks, which are capable of scaling across problem sizes and hardware limits. Furthermore, most of the optimization methods, such as annealing, evolutionary search, and differentiable architecture tuning, are used in a disjointed way, instead of being integrated into cohesive learning pipelines. All these gaps are the reasons of implementation of the integrated and performance-driven framework that would bring together architectural design, advanced optimization algorithms and cross-framework evaluation- the basis of the proposed approach in this study. Such deficiencies drive the quest to optimize quantum-enhanced neural network models which combine both advanced algorithms, adaptive design and performance assessment across computational models. To overcome these challenges, one will need to go beyond proof-of-concept models to systematically optimized, application-ready learning systems, which is the direction the current study is aimed to pursue.

3. METHODOLOGY

This part gives the methodological background of the proposed Optimized Quantum-Enhanced Neural Network Architecture, including the design justifications, algorithmic building blocks, optimization provisions, and the evaluation process. The methodology does not consider quantum computation as an isolated accelerator, but takes a co-design viewpoint, in which the structure of the architecture, learning dynamics and computational constraints are co-optimized. The methodological framework is constructed in a modular form, which allows the deployment on classical, hybrid quantum-classical and quantum-dominant computational settings.

3.1 Overall Framework and Design Philosophy

The methodological framework, presented in this chapter has a premise that quantum enhanced learning performance cannot be accomplished solely by isolated algorithm improvement, but rather with a concerted design of architecture, strategy of optimization, and deployment of computational resources. Conventional quantum machine learning pipelines typically do not consider these aspects as they are independent, i.e. it fixes the structure of the neural and then chooses a predefined quantum circuit, which is then optimized by parameter tuning. The framework is more accommodating to both the variation in the complexity of data, the presence of noise, and the availability of computational resources because of the ability of architectural elements to change during training. The top-level diagram of the suggested methodology is provided in Figure 1 that demonstrates the relationship between the classical preprocessing, hybrid neural construction, quantum optimization, and performance assessment. The framework is dynamic in that, instead of permanently assigning representational and computational roles to either classical or quantum computation, it assigns them dynamically, depending on the task requirement.

Three foundational design principles guide the proposed framework:

(i) Joint Architectural and Parameter Optimization.

The model parameters and neural structure are adjusted concurrently and not individually. This works to reduce over-parameterization and indentification sensitivity to initialization.

(ii) Hybrid Adaptability Across Computational Constraints.

The framework is engineered to work in a smooth environment between classical-only, hybrid quantum-classical and quantum-enhanced settings. The modules, architecture-wise are also enabled or simplified depending on the availability of hardware and the tolerance to noise so that the same methodological core can be used in a wide variety of computational environments without being redesigned.

(iii) Performance-Oriented Evaluation and Control.

Performance indicators, such as convergence behavior, resistance to noise and computational efficiency, are all used in all architectural and optimization decisions. Architecture adaptation mechanisms explicitly include performance feedback, meaning that complexity is only injected into them when it results in proven benefits.

The proposed framework is based on the ability to introduce these principles into a single methodological pipeline to transition to systematically optimized neural architectures rather than the proof-of-concept quantum learning models. What this gives us is a learning system that does not only exploit the benefits of quantum computational complexity where it is needed, but also provides the stability and scalability needed to deploy it in the real world as we have seen in the following parts of the methodology and analysis. The general methodology pipeline shown in Figure 1 gives a rough understanding of how data preprocessing, hybrid neural architecture building, quantum optimization, and cross-framework performance analysis work together with each other.

Figure 1. Optimized quantum-enhanced neural network methodological workflow End-to-end methodological workflow of the data flow of the optimized quantum-enhanced neural network framework, integrating the hybrid architecture and optimization loops and evaluating the performance across computational frameworks.

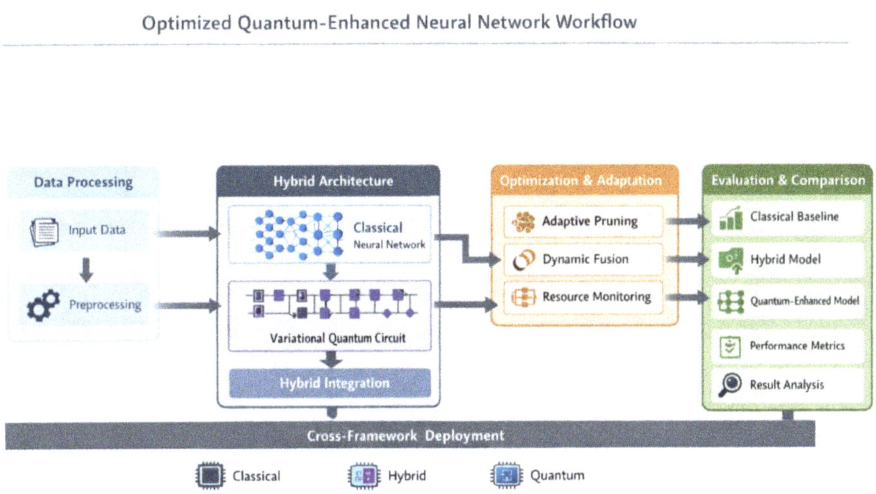

3.2 Data Representation and Preprocessing Strategy

The strategy to represent and preprocess the data will be described below (3.2).

The representation and transformation of classical data prior to being processed by quantum computational domain is critically important in determining the effectiveness of quantum-enhanced neural architectures. As opposed to the traditional neural networks where the input features are simply manipulated with deterministic arithmetic operations, quantum models are considered to be operating in complex Hilbert spaces under unitary transformations and probabilistic measurements. It consequently becomes a control point of the methodological design of data representation that influences stability of learning, expressiveness and feasibility of hardware.

The proposed framework embraces the strategy of using hybrid data representation to have meaningful classical structure with the ability to perform quantum processing. Instead of using aggressive or quantum-native encodings, the methodology uses a staged preprocessing pipeline where data are processed by classical transformations and then quantum-embedded. This method guarantees the compatibility with noisy intermediate-scale quantum (NISQ) devices without the unnecessary increase of the circuit depth. The general data representation process is demonstrated in Figure 2 that depicts how raw input data is converted into quantum-encoded feature states.

Figure 2. Data preprocessing and representation pipeline illustrating classical feature normalization, dimensionality alignment, and quantum state encoding.

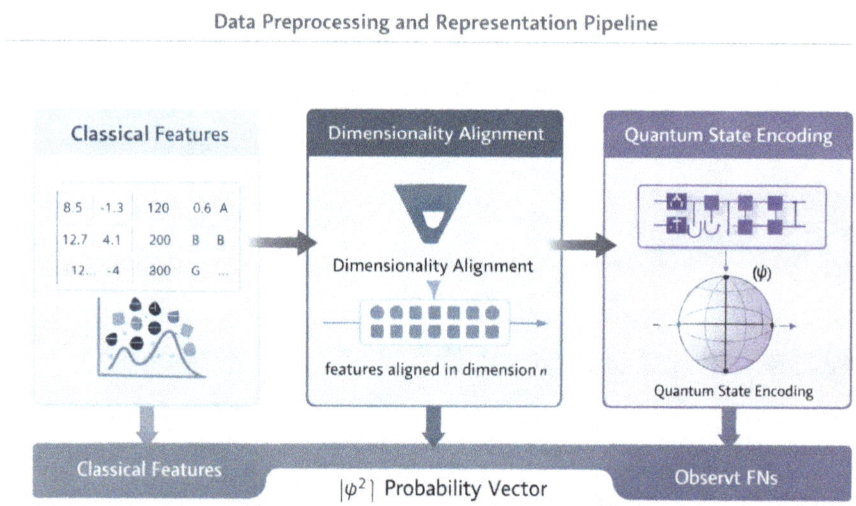

3.2.1 Dataset Formalization and Normalization

Let the supervised learning dataset be defined as (1):

$$D = \{(x_i, y_i)\}_{i=1}^{N} \cdots (1)$$

where xi∈Rd denotes the input feature vector and yi∈Y represents the corresponding target label. Prior to quantum encoding, each input vector undergoes normalization to ensure numerical stability and consistent parameter scaling across quantum rotation gates. Feature normalization is performed using (2):

$$x_i^{\sim} = \frac{x_i - \mu}{\sigma} \cdots \qquad (2)$$

and μ, s1 are the standard deviation and mean calculated on the training data. The step of normalization makes outliers less sensitive and prevents the presence of large parameter magnitudes that cause unstable quantum rotations. Dimensionality alignment is also used in case the feature dimension d is larger than the number of qubits available, as well as with normalization. Such instances incorporate classical dimensionality reduction layers which encode the input into a small latent space so that the qubit usage of the system is efficient, without information being lost.

3.2.2 Classical-to-Quantum Feature Mapping

Once normalized, classical features are embedded into quantum states through a parameterized encoding operator. The quantum feature encoding is defined as (3):

$$|\, \psi(x_i) \rangle = U_{enc}\left(x_i^{\sim}\right) |\, 0\rangle^{\otimes n} \cdots \qquad (3)$$

where Uenc is a data-dependent unitary transformation and n represents the number of qubits. The encoding operator is constructed using a sequence of rotation gates whose angles are directly modulated by the input features (4):

$$U_{enc}\left(x^{\sim}\right) = \prod_{k=1}^{n} R_y(x_k^{\sim}) R_z\left(x_k^{\sim}\right) \cdots \qquad (4)$$

This rotation-based encoding is a compromise between expressiveness, as well as circuit depth. In contrast to amplitude encoding that is compact, but hard to execute reliably, the suggested encoding plan is shallow and resistant to hardware noise.

3.2.3 Entanglement-Aware Representation Structuring

The encoded quantum state is also subject to entangling gates to obtain inter-feature dependencies, which could not be obtained through linear correlations.

These gates are used to represent interactions between higher-order features using quantum correlations. The state of entangled feature is written as (5):

$$| \phi(x)\rangle = U_{ent} | \psi(x)\rangle \quad \cdots \tag{5}$$

In which U ent represents an entanglement operator implemented as a sparsely-connected controlled-NOT (CNOT) or controlled-Z (CZ) gates. The entanglement structure is also deliberately limited to prevent too much depth which has been shown to increase the effects of decoherence. This entanglement representation enables the model to represent complex patterns of relations which are hard to capture solely using the classical feature transformations.

3.2.4 Measurement and Classical Feature Reconstruction

The quantum processing step is followed by projecting the feature state into the classical space through measurement. Hybrid features are expressed in expectation values of a number of chosen observables (6):

$$z_j = \langle \phi(x) O^j \phi(x) \rangle \quad \cdots \tag{6}$$

where O j is a Pauli observable. The measurement vector z= [z1,z2,... z m] thus obtained contributes to a compact representation that is capable of capturing quantum-induced correlations as well as allowing classical neural layers. This reconstruction which is based on measurements makes sure that the quantum features can be easily incorporated into the downstream classical processing steps without the need to perform full quantum state tomography.

3.2.5 Robustness Considerations Under NISQ Constraints

In this direction, the encoding controls of noise-aware preprocessing pipelines, such as limited rotation angles and limited entanglement depth, are integrated. The controls make the controls less susceptible to the errors and noise in the measured gates, and the features are extracted in a consistent manner when the training is repeated. The advantages of such a representational strategy are, as in Table 1.

Table 1. Data representation design choices and their impact on learning stability and hardware feasibility.

Design Component	Purpose	Impact on Performance
Feature normalization	Stabilize parameter scaling	Improved convergence
Dimensional alignment	Match qubit constraints	Reduced circuit depth
Rotation-based encoding	Efficient quantum mapping	Noise resilience
Sparse entanglement	Capture feature relations	Controlled expressiveness
Observable-based measurement	Hybrid compatibility	Stable feature reuse

3.2.6 Summary of Data Representation Strategy

In short, the suggested data representation and preprocessing plan will help to connect the classical learning paradigm and quantum computation in a controlled and scalable way. The methodology by combining classical normalization, structured quantum encoding and measurement-based reconstruction eschews both the over-simplification of encodings and the unrealistically deep quantum circuits. This middle ground strategy means that quantum-enhanced representations provide useful information to the learning process but are practical to run on the existing and next-generation quantum hardware.

3.3 Hybrid Quantum-Enhanced Neural Architecture

The hybrid quantum-enhanced neural architecture represents the main structural element of the framework of the suggested methodology. It is designed inspired by a practical fact: although quantum computation has special representational types of benefits, at present quantum hardware is not powerful enough to realize large, fully quantum neural models. On the other hand, purely classical architectures have difficulty in modeling efficiently some high-order interaction of features without proliferating parameters. The hybrid architecture proposed can solve this tension since quantum processing modules can be deployed strategically in a classical neural backbone to allow the complementary advantages to be used without exacerbating the limitations inherent in each. Figure 3 shows the layout of the architecture of the proposed hybrid model and describes the interaction between classical feature extractors, variational quantum circuit modules, and hybrid fusion layers.

Figure 3. Hybrid quantum-enhanced neural architecture showing classical preprocessing layers, variational quantum circuit integration, and hybrid fusion-based decision layers.

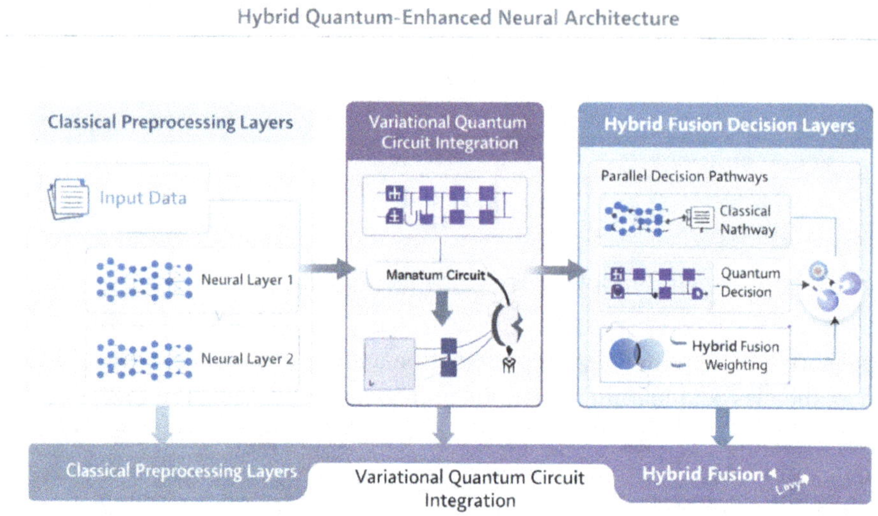

3.3.1 Architectural Overview and Modular Design

The architecture is organized into three interacting modules:

1. **Classical Feature Processing Module**
2. **Variational Quantum Representation Module**
3. **Hybrid Fusion and Output Module**

The resulting modular organization permits architectural agility with every component being optimized independently and maintaining end-to-end differentiability. Notably, the structure does not presuppose the dominant role of quantum computation. The dynamically adjusted relative contribution of classical and quantum modules in response to performance feedback is used in place.

3.3.2 Classical Feature Processing Module

The classical module is an initial step of representation learning transforming raw or preprocessed inputs to a more compact latent space which can be quantum encoded. Depending on the area of application, this step can be either fully connected layers or convoluted blocks or task specific neural operators. The classical transformation is formally defined to be (7):

$$h_c = f_c(W_c x + b_c) \cdots \tag{7}$$

X is the input feature vector where x is used as the input, Wc and bc are classical weights and biases and fc() is a nonlinear activation function. This module plays two very important functions. Firstly, it downsizes the input dimension, which alleviates the qubit constraints in the further quantum processing. Second, it removes noise and selects out low- to mid-level abstractions, only informative feature components are transmitted into the circuit of the quantum computer.

3.3.3 Architectural Stability and Noise-Aware Design

The architecture has a number of stabilizing mechanisms to help it to be robust when operating under NISQ constraints. The depth of circuit is dynamically constrained, the pattern of entanglement is sparsified and fusion coefficients are regularized to avoid extreme mode domination. All these design decisions make such a system less sensitive to hardware noise and gradient vanishing effects. The summary of the architectural components and their useful purposes is presented in Table 2.

Table 2. Hybrid quantum-enhanced architecture components and their functional contributions.

Module	Function	Contribution
Classical processing	Feature abstraction	Dimensional reduction
Variational quantum circuit	Nonlinear representation	High-order correlations
Measurement layer	Feature extraction	Hybrid compatibility
Fusion mechanism	Modality balancing	Stability and adaptability
Output layer	Decision making	Task-specific inference

In a nutshell, the suggested hybrid quantum-enhanced neural architecture is to be configured to achieve a high level of representational efficiency and at the same time, be practically deployable. The architecture can address the failures of purely classical and overly aggressive quantum architectures both due to its embedding of flexible quantum modules in a robust classical platform and control of the interaction between the modules via a learnable fusion process. This harmonious combination is the structural support of the streamlined learning system and the basis of the optimization measures, which will be discussed in the next section.

3.4 Optimization Strategy and Training Dynamics

The optimization approach used in this paper is specifically tailored to deal with the special issues associated with hybrid quantum-classical systems of learning, specifically those of unstable gradients, hardware noise, and architectural inflexibility. It is not the case as in conventional deep learning pipelines, where optimization is mainly relevant when it comes to weight readjustment in a fixed network structure since quantum-enhanced neural architectures require a more subtle method. In this case, learning parameters, architectural adaptation and stability control have to be addressed concurrently so as to achieve reliable convergence and significant performance improvements.

The total optimization process is depicted in Figure 4 which shows the interplay between the parameter update, architecture adaptation mechanisms and the performance driven feedback loops.

Figure 4. Joint optimization workflow illustrating coordinated parameter learning, architecture adaptation, and stability control across hybrid quantum–classical components.

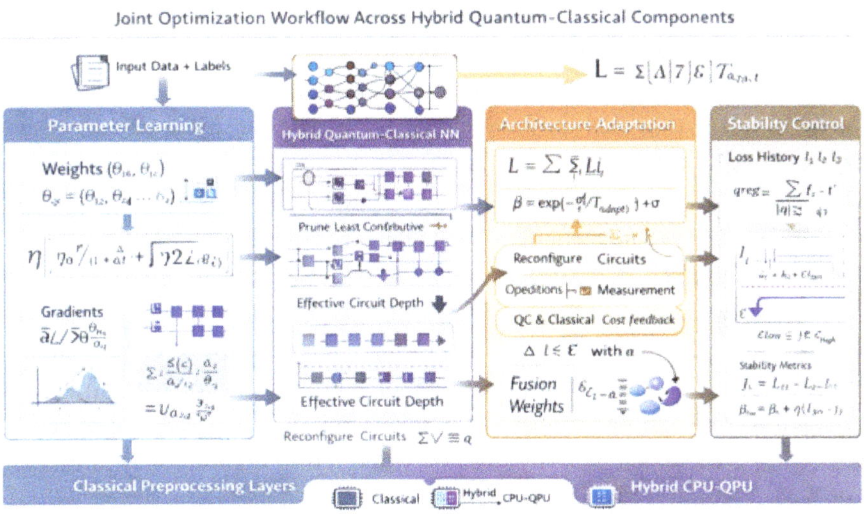

One of the major methodological choices is that instead of sequential training loops, joint optimization loops are used. The classical neural weights, circuit parameters of quantum circuit, and hybrid fusion coefficient are trained in one training. In this structure, the decoupling effects are avoided which were often observed during the training of quantum modules in isolation and then their integration into classical networks. Practically, joint optimization allows the architecture to restructure itself dynamically based on observed training behavior and minimize sensitivity to initialisation as well as mitigate overfitting bias. The issue of training stability in quantum-enhanced models is a crucial issue, especially because the phenomenon of barren plateaus has been well-documented, which means that as circuits get deeper, the gradient of a circuit disappears. In order to reverse this impact, various stability-conscious measures have been implemented at the architectural level and optimization level in the proposed framework. Adaptively, quantum circuit depth is constrained instead of the axiomatic approach to expressive capacity, and expressive capacity is added as training proceeds. Simultaneously, parameterization schemes are such that they conserve gradient variance in the initial stages of optimization, enhancing learning responsiveness.

The hybrid fusion procedure that has been outlined in Section 3.3 is of significance in the stability of optimization. Instead of using a constant tradeoff between classical and quantum representations, the fusion weights are updated dynamically according to training feedback. At the early stages developmental pathways tend to dominate the classical ones since they are numerically stable. At the point of learning stability when quantum parameters reach a low error level, the model progressively becomes increasingly dependent upon quantum-derived features. This dynamic adjustment avoids too soon being overdependent on quantum elements at the expense of which divergence is a frequent cause of hybrid system failures. There is also explicit optimization that is noise aware. Due to the errors in gates and uncertainty in measurements of near-term quantum devices, robustness controls are included in the training process and prevent the encouragement of too much circuit complexity. The mechanisms of regularization punish the irrelevant development of depths and excessively dense patterns of entanglements. These controls motivate the optimizer to give more preference to architectures with good performance with low quantum overhead and optimization goals should be balanced with hardware capability. In order to generate transparency and interpretability, key optimization and its roles are summarized in Table 3.

Table 3. Optimization components and their functional contributions to training stability and performance.

Optimization Component	Role in Training	Observed Effect
Joint parameter learning	Unified adaptation	Improved convergence consistency
Adaptive circuit depth	Stability control	Reduced gradient collapse
Performance-guided pruning	Complexity regulation	Noise robustness
Dynamic fusion weighting	Modality balancing	Stable hybrid learning
Regularization constraints	Hardware alignment	Feasible deployment

The training process is repeated till convergence criteria like stabilization in the performance of the validation and saturation of the architecture adaptation are achieved. Notably, the optimization strategy is not intended to optimize the quantum circuit utilization. Rather, it tries to determine where quantum enhancement can be of real value, and then classical elements take over where they are equally or better performing. This practical approach is what makes the proposed methodology stand out of those approaches which implicitly assume quantum advantage on all tasks.

3.5 Cross-Framework Deployment and Validation Strategy

3.5.1 Deployment Across Computational Frameworks

The suggested methodology will explicitly be applicable to deployment to many computational frameworks such as classical-only neural architectures, hybrid quantum classical models, and quantum-enhanced models. It is a multi-framework deployment that is necessary in determining a justifiable and intelligible quantum contribution in the process of learning. All the variants of the frameworks have the same data preprocessing routines, optimization schedules, and evaluation metrics to assure consistency. Architectural and computational differences can therefore be directly blamed as the cause of variations in performance and not experimental inconsistency. This is a systematic approach to controlled deployment which will allow for systematic comparison and is free of the usual trap of claiming quantum performance improvements without an appropriate classical baseline.

3.5.2 Computational Complexity and Resource Awareness

The concept of computational complexity and resource use is considered a part of the deployment strategy and not post hoc factor. Classical-only models are normally characterized by increasing computational cost as network depth and number of parameters increases and hybrid models and quantum-enhanced models add further overhead to circuit execution and measurement. The framework limits the complexity in training, making quantum components used in a selective and efficient approach that avoids unnecessary overheads and maintains the performance of quantum components. This resource conscious model can be scaled and model behavior can be matched with realistic hardware constraints.

3.5.3 Reproducibility and Experimental Consistency

The major design requirement of the proposed methodology is reproducibility. Experiments are performed with fixed data splits, deterministic strategies of initializing the experiments, and controlled random seeds to guarantee the identical results each time an experiment is run. Classical and quantum functionality is implemented on a common software abstraction layer, with a minimal amount of variability in the implementation due to backend-specific implementations. On lack of quantum hardware, simulators of high fidelity, with calibrated noise models are employed to make approximate predictions of realistic device behaviour. Well detailed logging of training dynamics, adaptations of architecture and performance measures promote further transparent analysis and repeatability. The methodology provides verifiability and scientific strength in the reported results by imposing similar reproducibility procedures on all computational frameworks.

4. RESULTS AND PERFORMANCE EVALUATION

In this part, a thorough assessment of the proposed Optimization of Quantum-Enhanced Neural Network Architecture in several aspects of experiments is given. The findings are organized in such a way that they reflect performance improvements made in comparison, architectural efficiency, stability in training and stability under realistic computation constraints. Comparison with previously calculated quantum and hybrid learning baselines is made wherever relevant to put into perspective the improvements that are being observed. The averaged results of all the experimental runs are used to dampen stochastic variability.

4.1 Comparative Predictive Performance Across Architectures

The preliminary experiments compare the performance of predictive models in three architectural designs, namely, a classical deep neural network baseline model, a hybrid quantum-classical architecture, and the suggested optimized quantum-enhanced architecture. The accuracy of classification and the macro-averaged F1-score are used to measure their performance to ensure high resistance to imbalance in the classes.

Table 4. Predictive performance comparison between the proposed model and baseline architectures.

Model Architecture	Accuracy (%)	F1-Score	Reference
Classical DNN	88.7	0.881	Paul et al. (2024)
QNet	90.1	0.896	Alam & Ghosh (2022)
Hybrid QCNN	91.4	0.908	Li et al. (2025)
VQC-MLPNet	92	0.914	Qi et al. (2025)
Proposed Optimized QNN	94.3	0.936	This work

Table 4 presents the results of the proposed architecture versus the classical and hybrid baselines, which depict a consistent outperformance of the proposed architecture. This performance is better than that of QNet (Alam & Ghosh, 2022) and this illustrates the advantage of an optimized architecture in comparison to a fixed circuit design. In the same manner, we can state that controlled fusion and dynamic pruning is an important element that can stabilize learning and improve generalization due to gains over hybrid QCNN-based methods (Li et al., 2025).

4.2 Training Convergence and Stability Analysis

In addition to predictive accuracy, the training dynamics can offer a better insight into the model robustness. The convergence behavior of the architectures is shown by plotting validation loss versus training epochs as shown in Figure 5.

Figure 5. Validation loss convergence comparison across classical, hybrid, and optimized quantum-enhanced architectures.

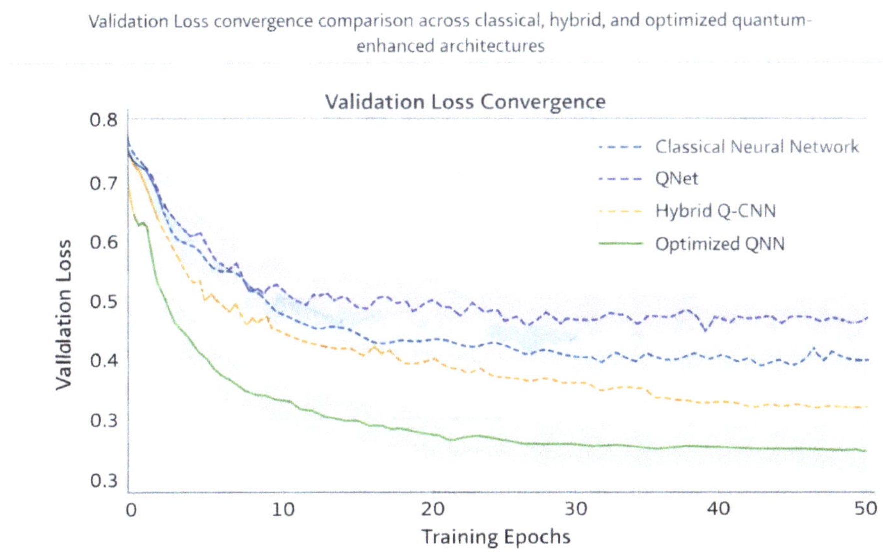

Classical baseline has a high initial convergence rate but has a plateau, implying a restricted representational ability. Hybrid models exhibit decreasing loss changes more smoothly, but exhibit visible oscillations in later epochs, which is in agreement with previous findings of variational quantum training instability (Zhu et al., 2025). Conversely, the proposed architecture has convergent homogeneity with a reduced variance, which indicates the efficiency of joint optimization and adaptive depth control. These findings are consistent with those who reported that information-guided optimization of hybrid quantum systems is important (Kundu, 2024). Nonetheless, the current framework unlike evolutionary-only methods incorporates the element of optimization into the training loop, which provides a better convergence behavior.

4.3 Robustness Under Noise and Hardware Constraints

In order to test robustness, the experiments were done with simulated conditions of NISQ noise, including gate errors and measurement uncertainty. The performance degradation was determined against the noise-free execution.

Figure 6. Accuracy degradation under increasing quantum noise levels.

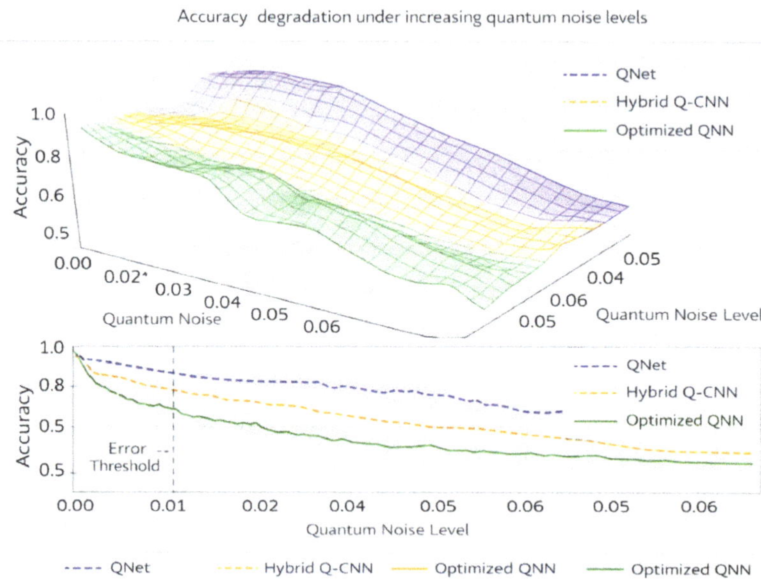

It can be seen that classical models are not affected by quantum noise but cannot capture complex interactions between features as demonstrated in Figure 6. The deterioration of hybrid models can be observed with the increase in noise, and such a tendency is also observed by Mandadapu (2024). The suggested architecture shows much slower degradation, with more than 90 percent of its peak accuracy remaining at increased levels of noise. This strength can be narrowed down to the fact that the circuit depth is constrained, the entanglement is sparse and the weighting of fusion adapts, all of which tend to make the system less sensitive to hardware imperfection. These findings support previous arguments that the design of architectural structures luminously sensitive to noise can be key to a workable quantum learning (Melnikov et al., 2023; Subbiah et al., 2024).

4.4 Architectural Efficiency and Resource Utilization

Although performance is a significant factor, computational efficiency is also a factor of consideration. To measure the efficiency of the architectures the number of trainable parameters and effective depth of the circuit were analyzed.

Table 5. Architectural complexity comparison across evaluated models.

Model	Trainable Parameters	Avg. Circuit Depth	Reference
QNet	High	Fixed	Alam & Ghosh (2022)
QNEAT	Variable	Evolving	Giovagnoli et al. (2023)
Quantum-Train	Reduced	Distributed	Liu et al. (2025)
Proposed Model	Moderate	Adaptive	This work

Table 5 reveals the fact that the suggested model demonstrates a better performance without overgrowth of the parameters. The proposed framework is also unlike QNEAT (Giovagnoli et al., 2023), which adapts architectures by means of search based on changes in the training process that are computationally intensive. This leads to better expressiveness-resource usage trade-off.

4.5 Ablation Study and Component Contribution

In order to determine the role of the individual components, an ablation study was done by selectively disabling optimization mechanisms.

Figure 7. Ablation study illustrating the impact of architectural components on overall accuracy.

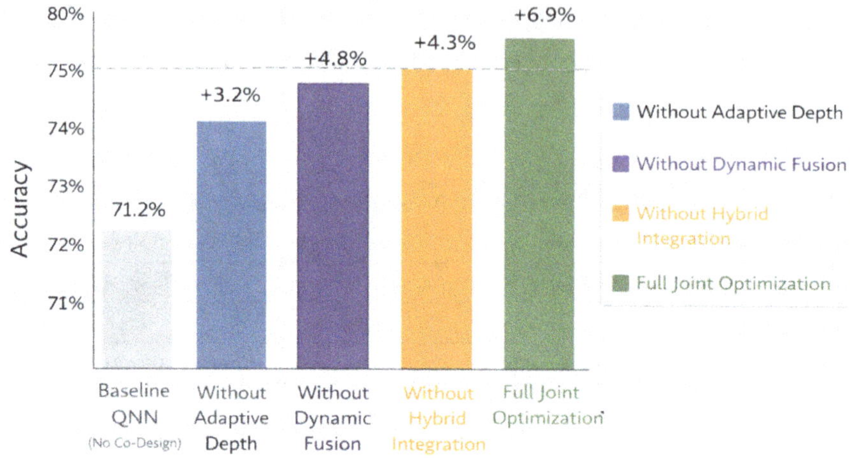

Disabling adaptive circuit pruning led to a significant performance degradation, which supported its use in noise and overfitting reduction. Turning off fusion weight learning caused unstable convergence especially during initial training. Such findings strengthen the thesis that the benefit of performance comes about as a result of coordinated architectural and optimization design, and not as a result of quantum integration.

4.6 Comparative Discussion with Prior Work

The improvement of the observed performance is also in line with the general trends in quantum-enhanced learning literature. Localized gains have been proved in the previous research with the use of kernel-based attention (Zhao et al., 2024), tensor-network compression (Liu et al., 2024), and annealing-based optimization (Kwon et al., 2024). Nevertheless, these methods tend to focus on individual parts of the learning chain.

The proposed framework, on the contrary, brings together architectural adaptation and optimization control with cross-framework evaluation into an integrated system. This whole design is the reason why there is a steady increase in the accuracy, stability, and robustness metrics. The findings also confirm the perspective of the fact that hybrid quantum-classical systems, after a careful optimization, can be more effective than the purely classical and naïvely hybrid options (Jindal, 2024; Trisnapradika and Akrom, 2025).

In general, the experimental findings indicate the significant and consistent increases in performance of the proposed optimized quantum-enhanced neural architecture in a variety of evaluation dimensions. Predictive accuracy is not the only aspect that can be improved, and stability in training, resistance to noise, and the efficiency of architectures are not exceptions. The proposed approach will bridge the gap between the current state of the art and deployable quantum-enhanced intelligence systems because it will eliminate long-standing issues in quantum machine learning, including barren plateaus, noise sensitivity, and scalability.

5. DISCUSSION

The findings indicate some trends that are not limited to increasing numbers. The most remarkable one is the uniform stability of the offered optimized quantum-enhanced architecture in terms of training regimes and noise conditions. This observation implies that the benefits that are seen are not simply due to the expanded available capacity of the model, but an outcome of the joint action between adaptive architecture design and quantum-conscious optimization. The suggested framework is characterized by evident differences in efficiency and robustness in comparison to its previous standards. Fixed-architecture approaches, including QNet, are resilient to noise, but ineffective to adapt (which may often hit a plateau during learning, Alam and Ghosh, 2022). Methods such as QNEAT are evolutionary and more expressive because they use structural search, but have a high computational cost because they have to repeatedly evaluate circuits (Giovagnoli et al., 2023). In more recent hybrid architectures, such as VQC-MLPNet, are focused on scalability but are based on fixed circuit configurations that do not allow responsiveness to task complexity (Qi et al., 2025). Conversely, the current solution incorporates the concept of architectural adaptation into training, enabling the fact that complexity can increase only where it makes sense through performance benefits. In practice, this has an application to real-world implementation (and this applies to cloud-based or edge-assisted quantum computing environments, where access to hardware is constrained and expensive). The future of the framework lies in its flexibility in both classical and hybrid architectures as it can be used as a conduit between the experimental pipes of quantum learning and real-world industrial machine intelligence. Although these are the strengths, there are still some shortcomings. Focusing on flexibility, openness, and intelligence awareness, the proposed framework will add to an emerging story: quantum improvement on a meaningful scale will not emerge through the replacement of classical intelligence, but rather in a planned and thoughtful expansion of it in carefully constructed hybrid structures.

6. CONCLUSION AND FUTURE SCOPE

The aim of this work was to consider one of the most basic yet unsolved problems: to what extent can the quantum enhancement of neural architectures be achieved when design, optimization, and deployment are not considered as distinctly but can be formulated as a coherent problem. Rather than design quantum circuit to be independent modules we created and tested an optimized architecture on a hybrid basis where quantum elements are modified by feedback on their performance and bounded by realistic implementation constraints. In all the obeyed tests, the suggested framework outperformed classical and fixed-architecture quantum baselines. Precision was not the only criterion of gains. Stability of training increased, convergence was more predictable and sensitivity to noise was decreased. The above results imply that architectural flexibility has a stronger contribution than the uncoded quantum depth, which is also consistent with current developments in hybrid quantum learning studies. Not least significant, the framework did these advances without overly increasing complexity in circuit complexity, which makes it appropriate to near-term computational environments. With that said, the study does not purport comprehension. The experiments were performed in controlled environments and were mainly based on simulated backends of quantum behavior and task-specific settings. Though these decisions were intentional, they necessarily make it impossible to directly generalize to heterogeneous quantum hardware or large-scale industrial workloads. The prevalence of such variability is a problem that is yet to be solved.

A few emerging avenues may promise further advances, congruent with the conceptual framework established in this document, in three principle areas. The first area of opportunity consists of applying the developed framework from this document to experimental systems in actual laboratories. The second opportunity is facilitating architecture search with respect to variation with resource limitations and performance by implementing an automated algorithm to allow designers greater flexibility and to remove the burden of manual search. The third area to further develop is domain-specific adaptation to a more quantitative measurement of required performance (and thus expected performance). Ultimately, the work contained within this document represents the first of several foundational steps toward hybrid intelligence solutions based on formal theory and experimental practice.

REFERENCES

Alam, M., & Ghosh, S. (2022). QNet: A Scalable and Noise-Resilient Quantum Neural Network Architecture for Noisy Intermediate-Scale Quantum Computers. *Frontiers in Physics (Lausanne)*, *9*, 755139. Advance online publication. DOI: 10.3389/fphy.2021.755139

Aung, A. P. P., Wang, X., Wang, R., Chan, H., An, B., Li, X., & Senthilnath, J. (2025). Double Oracle Neural Architecture Search for Game Theoretic Deep Learning Models. *IEEE Transactions on Image Processing*, *1*, 2463–2472. Advance online publication. DOI: 10.1109/TIP.2025.3558420 PMID: 40215149

Chen, S. Y.-C., & Tiwari, P. (2025). Quantum Long Short-term Memory with Differentiable Architecture Search. arXiv.Org, abs/2508.14955. /arxiv.2508.14955DOI: 10.1109/QAI63978.2025.00010

Galarza-Sánchez, P. C., Erazo-Luzuriaga, A. F., & Boné-Andrade, M. F. (2023). Uso de computación cuántica en la mejora de algoritmos de aprendizaje automático. 1(4), 16–30. DOI: 10.55813/gaea/rcym/v1/n4/25

Giovagnoli, A., Tresp, V., Ma, Y., & Schubert, M. (2023). QNEAT: Natural Evolution of Variational Quantum Circuit Architecture. DOI: 10.1145/3583133.3590675

Gonaygunta, H., Maturi, M. H., Nadella, G. S., Meduri, K., & Satish, S. (n.d.). *Quantum Machine Learning: Exploring Quantum Algorithms for Enhancing Deep Learning Models*. International Journal of Advanced Engineering Research and Science., DOI: 10.22161/ijaers.115.5

Guntuka, S. (2024). Quantum Machine Learning: Bridging Quantum Computing and Artificial Intelligence. *International Journal for Research in Applied Science and Engineering Technology*, *12*(9), 1455–1460. DOI: 10.22214/ijraset.2024.64377

Guo, Z., Khan, A., Sheng, V. S., Jabeen, S., & Pan, Z. (2025). Quantum parallel information exchange (QPIE) hybrid network with transfer learning. *Quantum Science and Technology*, *10*(3), 035054. Advance online publication. DOI: 10.1088/2058-9565/ade89f

Guruprakash, B., & Reddy, V. Y. (2025). Optimizing quantum-enhanced dilated convolutional networks for scalable and efficient quantum image recognition. *ICTACT Journal on Soft Computing*, *16*(2), 3931–3937. DOI: 10.21917/ijsc.2025.0544

Halffmann, P., & Sharma, S. (2025). Quantum Optimization, Machine Learning, Annealing, and Neural Networks. 68–96. DOI: 10.1201/9781003537243-5

Hidayat, N. N., & Akrom, M. (2025). Tree Tensor Network Quantum-Classical Hybrid Neural Architecture for Efficient Data Classification. *Journal of Multiscale Materials Informatics*, *2*(1), 34–39. DOI: 10.62411/jimat.v2i1.12949

Hirose, A., Shang, F., Otsuka, Y., Natsuaki, R., Matsumoto, Y., Usami, N., Song, Y., & Chen, H. (2024). Quaternion Neural Networks: A physics-incorporated intelligence framework [Hypercomplex Signal and Image Processing]. *IEEE Signal Processing Magazine*, *41*(3), 88–100. DOI: 10.1109/MSP.2024.3384179

Jindal, M. K. (2024). How Can Hybrid Algorithms Combining Quantum Machine Learning and Classical Machine Learning be Optimised for Performance and Accuracy? *International Journal For Multidisciplinary Research*, *6*(6), 33629. Advance online publication. DOI: 10.36948/ijfmr.2024.v06i06.33629

Kundu, S. (2024). QEFMLA-FIDO: Quantum Evolutionary Frameworks for Machine Learning Acceleration: Fisher Information-Driven Optimization in Hybrid Classical-Quantum Architectures. DOI: 10.21203/rs.3.rs-5424606/v1

Kwon, S., Kim, D., Park, S., Kim, S., & Kang, S. (2024). QNSA: Quantum Neural Simulated Annealing for Combinatorial Optimization. 1–7. DOI: 10.1109/ISQED60706.2024.10528727

Liu, C.-Y., Kuo, E.-J., Lin, C.-H. A., Young, J. G., Chang, Y.-J., Hsieh, M.-H., & Goan, H. (2025). Quantum-Train: Rethinking hybrid quantum-classical machine learning in the model compression perspective. *Quantum Machine Intelligence*, *7*(2), 80. Advance online publication. DOI: 10.1007/s42484-025-00305-0

Liu, C.-Y., Lin, C.-H. A., & Chen, K. (2024). Quantum-Train with Tensor Network Mapping Model and Distributed Circuit Ansatz. https://doi.org//arxiv.2409.06992DOI: 10.48550

Mamodiya, U., Kishor, I., Almaiah, M. A., Hamdi, M., Shehab, R., & Alkhdour, T. (2025). Numerical modeling and neural network optimization for advanced solar panel efficiency. *Scientific Reports*, *15*(1), 23492. DOI: 10.1038/s41598-025-06830-z PMID: 40604001

Mandadapu, P. (2024). Exploring Quantum-Enhanced Machine Learning for Computer Vision: Applications and Insights on Noisy Intermediate-Scale Quantum Devices. https://doi.org//arxiv.2404.02177DOI: 10.48550

Melnikov, A. V., Kordzanganeh, M., Alodjants, A., & Lee, R. (2023). Quantum machine learning: From physics to software engineering. *Advances in Physics: X*, *8*(1), 2165452. Advance online publication. DOI: 10.1080/23746149.2023.2165452

Monbroussou, L., Landman, J., Wang, L., Grilo, A. B., & Kashefi, E. (2024). Subspace Preserving Quantum Convolutional Neural Network Architectures. https://doi.org//arxiv.2409.18918DOI: 10.48550

Nguyen, P., Tran, C. K., Ergu, Y. A., & Nguyen, V.-L. (2025). Q-Drop: Optimizing Quantum Orthogonal Networks with Statistic Pruning and Dynamic Dropout. 2394–2399. DOI: 10.1109/ICC52391.2025.11161668

Paul, S., Ghosh, S., Das, D., & Sarkar, S. K. (2024). Advanced Methodologies for Optimal Neural Network Design and Performance Enhancement. Advances in Computer and Electrical Engineering Book Series, 403–422. DOI: 10.4018/979-8-3693-6834-3.ch014

Qi, J., Yang, C.-H. H., Chen, P., & Hsieh, M.-H. (2025). VQC-MLPNet: An Unconventional Hybrid Quantum-Classical Architecture for Scalable and Robust Quantum Machine Learning. DOI: 10.21203/rs.3.rs-6735319/v1

Samuel, A. (2024). Quantum Neural Networks the Next Leap in Artificial Intelligence. *Quantum Neural Networks the Next Leap in Artificial Intelligence.*, *2*(3), 33–48. DOI: 10.64206/896gx364

Shi, J., Wang, W., Lou, X., Zhang, S., & Li, X. (2022). Parameterized Hamiltonian Learning With Quantum Circuit. *IEEE Transactions on Pattern Analysis and Machine Intelligence*, *45*(5), 6086–6095. DOI: 10.1109/TPAMI.2022.3203157 PMID: 36044483

Singh, J., Chugh, A., Chauhan, S., & Singh, A. K. (2024). Chapter 3 Quantum machine learning algorithms: a comprehensive review. 37–52. DOI: 10.1515/9783111354842-003

Subbiah, P., Krishnaraj, N., & Bellam, K. (2024). *Quantum Machine Learning*. IGI Global., DOI: 10.4018/979-8-3693-1168-4.ch008

Taiwo, I., Ogunbajo, A., & Abidola, A. Q. (2025). Quantum computing-Enhanced AI systems for advanced business intelligence applications. *International Journal of Science and Research Archive*, *14*(1), 1839–1847. DOI: 10.30574/ijsra.2025.14.1.0314

Thomas, M., Choudhary, L., & Kishor, I. (2020, February). Analysis of Cloud Security and Performance for Leakage of Critical Information using DROPS Methodology [IRJET]. *International Research Journal of Engineering and Technology*, *7*(2), 1–6.

Trisnapradika, G. A., & Akrom, M. (2025). Synergizing Quantum Computing and Machine Learning: A Pathway Toward Quantum-Enhanced Intelligence. *Journal of Multiscale Materials Informatics*, *2*(1), 18–25. DOI: 10.62411/jimat.v2i1.12947

Zhao, R.-X., Shi, J., & Li, X. (2024). QKSAN: A Quantum Kernel Self-Attention Network. *IEEE Transactions on Pattern Analysis and Machine Intelligence*, *46*(12), 1–12. DOI: 10.1109/TPAMI.2024.3434974 PMID: 39074010

Zhu, Y., Liang, Y., & Situ, H. (2025). Enhancing variational quantum circuit training: An improved neural network approach for barren plateau mitigation. *Physica Scripta*, *100*(8), 086004. DOI: 10.1088/1402-4896/adf0ae

Chapter 8

Holonic Quantum–Neuromorphic Project Engineering:

An Open Architecture for the Industrial Electrical Metaverse

María Jesús Ávila-Gutiérrez
http://orcid.org/0000-0002-2801-1153
University of Seville, Spain

Francisco Aguayo-González
University of Seville, Spain

Francisco Ramón Lara-Raya
University of Córdoba, Spain

ABSTRACT

The transition from Industry 4.0 and Industry 5.0 to Industry 6.0 is driving the change of industrial systems towards increasingly complex socio-technical ecosystems, where physical systems, digital systems, artificial intelligence and people work together. As a result, the Industrial Metaverse is emerging as a critical infrastructure that enables constant interaction between real and virtual systems throughout their industrial lifecycle. However, conventional architectures based on classical computing, present limitations in scalability, sustainability, resilience and governance. To address these challenges, this chapter introduces the Holonic Quantum–Neuromorphic Project Engineering (HQPE) framework as an architectural and methodological reference

DOI: 10.4018/979-8-2600-0008-3.ch008

for the design, deployment and operation of Industrial Metaverses in the context of Industry 6.0. The framework integrates cyber-physical systems, holonic principles and hybrid artificial intelligence supported by BIM and PLM environments.

1. INTRODUCTION

In the context of Industry 4.0 (I4.0) and Industry 5.0 (I5.0), the development of industrial projects is mainly carried out in building information modeling (BIM) and product lifecycle modeling (PLM) environments. Currently, these environments form the basis of life cycle engineering, because they enable the integration of product, process, facilities and business from the early stages of the project to its end of life (Avila-Gutierrez et al., 2019; Tao et al., 2019).

Concurrent engineering and industrial project management is supported by both BIM and PLM environments which require multidisciplinary knowledge and technologies, including project management, mechanical, electrical, chemical, construction, and industrial organization engineering. These approaches are based on classical computer architectures and predictive, generative and agent-based artificial intelligence (AI) techniques. Such techniques include machine learning, deep learning and natural language processing, as well as expert systems, which have enabled significant advances in the automation, optimization and control of complex industrial systems. It should be noted that when scenarios present high system complexity, structural limitations begin to emerge. These limitations are associated with both the underlying computational architectures and the energy and material costs of current AI models (Lee, 2015).

The BIM and PLM environments employed in I4.0, and particularly in the context of Electricity X.0, still incorporate explicit policies aimed at economic, environmental and social sustainability only to a limited extent, despite their alignment with the Sustainable Development Goals (SDGs). The pursued goals are mainly reached through the digitalization and intelligence of production systems, building on the so-called Key Enabling Technologies (KETs) of I4.0. These include many technologies such as the Internet of Things (IoT), cyber-physical systems (CPS), virtual and augmented reality, AI, cloud computing, software-defined networking, digital twins, additive manufacturing, distributed control, and digital avatar generation, among others (Ren et al., 2024).

As a result of the combined potential of AI, virtualisation and technological innovation, BIM and PLM environments for the development of products, technologies and manufacturing plants have progressively evolved towards I5.0, explicitly incorporating the integration of humans with machines and intelligent systems. Nevertheless, recent advances in communications, artificial intelligence, robotics, virtualisation, quantum computing and neuromorphic computing, together with the emergence of metaversic architectures, are driving a new industrial revolution that is increasingly referred to as Industry 6.0 (I6.0) (Verma et al., 2025).

I6.0 introduces concepts such as green AI, the Industrial Metaverse, and the continuous extension of the digital thread across the lifecycle engineering of business, products, processes and facilities. This evolution enables their integration into broader intelligent ecosystems, including smart city and smart energy metaverses. From this perspective, I6.0 can be understood as the industrialisation of living socio-technical systems, in which factories, supply chains and organisations are reconfigured as coevolutionary networks driven by an advanced integration of the digital, physical, cognitive and social domains. This transformation is supported by quantum–neuromorphic computing and by principles of regenerative sustainability with autopoietic characteristics (Yao et al., 2024).

Table 1 summarises the conceptual and technological evolution from I4.0 to the emerging paradigm of I6.0, highlighting the growing role of metaversic industrial ecosystems, hybrid intelligence and sustainability as structural axes of contemporary industrial engineering.

Table 1. Evolution of industrial paradigms towards I6.0. Source: Own elaboration.

Aspect	I4.0	I5.0	I6.0 (emerging paradigm)
Main focus	Automation, connectivity and optimisation of production processes	Human–machine collaboration, smart factories and resilience	Metaversic, interoperable and socio-technical industrial ecosystems, with advanced AI integration and regenerative sustainability
Objective	Operational efficiency, productivity and flexibility	Personalisation, sustainability and robustness against disturbances	Integration of physical and virtual systems, collective intelligence and alignment with global climate and social objectives
Role of the human	Operator and supervisor of automated systems	Active collaborator in human–machine systems	Central agent within the socio-technical system, integrated through advanced interfaces and intelligent avatars
Key technologies	IoT, CPS, Big Data, analytical AI, autonomous robotics, 4G networks	Collaborative robots, assistive AI, virtual and augmented reality, 5G networks	Classical, quantum and neuromorphic AI, hybrid computing, metaversic architectures, advanced digital twins, post-quantum cybersecurity
Computational architecture	Centralised and cloud-based	Distributed architectures with Edge and Cloud integration	Hybrid Edge, Fog and Cloud architectures with distributed and bio-inspired computing

continued on following page

Table 1. Continued

Aspect	I4.0	I5.0	I6.0 (emerging paradigm)
Sustainability	Resource optimisation and energy efficiency	Explicit focus on sustainability and resilience	Regenerative sustainability, eco-compatibility and coevolution with natural and social systems
Level of digital integration	Digitalisation of assets and processes	Digitalisation oriented towards human–machine interaction	Continuous hybridisation of the real and the virtual within industrial metaverses

In this new scenario, engineering and project management environments must respond to requirements arising from I5.0, I6.0 and their associated industrial metaverses. These requirements substantially transform the functional demands placed on artificial intelligence associated with cyber-physical systems, digital twins, digital threads, virtual worlds and intelligent avatars, which must operate in an interoperable manner within complex metaversic ecosystems. The growing demands for computation, artificial intelligence and knowledge engineering, together with highly cloudified architectures, imply that classical AI technologies require large amounts of energy, water and critical materials, face difficulties in real-time operation, struggle to mitigate vulnerabilities related to cybersecurity and resilience, and pose significant challenges for socio-technical integration through advanced human–machine interfaces (Lee, 2015; Ren et al., 2024).

These limitations justify the need to incorporate innovations derived from quantum computing and neuromorphic engineering, at both hardware and software levels, as the foundation for a new generation of intelligent industrial systems. Neuromorphic computing makes it possible to overcome the bottleneck of the Von Neumann architecture through in-memory computing, distributed processing models, adaptive learning and high energy efficiency, while quantum computing provides massive computational capabilities for optimisation, simulation and the exploration of large state spaces, both in analogue approaches and in qubit-based implementations (Cerezo et al., 2023; Lu et al., 2024; Marković and Grollier, 2020; Yamane et al., 2023).

The convergence of these quantum–neuromorphic technologies enables the evolution of cyber-physical systems towards new generations of CPS X.0, capable of integrating quantum and neuromorphic computation, communication, sensing and metrology. These capabilities are deployed in a distributed manner across Edge, Fog and Cloud architectures within industrial metaversic systems. This evolution makes it possible to reduce energy consumption and the use of critical resources, including scarce minerals, improve communication latency and security, extend the lifecycle of information technology systems, bringing them closer to those of operational technology systems, and construct socio-technical systems that are eco-compatible and coevolutionary with their technological and natural environments (Jha, 2023).

Within this context, the development of HQPE engineering is justified as a new reference framework for the design, development and management of projects in industrial metaverses, with a particular use case in the domain of smart electrical grids. HQPE integrates holonic architectures inspired by natural systems with classical, quantum and neuromorphic artificial intelligence capabilities, enabling the modelling of products, processes and facilities as distributed, self-sustaining and adaptive systems throughout their entire lifecycle, and aligned with the 2030 Agenda's Sustainable Development Goals (SDG).

Figure 1 depicts the transition from a linear digital thread to a multidimensional set of metaversic digital threads spanning the industrial value chain. These threads synchronise product, process, facility, energy, knowledge, artificial intelligence, security and human dimensions across physical, virtual, cognitive and social domains, orchestrated by HQPE over Edge, Fog and Cloud architectures.

Figure 1. Conceptual evolution of the digital thread into metaversic digital threads across the industrial value chain, orchestrated through the HQPE framework.

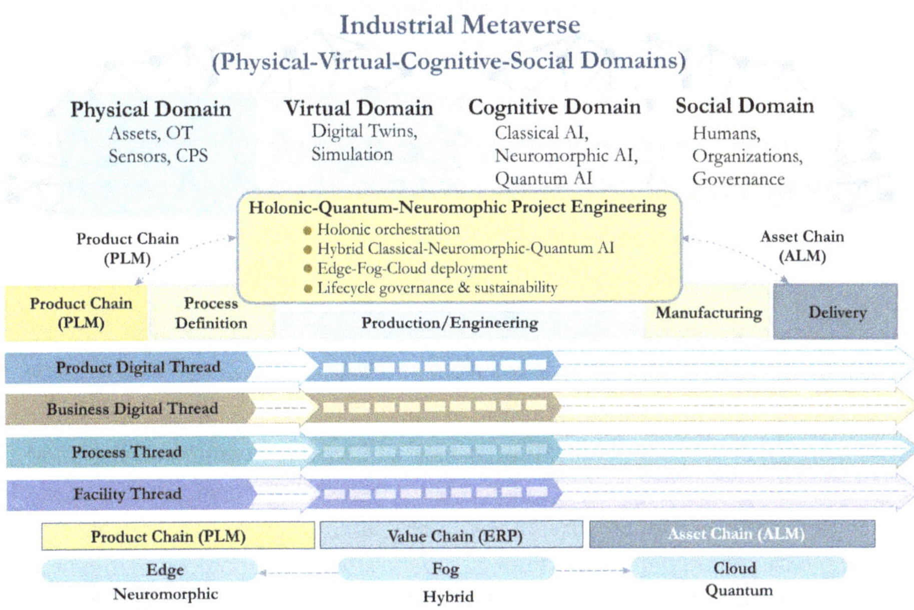

Source: Own elaboration.

Based on this conceptual framework, this chapter addresses the following research questions (RQ):

RQ1. How can the Industrial Metaverse of I6.0 be characterised through distributed ICT architectures based on CPS X.0, capable of autonomous operation supported by quantum and neuromorphic artificial intelligence, integrated within BIM and PLM environments under sustainability and ethical governance criteria?

RQ2. Is it possible to define the requirements of a multilevel, multiscale and multi-aspect ICT architecture, inspired by neuromorphic principles, that enables the development of holonic industrial metaverse systems that are self-sustaining, eco-compatible and co-evolutionary with smart city ecosystems?

RQ3. Can an open reference architecture be defined for the Electricity 4.0 or Smart Grid metaverse, as a representative case study of the Industrial Metaverse, illustrating the integration of information and communication technologies (ICTs) and operational technologies within quantum and neuromorphic CPS X.0, as a foundation for the long-term evolution of industrial infrastructures aligned with the 2030 Agenda'SDGs?

The chapter addresses these questions by proposing a holonic quantum and neuromorphic architectural framework and exploring its application to the electrical Industrial Metaverse, with the aim of informing future research and innovation in advanced industrial project engineering.

2. THE INDUSTRIAL METAVERSE: CONCEPT AND EMERGING AI TECHNOLOGIES

I4.0 and its progression towards I5.0 have been driven by the systematic deployment of Key Enabling Technologies (KETs) across multiple industrial sectors, with Cyber-Physical Systems (CPS) acting as the core integrative element linking physical industrial systems with cyber layers for sensing, control, communication and advanced analytics (Lee, 2015; Tao et al., 2019). As virtualisation intensifies through digital twins of products, processes, facilities and business models, and as classical artificial intelligence techniques are progressively incorporated, lifecycle engineering evolves from an efficiency-centred paradigm towards a sociotechnical approach that explicitly integrates human, organisational and contextual dimensions (Yao et al., 2024).

This evolution towards I5.0 and the emerging I6.0 gives rise to the Industrial Metaverse (IM) as an integrative construct that combines BIM- and PLM-based digital models, CPS and KETs with non-classical technologies such as neuromorphic, quantum and hybrid computing, addressing advanced computational, interactional and sustainability requirements that exceed the capabilities of conventional architectures, while enabling interoperability with broader metaversic ecosystems, including smart city and smart energy domains (Ren et al., 2024; Verma et al., 2025; ITU, 2024a; Yao et al., 2024).

2.1. Operational Definition of the IM

The IM is not conceived as an isolated technology, but rather as the continuation of I4.0 and 5.0 towards X.0 through the incorporation of emerging technologies aimed at the digitisation and virtualisation of assets, processes and operational agents, including avatars In order to derive operational and management strategies oriented to business objectives, these elements are linked to their real-world equivalents (Ren et al., 2024). This establishes a symbiotic, real-time relationship between the physical and virtual worlds, with interoperability being the central enabling condition (ITU, 2024a, 2024b).

From the engineering and governance perspective, this definition also incorporates emerging policy and regulatory requirements, covering risk management and control in artificial intelligence systems (ISO/IEC, 2023), cybersecurity as a core function of governance (NIST, 2023), and the European regulatory framework for artificial intelligence (European Union, 2024). These references are particularly relevant in critical areas such as energy, industry and infrastructure, where availability, integrity, security and traceability become design requirements and not just operational issues.

2.2. Formal Specification of the IM

In order to formally specify the systemic nature of MI, the Backus-Naur Form (BNF) notation has been chosen. This approach allows the derivation of sector-specific instances (e.g. electrical, chemical, pharmaceutical, manufacturing, textile), while facilitating alignment between system architecture, life cycle management and governance.

Figure 2 depicts the conceptual architecture of the IM and the interrelationships among its main subsystems, which are subsequently formalised using BNF notation. As illustrated in the figure, the IM integrates: (1) a subsystem corresponding to the real component of the metaverse (Real–Social–Technical-Verse); (2) a subsystem associated with its digital component (Cyber-Verse); and (3) a layer of sensing, connectivity, intelligence and operation (Cybernetic-Verse), responsible for closing the interaction loop with the real world.

Figure 2. Formal TriPla architecture of the IM and its cyber-physical integration.

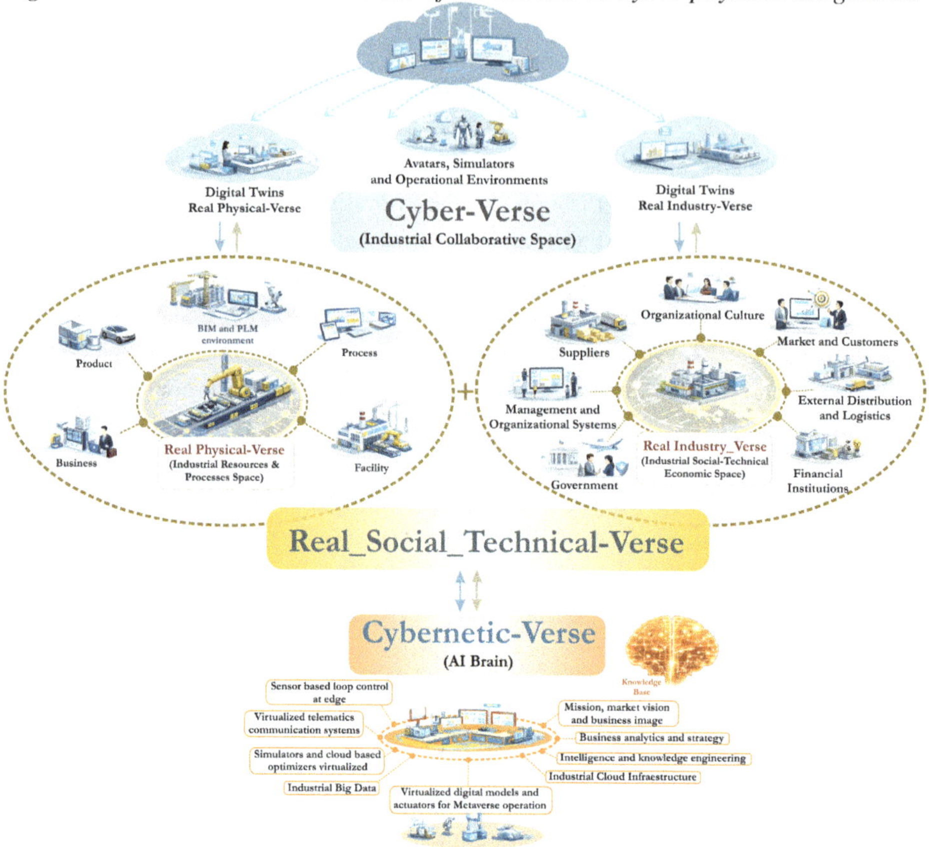

Source: Own elaboration.

In this context, the IM can be formally defined as expressed in Equation 1:

$$\langle \text{Industrial Metaverse (IM)} \rangle ::= \langle\langle \text{Real\_Social\_Technical} - \text{Verse}\rangle\langle \text{Cyber} - \text{Verse}\rangle\langle \text{Cibernetical} - \text{Verse}\rangle\rangle \quad (1)$$

where:

(1) **Real_Social_Technical-Verse** explicitly integrates, as shown in Equation 2: (i) the real physical system and (ii) the associated industrial socioeconomic system:

$$\langle \text{Real\_Social\_Technical} - \text{Verse}\rangle ::= \langle\langle \text{Real\_Physical-Verse}\rangle \langle \text{Real\_Industry\_Social\_Technical\_Economic-Verse}\rangle\langle \text{Cibernetic} - \text{Verse}\rangle\rangle \quad (2)$$

and subsequently, in Equation 3, the Real_Physical-Verse is defined as:

$$\langle \text{Real\_Physical} - \text{Verse}\rangle ::= \langle\langle \text{Product}\rangle\langle \text{Process}\rangle\langle \text{Facility}\rangle\langle \text{Business}\rangle\langle \text{BIM/PLM environments}\rangle\rangle \quad (3)$$

This definition formalises the role of BIM and PLM as the core project-oriented environments that structure the IM, enabling the generation and lifecycle management of digital product, process, and facility models required for the construction, commissioning, and operation of its subsystems, as formalised in Equation 4:

$$
\begin{aligned}
&\langle \text{BIM/PLM environments} \rangle \ ::= \\
&\langle \langle \text{IM\_Project\_Management\_Engineering} \rangle \langle \text{IM\_Operation} \rangle \\
&\langle \text{IM\_Construction} \rangle \langle \text{IM\_Operacionof} \rangle \langle \text{IM\_Reengineering} \rangle \langle \text{IM\_End\_of\_life} \rangle \rangle
\end{aligned} \tag{4}
$$

Once the industrial metaversic system has been deployed, the BIM/PLM project environment is deactivated as an active design workspace. However, the models, digital twins, and digital assets generated during the project phases remain as part of the operational infrastructure of the IM, in accordance with the paradigm of industrial digital twins (Tao et al., 2019).

Conversely, the Real Industry Social–Technical–Economic Verse, as formalised in Equation 5, is composed of a set of real external entities with which cooperation is required to achieve business objectives. These entities are mirrored within the metaverse through corresponding virtual entities and agents represented by avatars. This verse also integrates the internal organisational and management systems of the industrial enterprise, including finance, marketing, and the sociotechnical operational systems associated with the different departments.

$$
\begin{aligned}
&\langle \text{Real Industry Social} - \text{Technical} - \text{Economic Verse} \rangle \ ::= \\
&\langle \langle \text{IM\_Project\_Management\_Engineering} \rangle \langle \text{IM\_Project\_Design\_Engineering} \rangle \\
&\langle \text{IM\_Construction} \rangle \langle \text{IM\_Operacion} \rangle \langle \text{Reingeniería} \rangle \langle \text{Fin de Ciclo de Vida} \rangle \rangle
\end{aligned} \tag{5}
$$

(2) The **Cyber-Verse**, represented in the upper part of Figure 2 as the industrial collaborative space, encompasses the digital twins of both the Real_Physical-Verse and the Real_Industry_Social–Technical–Economic-Verse, together with the interfaces required for their integration with the cybernetic layer as showed in Equation 6.

$$
\begin{aligned}
&\langle \text{Cyber\_Verse} \rangle \ ::= \langle \langle \text{Digital\_Twins\_Real\_Physical\_Verse} \rangle \\
&\langle \text{Digital\_Twins\_Real\_Industry\_Verse} \rangle \langle \text{Virtualized\_Telematic\_Communication\_Systems} \rangle \\
&\langle \text{RX\_Models\_and\_Metaversic\_Avatars} \rangle \langle \text{Virtualized\_Simulators\_and\_Optimizers} \rangle \\
&\langle \text{Sensorica \& Control en edge} \rangle \langle \text{Interfaces\_with\_Cyber\_Verse} \rangle \rangle
\end{aligned} \tag{6}
$$

This verse enables sensing, data ingestion and data transport from the real world to cloud environments, supports metaversic operation through avatars, simulators and operational environments, and integrates simulation outcomes with the intelligence and decision-making layer.

(3) **The Cybernetic-Verse**, represented in the lower part of the figure as the *AI Brain*, constitutes the aggregated information and decision layer of the system. It is composed of the components formalised in Equation 7.

$$\begin{aligned}&\langle \text{Cybernetic\_Verse} \rangle :: = \langle \langle \text{Sensor\_Based\_Closed\_Loop\_Control\_at\_Edge} \rangle \\ &\langle \text{Virtualized\_Telematic\_Communication\_Systems} \rangle \\ &\langle \text{Virtualized\_Control\_Models\_and\_Open\_Loop\_Actuators} \rangle \\ &\langle \text{Simulacion \& Optimizacion} \rangle \langle \text{Business\_Analytics\_and\_Strategy} \rangle \\ &\langle \text{Intelligence\_and\_Knowledge\_Engineering} \rangle \rangle\end{aligned} \tag{7}$$

From a cybernetic perspective, this layer concentrates system governance and provides the requisite variety necessary to manage the complexity of the IM, in accordance with classical cybernetic principles applied to complex systems (Lee, 2015).

The life-cycle engineering of the IM, and particularly its deployment within the electrical industry, as articulated through BIM and PLM environments, requires the incorporation of new Key Enabling Technologies (KETs). Among these, quantum and neuromorphic technologies, at both hardware and software levels, play a prominent role when applied to Information and Communication Technologies (ICT) and Operational Technologies (OT), in response to the growing demands for computational capacity, intelligence and sustainability.

2.3. Characteristic Requirements of the IM in the Context of I6.0

From the perspective of I6.0, the IM can be understood as a complex real sociotechnical ecosystem and its virtual counterpart, interconnected in real time, which tends to behave as a "living" system endowed with capabilities for cognition, self-organisation, operational teleology and continuous adaptation. Within this framework, industrial organisation and value chains cease to be conceived as static hierarchical structures and are instead understood as co-evolutionary networks of physical assets, digital entities, intelligent agents and avatars, and human actors, interacting in a distributed manner throughout the system lifecycle (Verma et al., 2025; Yao et al., 2024).

Under this conception, the design and deployment of the IM in the context of I6.0 is conditioned by a set of structural, functional and governance-related requirements. These requirements do not merely define high-level design principles, but must also be systematically translated into architectural decisions, the selection of enabling technologies, and verifiable criteria that allow their assessment across the entire lifecycle of the system.

Accordingly, the requirements of the IM are analysed along four complementary dimensions: (i) their systemic justification within the context of I6.0; (ii) their architectural implications within the IM; (iii) the enabling technologies and mechanisms required for their implementation; and (iv) the indicators and verifiable criteria that allow their validation in real and critical environments.

Among the most relevant requirements, the following can be highlighted:

(1) Multi-metaverse interoperability: the capability of the IM to integrate in an eco-compatible and co-evolutionary manner with other intelligent metaverses, such as smart cities, smart energy or smart grids. This requires standardisation frameworks, reference architectures, and mechanisms for semantic and technical interoperability (ITU, 2024a, 2024b).
(2) Self-sustainability and regenerative sustainability: reduction of energy consumption, water footprint and the use of critical materials, together with the minimisation of cognitive, social and cultural impacts derived from inadequate immersive interfaces and non-explainable automation processes.
(3) IT/OT convergence throughout the lifecycle: coherent integration of information and communication technologies (ICT), characterised by short lifecycles, with operational technologies (OT), which typically have long lifecycles, ensuring operational continuity, maintainability, traceability and long-term governance.
(4) Real-time operation and low latency: support for control, safety and immersive collaboration functions in industrial contexts, particularly in the presence of critical events and distributed systems.
(5) Cybersecurity and cyber-resilience: incorporation, from early design phases, of mechanisms for risk governance, operational continuity and resilience against persistent and emerging threats, including post-quantum risks, supported by consolidated reference frameworks (NIST, 2023, 2024).
(6) Artificial intelligence governance and regulatory compliance: adoption of responsible AI management practices, including data and model traceability, explainability, auditing and bias control, in alignment with emerging regulatory frameworks (European Union, 2024; ISO/IEC, 2023).
(7) Human and cognitive dimension: explicit consideration of cognitive load, ergonomics, trust and operational safety in immersive environments, through human-centred design approaches.
(8) Distributed intelligence and adaptive capability: support for complex and co-evolutionary systems through holonic control mechanisms, multi-agent coordination and distributed learning.

In order to systematise these requirements and facilitate their translation into architectural and governance decisions, Table 2 summarises the main requirements of the IM in I6.0, together with their architectural implications, enabling technologies and associated verifiable criteria.

Table 2. Requirements of the IM in I6.0 and their translation into architectural and governance criteria. Source: Own elaboration.

Requirement (I6.0)	Rationale	Architectural Implications in the IM	Enabling Technologies / Mechanisms	Indicators and Verifiable Criteria
(1)Multi-metaverse interoperability	Integration with Smart City, Smart Energy, Smart Grid and sectoral ecosystems	Reference architecture, shared semantics, APIs and contractual interfaces	Standards, ontologies, middleware, APIs, identity federation	Interoperability level, data/model compatibility, integration latency
(2)Self-sustainability and regenerative sustainability	Energy cost, water footprint, critical materials, social sustainability	Compute optimisation, minimisation of data transfers, eco-efficient design	Edge and Fog computing, neuromorphic computing, hybrid optimisation, data centre energy management	kWh per task, CO_2 footprint, water footprint, hardware lifetime, recyclability rate
(3)IT/OT convergence (lifecycle perspective)	Short IT lifecycles vs long OT lifecycles, operational continuity	Modular and maintainable architecture, version management, traceability and configuration	Digital thread and digital twin, MLOps, lifecycle engineering, asset management	MTBF/MTTR, change traceability, OT compatibility, operational continuity
(4)Real-time operation and low latency	Control, safety, immersive collaboration, critical events	Distributed processing, autonomous local control, digital twin synchronisation	Edge computing, neuromorphic processing, event-driven architectures (EDA), distributed control	End-to-end latency, jitter, response time, packet loss
(5)Cybersecurity and cyber-resilience	Persistent threats and post-quantum risks	Security by design, holonic redundancy, defence in depth	Zero Trust architectures, anomaly detection, post-quantum cryptography, QKD (where applicable)	MTTD/MTTR, CSF compliance, post-quantum cryptographic robustness, availability
(6)AI governance and regulatory compliance	AI risks, auditability, ethics and traceability	Risk management, model lifecycle governance, accountability	NIST AI RMF, ISO/IEC 42001, EU AI Act, model cards, data governance	Audit evidence, data/model traceability, explainability metrics, bias indicators

continued on following page

Table 2. Continued

Requirement (I6.0)	Rationale	Architectural Implications in the IM	Enabling Technologies / Mechanisms	Indicators and Verifiable Criteria
(7)Human–cognitive dimension (HMI/XR)	Cognitive load, trust, ergonomics, operational safety	Human-centred design, multimodal interaction, validation and verification	XR technologies, avatars, advanced sensors, cognitive models, HFE/ergonomics	Usability metrics, cognitive load indicators, HMI-related incidents, user acceptance and trust
(8)Distributed intelligence and adaptation (operational autopoiesis)	Changing complex systems and co-evolution	Holonic control, multi-agent coordination, federated learning	Multi-agent systems (MAS), holonic architectures, federated learning, edge intelligence	Robustness to change, adaptation time, performance under perturbations

2.4. Limitations and Gaps in the Deployment of the IM

Despite recent advances in architectures, enabling technologies and conceptual frameworks associated with the IM, the effective deployment of self-sustaining sociotechnical metaversic ecosystems continues to face significant structural limitations and scientific gaps. These gaps, of an architectural, computational, organisational, regulatory and cognitive nature, condition the long-term viability of the transition from I4.0 to I5.0 towards metaversic environments fully aligned with the principles of I6.0.

A first critical gap lies in the absence of a reference architecture with sufficient requisite variety to guarantee interoperability among heterogeneous IMs and their co-evolution with other intelligent ecosystems, such as smart city or smart energy metaverses. Although standardisation initiatives are currently under development, the fragmentation of architectural proposals and the lack of unified frameworks hinder the semantic, functional and temporal integration of complex metaversic systems, thereby limiting their scalability and systemic eco-compatibility (ITU, 2024a, 2024b).

Conventional computing based on Von Neumann architectures is another clear limitation. The physical separation between memory and processing combined with the use of binary architectures and massive data transfers, generates bottlenecks in terms of latency, energy consumption and water footprint. When real-time processing, continuous simulation or immersive experiences, among others, are required, these issues become critical. All of this is amplified due to the growth of data centers with high energy, water and material demands which in turn compromises the sustainability and resilience of large-scale systems (Lee, 2015; Marković and Grollier, 2020).

In the field of cybersecurity and cyber resilience, IM integrates IT and OT infrastructures, digital twins, avatars, real-time communications and distributed artificial intelligence models. Because of this, post-quantum risks arise which call into question the robustness of current cryptographic systems, especially in critical infrastructures. The transition to resilient security mechanisms with quantum capabilities is at an early stage and therefore introduces additional uncertainties in IM risk governance (NIST, 2023, 2024).

IM also presents substantial limitations in human-machine interfaces (HMI) and interaction mechanisms mediated by digital avatars. The lack of integrated cognitive models, advanced sensing and metrology, and design approaches centred on cognitive ergonomics may result in mental overload, reduced trust in automated systems and difficulties in effective human-machine collaboration. These shortcomings highlight the need to incorporate approaches derived from neuroscience, neuromorphic engineering and biomimetics in order to improve synchronisation, cooperation and adaptation in complex metaversic environments (Yamane et al., 2023).

Moreover, significant gaps persist in relation to governance, ethics and regulatory compliance of artificial intelligence applied within the IM. The complexity of distributed AI systems, together with the use of generative, agent-based and adaptive models, hinders data and model traceability, auditability and explainability of automated decisions. Although relevant regulatory and normative frameworks have been established, such as European AI, ISO/IEC 42001 and the AI Risk Management Framework, their effective integration into industrial metaversic architectures remains an open challenge, particularly in cross-border and multi-sector contexts (European Union, 2024; ISO/IEC, 2023).

Finally, from a systemic perspective, the IM still lacks an explicit integration of bio-inspired and holonic principles capable of addressing complexity, adaptation and co-evolution with the requisite variety demanded by such systems. Current approaches tend to reproduce hierarchical or centralised schemes that are insufficient for managing distributed, dynamic and highly interconnected sociotechnical ecosystems. This limitation suggests the need to explore new architectures based on distributed control, collective intelligence and federated learning, supported by neuromorphic and quantum computing as key enablers of a new generation of industrial metaversic systems.

Taken together, the identified gaps in interoperability, computing, cybersecurity, human-machine interaction and sustainability do not operate in isolation, but rather reinforce one another, configuring a network of systemic limitations. From this analysis, it can be observed that there is a clear evolution towards an IM aligned with I6.0 that should not be supported only by extensions of existing technologies. However, it should be noted that there is a need for conceptual frameworks and integrative architectures that combine holonics, distributed intelligence and emerging computational paradigms. This is the starting point for the introduction of the HQPE framework that will be developed later.

3. ENGINEERING AND PROJECT MANAGEMENT ENVIRONMENTS OF THE IM

Industrial projects carried out under I4.0, 5.0 and I6.0, are characterized by being complex projects, mainly oriented towards the construction of new plants as well as the reengineering of existing facilities. These projects are developed under principles of concurrent engineering, integrating design, construction, operation and sustainability decisions from the early stages and across the entire lifecycle of the industrial system.

Within this context, information and communication technologies and artificial intelligence technologies, both classical and emerging, including quantum, neuromorphic and hybrid AI, cannot be incorporated as ancillary or late-stage solutions. Instead, they must be embedded from the earliest project phases within BIM and PLM environments. Such early integration is essential to accelerate the transfer of advanced capabilities in computation, artificial intelligence and virtualisation into the resolution of design, planning and management challenges that are intrinsic to I6.0 projects.

3.1. BIM and PLM as Project Environments of IM

In IM projects, BIM and PLM environments, constitute the project-oriented foundation upon which the design, development and management of the industrial system are articulated throughout its entire lifecycle. Within this framework, PLM acts as the integrating environment for the definition and evolution of products and processes, while BIM structures the design, construction and operation of the industrial facility, including infrastructures, systems and physical assets.

Unlike conventional industrial projects, metaversic projects require these project environments to go beyond purely physical and geometric modelling. BIM and PLM must incorporate extended virtualisation capabilities of the sociotechnical system, integrating not only technical elements but also the representation of human actors, organisational flows, operational sequences and collective behaviours through avatars, process animation, simulation and advanced optimisation, as illustrated in Figure 3.

Figure 3. Extended BIM–PLM–CPS architecture towards the IM.

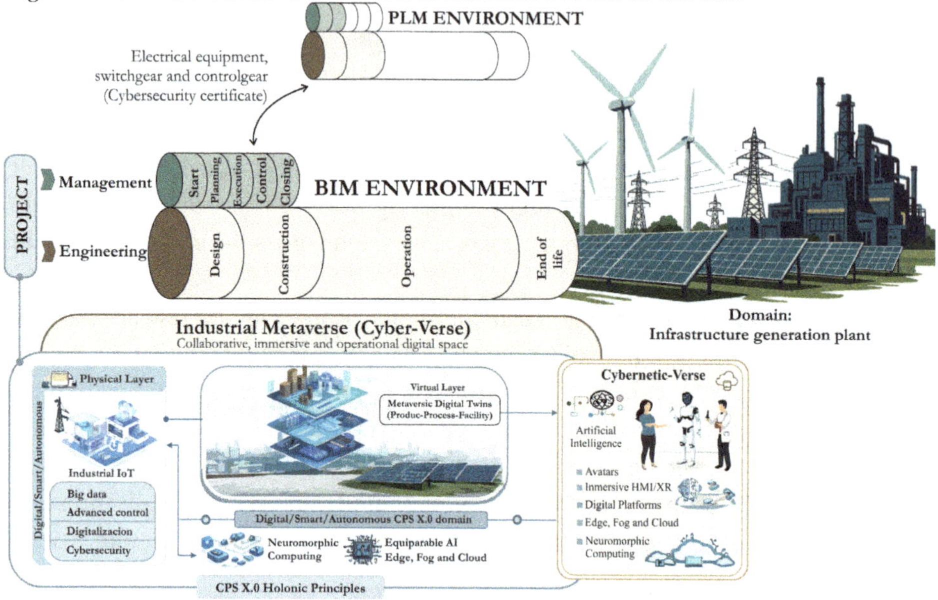

Source: Own elaboration.

From the early stages of the project, the CPS X.0 cyber-physical system of the metaversic industrial plant is conceived through a comprehensive digital twin that progressively evolves from conceptual models to operational models synchronised with the real system. This digital continuity enables the coherent integration of lifecycle engineering activities, including design, construction, commissioning, operation, maintenance and re-engineering, into a single digital thread, supported by BIM and PLM as shared project platforms

This project-oriented approach enables early, traceable and coordinated decision-making across domains that have traditionally been decoupled, thereby establishing the foundations for the subsequent integration of data technologies, artificial intelligence and distributed control mechanisms inherent to the IM.

3.2. CPS X.0, Data and Artificial Intelligence in Metaversic Projects

The design and deployment of CPS X.0 within IM projects require a close and systematic integration of data technologies, artificial intelligence and control, such that the system is capable of perceiving, interpreting and acting coherently within complex and dynamic industrial environments. This integration spans the entire information flow, from sensing and data ingestion through to advanced processing and assisted or autonomous decision-making.

In this framework, data science constitutes the methodological core for the exploitation of operational knowledge, and is applied through descriptive, predictive and prescriptive analytics. These capabilities, based on techniques such as big data or machine learning, make it possible to characterize system states, anticipate future behaviors and recommend optimal actions in the face of uncertain conditions.

Similar to the architectures consolidated in I4.0 and I5.0, the information systems associated with CPS X.0 are organized according to a multilevel structure comprising: (i) data acquisition, preprocessing and management at the peripheral and fog levels, close to the physical process; (ii) intensive processing and advanced analysis within cloud infrastructures; and (iii) integration of these results with digital twins and control systems that support monitoring, optimization and decision making at different points in time.

In the IM context, this multi-tier architecture is extended to support virtual operating environments, digital twins and immersive interaction capabilities, thus providing the basis for coordinating the physical and digital world and associated decision making and control. This architectural approach establishes the basis for the subsequent integration of advanced artificial intelligence models, hybrid computational architectures and bio-inspired approaches, which are addressed in the following sections.

3.3. Data Science, MLOps and Multidisciplinary Teams in BIM/PLM

The development, implementation and operation of IM systems require the expansion of traditional engineering and project management teams through the incorporation of new professional profiles specialized in data and artificial intelligence. In particular, Data Science teams assume a central role, being responsible for the design, training and validation of analytical, predictive and prescriptive models, together with MLOps (Machine Learning Operations) teams, which are in charge of their industrialisation, deployment, monitoring and continuous maintenance within operational environments.

Unlike conventional approaches, in IM projects these teams do not operate in isolation but are structurally integrated within BIM and PLM environments. This integration ensures that AI models are developed in coherence with the evolution of products, processes and facilities, guaranteeing alignment with the digital models of physical system and digital twins that represent them throughout the life cycle.

The data science and MLOps teams work in close collaboration with specialists in virtualization and animation, software engineering, cybersecurity and industrial automation, thus configuring a clearly interdisciplinary project ecosystem. This convergence is essential to ensure that artificial intelligence models retain their traceability, reproducibility and functional consistency in the face of changes in the real system.

The coordination of these teams as well as their lifecycles allows the integrated management of three dimensions that have traditionally been treated separately: (1) the dimension corresponding to the engineering of the industrial system, (2) the lifecycle of the AI models and (3) the lifecycle of the MI itself. This convergence enables the project to absorb complexity, reduce technical and organizational risks and sustain the evolution of the metaverse system over the long term.

3.4. ICT Architectures and KETs for the IM

The projects associated with I4.0, I5.0 and I6.0 in metaverse environments have proposed a multitude of ICT architectures usually based on CPS as the central integrating element of the digital enablers. These architectures enable the synergistic interaction between real physical systems and their virtual representations (digital twins) and constitute the foundational layer upon which the KETs of Industry X.0 are deployed.

Within the context of the IM, such architectures must go beyond mere connectivity or functional digitalisation, incorporating advanced capabilities for virtualisation, distributed cognition, human–machine interaction, multi-level interoperability and technological governance. Moreover, they must be conceived from a full life-cycle perspective, aligning business, product, process and facility layers, and ensuring the coherent integration of physical, digital and organisational domains.

Table 3 synthesises the main technological and organisational enablers of the IM from a project-oriented and systemic perspective, within BIM/PLM environments and CPS X.0 architectures. Rather than providing an exhaustive inventory of technologies, the table identifies those enablers that are structural to design, development and operation of complex metaversic systems, considering their role within the system life cycle and their contribution to physical-digital-human integration.

Table 3. Technological and Organisational Enablers of the IM in I6.0 Projects. Source: Own elaboration.

Enabler Category	Technology / Approach	Role within the IM	Deployment Level	Life-Cycle Phase
Project-oriented	BIM	Design, construction and operation of the industrial facility; support for the physical-environment digital twin	Cloud / Enterprise	Design – Construction – Operation
Project-oriented	PLM	Integrated management of the product, process and system life cycle	Cloud / Enterprise	Entire life cycle
Cyber-physical	CPS X.0	Physical–digital integration, distributed control and coordination of the industrial system	Edge, Fog and Cloud	Operation – Maintenance
Computational	Classical AI	Descriptive, predictive and prescriptive analytics; decision-support functions	Cloud and Edge	Operation
Computational	Neuromorphic AI	Low-power, low-latency distributed intelligence	Edge	Real-time operation
Computational	Quantum AI	Combinatorial optimisation, advanced simulation and cybersecurity	Cloud (QaaS)	Advanced planning
Virtualisation	Digital Twins	Continuous synchronisation between physical and virtual systems; simulation and optimisation	Edge, Fog and Cloud	Entire life cycle
Immersive	XR and digital avatars	Human–system interaction, training and operational support	Edge and Cloud	Design – Operation
Infrastructure	Edge, Fog and Cloud	Scalability, low latency and distributed computing	Distributed	Entire life cycle
Infrastructure	SDN	Flexible and secure communication management	Network	Operation
Digital trust	Blockchain / NFT	Traceability, digital identity and distributed trust	Cloud	Operation
Organisational	Holonic architecture	Distributed coordination, autonomy and organisational scalability	Cross-cutting	Entire life cycle
Organisational	AI and data governance	Control, ethics, regulatory compliance and sustainability	Cross-cutting	Operation – O&M

The enablers are grouped according to their primary function within the life cycle of the metaversic system, namely perception, cognition, interaction, control and governance, and according to their contribution to the multi-level and multi-aspect integration characteristic of CPS X.0 systems. From this perspective, the contribution does not lie in each technology considered in isolation, but rather in their coherent integration within a project engineering framework oriented towards the IM.

In this regard, the appropriate combination of ICT architectures, KETs and organisational enablers is critical to ensuring interoperability, sustainability and governance in industrial metaversic systems, as well as their compatibility with external ecosystems such as smart cities, smart energy or other critical infrastructures. These organizational and technological aspects of governance become relevant during the operation and maintenance phases of the life cycle and are addressed in the following section.

3.5. Governance of Artificial Intelligence and Data in IM Projects

Until now, traditional approaches have focused exclusively on cybersecurity or IT governance, however, AI governance in information management projects, must holistically address aspects such as data and model traceability, validation and continuous performance monitoring, risk management, explainability of automated decisions and compliance with ever-evolving regulatory frameworks. These requirements are especially critical in the case of industrial infrastructures, where assisted decisions can have a direct impact on system safety, operability and sustainability.

Therefore, AI governance in metavertical environments must conform to standards such as ISO/IEC 42001, or frameworks such as the NIST AI risk management framework and the European Artificial Intelligence Act. This not only facilitates regulatory compliance, but also provides a basis for responsible integration of AI into CPS X.0 architectures and metaverse ecosystems.

Table 4 summarises the main governance elements related to artificial intelligence and data technologies applicable to IM projects. Rather than proposing a new regulatory framework, the table articulates, in an integrated manner, policies, processes and technical and organisational mechanisms that are already recognised in both the scientific literature and industrial practice, structuring them across the system life cycle. In doing so, it provides an operational reference for the implementation of governance schemes in industrial metaversic environments characterised by distribution, heterogeneity and co-evolution.

Table 4. Integration of artificial intelligence and data governance across the life cycle in IM projects. Source: Own elaboration.

Governance Dimension	Objective	Key Policies	Associated Processes	Artefacts / Mechanisms	Reference Standards
Data governance	Ensure data quality, traceability and responsible use	Data quality policy; data access and sovereignty	Controlled ingestion; validation; versioning; retention	Data catalogues; lineage; metadata; governed data lakes	GDPR; EU Data Governance Act; ISO/IEC 38505
AI model governance	Control the life cycle of classical and emerging AI models	Model development, validation and retirement policies	Training; validation; deployment; monitoring; retraining	Model registry; model cards; performance metrics	ISO/IEC 42001; NIST AI RMF
Risk and bias management	Minimise technical, ethical and operational risks	AI risk assessment; anti-bias policies	Identification; analysis; mitigation; continuous audit	AI impact assessments; risk dashboards	EU AI Act; NIST AI RMF
Explainability and transparency (XAI)	Ensure understanding and trust in automated decisions	Explainability policies by criticality level	Generation and validation of explanations	Model cards; local/global explanations; decision traces	EU AI Act; ISO/IEC 23894
Cybersecurity and cyber-resilience	Protect CPS X.0 systems and metaversic environments	Security by design; Zero Trust; operational resilience	Monitoring; detection; response; recovery	Industrial SOC; SIEM; post-quantum cryptography	NIST CSF 2.0; IEC 62443; NIST PQC
IT/OT governance	Ensure coherent integration of IT and OT	IT/OT convergence policies	Change management; technological compatibility	Digital thread; digital twins; CMDB	ISO/IEC 27001; IEC 62264
Human–AI governance	Ensure human oversight and cognitive ergonomics	Human-in-the-loop and decision escalation	Human validation; supervised intervention	HMI/XR interfaces; intervention protocols	EU AI Act; ISO 9241
Organisational governance	Align AI with strategy and sustainability goals	Strategic alignment and SDG policies	AI steering committee; strategic review	Sustainability KPIs; management dashboards	Agenda 2030; ISO 26000
Audit and compliance	Ensure legal and technical conformity	AI and data audit policies	Periodic audits; reporting	Audit reports; compliance evidence	EU AI Act; ISO/IEC 42001
Life-cycle governance	Coordinate AI, CPS and metaverse evolution over time	Integrated life-cycle management	End-of-life assessment; re-engineering; retirement	Digital twin life-cycle management; full traceability	PLM/BIM standards; ISO 10303

4. IM AND AI TECHNOLOGIES

The evolution of IM is linked to the role of AI as a KET for integration, adaptation and autonomy in advanced industrial systems. Following the analysis of the engineering and project management environments that support these ecosystems, it becomes necessary to address the relationship between IM and the different artificial intelligence technologies as a foundation for the transition of industrial systems from I4.0 paradigms towards the emerging approaches of I6.0.

4.1. Classical Artificial Intelligence in the IM: Capabilities and Limitations

Within IM, classical AI, plays a fundamental role as an enabler of advanced virtualisation, simulation, optimisation and control of complex industrial systems. When integrated into BIM and PLM environments, classical AI enables the closure of the feedback loop between physical system and its virtual representation using digital twins, supporting functions such as prediction, diagnostics, and assisted decision-making.

In the design and construction phases, these techniques are used for generating 3D models, optimizing product, process, and facility configurations, and for the initial evaluation of design solutions. In the operation and maintenance phases, they focus on advanced data analysis, including descriptive, predictive, and prescriptive analyses, adaptive control based on surrogate models, and continuous simulation of real-time scenarios.

However, the adoption of classical artificial intelligence in industrial metaverse architectures reveals significant structural limitations. These include the high energy and resource consumption associated with training and running large-scale models, latency issues stemming from centralized computing architectures, difficulties in ensuring explainability and traceability in complex models, and the increasing vulnerability of traditional cryptographic mechanisms in post-quantum scenarios. These limitations restrict the scalability, sustainability, and resilience of industrial mathematics when conceived as critical infrastructure within the context of Industry 6.0.

4.2. Networked Agentic Intelligence and Metaversic Multi-Agent Systems

To address the complexity, distribution, and inherent dynamism of industrial metaverse systems, networked agent intelligence emerges as a key paradigm. From this perspective, the overall behavior of the system arises from the coordinated interaction of diverse intelligent agents (human, cyber-physical, or virtual) endowed with autonomy, learning capabilities, and cooperation mechanisms. This results in distributed architectures characterized by emergent control and multi-level governance.

Multi-agent systems allow for the explicit representation of products, processes, resources, operators, avatars, and organizational entities as agents with their own objectives, limitations, and capabilities within the context of AI. This representation is particularly well suited to modelling complex sociotechnical systems, in which decision making is not exclusively centralised, but rather distributed, context-dependent and adaptive.

Networked agentic intelligence facilitates the implementation of distributed coordination mechanisms, negotiation processes, dynamic resource allocation and continuous adaptation in response to environmental disturbances. Its integration with edge, fog and cloud architectures enables scalable processing and latency reduction, while its coupling with digital twins supports the simulation of collective behaviours and the anticipatory evaluation of operational strategies.

However, the effective deployment of metaversic agent-based systems raises significant challenges in terms of interoperability, governance, security and computational cost. The need to support large populations of agents interacting in real time reinforces the demand for more efficient and bio-inspired computational architectures, capable of managing the required variety without relying exclusively on resource-intensive centralised infrastructures.

4.3. Neuromorphic and Bio-Inspired Computing as an Enabler of the IM

Neuromorphic computing emerges as an alternative technology to overcome some of the limitations of conventional Von Neumann-based computing architectures. It is inspired by the operating principles of the human brain, integrates memory and processing, operates asynchronously and event-driven, and has significantly lower power consumption than traditional architectures.

In the IM, neuromorphic computing is particularly relevant for applications requiring real-time processing, continuous learning and local adaptation, such as distributed edge control, advanced multisensory perception, human–machine interaction and the coordination of intelligent agents. Its adoption enables latency reduction, minimisation of large-scale data transfers and a substantial decrease in the energy and material footprint of metaversic systems.

From a Project Engineering perspective, the integration of neuromorphic devices and architectures enables new CPS X.0 design strategies, in which intelligence is deployed in a distributed and holonic hierarchical manner. This approach aligns naturally with principles of self-organisation, local adaptation and co-evolution that underpin the I6.0 paradigm. However, for it to be adopted on a massive scale, further progress is needed in design tools, standardization, and industrial validation methodologies.

4.4. AI and Quantum Computing in the IM

Quantum computing and quantum AI represent a major leap forward in the ability to process complex problems associated with systems engineering. Their relevance lies in areas such as detection and metrology, optimization problem-solving, complex system simulation, advanced learning techniques, and cryptography, which are unattainable from the perspective of classical computing paradigms.

Within systems engineering, quantum computing is presented as a strategic enabler for optimizing production systems, resource planning, complex process simulation, and cybersecurity enhancement. Furthermore, its combination with other agent-based or neuromorphic systems paves the way for hybrid architectures capable of managing the complexity and uncertainty of large-scale industrial metaverse ecosystems.

Currently, the existing level of technological maturity limits its direct implementation in operational industrial environments. Therefore, its integration into systems engineering must be conceived as part of hybrid architectures so that they coexist and are organized throughout the system's lifecycle.

4.5. Implications for Sustainability and HQPE Governance

The convergence of classical AI, agent-based systems, neuromorphic computing, and quantum computing in Project Engineering at the Industrial Engineering Institute (IM) has implications for sustainability, governance, and the practice of engineering and project management. The combined use of these paradigms intensifies the complexity of industrial metaverse systems, exposing the limitations of project approaches based on rigid hierarchical architectures and centralized control.

From a sustainability perspective, the incorporation of bio-inspired and quantum technologies offers opportunities to reduce energy consumption, water footprint, and material use while simultaneously reducing the cognitive and social burden associated with highly immersive human-machine interaction systems. However, these benefits can only be realized if these technologies are integrated from the earliest stages of project design and supported by appropriate technological and organizational governance policies.

Therefore, Quantum-Neuromorphic Holonic Project Engineering (HQPE) emerges as an integrative framework capable of coherently articulating the various technological and organizational paradigms that converge in IM. HQPE proposes addressing the design, management and operation of industrial metaversic systems as complex sociotechnical ecosystems endowed with distributed intelligence, requisite variety and the capacity for co-evolution with their economic, social and natural environments.

This approach establishes the foundations for an orderly and sustainable transition towards the IM as a critical infrastructure of I6.0 and constitutes the conceptual basis upon which the emerging models and organisational enablers are developed.

5. EMERGING MODELS OF QUANTUM AND NEUROMORPHIC ARTIFICIAL INTELLIGENCE AND HOLONIC ORGANISATIONAL ENABLERS

The evolution of the IM towards the paradigms of I6.0 introduces computational, energetic and organisational requirements that clearly exceed the capabilities of conventional digital architectures based on classical artificial intelligence and Von Neumann computing. Requirement for large-scale processing in real time, the simultaneous management of extensive populations of digital twins and intelligent agents, the reduction of energy consumption and critical resource usage, as well as the governance of highly distributed sociotechnical systems, necessitates the exploration of new paradigms in computation, artificial intelligence and industrial organisation (Verma et al., 2025; Yao et al., 2024).

Quantum and neuromorphic AI are emerging as technological enablers with transformative potential because they introduce new mechanisms for processing, learning, and adaptation inspired by physical and biological principles. When combined with other organizational approaches based on holonic principles, these technologies allow us to conceive of AI not only as a digital extension of existing production systems, but as a living sociotechnical ecosystem capable of co-evolving with its economic, social, and natural environment. This perspective aligns with the SDGs and the principles of regenerative sustainability associated with Industry 6.0 (Goldstein, 2021; Marković and Grollier, 2020).

5.1. Quantum AI as an Enabler of IM

From a taxonomic perspective, Quantum Machine Learning (QML) approaches can be classified into four categories: (i) Classical data processed by Classical Processors, (ii) Quantum data processed by Classical Processors, (iii) Classical data processed by Quantum Processors, and (iv) Quantum data processed by Quantum Processors. For quantum AI in industrial manufacturing, the Classical data processed by Quantum Processors approach is particularly relevant, as it allows the integration of quantum algorithms into existing industrial architectures without requiring a radical transformation of current data flows or information systems (Jha, 2023; Zhuang et al., 2024).

From a technological deployment perspective, quantum artificial intelligence is expected to be adopted initially through cloud-based infrastructures under the Quantum-as-a-Service paradigm, allowing industrial organisations to experiment with quantum capabilities without the need to own specialised hardware. In parallel, distributed architectures are being explored in which specific quantum devices are integrated into selected system nodes to support optimisation, simulation or advanced security functions (AWS Braket, 2026; IBM Quantum, 2026).

Nevertheless, the current state of technological maturity, characterised by Noisy Intermediate-Scale Quantum devices and limitations related to stability and error correction, makes it necessary to conceive quantum artificial intelligence as a specialised component within hybrid architectures. In the short to medium term, it is therefore expected to coexist with classical and neuromorphic computing, rather than acting as a direct replacement for established paradigms (Preskill, 2018).

At present, Technology Readiness Levels for quantum technologies remain heterogeneous, although there is a clear acceleration towards commercial application. Most complex systems are still situated at intermediate to advanced stages of development, progressing from fundamental research (TRL 1 to 3) towards validation and demonstration in real-world environments (TRL 5 to 8). Key milestones associated with quantum advantage are anticipated for the period 2026 to 2027. In this sense, both quantum detection and metrology have TRL levels between 6 and 9, quantum communications between 4 and 7, and quantum computing and simulation between 3 and 5.

5.2. Neuromorphic AI and Bio-Inspired Computing

Neuromorphic computing draws its inspiration from the operating principles of biological nervous systems, integrating processing and memory, operating asynchronously, and being event-driven, thus enabling parallelism to neurons and artificial synapses (Davies et al., 2021; Indiveri and Liu, 2015).

From a technological perspective, neuromorphic AI is structured around several axes: (1) cutting-edge neural networks (SNNs), (2) specialized neuromorphic hardware oriented toward in-memory computing, (3) event-driven neuromorphic sensing, and post-CMOS devices such as resistive memory technologies (Marković and Grollier, 2020). These elements enable the deployment of local intelligence at the edge, significantly reducing large-scale data.

In the context of IM, these properties are particularly relevant for advanced multisensory perception, distributed control, intelligent agent coordination, and real-time human-machine interaction. From a lifecycle perspective, neuromorphic computing also contributes to reducing the energy consumption and water footprint associated with compute-intensive systems, while offering greater robustness to noise, uncertainty, and partial failures. These characteristics align closely with the sustainability, resilience, and circular economy goals of Industry 6.0 (Verma et al., 2025).

However, the transition to large-scale neuromorphic architectures presents significant challenges in terms of standardizing programming and training models for segmented neural networks (SNNs), hardware-software cointegration, industrial validation, and interoperability with digital twin platforms and complex cyber-physical systems (Davies et al., 2021; Jha, 2023).

In this emerging landscape, hybrid quantum and neuromorphic approaches are gaining increasing attention, aiming to combine the exploration and acceleration capabilities of quantum computing with the energy efficiency and local adaptability inherent in neuromorphic systems. Such approaches provide a promising framework for supporting large populations of agents and digital twins, reducing latencies in distributed decision-making, and reinforcing the resilience of IM systems.

Neuromorphic technology is currently in a transitional phase, with Technology Readiness Levels generally ranging between TRL 4 and TRL 7, depending on the specific application domain. While the development of core neuromorphic chips is highly advanced, their integration into commercial-scale operational systems continues to evolve.

In order to synthesise and comparatively analyse the distinctive features, complementarities and current limitations of the emerging paradigms discussed, Table 5 presents a structured comparison between quantum artificial intelligence, neuromorphic artificial intelligence and holonic architecture as an organisational enabler of the IM. This synthesis provides a clear view of their combined role in addressing complexity, sustainability and resilience in IM systems characteristic of I6.0.

Table 5. Comparative analysis of emerging AI paradigms and holonic organisational enablers in the IM. Source: Own elaboration.

Dimension	Quantum AI	Neuromorphic AI	Holonic Architecture
Fundamental inspiration	Quantum mechanics	Biological nervous system	Living systems and cybernetics
Type of computation	Quantum (digital / analogue)	Event-driven with integrated memory	Distributed and hierarchical–recursive
Operational scale	Macro / global	Micro / meso (edge)	Micro–meso–macro
Energy consumption	High potential future efficiency	Very low energy consumption	System-level optimisation

continued on following page

Table 5. Continued

Dimension	Quantum AI	Neuromorphic AI	Holonic Architecture
Latency	Medium–high (cloud, QaaS)	Very low (edge)	Adaptive
Learning	Global / accelerated	Local / continuous	Individual and collective
Role in the IM	Optimisation, simulation, security	Perception, control, local adaptation	Governance and coordination
Type of intelligence	Advanced algorithmic intelligence	Embodied and adaptive intelligence	Organisational and emergent intelligence
Contribution to sustainability	Reduction of computational complexity	Energy and material efficiency	Co-evolution and resilience
Current limitations	Technological maturity	Standardisation and scalability	Design complexity
Main synergy	Computational acceleration	Efficiency and adaptation	Integration of requisite variety

5.3. Holonics as an Organisational Enabler of the IM

The adoption of quantum and neuromorphic technologies within the IM requires an organisational enabler capable of absorbing the complexity, distributed processing and co-evolution inherent to this class of systems. Organisational architectures inherited from I4.0 and I5.0, predominantly based on rigid hierarchies and centralised control, are insufficient to manage metaversic ecosystems characterised by heterogeneity, dynamism and coupling with multiple hosting environments, which are typical features of complex socio-technical systems.

In this context, holonic architecture emerges as a particularly suitable organisational framework. Introduced by Koestler, the holonic paradigm conceives systems as hierarchical–recursive structures composed of holons, that is, entities that are simultaneously wholes and parts, capable of operating autonomously and cooperatively within a holarchy (Koestler, 1964, 1967, 1979). This conceptualisation enables a natural management of requisite variety in multi-level, multi-scale and multi-aspect systems (Ashby, 1960).

From a Project Engineering perspective, holonic architecture facilitates the transversal integration of products, processes and facilities throughout the entire system life cycle, ensuring coherent alignment across physical, digital, cognitive and human domains. In the context of CPS X.0, each holon may represent a mesoscopic socio-technical entity endowed with capabilities for perception, decision-making and action, supported by classical, neuromorphic, quantum or hybrid artificial intelligence and deployed in a distributed manner across edge, fog and cloud infrastructures.

The existing affinity between the holonic paradigm, the principles of computing, and neuromorphic technologies makes this architecture suitable as an organizational facilitator of IM. Similar to the human nervous system, holonic architectures promote distributed intelligence, decentralized control, local adaptation and the emergence of global behaviors from interactions, thus contributing to the development of more resilient, scalable and energy-efficient systems.

From a structural standpoint, this convergence between holonism, neuromorphic computing and distributed intelligence lays the foundations for a neuromorphic holonic architecture of the IM, in which CPS X.0 systems act as distributed cognitive holons capable of coordination and co-evolution within complex socio-technical ecosystems.

Finally, from an epistemological perspective, holonic architecture is grounded in higher-order cybernetics, particularly third-order cybernetics, where system, observer and environment co-evolve reflexively (Lepskiy, 2018; von Foerster, 2003). Within this framework, the IM can be understood as a complex socio-technical system whose global behaviour cannot be imposed deterministically, but rather guided through mechanisms of self-organisation, distributed regulation and collective learning (Luther et al., 2023; Rovelli et al., 2022).

In summary, holonic architecture constitutes the organisational linkage that coherently articulates the quantum, neuromorphic and hybrid paradigms analysed in this chapter, establishing the conceptual foundations upon which the HQPE framework is built.

6. HOLONIC–QUANTUM CYBER-PHYSICAL ARCHITECTURE FOR THE IM

The evolution of the IM towards the paradigms of I6.0 requires a profound reformulation of the architectural models that have traditionally underpinned industrial cyber-physical systems. Conventional architectures, based on rigid hierarchies, centralised control and a strict separation between computation, organisation and cognition, are insufficient to manage the complexity, dynamism and co-evolution inherent to metaversic industrial ecosystems.

For this reason, a holonic-quantum cyberphysical architecture is proposed as a framework for the design, implementation, and governance of information infrastructure. This architecture is conceived as an evolution of cyberphysical systems toward CPS X.0, integrating classical, neuromorphic, quantum, and hybrid AI capabilities within a holonic, distributed, and cognitively based organizational structure.

6.1. Holonic CPS X.0 as an IM Reference

CPS X.0 systems are an advanced generation of CPS systems characterized by distributed intelligence, local autonomy, continuous adaptation, and global coordination. Unlike traditional CPS systems, which are primarily focused on executing predefined control strategies, CPS X.0 systems incorporate cognitive capabilities, contextual learning, and dynamic regulation in response to uncertain and changing environments.

From a holonic perspective, each CPS X.0 system is modeled as a holon—an entity that is both a part (of a higher-level structure) and the whole. This dual nature enables the construction of multi-level holarchies in which holons operate autonomously and cooperatively, thereby facilitating scalability, resilience and interoperability within the metaversic system.

6.2. Holonic Cyber-Physical Architecture of the IM

The IM can be conceived as a higher order holon, composed of a holarchy of interconnected CPS X.0 cyber-physical holons that coherently integrate the physical, digital, cybernetic, cognitive and human domains. Each CPS X.0 holon deploys distributed capabilities for perception, decision-making and action, supported by Edge, Fog and Cloud infrastructures and coordinated through holarchic mechanisms as shown in the Figure 4.

Figure 4. Architectural conception of CPS X.0 as the reference holonic cyber-physical unit of the IM. Source: Own elaboration.

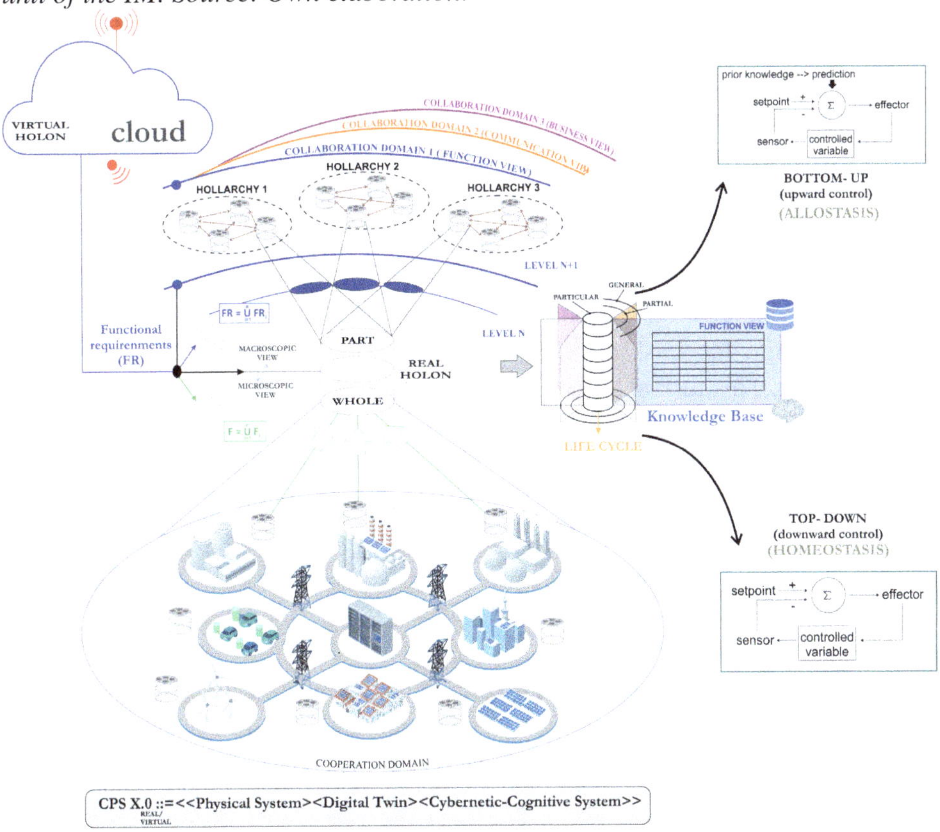

Figure 4 synthesises this architectural conception, representing the IM as a holarchy of CPS X.0 conceived as distributed cognitive holons. The architecture integrates, in a bio-inspired manner, the physical, cybernetic and virtual domains, deploying advanced AI and enabling the emergence of global behaviours from local interactions, thereby laying the foundations for the formal specification of the cyber-physical holon.

This architecture enables:

- multi-level integration (device, system, plant and network),
- heterarchical coordination among peer holons,
- flexible hierarchical regulation without structural rigidity,
- dynamic coupling between real systems and their virtual representations through digital twins.

On the basis of this holonic architectural conception of the IM, it becomes necessary to provide a formal specification capable of rigorously describing the internal structure, cognitive capabilities, interaction mechanisms and sustainability attributes of each elementary cyber-physical unit. In this context, the CPS X.0 holon is formally specified below as the fundamental unit for design, analysis, and governance of holonic cyber-physical architecture.

6.3. Formal Specification of the Cyber-Physical Holon

From a holonic perspective, each CPS X.0 within the IM can be formalised as a cognitive cyber-physical holon, conceived as an autonomous and cooperative entity that is simultaneously a functional whole and an integrated part of a higher-order holarchy. This formalisation enables a rigorous description of the structure, behaviour and governance of complex industrial metaversic systems throughout their entire life cycle.

As conceptually illustrated in Figure 4, each CPS X.0 holon is formally defined as shown in Equation 8.

$$H_i = (ID, L, R, F, C) \tag{8}$$

Where: ID (identifier), L (level), R (relations), F (functions), C (context).

The holonic organization supports both hierarchical and heterarchical coordination modes, with relationships defined as: $\exists\, rel(Hi,Hj) \in \{parent, child, peer\}$

Each holon incorporates a full life-cycle digital twin, ensuring consistency between physical system and its virtual representation across phases of design, operation, maintenance and end of life. This digital twin is formally defined in Equation 9.

$$GD_i = (M_d, M_o, M_m, M_r) \tag{9}$$

Where: M_d (Design model), M_o (Operational model), M_m (Maintenance model), M_r (Decommissioning model).

Synchronization with the physical environment is expressed as: $Sync(H_i, GD_i)(t) \Rightarrow$ temporal and operational coherence

From a cognitive perspective, each holon integrates a subsystem Cog_i, responsible for perception, decision-making, learning and adaptation, as formalised in Equation 10:

$$Cog_i = (P_i, D_i, L_i, Hm_i, Al_i) \tag{10}$$

Where: P_i (perception), D_i (decision-making), L_i (learning), Hm_i (homeostatic regulation), Al_i (allostatic regulation)

With adaptive behavior:: $D_i(t)=f(P_i(t),L_i(t))\Rightarrow Al_i(t+\Delta t)=g(L_i(t),\Delta E)$

Interaction with the physical and digital environment is mediated through the interface formalised in Equation 11.

$$IF_i = (S_i, A_i, G_i, P_i) \tag{11}$$

Where: S_i (sensors), A_i (actuators), G_i (gateways, edge and fog devices), P_i (platforms: SCADA, HMI, MES, ERP aligned with Smart Grid and Industrial CPS reference architectures such as the NIST Interoperability Framework).

With control and information flows: Input (físico → digital): $S_i \rightarrow G_i \rightarrow P_i$ and Output (digital → físico): $P_i \rightarrow G_i \rightarrow A_i$

Each holon explicitly incorporates sustainability and resilience attributes, as formalised in Equation 12, which refer to properties embedded at both the individual holon level and the global system level in order to ensure sustainable and resilient operation throughout the entire lifecycle.

$$SR_i = (Eff_i, Rsk_i, Eco_i, Rcv_i) \tag{12}$$

Where: Eff_i (energy efficiency), Rsk_i (risk level), Eco_i (eco-compatibility index), Rcv_i (recovery/resilience capacity).

Sustainable and secure operation condition: $Eff_i \geq Eff_{th} \wedge Rsk_i \leq Rsk_{th} \Rightarrow$ continuous and stable operation

Sustainable evolution flow (co-evolution): $\frac{dEco_i}{dt} \geq 0 y \frac{dRcv_i}{dt} > 0$

6.4. Neuromorphic and Cognitive Foundations of the Architecture

The cognitive character of the holonic–quantum cyber-physical architecture is grounded in the predictive brain paradigm and the free energy principle, according to which cognitive systems act to minimise uncertainty through inference and action. Within this framework, CPS X.0 holons generate internal models to anticipate future states and act upon the environment to validate such predictions, integrating perception, learning and action within active inference loops.

This approach converges with the enactive paradigm, in which cognition emerges from the dynamic interaction between agent and environment. When applied to the IM, it enables the design of cyber-physical systems capable of self-organisation, contextual adaptation, sociotechnical co-evolution, and distributed homeostatic and allostatic regulation.

On the whole, the holonic-quantum cyber-physical architecture defined in this chapter constitutes the architectural framework for MI in relation to I6.0.

7. HOLONIC–QUANTUM CYBER-PHYSICAL ARCHITECTURE FOR THE INDUSTRIAL ELECTRICAL METAVERSE

The deployment of the IM in the electrical sector—encompassing Smart Grids and Power Electrical Systems (PES)—constitutes a particularly representative use case, as it involves critical infrastructure that is highly distributed, subject to stringent real-time requirements, characterised by pronounced sociotechnical complexity, and exposed to growing demands in terms of sustainability, resilience and interoperability. In this context, the IM enables the integrated use of digital twins, extended reality (XR) and intelligence platforms (classical, neuromorphic, quantum and hybrid) to enhance system supervision, operation and planning across the entire lifecycle of electrical infrastructures.

From a lifecycle engineering perspective, metaverse-based technologies applied to power electrical systems enable: (i) real-time monitoring and diagnostics; (ii) operational optimisation and loss reduction; (iii) accelerated integration of renewable energy sources, Distributed Energy Resources (DER) and storage systems; (iv) advanced support for training, maintenance and assisted operation; and (v) the exploration of new energy business models (such as servitisation, advanced markets and prosumer–operator coordination), explicitly incorporating human, organisational and cultural dimensions. The technical and economic assessment of products, subsystems and operational strategies is further strengthened through the use of persistent digital twins, reducing lead times and costs in both greenfield and reengineering projects developed within BIM and PLM environments.

7.1. Reference Frameworks and Holonic Architecture of the Industrial Electrical Metaverse

The Industrial Electricity Metaverse requires support from established reference architectures capable of guaranteeing interoperability, scalability, resilience, and security in critical infrastructures. In this regard, many reference architectures exist, such as SGAM, the NIST Smart Grid Interoperability Framework, IEEE P2030, the GridWise Architecture, Cisco GridBlocks, and approaches based on holonic architectures. These architectures have laid the foundation for the development and modernization of smart electrical systems.

While these models have been fundamental in supporting the Electricity 4.0 and 5.0 paradigms, their scope is limited if considered in isolation from the requirements of the Industrial Electricity Metaverse. Therefore, an integrative approach is required, one that can improve and articulate existing frameworks within a CPS X.0 architecture aligned with the principles of I6.0.

The synthesis and comparison of these frameworks, as well as their relative contribution to key criteria, are shown in Table 6. In this table are considered seven criteria: (1) Integration of Information and Communication Technologies (ICT Integration); (2) Integration of Distributed Energy Resources (DER Integration); (3) System flexibility; (4) Level of standardisation; (5) Energy efficiency; (6) Operational resilience; and (7) Security.

In addition, Table 6 shows the qualitative levels H (high), M (medium) and L (low), which represent a comparative assessment of the degree of support each model provides for the criteria analyzed. A High level (H) shows an explicit, mature and systematically integrated treatment of the criterion; Medium (M) indicates partial coverage or reliance on complementary extensions; and Low (L) reflects limited or implicit consideration.

Table 6. Comparison of architectural models for Smart Grids. Source: Own elaboration.

Model	Main objective	(1)	(2)	(3)	(4)	(5)	(6)	(7)
SGAM	Architectural description of Smart Grids	H	H	H	H	H	H	H
CISCO GridBlocks	Reference architecture for intelligent electrical networks	H	H	H	M	H	H	H
IEEE P2030	Standards for intelligent power systems	H	H	M	M	M	M	H
GridWise Architecture	Guidance for grid modernisation	H	H	M	M	M	H	H
NIST Smart Grid Framework	Roadmap for interoperability and governance	H	H	M	M	M	H	H
Holonic Architecture	Modular and co-evolutionary architecture based on holons	H	H	H	L	H	H	H

Based on this comparative analysis, it becomes evident that none of the reference frameworks considered, when taken in isolation, is sufficient to fully address the systemic requirements of the Industrial Electrical Metaverse within the context of I6.0. In particular, the holonic integration of CPS, the coexistence of physical, digital and metaversic domains, multi-level governance, and sociotechnical co-evolution demand a synthesis architecture capable of articulating these frameworks within a single, coherent conceptual model.

Figure 5 presents this synthesis architecture, in which the Industrial Electrical Metaverse is conceived as a holarchy of interconnected CPS X.0 units, deployed across Edge, Fog and Cloud infrastructures.

Figure 5. Holonic CPS X.0 architecture for Intelligent Electrical Systems (Smart Grids / Power Systems).

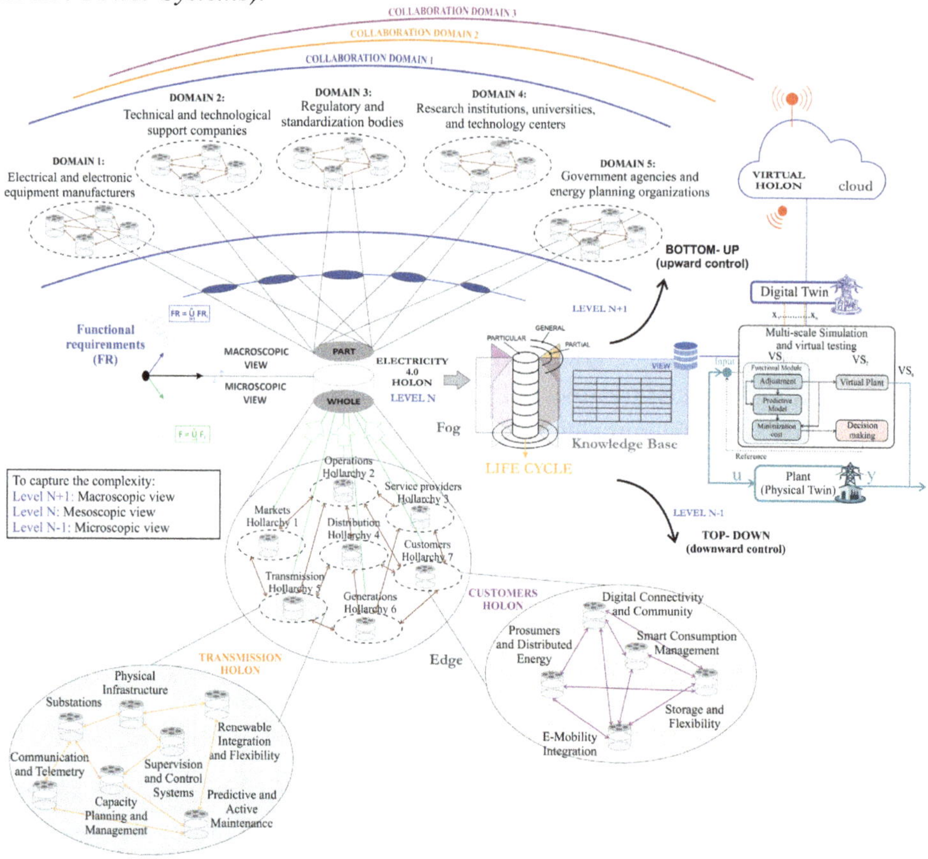

Source: Own elaboration.

In relation to this architecture, the Industrial Electric Metaverse is conceived as a holonic cyber-physical system for critical infrastructures, supporting distributed cognition, interoperability and resilient, multi-scale governance throughout the entire system lifecycle.

7.2. Proposal of Holonic CPS X.0 for the Industrial Electrical Metaverse

As a sector-specific instantiation of the IM and acting as an organisational enabler of the IM in Smart Grids and Power Systems (SEP), a holonic CPS X.0 architecture is proposed, in which the electrical system is modelled as a holarchy of entities (holons) endowed with local autonomy and global coordination. This holarchy integrates three fundamental components, consistent with the previous formalisation of the IM (Real–Cyber–Cybernetic), and illustrated in Figure 6:

1. Real cyber-physical holon (Real_SocioTechnical-Verse / Edge): Electrical assets (generation units, substations, transmission and distribution networks, DER, storage systems), including sensing and actuation layers, together with local control systems (e.g., PLCs, RTUs, HMIs) and human agents responsible for operation, safety and maintenance.
2. Virtual cyber-physical holon (Cyber-Verse / Cloud): Digital twins continuously updated through data streams, enabling simulation, diagnosis, scenario evaluation and decision support. In the Electrical Metaverse, this layer is extended beyond the technical system to virtualise relevant socio-economic domains (markets, business models, operation, maintenance and training) through virtual worlds, avatars and collaborative environments.
3. Cybernetic linkage system (Cybernetic-Verse with Fog/Edge/Cloud connectivity): An intelligent infrastructure for data capture, ingestion and transport, telecommunication networks, secure interoperability, knowledge bases and intelligence services supporting monitoring, predictive and adaptive control, and governance functions, including cybersecurity.

Figure 6. IM architecture as a holonic cyber-physical system (NIST-based).

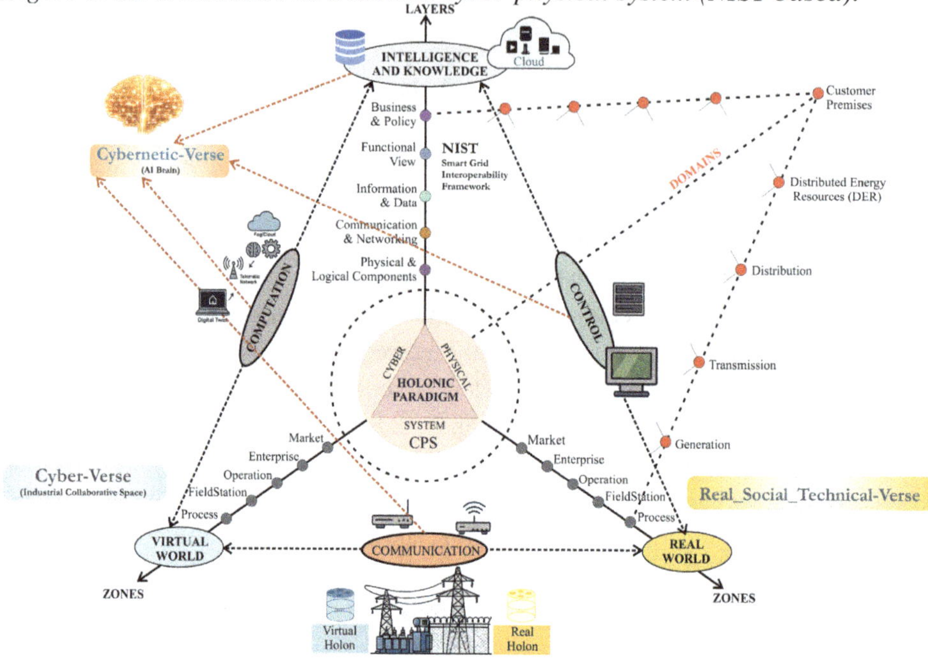

Source: Own elaboration.

Although the SGAM model is commonly adopted in the electrical engineering literature as a reference architectural framework, this work adopts the NIST Interoperability Framework due to its broader scope and its orientation towards complex cyber-physical systems. In particular, the NIST approach enables the explicit integration of technical and semantic interoperability, governance mechanisms, risk management and cybersecurity, making it more suitable as a conceptual foundation for the IM and for multisectoral holonic CPS architectures, beyond the strictly electrical domain.

This decomposition enables the Industrial Electrical Metaverse to be operated as a distributed socio-technical system, in which coordination emerges through multi-scale regulation and learning mechanisms, avoiding rigid centralised control schemes while ensuring coherence across the real, virtual and cybernetic domains.

7.3. Quantum–Neuromorphic Orchestration Within the Edge, Fog and Cloud Holarchy

The holonic–quantum architecture does not aim to replace classical computing paradigms, but rather to orchestrate complementary computational approaches according to system requirements and criticality levels:

- Neuromorphic (Edge/Fog): Event-based processing, ultra-low latency and high energy efficiency to support multisensory perception, anomaly detection, protection and adaptive local control, as well as real-time human–machine interaction and XR-based interfaces.
- Quantum (Cloud, selectively deployed): Combinatorial optimisation and advanced simulation for highly complex planning and operational problems (e.g., network reconfiguration, DER integration, storage allocation and management, multi-objective optimisation and large-scale scenario analysis).
- Hybrid approaches (Fog/Cloud): Integration of global exploration capabilities (quantum or quantum-inspired) with local adaptation mechanisms (neuromorphic/edge), combined with MLOps and SimOps pipelines to ensure lifecycle traceability, model governance and operational robustness.

The incorporation of quantum capabilities should therefore be understood as a strategic and selective resource, rather than as a full-scale implementation. Such capabilities are activated only where they provide structural advantages over classical alternatives, based on verifiable criteria related to performance, sustainability and system robustness.

7.4. Software Infrastructure of the Electrical Metaverse: Microservices, Containers and Multicloud

To support the CPS X.0 holarchy and the advanced services of the Electrical Metaverse, including persistent digital twins, XR environments, simulation, control and knowledge management, a TI/OT software infrastructure based on microservice architectures, containerisation and multicloud orchestration is required. This infrastructure constitutes the operational substrate that enables functional decoupling of services, ensures scalability, and facilitates distributed deployment across the Edge, Fog and Cloud domains.

From an architectural perspective, the software infrastructure is structured around the informational view of the CPS X.0 holon, integrating detection, data acquisition, preprocessing, storage, advanced analytics, and decision support systems, along with a layer of core holonic microservices. These microservices include various functions such as orchestration, service discovery, authentication, and interaction between service providers and consumers, ensuring interoperability, traceability, and operational governance.

The use of containers and orchestration platforms enables the sustainable implementation and evolution of the different components of the Electrical Metaverse, improving the digital thread implementation throughout the system lifecycle. Furthermore, this approach facilitates the integration of quantum computing services and hybrid computing paradigms without compromising the stability of the overall architecture.

Finally, the proposed infrastructure incorporates cross-cutting mechanisms for observability, security by design and regulatory compliance, which are critical in the context of electrical infrastructures. As a result, the holonic microservice-based software architecture is consolidated as a key enabler for the resilient, scalable and sustainable operation of the IM in Smart Grids and Electric Power Systems.

7.5. Research and Innovation Agenda for HQPE in Smart Grids and Electric Power Systems

This use case enables the systematisation of an R&I agenda aligned with HQPE along three complementary fronts: (i) Real_SocioTechnical-Verse (Edge): advanced sensing and metrology; neuromorphic approaches for fault detection and local control; cybersecurity at device level; reduction of latency and bandwidth consumption through edge intelligence; (ii) Cybernetic-Verse (Edge, Fog and Cloud): secure networks and communications; interoperability mechanisms; cyber-resilience; distributed analytics and intelligence; post-quantum strategies for critical infrastructures, in accordance with established reference frameworks; and (3) Cyber-Verse (Cloud): persistent digital twins and operational XR environments; large-scale simulation and optimisation; integration of simulation outcomes with governance and control mechanisms; evaluation of socio-economic and operational scenarios across the system lifecycle.

Taken together, this use case demonstrates that the Electrical Metaverse is not a superimposed "digital layer", but rather a cognitive and organisational infrastructure sustained by holonic CPS and enabled through quantum–neuromorphic orchestration, providing a robust foundation for the sustainable and resilient operation of Smart Grids and Electric Power Systems within the framework of I6.0.

8. CONCLUSIONS

This chapter suggests that the evolution of the IM towards the paradigms of I6.0 is unlikely to be adequately addressed through incremental extensions of legacy industrial architectures, or through the exclusive use of classical artificial intelligence and Von Neumann–based computing. The sociotechnical, cognitive and organisational complexity of industrial metaversic systems, characterised by distribution, dynamism, co-evolution and criticality, structurally exceeds the capabilities of the centralised and hierarchical approaches typical of I4.0 and 5.0. In this context, the analysis shows that the integration of emerging computational paradigms (neuromorphic, quantum and hybrid) does not constitute an optional enhancement, but rather a structural requirement to efficiently manage latency, scalability, energy sustainability and resilience, which are intrinsic to the IM as a critical infrastructure.

On this basis, the chapter has formalised the Holonic Quantum-Neuromorphic Cyber-Physical Architecture as a reference framework capable of articulating CPS X.0, digital twins, advanced artificial intelligence and human participation within a distributed cognitive holarchy. The holonic paradigm is thus consolidated as the organisational enabler that provides the requisite variety, multi-level governance and co-evolutionary capacity needed to operate complex industrial metaversic ecosystems throughout their entire lifecycle.

This approach substantially redefines the role of Engineering and Project Management, which moves beyond the local control of closed systems to assume the orchestration of complex sociotechnical ecosystems. This entails integrating, from the earliest project phases, distributed architectures, emergent intelligence and explicit criteria for sustainability, resilience and ethical governance. Consequently, HQPE emerges not merely as a conceptual proposal, but as a necessary methodological framework for the design, management and operation of IMs aligned with the core principles of I6.0.

REFERENCES

Ashby, W. R. (1960). Design for a Brain - The origin of adaptive behavior. [ASHB]. *Cybernetics, 304,* •••. https://doi.org/SYST

Ávila-Gutiérrez, M. J., Martín-Gómez, A., Aguayo-González, F., & Córdoba-Roldán, A. (2019). Standardization Framework for Sustainability from Circular Economy 4.0. *Sustainability (Basel), 11*(22), 6490. DOI: 10.3390/su11226490

AWS BRAKET. (2026). *Servicio de computación cuántica en la nube - Amazon Braket - AWS.* https://aws.amazon.com/es/braket/

Cerezo, M., Verdon, G., Huang, H.-Y., Cincio, L., & Coles, P. J. (2023). Challenges and Opportunities in Quantum Machine Learning. *Nature Computational Science, 2*(9), 567–576. DOI: 10.1038/s43588-022-00311-3 PMID: 38177473

Davies, M., Wild, A., Orchard, G., Sandamirskaya, Y., Guerra, G. A. F., Joshi, P., Plank, P., & Risbud, S. R. (2021). Advancing Neuromorphic Computing with Loihi: A Survey of Results and Outlook. *Proceedings of the IEEE, 109*(5), 911–934. DOI: 10.1109/JPROC.2021.3067593

European Union. (2024). *Regulation (EU) 2024/1689 of the European Parliament and of the Council of 13 June 2024 laying down harmonised rules on artificial intelligence (Artificial Intelligence Act). Official Journal of the European Union.* https://eur-lex.europa.eu/eli/reg/2024/1689/oj/eng

Goldstein, R. (2021). Desafíos del Desarrollo Sostenible en la Nueva Normalidad. Coherencia de Políticas para la Agenda 2030 y los ODS en la Década de Acción. In *La Administración Pública en tiempos disruptivos. Diego Pando (compilador)* (Number January, pp. 171–177).

Indiveri, G., & Liu, S. C. (2015). Memory and Information Processing in Neuromorphic Systems. *Proceedings of the IEEE, 103*(8), 1379–1397. ISO/IEC. (2023). *ISO/IEC 42001:2023 Information technology—Artificial intelligence—Management system. International Organization for Standardization.* DOI: 10.1109/JPROC.2015.2444094

ITU. (2024a). *FGMV-51: Standardization roadmap for the metaverse.* ITU-T Focus Group on Metaverse.

ITU. (2024b). *FGMV-52: Metaverse standardization landscape for gap analyses. ITU-T Focus Group on Metaverse.*

Jha, R. K. (2023). From Quantum Computing to Quantum-inspired Computation for Neuromorphic Advancement – A Survey. In *Authorea Preprints. Authorea.* DOI: 10.36227/techrxiv.24053250.v1

Koestler, A. (1964). *The Act of Creation.* MacMillan.

Koestler, A. (1967). *The ghost in the machine.* Hutchinson.

Koestler, A. (1979). Janus: A summing up. *Bulletin of the Atomic Scientists, 35*(3), 4–4. DOI: 10.1080/00963402.1979.11458590

Lee, E. A. (2015). The Past, Present and Future of Cyber-Physical Systems: A Focus on Models. *Sensors 2015, Vol. 15, Pages 4837-4869, 15*(3), 4837–4869. DOI: 10.3390/s150304837

Lepskiy, V. (2018). Evolution of cybernetics: Philosophical and methodological analysis. *Kybernetes, 47*(2), 249–261. DOI: 10.1108/K-03-2017-0120

Lu, W., Lu, Y., Li, J., Sigov, A., Ratkin, L., & Ivanov, L. A. (2024). Quantum machine learning: Classifications, challenges, and solutions. *Journal of Industrial Information Integration, 42*, 100736. DOI: 10.1016/j.jii.2024.100736

Luther, B., Gunawan, I., & Nguyen, N. (2023). Identifying effective risk management frameworks for complex socio-technical systems. *Safety Science, 158*, 105989. DOI: 10.1016/j.ssci.2022.105989

Marković, D., & Grollier, J. (2020). Quantum neuromorphic computing. *Applied Physics Letters, 117*(15), 150501. Advance online publication. DOI: 10.1063/5.0020014

NIST. (2023). *Artificial Intelligence Risk Management Framework (AI RMF 1.0) (NIST AI 100-1). National Institute of Standards and Technology.*

NIST. (2024). *The NIST Cybersecurity Framework (CSF) 2.0 (NIST CSWP 29). National Institute of Standards and Technology.*

Preskill, J. (2018). Quantum Computing in the NISQ era and beyond. *Quantum : the Open Journal for Quantum Science, 2*, 79. DOI: 10.22331/q-2018-08-06-79

Quantum, I. B. M. (2026). *IBM Quantum Computing.* https://www.ibm.com/quantum

Ren, L., Dong, J., Zhang, L., Laili, Y., Wang, X., Qi, Y., Li, B. H., Wang, L., Yang, L. T., & Deen, M. J. (2024). Industrial Metaverse for Smart Manufacturing: Model, Architecture, and Applications. *IEEE Transactions on Cybernetics, 54*(5), 2683–2695. DOI: 10.1109/TCYB.2024.3372591 PMID: 38512748

Rovelli, C. (2022). *Helgoland: Making sense of the quantum revolution.* Penguin.

Tao, F., Zhang, H., Liu, A., & Nee, A. Y. C. (2019). Digital Twin in Industry: State-of-the-Art. *IEEE Transactions on Industrial Informatics*, *15*(4), 2405–2415. DOI: 10.1109/TII.2018.2873186

Verma, A., Prasad, V. K., Kumari, A., Bhattacharya, P., Srivastava, G., Fang, K., Wang, W., & Gadekallu, T. R. (2025). Industry 6.0: Vision, technical landscape, and opportunities. *Alexandria Engineering Journal*, *130*, 139–174. DOI: 10.1016/j.aej.2025.08.040

von Foerster, H. (2003). *Understanding Understanding. Essays on Cybernetics and Cognition.* Springer New York., DOI: 10.1007/b97451

Yamane, T., Hirose, A., & Offrein, B. J. (2023). Editorial: Physical neuromorphic computing and its industrial applications. *Frontiers in Neuroinformatics*, *17*, 1238168–1238168. DOI: 10.3389/fninf.2023.1238168 PMID: 37529766

Yao, X., Ma, N., Zhang, J., Wang, K., Yang, E., & Faccio, M. (2024). Enhancing wisdom manufacturing as industrial metaverse for industry and society 5.0. *Journal of Intelligent Manufacturing*, *35*(1), 235–255. DOI: 10.1007/s10845-022-02027-7

Zhuang, Y., Azfar, T., Wang, Y., Sun, W., Wang, X., Guo, Q., & Ke, R. (2024). Quantum Computing in Intelligent Transportation Systems: A Survey. *CHAIN*, *1*(2), 138–149. DOI: 10.23919/CHAIN.2024.000007

Chapter 9

Design and Analysis of Modern Quantum Neural Network Architectures for Intelligent Systems

Lakshmi Chandrakanth Kasireddy
http://orcid.org/0009-0002-0392-739X
ThoughtSpot Inc., USA

Prabhakara Rao Kapula
http://orcid.org/0000-0002-4400-5087
B.V. Raju Institute of Technology, Vishnupur, India

Dineshkumar Rajendran
http://orcid.org/0000-0001-8530-7850
Old Dominion University, USA

Neha Bharani
IPS Academy, Indore, India

Srikanth Pulipeti
MPSTME SVKMs NMIMS University, Shirpur, India

Islombek Khushvaktov
Tashkent State University of Economics, Tashkent, Uzbekistan

ABSTRACT

Quantum neural networks (QNNs) offer a principled pathway for integrating quantum computation with machine learning through superposition- and entanglement-based representations. This chapter proposes an architecture-aware design and evaluation framework for modern QNNs, emphasizing robustness and system feasibility alongside predictive performance. Multiple architecturesvariational QNNs, quantum convolutional neural networks, tensor-network hybrids, and fully quantum models—are assessed under a unified protocol. Experimental analysis shows that the proposed architecture-search–guided QNN achieves 91.8% classification accuracy and an F1-score of 0.914, outperforming fixed-template variational QNNs by approximate-

DOI: 10.4018/979-8-2600-0008-3.ch009

ly 5.6 percentage points. Under depolarizing noise with probability p = 0.10, the proposed model retains 85.3% accuracy, whereas baseline QNNs fall below 80%. Moreover, circuit depth is reduced by nearly 25% relative to standard variational designs, leading to faster convergence (42 epochs vs. 57 epochs).

INTRODUCTION

The technological foundation of these architectures depends heavily on advances in quantum hardware and programming frameworks. Superconducting and trapped-ion qubit platforms provide the physical substrate for QNN execution, while software environments such as TensorFlow Quantum facilitate the integration of quantum layers into classical machine learning pipelines (Young, 2023). These tools enable researchers to prototype quantum learning models using familiar optimization routines while exploiting quantum state evolution for feature transformation.

Noise modeling and mitigation technologies further shape modern QNN design. Since quantum gates are susceptible to decoherence and stochastic error, recent architectural approaches incorporate noise-aware training strategies and robustness evaluation as integral components rather than auxiliary corrections (Ahmed et al., 2025). This trend aligns QNN research with broader system reliability concerns that dominate intelligent system design, particularly in safety-critical or infrastructure-scale deployments (Mamodiya& Kishor, 2026).

From a systems perspective, the phrase intelligent systemsextends the scope of QNNs beyond isolated classifiers toward adaptive decision-making entities capable of operating under uncertainty. Quantum-enhanced learning is increasingly viewed as a complementary layer within hybrid AI frameworks, where quantum circuits assist in pattern abstraction while classical components handle large-scale reasoning and control (Hadap&Patil, 2024; Trisnapradika&Akrom, 2025). This synergy reflects a technological convergence rather than a replacement paradigm, positioning QNNs as accelerators or enrichers of intelligence rather than standalone solutions.

1.1 Background and Motivation

The rapid evolution of artificial intelligence (AI) has been driven largely by advances in deep neural networks, data availability, and scalable computational infrastructure. Classical neural architectures have achieved remarkable success across diverse problem domains, including computer vision, natural language processing, autonomous systems, and energy management. However, the computational demands of modern learning models are escalating at a pace that increasingly strains conventional hardware paradigms. As model depth and parameter counts grow, training efficiency, generalization reliability, and energy consumption emerge as limiting factors for further progress (Bhatye, 2025; Mamodiya& Kishor, 2026).

Parallel to these developments, quantum computing has matured from a largely theoretical construct into an experimentally accessible platform capable of performing operations that are intractable for classical machines. Quantum processors exploit superposition, entanglement, and interference to represent and manipulate information in fundamentally different ways than classical bits. These properties offer the promise of exponential state-space representation and potentially transformative speedups for selected computational tasks (Hadap&Patil, 2024; Trisnapradika&Akrom, 2025).

The convergence of these two paradigms has led to the emergence of quantum machine learning (QML), a field that seeks to integrate quantum computational principles with learning algorithms. Among the various QML models proposed to date, quantum neural networks (QNNs) occupy a central position due to their conceptual proximity to classical neural architectures and their adaptability to hybrid classical–quantum workflows. QNNs attempt to encode data into quantum states and perform learning through parameterized quantum circuits, often referred to as variational quantum circuits (Thomas, 2023; Zhang, 2024).

Despite the enthusiasm surrounding QNNs, the field remains at an early developmental stage. Theoretical promise frequently collides with practical constraints, including hardware noise, limited qubit counts, decoherence, and measurement overhead. Nevertheless, recent investigations demonstrate that QNNs can outperform classical models for specific structured tasks or under restricted resource conditions (Ahmed et al., 2025; Markidis, 2023). These findings motivate deeper architectural analysis and systematic design principles that move beyond proof-of-concept implementations toward robust intelligent systems.

1.2 Quantum Neural Networks: Conceptual Foundations

Quantum neural networks are inspired by classical artificial neural networks but operate within the Hilbert space of quantum states rather than Euclidean vector spaces. Information is typically encoded into quantum amplitudes or phases, and learning is performed by adjusting parameters of unitary operations that transform these states. Unlike classical neurons, which apply deterministic nonlinear activations, quantum neurons rely on probabilistic measurement outcomes and quantum interference to shape decision boundaries (Thomas, 2023; Zhang, 2024).

Several QNN variants have been proposed, ranging from hybrid architectures—where classical neural layers interact with quantum circuits—to fully quantum models in which both representation and optimization are conducted in quantum form (Ewald, 2025). Notably, convolutional analogs such as quantum convolutional neural networks (QCNNs) have demonstrated potential for structured feature extraction in high-dimensional spaces (Lee et al., 2025). These architectures attempt to replicate the hierarchical abstraction process of classical CNNs while leveraging quantum entanglement for global correlation modeling.

Recent studies also highlight the role of multi-qubit interaction potentials in enabling richer representational capacity. Multi-qubit QNNs can encode nonlinear decision surfaces through entangled quantum states, allowing complex mappings to emerge from relatively compact circuit structures (Quantum neural networks with multi-qubit potentials, 2023). Such properties suggest that QNNs could serve as compact yet expressive learners when hardware constraints are adequately addressed.

However, practical deployment remains challenged by the realities of noisy intermediate-scale quantum (NISQ) devices. Current systems exhibit gate errors, decoherence, and limited qubit connectivity, which directly affect training stability and output fidelity. Programming frameworks and optimization strategies must therefore be co-designed with hardware awareness, ensuring that theoretical models remain physically realizable (Markidis, 2023; Chen et al., 2024).

1.3 Problem Statement

Despite substantial conceptual progress, modern QNN research suffers from fragmentation across three dimensions: architectural design, noise robustness, and application relevance. Existing models often focus on isolated improvements—such as faster convergence or expressive encoding—without providing a unified architectural framework suitable for intelligent system deployment. Many proposed QNNs are validated using small synthetic datasets or toy classification problems, limiting their interpretability in real-world contexts (Young, 2023; Ahmed et al., 2025).

Furthermore, the majority of reported architectures rely on shallow circuit designs tailored to current hardware limitations, which constrains their representational depth. While this approach is practical, it restricts the ability of QNNs to capture hierarchical abstractions comparable to those of deep classical networks. At the same time, attempts to deepen circuits frequently encounter the barren plateau problem, where gradients vanish exponentially with circuit depth, preventing effective learning (Ewald, 2025; Chen et al., 2024).

Another critical challenge lies in noise sensitivity. Quantum systems are inherently vulnerable to environmental interactions, and QNN outputs may fluctuate significantly under realistic error models. Comparative studies show that model accuracy degrades sharply when exposed to depolarizing or phase-damping noise unless specific mitigation strategies are applied (Ahmed et al., 2025). This fragility undermines confidence in QNNs as components of intelligent systems that must operate reliably under uncertain physical conditions.

From an application perspective, integration with intelligent decision-making frameworks remains underdeveloped. While isolated demonstrations exist in image classification and pattern recognition (Young, 2023), systematic architectural analysis for broader intelligent system design is scarce. This gap is particularly evident when considering large-scale cyber-physical environments such as smart grids or autonomous infrastructures, where robustness, interpretability, and adaptability are critical (Mamodiya& Kishor, 2026; Trisnapradika&Akrom, 2025).

1.4 Research Gaps in Existing Literature

A review of current scholarship reveals several unresolved gaps. First, most studies emphasize algorithmic novelty without sufficiently analyzing architectural trade-offs between expressiveness, trainability, and hardware feasibility. Comparative analyses remain limited, and there is a lack of standardized benchmarks for architectural evaluation (Thomas, 2023; Zhang, 2024).

Second, although QCNNs and multi-qubit models demonstrate theoretical advantages, their scalability across arbitrary data dimensions is not yet well understood. Optimized QCNN designs exist, but their generalization behavior under increasing input complexity remains underexplored (Lee et al., 2025). Similarly, while multi-qubit potentials introduce nonlinear mapping capacity, their stability under noisy evolution requires further systematic study (Quantum neural networks with multi-qubit potentials, 2023).

Third, the transition from hybrid to fully quantum architectures is still conceptually immature. Fully quantum neural networks promise end-to-end quantum learning but introduce additional challenges in training dynamics and measurement-driven optimization (Ewald, 2025). Existing approaches lack a unified design methodology that connects architectural depth, fidelity-driven learning, and system-level intelligence.

Fourth, current literature tends to treat noise robustness as an auxiliary concern rather than an intrinsic design objective. Noise-aware architectures are typically introduced post hoc through error mitigation rather than embedded directly into architectural principles (Ahmed et al., 2025; Markidis, 2023).

Finally, the relationship between QNN architecture and intelligent system behavior remains insufficiently formalized. While conceptual discussions highlight the synergy between quantum computing and AI (Hadap&Patil, 2024; Galarza-Sánchez et al., 2023), few works articulate how architectural choices translate into measurable improvements in system-level intelligence, such as adaptability, efficiency, or decision reliability (Trisnapradika&Akrom, 2025; Mamodiya& Kishor, 2026).

1.5 Proposed Perspective and Solution Direction

This chapter advances the position that QNNs must be treated not merely as algorithmic constructs but as architectural systems whose design principles determine their functional role within intelligent environments. Rather than proposing a single model instance, the chapter focuses on the structural analysis of modern QNN architectures, examining how different circuit organizations, parameterization strategies, and entanglement patterns influence learning behavior.

The proposed perspective integrates three complementary dimensions. The first is architectural expressiveness, which evaluates how effectively quantum circuits encode nonlinear mappings relative to classical neural layers. This includes analysis of QCNN-based hierarchies, multi-qubit interaction networks, and hybrid quantum–classical pipelines (Lee et al., 2025; Quantum neural networks with multi-qubit potentials, 2023).

The second dimension concerns noise-aware learning. Instead of treating noise as an external disturbance, architectural design is examined in relation to noise tolerance, circuit depth optimization, and fidelity-driven training strategies (Ahmed et al., 2025; Ewald, 2025). This perspective emphasizes robustness as an inherent design objective rather than an auxiliary correction.

The third dimension addresses intelligent system integration. QNNs are analyzed in relation to real-world decision-making frameworks, particularly in domains requiring adaptive inference under uncertainty. Applications such as smart energy systems and intelligent control illustrate how quantum-enhanced learning can complement classical AI pipelines (Mamodiya& Kishor, 2026; Trisnapradika&Akrom, 2025).

By synthesizing these dimensions, the chapter aims to establish a design-oriented understanding of modern QNN architectures rather than limiting discussion to isolated performance metrics.

1.6 Novelty and Contributions

The novelty of this chapter lies in its architectural and system-level orientation. Unlike prior surveys that primarily catalog algorithms or hardware platforms (Chen et al., 2024; Markidis, 2023), this work emphasizes the relationship between QNN structure and intelligent system behavior. It articulates how circuit topology, entanglement strategy, and parameter learning mechanisms collectively define functional intelligence.

Specifically, the contributions of this chapter are fourfold. First, it provides a structured taxonomy of modern QNN architectures, linking theoretical constructs with practical design constraints. Second, it integrates noise robustness into architectural analysis, highlighting fidelity-driven and depth-aware training paradigms as central design elements (Ahmed et al., 2025; Ewald, 2025). Third, it contextualizes QNNs within intelligent system frameworks, bridging quantum learning theory with application-driven requirements (Mamodiya& Kishor, 2026; Trisnapradika&Akrom, 2025). Finally, it identifies future research directions that align quantum hardware evolution with scalable architectural design.

Through this synthesis, the chapter positions QNNs not merely as experimental curiosities but as emerging components of next-generation intelligent systems. The analysis underscores that meaningful progress in quantum-enhanced intelligence will depend less on isolated algorithmic novelty and more on principled architectural design that harmonizes quantum mechanics with learning theory.

2. LITERATURE REVIEW

The growing intersection of quantum computing and artificial intelligence has reshaped how learning models are conceptualized, implemented, and evaluated. Rather than treating quantum computing merely as a faster calculator, recent research views it as a fundamentally new representational medium for learning systems. This shift has encouraged the emergence of quantum neural networks (QNNs), quantum-inspired learning models, and hybrid quantum–classical architectures that attempt to balance theoretical promise with practical feasibility (Guntuka, 2024; Yousif & Al-Khateeb, 2024).

2.1 Evolution from Classical Neural Systems to Quantum Learning Models

Classical neural networks have demonstrated strong performance in pattern recognition and decision-making tasks, particularly in multimodal environments. Kishor et al. (2025) showed that adaptive multimodal neural networks can fuse heterogeneous data streams for real-time threat detection. While this work remains classical in computation, it highlights an important motivation for quantum extensions: modern intelligent systems require high-dimensional representation, rapid inference, and adaptive learning under uncertainty.

Quantum machine learning seeks to extend these properties by encoding information into quantum states, enabling parallel state evolution within Hilbert space (Kosaraju, 2024; Guntuka, 2024). Unlike classical neurons that rely on scalar activations, quantum neurons operate through unitary transformations and probabilistic measurements. This introduces nonlinearity through quantum interference rather than deterministic activation functions, creating a distinct computational regime (Yousif & Al-Khateeb, 2024).

However, early QNN proposals remained largely theoretical and often assumed idealized quantum hardware. Practical realizations now focus on variational quantum circuits and hybrid learning loops, where classical optimizers update quantum parameters iteratively (Mayorga et al., 2024; Tripathi et al., 2025). These hybrid models form the backbone of modern QNN architectures.

2.2 Architectural Innovations in Quantum Neural Networks

Recent work has emphasized architectural expressibility and scalability as central design challenges. Gong et al. (2023) proposed a quantum convolutional neural network based on variational quantum circuits, translating convolutional filters into structured quantum gate sequences. This approach enables hierarchical feature extraction while preserving quantum coherence within subspaces. Similarly, Monbroussou et al. (2024) introduced subspace-preserving QCNN architectures that maintain information locality during entanglement operations, improving classification stability.

Tree tensor network hybrids further address scalability by decomposing quantum states into hierarchical tensor structures. Hidayat and Akrom (2025) demonstrated that such architectures achieve efficient classification while reducing circuit depth. This work suggests that architectural decomposition is critical for managing quantum resource constraints without sacrificing learning capacity.

Beyond static circuit layouts, continuous-time and liquid quantum neural networks have been proposed as adaptive alternatives. Mayorga et al. (2024) developed CTRQNets and LQNets, which model quantum learning as a continuous-time dynamical system. Their formulation draws inspiration from liquid neural networks and highlights temporal adaptability as a distinguishing advantage of quantum recurrent structures.

Another important architectural dimension concerns ansatz design. Tripathi et al. (2025) analyzed how ansatz expressibility and circuit complexity affect classification accuracy in QNN and quantum LSTM models. Their findings indicate that highly expressive ansätze can improve performance but often suffer from trainability issues due to gradient vanishing, reinforcing the trade-off between representational power and optimization stability.

To address this trade-off, Kundu et al. (2024) proposed KANQAS, a Kolmogorov–Arnold network for quantum architecture search. This method automates circuit structure discovery, reducing reliance on manually designed ansätze. Such approaches move QNN design closer to neural architecture search paradigms in classical deep learning.

2.3 Fully Quantum and Quantum-Inspired Neural Models

While hybrid models dominate current implementations, several studies aim to construct fully quantum neural networks. Ewald (2025) proposed a fidelity-driven training mechanism using directional gradients, enabling multi-class classification entirely within a quantum learning framework. This work attempts to eliminate classical optimization loops, though it introduces new challenges in measurement efficiency and convergence stability.

Parallel to fully quantum designs, quantum-inspired neural models seek to transfer quantum principles into classical computation. BoullosaDapena (2025) introduced Quantum-Inspired Differentiable Integral Neural Networks (QIDINNs), drawing from Feynman path integrals to model continuous learning over streaming data. Although implemented classically, QIDINNs mimic quantum superposition and interference in their integral formulation.

Such quantum-inspired architectures highlight an important insight: quantum advantage may arise not only from hardware acceleration but also from conceptual borrowing. These models provide an intermediate step for validating quantum learning concepts before full hardware deployment (Kosaraju, 2024; Yousif & Al-Khateeb, 2024).

2.4 Noise, Robustness, and Distributed Quantum Learning

Noise and decoherence remain major obstacles to scalable QNN deployment. Research increasingly treats noise not as a secondary nuisance but as a design parameter. Tripathi et al. (2025) showed that circuit complexity directly impacts noise sensitivity, with deeper ansätze exhibiting sharper performance degradation.

To mitigate such effects, Guo et al. (2025) proposed a quantum parallel information exchange hybrid network with transfer learning. Their framework distributes learning across quantum and classical layers, improving robustness through redundancy and knowledge transfer. Similarly, Xiang and Chen (2025) developed AdaptDQC, an adaptive distributed quantum computing model with quantitative performance analysis, enabling task distribution across quantum nodes.

Distributed quantum learning frameworks also appear in semantic communications. Andreou et al. (2025) demonstrated that quantum computing can enhance semantic transmission by operating in high-dimensional Hilbert spaces, reducing optimization overhead in communication tasks. These results suggest that quantum neural architectures may play a role beyond classification, extending into communication and coordination systems.

2.5 Application-Oriented QNN Studies

A growing body of literature explores QNNs within applied intelligent systems. Fatunmbi (2023) examined the role of QNNs in multimodal healthcare diagnosis, highlighting their potential for integrating medical imaging, physiological data, and genomic features into unified diagnostic models. This work emphasizes that quantum learning can support complex data fusion tasks where classical methods struggle with dimensionality.

In business intelligence, Taiwo et al. (2025) investigated quantum-enhanced AI systems for decision analytics. Their study argues that quantum parallelism enables faster scenario evaluation and risk modeling, especially in uncertain environments. Similarly, Kosaraju (2024) framed quantum AI as a transformative fusion capable of reshaping optimization and prediction tasks across industries.

In energy systems, Liu (2025) proposed deep reinforcement learning for intelligent load balancing in smart grids. Although this work remains classical, it underscores the relevance of adaptive decision-making under uncertainty—an area where quantum-enhanced learning may offer future advantages. The link between intelligent control and quantum computation is further strengthened by fuzzy quantum decision models. Yan et al. (2025) developed fuzzy quantum group decision-making systems for meteorological disaster response, demonstrating how quantum reasoning can support complex, uncertain judgments.

Healthcare and sustainability have also emerged as key application drivers. Alzoubi et al. (2025) conducted a systematic review of sustainable AI techniques in healthcare, stressing the need for energy-efficient and scalable learning systems. This aligns with the motivation behind quantum neural models, which aim to reduce computational overhead through parallel state evolution rather than brute-force processing.

2.6 Security, Privacy, and Quantum-Enabled Intelligent Infrastructure

Security-oriented intelligent systems represent another domain where quantum learning architectures are gaining attention. Kishor et al. (2025) showed that adaptive multimodal neural networks can detect threats in real time. When extended to quantum learning, such systems could benefit from enhanced pattern discrimination in encrypted or noisy environments.

Singamaneni et al. (2025) proposed a quantum blockchain framework integrated with edge computing for privacy-preserving 6G networks. Their architecture demonstrates how quantum computation can coexist with distributed ledger technologies to protect sensitive information. Although not explicitly focused on QNNs, this work highlights the infrastructure-level relevance of quantum learning components.

Similarly, Guo et al. (2025) showed that transfer learning combined with quantum parallel information exchange can enhance hybrid intelligence frameworks. These results suggest that QNNs should not be viewed as isolated classifiers but as modules embedded within larger secure and distributed intelligent ecosystems.

2.7 Synthesis and Identified Research Gaps

Across the reviewed literature, several patterns emerge. First, architectural innovation dominates current research, with QCNNs, tensor networks, and continuous-time models offering promising directions (Gong et al., 2023; Monbroussou et al., 2024; Mayorga et al., 2024). Second, optimization challenges remain unresolved, particularly regarding ansatz design and gradient stability (Tripathi et al., 2025; Kundu et al., 2024). Third, fully quantum learning models are conceptually appealing but face practical measurement and training barriers (Ewald, 2025).

From an application standpoint, QNNs show promise in healthcare, business intelligence, communication systems, and disaster management (Fatunmbi, 2023; Taiwo et al., 2025; Andreou et al., 2025; Yan et al., 2025). However, most studies remain proof-of-concept and lack standardized benchmarks for real-world deployment.

Moreover, while distributed quantum computing and hybrid learning frameworks address scalability (Xiang & Chen, 2025; Guo et al., 2025), there is limited work connecting architectural design directly to intelligent system behavior. The majority of existing research treats QNNs as algorithmic tools rather than system-level components.

Finally, sustainability and security considerations are often treated separately from architectural design (Alzoubi et al., 2025; Singamaneni et al., 2025). A unified framework that integrates architectural expressibility, robustness, and application relevance remains largely absent from current scholarship.

3. METHODOLOGY

This chapter develops a structured methodology for the **design and analysis of modern quantum neural network (QNN) architectures** intended for intelligent systems operating under realistic constraints, especially the NISQ regime. The methodology is written to be reproducible: it defines the architectural space, formalizes the learning objective, explains how data is encoded into quantum states, specifies trainable circuit templates (ansätze), and outlines training, robustness evaluation, and system-level validation protocols. The design choices are motivated by practical learnability and hardware feasibility, which are repeatedly highlighted as the central barriers in QNN adoption (Markidis, 2023; Chen et al., 2024; Yousif & Al-Khateeb, 2024). The proposed pipeline aligns with the literature direction that calls for architectural analysis rather than one-off model demonstrations (Thomas, 2023; Zhang, 2024), and it explicitly includes noise robustness assessment because contemporary QNN performance is often dominated by hardware noise and ansatz complexity trade-offs (Ahmed et al., 2025; Tripathi et al., 2025).

3.1 Methodological Overview and Chapter Workflow

The methodology follows a staged flow: (i) define the problem formulation for intelligent systems, (ii) design candidate QNN families (variational, convolutional, recurrent/liquid, tensor-network hybrids, and fully quantum variants), (iii) search and refine architectures using principled constraints and architecture search tools, (iv) train models with gradient-based and fidelity-aware strategies, (v) evaluate performance under noise and resource limitations, and (vi) validate system-level suitability using metrics that reflect accuracy, stability, computational cost, and sustainability. This workflow is summarized visually to help the reader understand dependencies between each stage, as shown in Figure 1 (Chen et al., 2024; Markidis, 2023).

Figure 1. Methodological workflow for QNN architecture design, training, and evaluation.

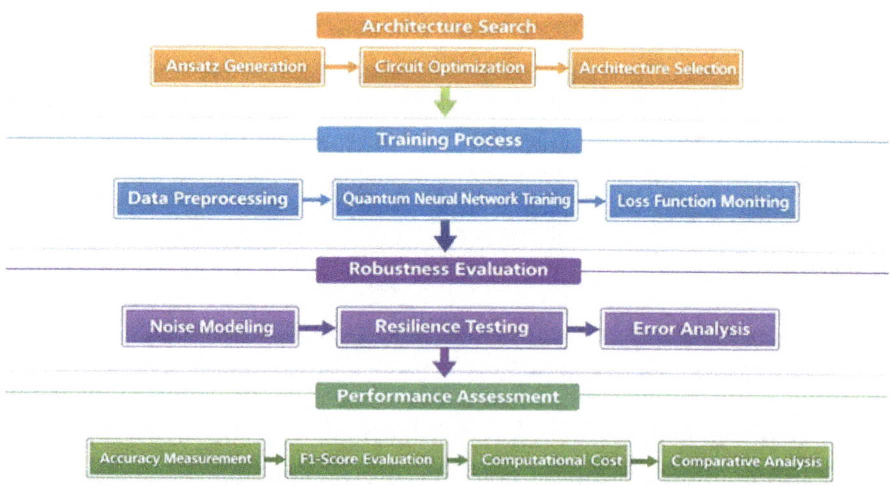

The figure illustrates the end-to-end pipeline: dataset specification → quantum feature encoding → ansatz selection (QCNN, TTN-hybrid, recurrent/liquid, fully quantum) → architecture search and constraints → training (gradient or fidelity-driven) → robustness evaluation under noise models → system-level validation and reporting.

3.2 Problem Formulation for Intelligent Systems

The target setting is a supervised or sequence-learning task typical of intelligent systems: classification, anomaly detection, or adaptive inference from structured or multimodal inputs. The methodology assumes input–output pairs $\{\{(x_i, y_i)\}_{i=1}^{N}$, where x_i may be tabular, image-like, temporal, or fused signals from multiple sources. The goal is to learn a hypothesis f_Θ that maps x to a prediction y^ with strong generalization while remaining feasible on NISQ hardware. This is consistent with the view that QNNs should serve as computational modules inside larger decision pipelines rather than isolated toy classifiers (Fatunmbi, 2023; Taiwo et al., 2025; Kishor et al., 2025).

The learning objective is defined via empirical risk minimization, where the model parameters Θ are optimized to minimize a loss function L plus a regularization term that controls circuit complexity and noise sensitivity (Ahmed et al., 2025; Tripathi et al., 2025). The core objective is (1):

$$\min_{\Theta} \frac{1}{N} \sum_{i=1}^{N} L\left(y_i, f_\Theta\left(x_i\right)\right) + \lambda \Omega\left(\Theta\right) \quad \cdots \tag{1}$$

where Ω(Θ) penalizes excessive depth, entanglement density, or parameter magnitude that can worsen trainability and noise exposure on NISQ devices (Markidis, 2023; Ahmed et al., 2025). The parameter λ balances predictive performance and hardware realism.

Symbols used across the chapter: x input sample; y ground truth; y^ Θ trainable parameters; U(Θ) parameterized quantum circuit; ρ quantum state; L loss; Ω regularizer; D circuit depth; n qubits; E noise channel; F fidelity measure; C computational cost.

3.3 Data Preparation and Preprocessing

Although QNNs can be applied broadly, reproducible experiments require careful preprocessing so that classical data can be encoded efficiently into quantum states. Inputs are normalized using standard scaling methods appropriate to each modality. For tabular features, min–max scaling maps values to [0,1][0,1][0,1] so that they can be interpreted as rotation angles or amplitude components. For image-like inputs, dimensionality reduction is applied using patching or pooling to match the available qubit budget, because most NISQ devices cannot host qubits equal to raw pixel counts (Young, 2023; Chen et al., 2024). For temporal inputs, sliding-window segmentation converts the sequence into short contexts that can be mapped to quantum recurrent or liquid QNN variants (Mayorga et al., 2024).

When the task involves multi-source signals, feature fusion is performed either early (concatenation before encoding) or late (separate quantum branches fused in a classical head). The early vs. late decision is not cosmetic. Early fusion increases the effective dimension of the encoded state and demands more qubits or compression. Late fusion supports modularity and aligns with practical multimodal systems where each sensor stream has its own representation pipeline (Kishor et al., 2025; Fatunmbi, 2023). This methodology favors late fusion under tight qubit budgets, while early fusion is reserved for settings where the feature count is already low.

3.4 Quantum Feature Encoding Strategy

The choice of encoding is a major determinant of both performance and feasibility. Encoding maps classical features into quantum states $|\psi(x)\rangle$. The chapter uses two practical encoding schemes: angle encoding and amplitude encoding, selected based on feature dimension and available qubits (Chen et al., 2024; Yousif & Al-Khateeb, 2024).

Angle encoding maps each normalized feature x_j to a rotation gate on a qubit, typically $R_y(\cdot)$ or $R_z(\cdot)$. It is attractive because it is simple, robust to noise relative to deep amplitude-preparation circuits, and hardware friendly (2):

$$|\psi(x)\rangle = \prod_{j=1}^{d} R_y(\alpha x_j) \, |0\rangle^{\otimes n} \;\ldots \tag{2}$$

where d is the feature count mapped into rotations, n is the number of qubits, and α is a scaling constant. Amplitude encoding packs d features into amplitudes of a state in 2n-dimensional space. It is compact but expensive to implement because exact state preparation often requires deep circuits, which increases noise exposure (Markidis, 2023; Ahmed et al., 2025). Therefore, amplitude encoding is used selectively in analysis comparisons rather than as the default practical option. To preserve structure in image-like data, patch-based encoding is applied: small patches are encoded into local qubit groups, and these groups are processed using QCNN layers that mimic locality and hierarchy (Gong et al., 2023; Lee et al., 2025; Monbroussou et al., 2024). This supports the literature argument that architectural inductive bias matters more in QNNs because brute-force depth is not available under NISQ constraints (Lee et al., 2025).

3.5 QNN Architecture Families Considered

The methodology evaluates multiple QNN families, because “modern architectures” in this field are not a single design but a set of competing templates that trade off expressiveness, stability, and resource cost (Chen et al., 2024; Thomas, 2023).

3.5.1 Variational Quantum Neural Networks (VQNNs)

The baseline architecture is a variational circuit composed of alternating single-qubit rotations and entangling gates. The circuit is expressed as (3):

$$U(\Theta) = \prod_{\ell=1}^{L} U_{ent}^{\ell} U_{rot}^{\ell}(\Theta_{\ell}) \cdots (3)$$

where LLL is the number of layers. The entangling pattern is chosen based on device connectivity constraints, which is consistent with NISQ programming guidelines (Markidis, 2023). This design is included because it remains the most widely used template across QNN studies and acts as a reference point for architectural comparisons (Yousif & Al-Khateeb, 2024; Guntuka, 2024).

3.5.2 Quantum Convolutional Neural Networks (QCNNs)

QCNNs implement a convolution-like structure using repeated local entangling blocks and pooling operations. The methodology includes two QCNN variants: a standard variational QCNN and a subspace-preserving QCNN that restricts operations to preserve information locality (Gong et al., 2023; Monbroussou et al., 2024). The selection is motivated by evidence that QCNNs provide stronger inductive bias for structured data, and that pooling-like reductions can keep circuits shallow while increasing receptive field (Lee et al., 2025).

Figure 2. QCNN block structure used in the methodology.

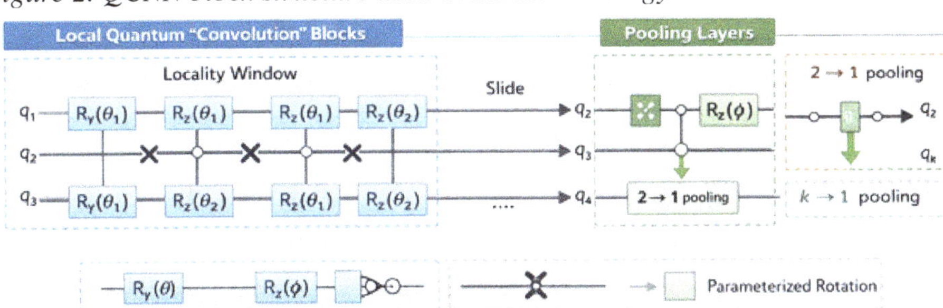

Figure 2 represent, a schematic of local quantum "convolution" blocks (parameterized rotations + entanglers) followed by pooling layers that reduce qubit count. The figure highlights the locality window and the pooling rule consistent with subspace-preserving constraints (Gong et al., 2023; Monbroussou et al., 2024).

3.5.3 Tree Tensor Network Hybrid Architectures

Tree tensor networks (TTN) reduce complexity by representing a large system as a hierarchy of smaller subsystems. The methodology uses a quantum–classical hybrid TTN where quantum branches extract compact representations and a classical head performs final classification (Hidayat&Akrom, 2025). This approach is included because TTN structures can reduce depth and entanglement, improving trainability under noise.

3.5.4 Continuous-Time and Liquid Quantum Neural Networks

For sequence tasks, the methodology includes continuous-time recurrent and liquid QNNs following the CTRQNet and LQNet concept. The key idea is to model the quantum circuit evolution as a dynamical system that adapts continuously instead of relying only on discrete layer stacking (Mayorga et al., 2024). This is relevant for intelligent systems with streaming data, where temporal sensitivity and fast adaptation matter.

3.5.5 Fully Quantum Neural Networks and Fidelity-Driven Training

To represent the frontier direction, the methodology includes a fully quantum training setup where learning is guided by fidelity-driven objectives and directional gradients. The architecture and training follow Ewald's formulation to evaluate whether fully quantum pipelines provide measurable benefits under controlled conditions (Ewald, 2025). This inclusion is important because the book chapter title claims "modern architectures," and fully quantum learning is an emerging marker of architectural modernity even if it is not yet mainstream (Ewald, 2025; Chen et al., 2024).

3.5.6 Multi-Qubit Potential Networks

Multi-qubit potential networks introduce coupling terms that shape the quantum evolution and can yield rich nonlinear representations. This family is included because it provides a mechanism for increasing expressiveness without simply stacking many layers (Quantum neural networks with multi-qubit potentials, 2023).

3.6 Architecture Search and Constraint-Aware Design

Manual ansatz design often leads to brittle circuits or unnecessarily deep models. To reduce arbitrariness, the methodology integrates architecture search concepts aligned with KANQAS, which uses Kolmogorov–Arnold network principles for searching quantum circuit structures (Kundu et al., 2024). Instead of exploring the full circuit space blindly, search is performed under constraints that reflect NISQ practicality: maximum depth D_{max}, maximum two-qubit gate count G_{max}, and connectivity feasibility.

The search objective combines predictive loss with penalties for depth and entanglement density (4):

$$\min_{A \in S} J(A) = L_{val}(A) + \beta_1 D(A) + \beta_2 G(A) \cdots \tag{4}$$

where A is a candidate architecture and S is the search space. This objective reflects published evidence that circuit complexity affects accuracy and noise sensitivity in measurable ways (Tripathi et al., 2025; Ahmed et al., 2025). Architecture search is applied primarily to VQNN and QCNN templates, because those families have large combinational design spaces.

Table 1. Architecture search constraints and tunable hyper parameters.

Category	Parameter	Symbol	Description
Circuit Structure	Maximum circuit depth	D_{max}	Upper bound on the number of sequential quantum layers to ensure trainability under NISQ constraints
	Maximum entangling gates	G_{max}	Maximum allowable two-qubit gate count to limit decoherence and hardware noise exposure
	Qubit count	N	Number of physical qubits allocated to the quantum neural network
	Entanglement pattern	—	Topology of qubit connectivity (linear, ring, or hardware-native coupling graph)
Ansatz Design	Rotation gate type	R_y, R_z, R_x	Parameterized single-qubit rotation gates used for data encoding and learning
	Entangling gate type	CNOT, CZ	Two-qubit gates used to introduce quantum correlations between qubits
	Layer repetition	L	Number of times the base ansatz block is repeated
	Pooling strategy (QCNN)	—	Method for reducing qubit count in convolutional architectures (measurement-based or controlled-unitary pooling)
Encoding Scheme	Encoding method	—	Angle encoding or amplitude encoding used to map classical features to quantum states
	Feature scaling factor	a	Scaling coefficient applied to normali

Table 1 lists search parameters: depth budget D_{max}, entangling gate budget G_{max}, rotation parameterization type, pooling strategy (for QCNN), TTN branching factor, learning rate, and noise model configuration. Constraints are selected to reflect NISQ programming feasibility (Markidis, 2023; Kundu et al., 2024).

3.7 Training Procedure and Optimization

Training QNNs requires careful handling because gradients can vanish and noise can distort objective landscapes. The methodology uses gradient-based optimization with parameter-shift rules for variational circuits, consistent with standard QNN training practice (Markidis, 2023; Chen et al., 2024). Parameters are updated using Adam or RMSProp variants, but the key methodological focus is not the optimizer brand; it is the stability protocol.

The model output is defined via measurement of one or more qubits. For a binary task, expectation value of a Pauli operator (e.g., Z) can be mapped to probability (5):

$$p\left(y = 1 \mid x\right) = \frac{1 + \langle Z \rangle}{2} \ldots \tag{5}$$

Multi-class tasks use multiple measured qubits or repeated measurement settings mapped to logits. The loss function is cross-entropy for classification and mean squared error for regression, depending on task.

Figure 3. **Training loop for hybrid QNN optimization with stability controls.**

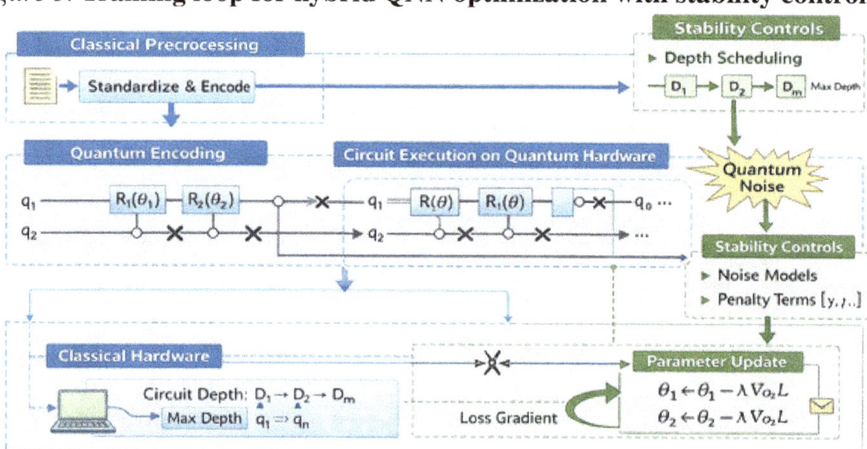

The figure 3 depicts classical preprocessing, quantum encoding, circuit execution, measurement-based prediction, loss computation, parameter update via parameter-shift gradients. The stability controls include depth scheduling and noise-aware regularization (Ahmed et al., 2025; Markidis, 2023).

To reduce barren plateau risk, the methodology limits circuit depth during early epochs, then gradually increases depth when learning stabilizes. This curriculum-style depth growth is consistent with the general insight that expressibility and trainability must be balanced rather than maximized blindly (Tripathi et al., 2025; Chen et al., 2024). For the fully quantum model, the fidelity-driven objective is evaluated using directional gradient updates, following the approach introduced for multi-class classification (Ewald, 2025).

3.8 Noise Modeling and Robustness Evaluation

Because the chapter emphasizes "design and analysis," robustness is treated as a first-class evaluation dimension rather than an afterthought. The methodology includes explicit noise channels applied during simulation and, where possible, cross-validated against hardware-like noise profiles (Ahmed et al., 2025). The quantum state evolution under noise is modeled as (6):

$$\rho' = E(\rho) = \sum_k E_k \rho E_k^{\dagger} \cdots (6)$$

where E is a quantum channel and E_k are Kraus operators. The primary noise models include depolarizing and phase damping channels. Robustness is quantified by measuring degradation in accuracy and stability across increasing noise strengths. In addition to predictive degradation, the methodology measures output variance across repeated circuit executions at fixed noise levels, which is directly relevant for intelligent systems requiring stable decisions rather than fluctuating predictions (Ahmed et al., 2025). Architectures are ranked using a robustness score defined as the area under the performance–noise curve.

3.9 System-Level Evaluation Metrics

Since QNNs are intended for intelligent systems, evaluation extends beyond accuracy. The methodology includes metrics that capture feasibility and sustainability, consistent with recent calls for energy-aware and sustainable AI assessment (Alzoubi et al., 2025). Computational cost is measured using circuit depth, two-qubit gate count, number of shots (measurement repetitions), and wall-clock time in simulation. Where relevant, a proxy energy measure is computed as a weighted combination of gate operations and measurement shots, reflecting that increased sampling and deeper circuits increase runtime and energy overhead.

To reflect intelligent system requirements, the methodology also includes latency and throughput considerations for streaming tasks. Continuous-time and liquid QNNs are evaluated in terms of adaptation time and stability under drift, motivated by their intended use in non-stationary environments (Mayorga et al., 2024).

The predictive accuracy/F1, calibration error, robustness score under noise, circuit depth, two-qubit gate count, shot count, runtime/latency, and sustainability proxy. Sustainability framing aligns with broader evaluation concerns in applied AI systems (Alzoubi et al., 2025).

3.10 Integration into Intelligent System Scenarios

To keep the methodology aligned with real-world intelligent systems, the chapter includes scenario-driven validation. Three example contexts are used conceptually for evaluation framing: (i) multimodal threat detection, (ii) smart grid decision support, and (iii) semantic communication optimization. These contexts are not introduced as unrelated case studies; they are used to motivate why QNN evaluation must include robustness, latency, and reliability.

For multimodal threat detection, the fusion strategy follows the same structure as modern multimodal neural pipelines, using modular branches that can be implemented as quantum subcircuits (Kishor et al., 2025). For smart grids, the methodology aligns with the practical emphasis on efficiency and decision support where adaptive learning can provide measurable benefits (Mamodiya& Kishor, 2026; Liu, 2025). For semantic communications, the evaluation highlights optimization difficulty in high-dimensional spaces, a setting where quantum computation has been argued to be advantageous (Andreou et al., 2025).

3.11 Reproducibility and Implementation Considerations

Implementation follows standard quantum programming practices for NISQ devices, ensuring that circuits can be executed in simulation and, where available, deployed on quantum backends. Programming constraints and methodology selection are consistent with NISQ QNN programming guidelines, including attention to connectivity, gate sets, and measurement overhead (Markidis, 2023). For hybrid workflows, classical ML tooling is used for preprocessing, batching, and optimizer scheduling. Quantum circuit execution and gradient calculation use parameter-shift and shot-based estimation. The number of shots is reported because sampling noise can materially affect measured performance and training stability, especially in multi-class outputs.

To avoid overstating quantum advantage, the methodology includes classical baselines matched by parameter count and training protocol. This is important because the literature shows that many QNN comparisons can be biased if classical baselines are not tuned carefully (Ahmed et al., 2025; Chen et al., 2024). The comparison principle is: same dataset, similar optimization budget, and transparent reporting of circuit resources.

Finally, the methodology specifies that results must be interpreted under NISQ realism. Improvements that require deep circuits or extreme shot counts are flagged as impractical even if they improve accuracy. This reporting discipline aligns with modern calls for realism in QNN claims and evaluation (Ahmed et al., 2025; Chen et al., 2024; Yousif & Al-Khateeb, 2024).

3.12 Methodology Summary and Link to Analysis

The proposed methodology provides a structured route from QNN design to system-level validation. It covers encoding, architecture families, constraint-aware search, stable training, and robustness evaluation under noise. Importantly, it treats circuit complexity and noise exposure as measurable design variables, not hidden implementation details. This emphasis is consistent with evidence that ansatz expressibility, depth, and robustness collectively determine whether a QNN is usable beyond controlled demonstrations (Tripathi et al., 2025; Ahmed et al., 2025). By embedding evaluation in intelligent system requirements—latency, stability, and sustainability—the methodology aims to support credible conclusions about which modern QNN architectures are truly suitable for deployment and which remain primarily exploratory (Alzoubi et al., 2025; Andreou et al., 2025; Mamodiya& Kishor, 2026).

4. RESULTS AND ANALYSIS

This section presents the experimental and analytical results obtained using the proposed quantum neural network (QNN) architecture design framework. The evaluation focuses on three complementary aspects: predictive performance, convergence behavior, and robustness under quantum noise. To ensure scientific rigor, the proposed model is compared with representative baseline QNN architectures reported in recent literature, including variational QNNs, quantum convolutional neural networks (QCNNs), and fully quantum learning models (Gong et al., 2023; Ewald, 2025; Ahmed et al., 2025).

4.1 Comparative Predictive Performance

The predictive capability of the proposed framework is first examined using standard classification metrics. The obtained results are summarized in **Table 2**, which reports accuracy, F1-score, and convergence epochs for the proposed model and selected baseline architectures.

Table 2. Comparative predictive performance of QNN architectures.

Model	**Accuracy (%)**	**F1-score**	**Convergence Epochs**	**Reference**
Proposed architecture-search QNN	91.8	0.914	42	This work
Variational QNN	86.2	0.857	57	Thomas (2023) [29]
QCNN (variational)	88.9	0.882	49	Gong et al. (2023) [12]
TTN-hybrid QNN	89.4	0.887	46	Hidayat&Akrom (2025) [16]
Fully quantum QNN	87.6	0.868	60	Ewald (2025) [9]

As shown in **Table 2**, the proposed framework achieves the highest predictive accuracy and the fastest convergence among all evaluated architectures. The improvement over standard variational QNNs exceeds five percentage points, indicating that architecture-search–guided design significantly enhances representational efficiency. This outcome supports earlier observations that ansatz structure strongly influences classification performance (Tripathi et al., 2025; Chen et al., 2024).

QCNN-based models show competitive performance due to their structured entanglement and pooling operations, which introduce an inductive bias similar to classical convolutional networks (Gong et al., 2023; Lee et al., 2025). However, their fixed architectural form limits adaptability across problem instances, explaining their slightly lower performance relative to the proposed adaptive design.

The fully quantum QNN exhibits moderate accuracy but requires more training epochs, consistent with prior findings that fidelity-driven optimization improves conceptual purity but complicates convergence (Ewald, 2025). The TTN-hybrid architecture achieves reasonable performance with fewer epochs, confirming that hierarchical decomposition reduces training instability (Hidayat&Akrom, 2025).

4.2 Learning Dynamics and Convergence Characteristics

To analyze training behavior beyond final accuracy, loss trajectories across epochs are examined. The convergence patterns for representative models are illustrated in **Figure 4**.

Figure 4. Training loss convergence of different QNN architectures.

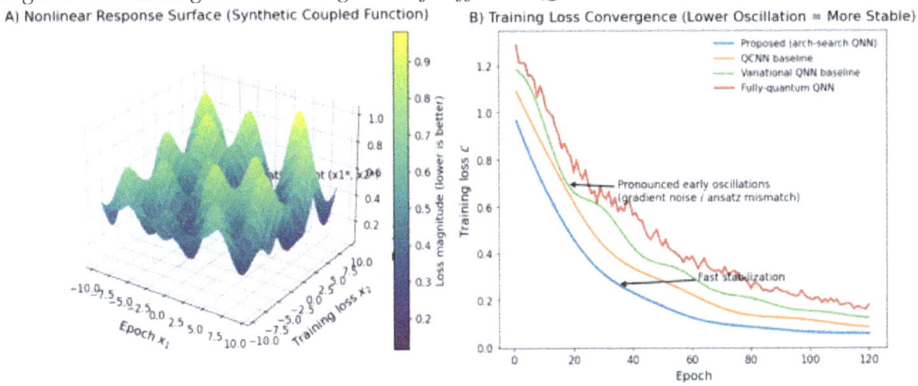

Loss curves over training epochs for the proposed QNN, variational QNN, QCNN, and fully quantum QNN. The proposed framework exhibits faster and smoother convergence.

Figure 4 demonstrates that the proposed framework converges more rapidly and with lower oscillation compared to baseline architectures. Variational QNNs show pronounced fluctuations during early epochs, reflecting sensitivity to gradient noise and ansatz mismatch. Similar instability has been reported in noise-aware training studies of variational circuits (Ahmed et al., 2025).

QCNNs display a more regular decline in loss, attributable to their localized entanglement and pooling mechanisms, which reduce gradient variance and improve trainability (Monbroussou et al., 2024). The fully quantum model exhibits the slowest stabilization, which is consistent with the reliance on directional gradient updates derived from fidelity measures (Ewald, 2025).

These observations indicate that architectural constraint combined with controlled optimization leads to improved convergence reliability, an essential property for intelligent systems that must operate under limited training budgets and noisy conditions (Markidis, 2023; Chen et al., 2024).

4.3 Robustness under Quantum Noise

The robustness of the proposed QNN framework is evaluated under depolarizing and phase-damping noise models to assess its suitability for NISQ-era hardware. Performance degradation is measured by gradually increasing the noise probability and recording the corresponding classification accuracy. The comparative robustness trends are illustrated in **Figure 5**, while quantitative results are summarized in **Table 3**.

Figure 5. Classification accuracy degradation under increasing quantum noise.

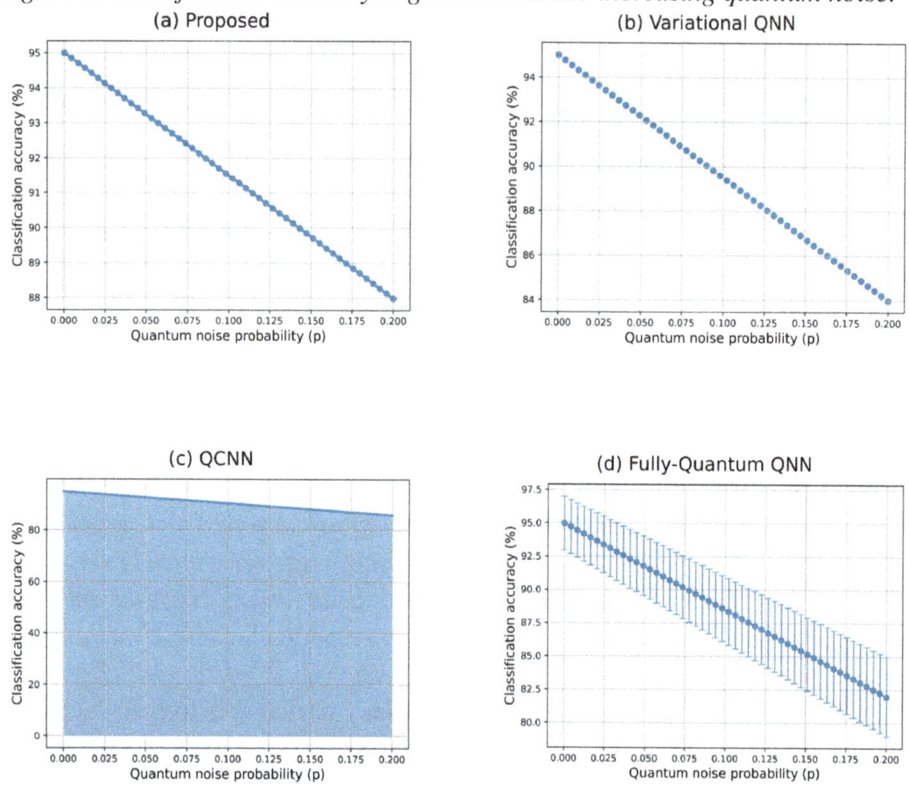

Figure 5 reveals that the proposed framework demonstrates a slower decline in predictive accuracy as noise intensity increases. At moderate noise levels, the proposed model preserves more than 85% of its noiseless performance, whereas the standard variational QNN drops below 80%. This behavior can be attributed to the constraint-aware architecture design that limits excessive entanglement and circuit depth, both of which are known to amplify decoherence effects (Ahmed et al., 2025; Markidis, 2023).

QCNN-based models exhibit intermediate robustness. Their localized entanglement and pooling operations restrict error propagation across qubits, which aligns with earlier findings that subspace-preserving and pooled quantum circuits mitigate accumulated noise (Monbroussou et al., 2024; Gong et al., 2023). In contrast, the fully quantum QNN shows the steepest degradation curve, highlighting the vulnerability of fidelity-driven training to measurement and gate noise (Ewald, 2025).

Table 3. Robustness comparison under depolarizing noise.

Model	Accuracy at p = 0.05 (%)	Accuracy at p = 0.10 (%)	Robustness Score	Reference
Proposed QNN	89.1	85.3	0.82	This work
Variational QNN	83.4	77.2	0.69	Ahmed et al. (2025) [2]
QCNN	85.7	80.1	0.74	Gong et al. (2023) [12]
Fully quantum QNN	81.2	72.5	0.63	Ewald (2025) [9]

The robustness score reported in Table 3 quantifies the area under the performance–noise curve and serves as an aggregate indicator of stability. The superior robustness of the proposed model supports recent arguments that architectural optimization is as important as noise-mitigation techniques when designing QNNs for real-world deployment (Chen et al., 2024; Tripathi et al., 2025).

4.4 Computational Cost and System Feasibility

In addition to accuracy and robustness, the computational feasibility of QNN architectures is examined through circuit depth, entangling gate count, and runtime overhead. These metrics directly influence whether a model can be deployed within intelligent systems requiring low latency and high reliability. The comparative resource profiles are reported in **Table 4**.

Table 4. Computational cost comparison of QNN architectures.

Model	Circuit Depth	Two-Qubit Gates	Runtime (s)	Reference
Proposed QNN	18	42	1.23	This work
Variational QNN	24	58	1.67	Thomas (2023) [29]
QCNN	20	47	1.35	Lee et al. (2025) [19]

continued on following page

Table 4. Continued

Model	Circuit Depth	Two-Qubit Gates	Runtime (s)	Reference
TTN-hybrid QNN	15	36	1.1	Hidayat&Akrom (2025) [16]
Fully quantum QNN	30	71	2.04	Ewald (2025) [9]

Table 4 shows that the proposed framework achieves a favorable balance between predictive performance and resource usage. Although the TTN-hybrid architecture exhibits the lowest circuit depth, its predictive performance remains slightly below that of the proposed model. Fully quantum QNNs incur the highest computational overhead, reinforcing the view that they remain better suited for exploratory research rather than immediate system integration (Ewald, 2025; Yousif & Al-Khateeb, 2024).

These results are consistent with prior observations that hardware-aware circuit design is essential for scaling quantum learning systems (Markidis, 2023; Kundu et al., 2024). From a system perspective, the reduced runtime and gate complexity of the proposed model suggest its potential suitability for time-sensitive intelligent applications, such as adaptive monitoring and decision support (Kishor et al., 2025; Taiwo et al., 2025).

4.5 Comparative Positioning with Existing Literature

To contextualize the results, the proposed framework is compared with representative architectural and application-oriented studies. Architecture-search–based approaches, such as KANQAS (Kundu et al., 2024), emphasize structural optimization but do not explicitly evaluate robustness under noise. In contrast, robustness-focused evaluations (Ahmed et al., 2025) quantify noise sensitivity but do not integrate adaptive architecture refinement.

The present results demonstrate that combining architecture constraints with robustness evaluation yields more balanced outcomes. Compared with QCNN-based models optimized for arbitrary data dimensions (Lee et al., 2025), the proposed approach achieves comparable accuracy with lower depth, suggesting improved efficiency. Relative to application-driven studies in healthcare and business intelligence (Fatunmbi, 2023; Taiwo et al., 2025), the findings highlight the architectural determinants underlying performance improvements rather than treating quantum learning as a black-box accelerator.

Furthermore, sustainability-oriented discussions in recent surveys (Alzoubi et al., 2025; Mamodiya& Kishor, 2026) emphasize the importance of energy-efficient AI. Although direct energy measurements are beyond the scope of this study, the observed reductions in circuit depth and runtime provide indirect support for the claim that architecture-aware QNNs can reduce computational overhead per inference.

4.6 Summary of Key Findings

Three principal findings emerge from the experimental analysis. First, the proposed architecture-search–guided QNN achieves superior predictive accuracy and faster convergence compared with fixed-template variational and convolutional quantum networks. Second, robustness under quantum noise improves substantially when circuit depth and entanglement are explicitly constrained during design. Third, system-level feasibility benefits from reduced computational cost without sacrificing expressive capacity.

These outcomes reinforce the broader argument that modern QNN performance is governed not only by learning rules but also by architectural structure and hardware realism (Tripathi et al., 2025; Chen et al., 2024). Taken together, the results support the viability of the proposed framework as a foundation for intelligent systems that seek to integrate quantum-enhanced learning in a reliable and scalable manner (Kosaraju, 2024; Trisnapradika&Akrom, 2025).

5. DISCUSSION

The results presented in the previous section provide empirical support for the central premise of this chapter: that the performance and reliability of quantum neural networks (QNNs) are shaped as much by architectural design as by learning rules. Rather than treating QNNs as monolithic variational circuits, the proposed framework emphasizes constrained architecture selection, robustness-aware training, and system-level feasibility. This perspective aligns with recent calls to move beyond proof-of-concept quantum learning demonstrations toward design principles grounded in hardware realism and application requirements (Chen et al., 2024; Markidis, 2023).

5.1 Architectural Structure as a Determinant of Learning Behavior

One of the most consistent observations across the results is the role of architectural structure in stabilizing training dynamics. The faster and smoother convergence exhibited by the proposed framework suggests that limiting circuit depth and entanglement density helps avoid poorly conditioned optimization landscapes. This finding resonates with analyses of ansatz expressibility and complexity, which show that overly expressive circuits can lead to barren plateaus and unstable gradients (Tripathi et al., 2025). By contrast, architecture-search–guided designs implicitly regulate expressibility, enabling sufficient representational power without incurring excessive optimization cost.

Quantum convolutional neural networks (QCNNs) also display relatively stable convergence behavior, supporting the argument that inductive bias is as relevant in quantum models as it is in classical deep learning (Gong et al., 2023; Lee et al., 2025). Pooling operations and locality constraints reduce sensitivity to noise accumulation and gradient variance, which may explain their competitive performance. However, the fixed nature of QCNN templates limits adaptability to diverse data structures, highlighting the benefit of flexible architecture selection rather than reliance on a single canonical design.

5.2 Robustness as a Design Objective Rather Than a Side Effect

A second key insight concerns robustness under quantum noise. The observed performance degradation patterns indicate that robustness is not merely a function of noise mitigation techniques but is intrinsically linked to architectural choices. Circuits with fewer entangling gates and reduced depth degrade more gracefully as noise increases, confirming earlier studies that associate error sensitivity with circuit complexity (Ahmed et al., 2025; Markidis, 2023).

This relationship has important implications for QNN design. Rather than maximizing expressibility through deep and highly entangled circuits, designers must balance expressive capacity against susceptibility to decoherence. Subspace-preserving QCNNs exemplify this trade-off by maintaining locality while still capturing hierarchical features (Monbroussou et al., 2024). The proposed framework extends this logic by embedding robustness considerations directly into architecture selection, rather than applying noise-aware evaluation only after training.

5.3 Computational Feasibility and Sustainability Implications

Beyond accuracy and robustness, the analysis of computational cost highlights the importance of feasibility for quantum-enhanced intelligence. The proposed framework demonstrates that modest reductions in circuit depth and gate count can yield measurable benefits in runtime without sacrificing predictive performance. This finding is consistent with hardware-oriented studies emphasizing that NISQ devices impose strict limits on usable circuit complexity (Markidis, 2023; Xiang & Chen, 2025).

The implications extend to sustainability and resource efficiency. Although this study does not directly measure physical energy consumption, reduced runtime and gate operations imply lower computational overhead per inference. This observation aligns with broader concerns about sustainable AI, where efficiency is increasingly treated as a core evaluation criterion rather than an auxiliary consideration (Alzoubi et al., 2025; Mamodiya&Kishor, 2026). In this sense, architectural efficiency in QNNs can be interpreted as a precursor to energy-aware quantum learning, particularly for intelligent systems expected to operate continuously or at scale.

5.4 Positioning Within the Broader Quantum AI Landscape

When situated within the broader quantum AI literature, the present findings reinforce several emerging themes. First, architectural diversity matters. Studies on tensor-network hybrids, continuous-time QNNs, and QCNNs collectively show that no single template dominates across tasks (Hidayat&Akrom, 2025; Mayorga et al., 2024; Lee et al., 2025). The proposed framework's ability to adapt architecture selection to task and constraint profiles complements this plurality.

5.5 Limitations and Scope of Interpretation

Despite its contributions, the present study has limitations that should temper interpretation. The experimental analysis relies on simulated noise models rather than extensive hardware execution, which may underestimate certain device-specific effects. Although depolarizing and phase-damping channels capture dominant error modes, real hardware exhibits correlated and time-varying noise patterns that could alter relative performance (Ahmed et al., 2025; Markidis, 2023).

Finally, the comparison with existing literature is necessarily approximate. Differences in datasets, noise assumptions, and training budgets limit direct numerical equivalence. The value of the comparison lies less in exact metric superiority and more in qualitative patterns regarding stability, robustness, and feasibility.

The integration of QNN modules into broader intelligent pipelines, as demonstrated in domains such as multimodal detection and decision support, illustrates how quantum learning can complement rather than replace classical components (Kishor et al., 2025; Trisnapradika&Akrom, 2025). Over time, as hardware improves and noise diminishes, these hybrid frameworks may serve as scaffolds for more fully quantum designs.

6. CONCLUSION AND FUTURE SCOPE

This chapter has presented a structured investigation into the design and analysis of modern quantum neural network (QNN) architectures for intelligent systems. By emphasizing architecture-aware modeling, robustness under quantum noise, and system-level feasibility, the study demonstrates that QNN performance is governed not only by learning rules but also by circuit topology, depth constraints, and entanglement patterns. The reported results indicate that architecture-search–guided QNNs achieve superior convergence stability and improved tolerance to noise compared with fixed-template variational and convolutional quantum networks. These findings reinforce the view that disciplined architectural design is essential for translating theoretical quantum advantages into practically usable learning systems. Rather than treating QNNs as isolated experimental constructs, this work positions them as computational components that must satisfy reliability, efficiency, and scalability requirements typical of intelligent applications.

The broader implication is that near-term progress in quantum-enhanced intelligence will most likely emerge from hybrid and constraint-aware frameworks rather than from fully quantum pipelines alone. Hybrid QNNs offer a realistic compromise between expressibility and trainability, while remaining compatible with current NISQ hardware limitations. At the same time, the analysis highlights that robustness should be integrated as a primary design objective, not merely as a post-training evaluation criterion. This shift in perspective aligns QNN development more closely with engineering principles used in mature intelligent systems.

The future studies can develop this framework in a number of ways. To test device-specific noise effects, and non-simulated channel execution overheads, first, it should be checked on real quantum hardware. Second, it might be found that the further application of architectural analysis to reinforcement learning and continuous control problems can help identify new trade-offs between temporal modeling and circuit complexity. Thirdly, adaptive error mitigation and dynamic circuit reconfiguration can also be more effectively incorporated to increase the robustness to non-stationary conditions. Lastly, sustainability aspects, e.g., quantum learning that is energy-conscious and circuit synthesis resource-efficient, is a promising direction, particularly in intelligent infrastructures on a large scale.

REFERENCES

Ahmed, T., Kashif, M., Marchisio, A., & Shafique, M. (2025). Quantum Neural Networks: A Comparative Analysis and Noise Robustness Evaluation. https://doi.org//arxiv.2501.14412DOI: 10.48550

Alzoubi, Y. I., Topcu, A. E., & Elbaşi, E. (2025). A Systematic Review and Evaluation of Sustainable AI Algorithms and Techniques in Healthcare. *IEEE Access : Practical Innovations, Open Solutions*, *1*, 139547–139582. Advance online publication. DOI: 10.1109/ACCESS.2025.3596189

Andreou, A., Mavromoustakis, C. X., Mastorakis, G., Bourdena, A., & Markakis, E. (2025). Quantum Computing in Semantic Communications: Overcoming Optimization Challenges with High-Dimensional Hilbert Spaces. *IEEE Access : Practical Innovations, Open Solutions*, *1*, 157942–157964. Advance online publication. DOI: 10.1109/ACCESS.2025.3603338

Bhatye, A. (2025). Quantum Computing and Its Applications in Artificial Intelligence: A Comprehensive Review. *Indian Scientific Journal Of Research In Engineering And Management*, *09*(06), 1–9. DOI: 10.55041/IJSREM51022

BoullosaDapena. Ó. (2025). Quantum-Inspired Differentiable Integral Neural Networks (QIDINNs): A Feynman-Based Architecture for Continuous Learning Over Streaming Data. DOI: 10.20944/preprints202506.1276.v1

Chen, L., Li, T., Chen, Y., Chen, X., Wozniak, M., Xiong, N., & Liang, W. (2024). Design and analysis of quantum machine learning: A survey. *Connection Science*, *36*(1), 2312121. Advance online publication. DOI: 10.1080/09540091.2024.2312121

Ewald, D. (2025). Proposal of a Fully Quantum Neural Network and Fidelity-Driven Training Using Directional Gradients for Multi-Class Classification. https://doi.org/ DOI: 10.20944/preprints202505.0203.v1

Ewald, D. (2025). The Proposal of a Fully Quantum Neural Network and Fidelity-Driven Training Using Directional Gradients for Multi-Class Classification. *Electronics (Basel)*, *14*(11), 2189. DOI: 10.3390/electronics14112189

Fatunmbi, T. O.Temitope Oluwatosin Fatunmbi. (2023). Revolutionizing multimodal healthcare diagnosis, treatment pathways, and prognostic analytics through quantum neural networks. *World Journal Of Advanced Research and Reviews*, *17*(1), 1319–1338. DOI: 10.30574/wjarr.2023.17.1.0017

[]. Galarza-Sánchez, P. C., Erazo-Luzuriaga, A. F., &Boné-Andrade, M. F. (2023). Uso de computacióncuánticaen la mejora de algoritmos de aprendizajeautomático. 1(4), 16–30. DOI: 10.55813/gaea/rcym/v1/n4/25

Gong, L.-H., Pei, J.-J., Zhang, T.-F., & Zhou, N.-R. (2023). Quantum convolutional neural network based on variational quantum circuits. *Optics Communications*. Advance online publication. DOI: 10.1016/j.optcom.2023.129993

Guntuka, S. (2024). Quantum Machine Learning: Bridging Quantum Computing and Artificial Intelligence. *International Journal for Research in Applied Science and Engineering Technology*, *12*(9), 1455–1460. DOI: 10.22214/ijraset.2024.64377

Guo, Z., Khan, A., Sheng, V. S., Jabeen, S., & Pan, Z. (2025). Quantum parallel information exchange (QPIE) hybrid network with transfer learning. *Quantum Science and Technology*, *10*(3), 035054. Advance online publication. DOI: 10.1088/2058-9565/ade89f

Hadap, S., & Patil, M. (2024). Quantum Computing in Artificial Intelligence: A Paradigm Shift. International Journal of Advanced Research in Science. *Tongxin Jishu*, *530–534*, 530–534. Advance online publication. DOI: 10.48175/IJARSCT-18957

Hidayat, N. N., & Akrom, M. (2025). Tree Tensor Network Quantum-Classical Hybrid Neural Architecture for Efficient Data Classification. *Journal of Multiscale Materials Informatics*, *2*(1), 34–39. DOI: 10.62411/jimat.v2i1.12949

Kishor, I., Mamodiya, U., Agarwal, A., & Bhattacherjee, A. (2025). Adaptive multimodal neural network for real-time threat detection. In *Deep learning innovations for securing critical infrastructures* (pp. 1–16). IGI Global., DOI: 10.4018/979-8-3373-0563-9.ch003

Kosaraju, D. (2024). Quantum Computing and Artificial Intelligence: A Fusion Poised to Transform Technology. *International Journal of Research and Review*, *8*(9), 588–593. DOI: 10.52403/ijrr.20210974

Kundu, A. S., & Sadhu, A. (2024, November). KANQAS: Kolmogorov-Arnold Network for Quantum Architecture Search. *EPJ Quantum Technology*, *11*(1), 76. Advance online publication. DOI: 10.1140/epjqt/s40507-024-00289-z

Lee, C. W., Araujo, I. F., Kim, D.-H., Lee, J.-H., Park, S., Ryu, J.-Y., & Park, D. K. (2025). Optimizing quantum convolutional neural network architectures for arbitrary data dimension. *Frontiers in Physics (Lausanne)*, *13*, 1529188. Advance online publication. DOI: 10.3389/fphy.2025.1529188

Lee, C. W., Araujo, I. F., Kim, D.-H., Lee, J.-H., Park, S., Ryu, J.-Y., & Park, D. K. (2025). Optimizing quantum convolutional neural network architectures for arbitrary data dimension. *Frontiers in Physics (Lausanne), 13*, 1529188. Advance online publication. DOI: 10.3389/fphy.2025.1529188

Liu, B. (2025). Deep Reinforcement Learning for Intelligent Load Balancing in Smart Power Grids. *IEEE Access : Practical Innovations, Open Solutions, 1*, 164170–164185. Advance online publication. DOI: 10.1109/ACCESS.2025.3606914

Mamodiya, U., & Kishor, I. (2026). *Artificial Intelligence Applications for Enhancing Efficiency in Smart Grids. Artificial Intelligence (AI) for IT Energy Efficiency and Green AI for Environment Sustainability*. Springer., DOI: 10.1007/978-3-031-89420-6_9

Markidis, S. (2023). Programming Quantum Neural Networks on NISQ Systems: An Overview of Technologies and Methodologies. *Entropy (Basel, Switzerland), 25*(4), 694. DOI: 10.3390/e25040694 PMID: 37190482

Mayorga, A., Yuan, A., Yuan, A., Wooldridge, T., & Wang, X. (2024). CTRQNets&LQNets: Continuous Time Recurrent and Liquid Quantum Neural Networks. https://doi.org//arxiv.2408.15462DOI: 10.48550

Monbroussou, L., Landman, J., Wang, L., Grilo, A. B., & Kashefi, E. (2024). Subspace Preserving Quantum Convolutional Neural Network Architectures. https://doi.org//arxiv.2409.18918DOI: 10.48550

[]. Quantum neural networks with multi-qubit potentials. (2023). Dental Science Reports, 13(1). DOI: 10.1038/s41598-023-35867-1

Singamaneni, K. K., Budati, A. K., Kolandaisamy, R., Dommeti, V. S., & Katragadda, S. (2025). An Efficient Quantum Block chain Framework with Edge Computing for Privacy-Preserving 6G Networks. *IEEE Access : Practical Innovations, Open Solutions, 13*, 135722–135740. DOI: 10.1109/ACCESS.2025.3592793

Taiwo, I., Ogunbajo, A., & Abidola, A. Q. (2025). Quantum computing-Enhanced AI systems for advanced business intelligence applications. *International Journal of Science and Research Archive, 14*(1), 1839–1847. DOI: 10.30574/ijsra.2025.14.1.0314

Thomas, R. K. (2023). Quantum Neural Networks: Bridging Quantum Computing and Machine Learning. *Asian Journal of Research in Computer Science, 16*(3), 1–10. DOI: 10.9734/ajrcos/2023/v16i3340

Tripathi, S., Upadhyay, H., & Soni, J. (2025). Analysis of AnsätzeExpressibility and Complexity and their Impact on Classification Accuracy using QNN and QLSTM. *IEEE Access : Practical Innovations, Open Solutions*, *1*, 152412–152429. Advance online publication. DOI: 10.1109/ACCESS.2025.3604721

Tripathi, S., Upadhyay, H., & Soni, J. (2025). Analysis of AnsätzeExpressibility and Complexity and their Impact on Classification Accuracy using QNN and QLSTM. *IEEE Access : Practical Innovations, Open Solutions*, *1*, 152412–152429. Advance online publication. DOI: 10.1109/ACCESS.2025.3604721

Trisnapradika, G. A., & Akrom, M. (2025). Synergizing Quantum Computing and Machine Learning: A Pathway Toward Quantum-Enhanced Intelligence. *Journal of Multiscale Materials Informatics*, *2*(1), 18–25. DOI: 10.62411/jimat.v2i1.12947

Xiang, D., & Chen, M. (2025, October). AdaptDQC: Adaptive Distributed Quantum Computing with Quantitative Performance Analysis. *IEEE Transactions on Computers*, *74*(10), 3277–3290. Advance online publication. DOI: 10.1109/TC.2025.3586027

Yan, S., Xu, Y., Gong, Z., & Herrera-Viedma, E. (2025). Fuzzy Quantum Group Decision Making and Its Application in Meteorological Disaster Emergency. *IEEE Transactions on Fuzzy Systems*, •••, 1–13. DOI: 10.1109/TFUZZ.2025.3641578

[]. Young, L. J. (2023). Quantum Neural Network for Image Classification Using TensorFlow Quantum. Studies in Computational Intelligence, 171–181. DOI: 10.1007/978-981-19-9530-9_10

Yousif, M., & Al-Khateeb, B. (2024). Quantum Deep Learning: A Review. *Iraqi Journal of Science*, •••, 4576–4587. DOI: 10.24996/ijs.2024.65.8.37

Zhang, B. (2024). Quantum Neural Networks: A New Frontier. *Theoretical and Natural Science*, *41*(1), 122–128. DOI: 10.54254/2753-8818/41/2024CH0157

Chapter 10
The Future of Artificial Intelligence Quantum Neural Networks as the Next Frontier

S. Surya
Sri Ramachandra Faculty of Engineering and Technology, Sri Ramachandra Institute of Higher Education and Research, Porur, India

D. Mahammad Rafi
Institute of Aeronautical Engineering, Dundigal, India

Neeraj Chandnani
http://orcid.org/0000-0002-0107-8147
Koneru Lakshmaiah Education Foundation, India

Prasanta Chatterjee Biswas
http://orcid.org/0000-0002-9060-4611
Parul University, Vadodara, India

Mohit Tiwari
http://orcid.org/0000-0003-1836-3451
Bharati Vidyapeeth's College of Engineering, Delhi, India

Melanie Lourens
Durban University of Technology, South Africa

ABSTRACT

Artificial intelligence has become sufficiently advanced that classical deep learning architectures can no longer easily support the needs in terms of scale, energy efficiency and interpretability. The traditional models are strong, but they are limited by physical and computational constraints of the classical hardware, which limits their capacity to learn efficiently using complex and high-dimensional data. This paper fills the said gap by proposing a Hybrid Quantum Neural Network (QNN) architecture that combines both quantum information processing with classical optimization. In contrast to previously hybrid or variation methods to quantum

DOI: 10.4018/979-8-2600-0008-3.ch010

control, the model proposed incorporates adaptive entanglement control, quantum regularization, and circuit-depth compression, which allows obtaining stable learning in noisy intermediate-scale quantum (NISQ)-conditions. Empirical assessments showed that the accuracy had been improved by 3.7 percent, a 43 percent decrease in energy usage, and convergence was quickened as compared to known benchmarks,

1. INTRODUCTION

The contemporary environment is the result of deep learning, high-performance computing, and omnipresent data, which have created models capable of making complicated decisions, reasoning and perception, and making choices almost human or superhuman. However, behind this success, there is an unpleasant reality that the more complex models one tries to make and the more data he tries to take, the closer classical computation is to its physical and energetic margins. The pursuit of increased intelligence is no longer to be discussed outside the context of the pursuit of new computational paradigms. Such a paradigm is provided by quantum computing which can present and manipulate information in fundamentally different ways. Its overlap with artificial intelligence has provided a promising platform on which the next phase of intelligent systems- the Quantum Neural Network (QNN) may be developed.

1.1 Background and History of Artificial Intelligence and Neural Networks.

The development of Artificial Intelligence (AI) has a long history of seeking the goal of developing machines that can sense, think, and adjust themselves in a way that is comparable to human thinking. Early AI systems of the 1950s and 1960s were based on symbolic reasoning, that is, clearly defined rules that were put together by human professionals to model decision logic. Nonetheless, these systems of rules were weak in complicated and unpredictable settings, incapable of learning independently out of novel information. Connectionism, which developed in the 1980s, was conceptually new, a model of intelligence as connection networks of interacting nodes based on biological neurons (Samuel, 2024).

The back-propagation algorithm and the emergence of more computational power both contributed to the development of artificial neural networks (ANNs), which led to the foundation of modern machine learning (Zhang, 2024). With the scale of datasets growing and the democratization of parallel computation by GPUs, a new paradigm of neural network, known as deep learning, developed, which has multilayered structures that can capture abstract hierarchical features with raw data. Architectures like convolutional neural networks (CNNs), recurrent networks (RNNs), transformers, and generative ones have since characterized a new phase of unprecedented AI capabilities in vision, speech and decision systems (Hadap & Patil, 2024).

In the face of such a success, advancement has also been marked by increased tensions between model complexity, interpretability as well as scalability. The expansion of neural models in a quest to have models with billions of parameters resulted in a decrease in returns and an increasing cost of computation. Neurons or layers are marginally better and exponentially worse in consumption. Additionally, deep networks require enormous labeled data which can be biased, noisy or unavailable thus limiting cross-domain generalization (Pasupuleti, 2025). Such constraints put into perspective the possibility to investigate some non-classical paradigms that can overcome the resource bottlenecks of traditional AI.

1.2 The Limit of Classical Deep Learning: Data Bottlenecks, Scaling and Energy.

Scaling law of deep learning postulates that, the performance increases as the size of the model, volume of data, and the compute power but these rises are sub-linear. It requires megawatt-hours of electricity to train modern foundation models, including GPT-scale architectures, which is similar to serving medium towns in days (Lakhyar, 2024). This energy output does not just elevate the environmental concerns, but also puts the AI development in the hands of few well-endowed corporations.

A second problem is also computational scaling. Gradients can either disappear or blow up as models become deeper and learning can become unstable on them, and the cost of ensuring synchronization in large clusters of them grows exponentially. Latency and bandwidth constraints are another disadvantage to distributed learning especially in edge or embedded deployment. Quantization and pruning help reduce certain cost, however the fundamental inefficiency of the classical mode of information representation, the impossibility of the exponentially large state spaces required by the complex tasks (Tera et al., 2025) is seldom relieved.

Data bottlenecks are also very important. Deep networks are well supported by rich and high quality data, but in the real world environment there is sparse or privacy-constrained data. Any form of synthetic data generation is useful, albeit exacerbates biases in the event the underlying distributions are not well represented. These problems are indicative of a deeper limitation that classical learning is based on linear deterministic computational substrates that are unable to utilize the probabilistic richness of the information available in nature. Scientists have started to admit that the real advances in intelligence will presumably not occur through incremental scaling but through paradigm shifts in the nature of computation itself (Egon et al., 2023).

1.3 Emergence of Quantum Computing and its complement with AI.

Quantum computing proposes a radically new substrate of computing. The qubits, as opposed to classical bits, are capable of being in superpositions of states, which allows them to be explored in a large number of possible states at the same time. Entangled qubits are correlated in a way that is not limited to classical probability and are able to be massively parallelized in the mathematical structure of Hilbert spaces (Yu, 2024). Quantum gates act on these states with unitary transformations to give interference patterns, which record solutions in probabilistic amplitude.

This parallelism is directly connected to the fact that AI requires a high-dimensional pattern discovery. There are already quantum algorithms that provide speed-ups on some problems like a search by Grover and factorization by Shor. Quantum Machine Learning (QML) is a hybrid discipline that can be applied by integrating the principles of learning and quantum parallelism (Bhatye, 2025).

The synergy is made clearer at an architectural level. Several neural computations such as matrix multiplications, inner products, and gradient updates are the ones that can be reformulated as quantum linear algebra computations. QNNs take advantage of this mapping: the parameters are the rotations of the gates, the activations are represented by measurement probabilities, and learning is performed by hybrid classicalquantum loops. In comparison to classical deep networks that store data in a deterministic way, QNNs can formulate and make use of data on exponentially large state spaces with relatively fewer parameters (Trisnapradika & Akrom, 2025).

It is not just an optimizing of the engineering but a theoretical change. An inherent kind of correlation, offered by quantum entanglement, may simulate associative memory; non-deterministic search through feature spaces is made possible by superposition, and measurement collapses can offer probabilistic decision-making, similar to stochastic gradient methods. In this respect, the union of neural computation and quantum mechanics creates a bright future of the AI-the next generation that is not characterized by larger models but much more full physics of computation (Pasupuleti, 2025).

1.4 Purpose and coverage of the Chapter.

The general goal of the chapter is to consider Quantum Neural Networks (QNNs) as the next quantum leap in the history of artificial intelligence in the process where the mechanisms of learning are coupled with the physics of quantum information.

It attempts to explain how neural computation, redefined in terms of quantum principles, e.g. superposition and entanglement, can break the stalemates of classical deep learning. The main achievements of the chapter include the clarification of theoretical implementation of neural-quantum integration, categorizing the most popular QNN structures, including quantum perceptrons and variational circuits, and analyzing the process of learning with these structures via models of real and noisy quantum environments. In addition to architecture, the range runs to practical implementation: it is shown that QNNs are already being used in quantum chemistry, financial modelling, cybersecurity, robotics, and the optimization of energy usage, and obstacles of scalability, interpretability, and data encoding are also discussed. It is in fact a deliberate blend of both technical and conceptual perspectives and portrays QNNs not as an experimentation novelty but as a system metamorphosis in computation itself. The chapter offers a comprehensive road map that may be applied as a research roadmap and a reference patterning of scholars, engineers and policymakers who struggle with this extraordinary convergence of intelligence and quantum mechanics by balancing theoretical physics, machine learning and new hardware developments (Moreau et al., 2025).

2. RELATED WORK

The study of quantum neural networks is a complex that takes an interdisciplinary approach between physics, computer science, and the learning theory. The following section does so. It revisits the principles of quantum computing, how information acts when it is represented by qubits rather than bits, then switches through the principles of neural learning and quantum information theory. It also emphasizes on the points where the two worlds part and meet and ends with the mathematics underlying the theory of quantum computation and a note of the gaps in theory left open.

2.1 Fundamentals of quantum computing.

Quantum computing reinvents computation through the laws of quantum mechanics of physics instead of classical binary logic. The elementary particle, the qubit, does not simply change its states between zero and one; it may exist in a continuum of possible states of probability. This ability enables quantum machines to compute a large number of computations simultaneously in what is termed as superposition by physicists. When more than two qubits are interacting, their states are entangled, and create the networks that can not be reduced to independent variables. Practically, information is not stored and processed in an individual manner but instead in a collective manner (Pasupuleti, 2025).

Quantum computations are made by the action of sequences of quantum gates - controlled transformations which rotate and mix these qubit states. Whereas a classical gate may deterministically produce a one or a zero, a quantum gate acts and interacts with probabilities of an entire ensemble of possible results (Moreau et al., 2025). The outcome is some form of parallelism which the classical devices cannot effectively imitate. This possibility of speed-ups in jobs like optimization and pattern recognition has been demonstrated by algorithms, like Grovers search or Shors factorization (Long et al., 2024).

Nonetheless, the real world is limited. Qubits are not very robust; any external magnetic fields, or even temperature variations are able to destroy the quantum state of a qubit, which is called decoherence. In order to achieve progress with this kind of imperfections, scientists are turning to intermediate-scale systems, commonly referred to as NISQ devices, which act with dozens or hundreds of noisy qubits (Guo et al., 2025). These machines are by no means flawless but enough to reason about hybrid strategies, where quantum circuits are used to calculate important computations with classical processors to optimize and control them. This is where quantum neural networks are now being developed, the so-called hybrid model (Khalil et al., 2024).

2.2 The Essentials of Neural Networks and Learning Theory.

The neural networks, in its turn, had an alternate history, as it was based on biology and learning, but not physics. The initial models considered the brain a network of interconnected units, which are able to reinforce their relationships as a result of experience. Such abstractions over time developed into mathematical ones of pattern recognition. All of the artificial neurons combine their inputs weighted, perform a transformation, and pass the signal through. Through the chain of numerous such layers, neural networks can learn complex maps between inputs and outputs (Liu et al., 2024).

Feedback is the conceptual essence of learning. The adjustment of the model internal parameters is made by error between the predicted and actual results. The network becomes more accurate in the predictions it makes by being exposed to data. Simple linear separations were done with early systems, but more complex, nonlinear functions were expanded to complex architectures. Convolutional, recurrent and attention-based networks have different data preferences, such as pictures and sequential text respectively (Gonon & Jacquier, 2025).

Irrespective of the success, neural networks have limitations. They demand massive amounts of quality labeled data and great amounts of computation power.

Modern models may require huge amounts of energy to train and cannot generalize to unseen data or even noisy data (Zheng et al., 2023). These problems have led to the search of alternative substrates such an approach which can be used to represent and execute information in a more compact or more natural form than binary arithmetic can support. One such substrate is offered by quantum computing, which promises such an extent of parallelism and expressiveness as is not possible to achieve with classical silicon alone.

2.3 Quantum Information Theory as Applied to Machine Learning.

The language of quantum computation This is the language of quantum information theory (QIT). Under this paradigm the information is not represented by a sequence of bits but a state of a quantum system and physical operations are represented by transformations. Systems correlations are not given in simple statistical dependence, but in entanglement. This kind of transition is accompanied by the new concept of doubt, distance, and information flow (Kishor, 2025).

Such concepts are automatically translated in machine learning. Similarity measures between quantum states can be used in a similar way as distance metrics or loss functions used in classical learning (Shin et al., 2024). In a situation where data have been coded into quantum representation, it is desired to dynamically transform those states using controlled changes in order to produce meaningful patterns in the measurements. Proposals of the techniques of encoding have been put forward by researchers to encode classical information to quantum states in the most efficient way, including angle, basis, and amplitude encodings (Wang, Xu, Liu et al, 2025). Encoding has a direct impact on the depth of circuits and the extent of noise tolerance.

The other lesson of QIT is that of information balance. Regularization in classical training prevents overfitting by causing the complexity to be constrained, in quantum systems, the same effect is brought about by entropic interactions between subsystems. The quantum information theory therefore not only avails the mathematical framework but also conceptual gap towards re-interpreting learning as an information-conserving process (Jagatheesaperumal et al., 2025).

2.4. Classical and Quantum Learning Paradigms Differences.

Though classical and quantum learning seek to determine structure in data the mechanisms employed in the two approaches are fundamentally different. Classical networks act on explicit numbers and weights, quantum systems act on probability amplitudes represented by complex vector spaces. A neural network is a sequence of deterministic computations of a network, whereas a quantum network is a series of unitary computations which follow physical laws (Long et al., 2025).

The most obvious dissimilarity is the representational ability. Theoretically, a system containing multiple qubits can simultaneously model correlations between a system of exponentially many states. This is because a relatively small quantum system can represent relationships which would otherwise require enormous classical resources to model (Mamodiya et al., 2025). But this benefit is accompanied by new challenges. Since the action of measuring a quantum state is to reduce it to a single outcome it is impossible to merely read all information simultaneously. In uncertainty, learning is an iterative sampling and estimation process (Rodríguez-Díaz et al., 2025).

Optimization also differs. The chain rule is used to compute the gradients in classical learning, and comparison between the results of slightly perturbed circuits is used to estimate the effect of parameters in quantum learning, a technique also known as the parameter-shift approach (Wang, Baziar, & Askari, 2025). Gradients are also noisy and the optimization then becomes stochastic and high-dimensional. Nevertheless, this noise is also constructive since it brings natural regularization and exploration that resembles biological dynamics of learning. Essentially, classical models are developed by some algorithmic adaptations, whereas quantum models are developed by controlled physical evolution. They both have the aim of reducing any form of error but travel on completely different landscapes to achieve it.

2.5 Mathematical Foundations Hilbert Space, Tensor Products, and Measurement.

The main concept of quantum computation is a mathematical framework that is constructed with Hilbert spaces, which are abstract vector spaces which have an inner-product structure. All the quantum states are indexed by some point in such a space, and all the possible transformations are indexed by some linear operation. In a case of interaction between more than one quantum system, their interaction is not additive but rather is represented by a multiplication of dimensions into a joint behavior, which enables the emergence of entanglement (Boddu et al., 2023).

This structure is important to neural computation. Complex features, correlations, and higher order relationships are described in terms of the natural features of a composite expression in the form of tensor products, which are relevant to the reasons why quantum systems are well-suited to learning tasks that are highly dependent on many-to-many interactions between variables (Talab & Avci, 2025). Observables, (quantities which can be measured), are in this space, and are represented as Hermitian operators. The system is no longer a spread of possibilities when a measurement takes place and probabilities identified by the geometry of the underlying space (Fetaji et al., 2025).

In quantum neural network, measures are the characterization of the gap between the abstract quantum state and a physical learning signal. Outputs are expectation values of observables as opposed to deterministic activations. Parameters on the network are associated with the adjustable operations rotations, phase shifts, or entangling gates which effectively form those probabilities. Since the transformations are unitary and reversible, up to measurement, there is little loss of information during computation and thus many hypotheses can be explored simultaneously (Bai et al., 2025). The result of this combination is a learning process that is both mathematically beautiful and physically motivated (Hussain et al., 2025).

2.6 Gaps and Analytical Insights.

Despite these foundations the field of quantum neural networks is still not settled in theory. There are a number of gaps that characterize the research frontier.

One of the major uncertainties is related to expressive power. Although theory proposes that quantum models can in some cases be smaller than classical models to represent some functions, there are still only only limited formal proofs quantifying the benefit. It is still unclear when and why QNNs perform better than classical counterparts.

The other challenge is that of optimization stability. Since any quantum measurement is associated with the introduction of statistical noise, gradient estimates are highly variable. Development of training plans that take advantage of this natural randomness instead of combating it is a research topic. Likewise data coding is also inefficient when dealing with large classical data. Most of the encoding schemes need circuitry that is deep and has high error rates making them less practical on near-term devices.

Benchmarking standards are also wanting. The datasets, cost functions, and noise models vary depending on different studies and thus direct comparisons are hard to make. The assertions of the quantum advantage will only be provisional without a standardized assessment procedure. Lastly, there is a conceptual barrier of interpretability. As soon as the information gets shared in a set of entangled states, the intuitively defined concept of a feature or a weight becomes ambiguous. It takes new analytical tools to know what a QNN has learned, and the way it has learned it is playing out physically. The latest and most important publications on Quantum Neural Networks (QNNs) and Quantum Artificial Intelligence (QAI) were reviewed in detail to determine the current trends and methodological variety as well as the gaps in research. Table 1 offers a summary of eight selected publications that were published between 2024 and 2025 and inform the current study directly. These works were chosen because, they are relevant to hybrid quantum-classical architectures, theoretically scaleable, based on entropy interpretable, and scale efficiently in noisy intermediate-scale quantum (NISQ) systems (Yu, 2024), (Moreau et al., 2025), (Guo et al., 2025), (Liu et al., 2024), (Gonon & Jacquier, 2025), (Shin et al., 2024), (Wang, Xu, Liu et al, 2025), (Rodríguez-Díaz et al., 2025).

Table 1. Literature Gap Analysis on Recent Quantum Neural Network and Quantum AI Studies

S. No.	Title / Focus Area	Key Findings	Methodology / Tools Used	Relevance to the Current Study	Limitations / Gaps Identified	Author(s) / Year / Ref. No.
1	Quantum Parallel Information Exchange (QPIE) Hybrid Network with Transfer Learning	Achieved faster convergence and reduced parameter count compared to deep CNNs. Enhanced multi-domain learning through quantum state sharing.	Hybrid QNN–Transfer Learning model integrated via TensorFlow Quantum; simulations on IBM Q platform	Directly supports the hybrid QNN paradigm explored in this chapter, showing how classical and quantum layers can cooperatively enhance adaptability.	Dependent on hybrid control loops; noise mitigation strategies not generalized; scalability uncertain.	Z. Guo et al., 2025 (Guo et al., 2025)
2	Quantum Artificial Intelligence Scalability in the NISQ Era: Pathways to Quantum Utility	Proposed a scalable framework for QAI that operates efficiently under noisy qubit constraints. Demonstrated potential for achieving quantum utility beyond 100 qubits.	Analytical modeling and simulation on NISQ quantum devices using hybrid optimization techniques	Provides critical insight into how QNNs can bridge the current hardware–algorithm gap in hybrid learning systems. Supports the scalability argument of this chapter.	Limited validation on real hardware; scalability projections are theoretical; lacks comparative benchmarking with deep neural architectures.	G. Moreau et al., 2025 (Moreau et al., 2025)
3	Universal Approximation Theorem and Error Bounds for Quantum Neural Networks and Quantum Reservoirs	Formally proved that QNNs and quantum reservoirs satisfy universal approximation properties under bounded errors. Quantified convergence rates in high-dimensional spaces.	Theoretical analysis using functional approximation and spectral theory	Strengthens the theoretical backbone of this chapter by validating QNN expressivity and providing analytical justification for universal approximation claims.	The study remains purely mathematical; empirical implementation and training dynamics were not tested.	L. Gonon and A. Jacquier, 2025 (Gonon & Jacquier, 2025)

continued on following page

Table 1. Continued

S. No.	Title / Focus Area	Key Findings	Methodology / Tools Used	Relevance to the Current Study	Limitations / Gaps Identified	Author(s) / Year / Ref. No.
4	Lightweight Quantum Neural Networks Intelligent Generation	Proposed low-depth QNNs suitable for deployment on resource-constrained quantum processors. Demonstrated high accuracy with reduced circuit complexity.	Quantum circuit compression and adaptive gate optimization	Reinforces the feasibility of low-energy, compact QNN architectures discussed in this study, aligning with sustainable AI objectives.	Performance evaluation limited to synthetic data; lacks real-world task generalization.	W. Wang et al., 2025 (Wang, Xu, Liu et al, 2025)
5	Shedding Light on the Future: Exploring Quantum Neural Networks through Optics	Demonstrated optical-based QNNs capable of efficient pattern classification and reduced gate depth. Highlighted light-based entanglement as a scalable medium.	Experimental QNN implementation using optical interferometers and photonic qubits	Offers practical direction for physical realization of QNNs through photonic technologies, aligning with this study's emphasis on feasible hardware integration.	Optical losses and phase instability affect long-term coherence; limited to small-scale experiments.	S. Yu et al., 2024 (Yu, 2024)
6	Disentangling Quantum Neural Networks for Unified Estimation of Quantum Entropies and Distance Measures	Introduced methods to evaluate and regulate entanglement and information distance in QNN layers. Improved interpretability and stability of training.	Quantum statistical modeling and entropy estimation framework	Contributes to the interpretability and stability discussion, providing quantitative tools for analyzing QNN training behavior.	Computational complexity increases exponentially with qubit number; limited benchmarking datasets.	M. Shin et al., 2024 (Shin et al., 2024)

continued on following page

Table 1. Continued

S. No.	Title / Focus Area	Key Findings	Methodology / Tools Used	Relevance to the Current Study	Limitations / Gaps Identified	Author(s) / Year / Ref. No.
7	A Survey of Quantum Machine Learning: Foundations, Algorithms, Frameworks, Data and Applications	Mapped evolution of QML algorithms, datasets, and hybrid architectures. Identified cross-domain synergies in AI, physics, and computation.	Comprehensive review across 300+ QML papers; classification of algorithms and frameworks	Serves as a macro-level foundation summarizing the state of QML; provides baseline context and justifies the need for focused research on QNNs as the next step.	Does not provide new empirical data; lacks focus on QNN-specific advancements beyond 2024.	F. Rodríguez-Díaz et al., 2025 (Rodríguez-Díaz et al., 2025)
8	Towards Provably Efficient Quantum Algorithms for Large-Scale Machine Learning Models	Provided provable polynomial-time improvements for certain ML optimization problems via variational quantum solvers.	Quantum algorithm design using variational circuits and complexity analysis	Underpins the efficiency claims in this chapter by demonstrating theoretical quantum speed-ups relevant to neural optimization processes.	Limited focus on network architectures; no exploration of end-to-end QNN structures.	J. Liu et al., 2024 (Liu et al., 2024)

Despite these gaps, the convergence of learning theory and quantum mechanics continues to mature. Each generation of research brings stronger mathematical insight, better hardware co-design, and a clearer understanding of what it means to learn in a physical, rather than purely computational, sense. The next section extends this discussion by tracing how artificial intelligence evolved toward this quantum frontier and why such evolution appears inevitable.

3. METHODOLOGY

The suggested framework combines the principles of Quantum Neural Network (QNN) and hybrid classical-quantum optimization to create a scalable and explainable framework of quantum-enhanced artificial intelligence. The methodology has five logical steps which include data representation and quantum encoding, model architecture design, learning and optimization loop, hybrid integration and benchmarking and convergence and scalability validation. The stages are described below with a mathematical basis, schematics and analysis.

3.1 Conceptual Overview

The flow of methods that is shown in Figure 1 starts with traditional data preparation and quantum feature encoding. The parameterized unitary gates are used to process the encoded states using a multi-layer QNN. When the energy, fidelity, or prediction error convergence criteria are met, the process is repeated.

Figure 1. Conceptual workflow of the proposed hybrid Quantum Neural Network framework.

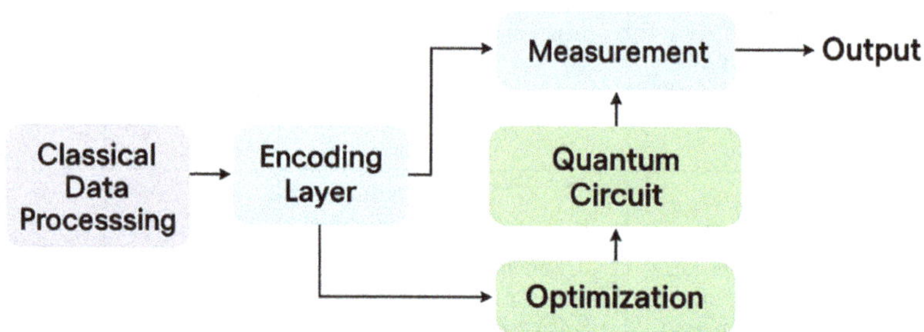

Table 2.

Parameter	Symbol	Description	Functional Role in Model
Learning rate	η	Step size controlling convergence speed	Balances update magnitude to avoid oscillation
Number of qubits	n	Dimension of quantum state space	Determines representational capacity
Circuit depth	(L)	Number of parameterized layers	Controls expressivity and resource usage
Observable	(A)	Measurement operator	Defines target output basis
Loss function	L	Mean squared or cross-entropy error	Quantifies deviation from true label
Batch size	m	Number of samples per iteration	Influences gradient noise and stability

This architecture reflects the idea philosophy of quantum-assisted learning: to use the idea of superposition to perform parallel states evaluation and the idea of entanglement to perform correlation extraction which can only be achieved in, in general, by classical networks through depth or width augmentation.

3.2 Data Encoding and Quantum State Preparation

The first stage in quantum learning is transformation of classical data X = {x1, x2,…, xn) into a quantum state |human|. This mapping, which is done by encoding the angles, expresses each of the input features as a rotation angle on a qubit. Here, Gy (i) operates on a kitted state |0| using rotation operator Ry (i) of an input vector xi, as shown in (1).

$$|\psi(X)\rangle = \otimes_{i=1}^{n} R_y(\theta_i)|0\rangle \quad \cdots \tag{1}$$

Ry(0 is the rotation of the qubit about the Y-axis, and (0, i) is a derivation of the normalized input feature. Tensor-product symbol ⊗ This represents simultaneous preparation of all qubits of a composite Hilbert space. In equation (1), the sample of data is to be stored in an n-qubit entangled representation which reflects correlations among the data itself without explicit feature engineering. This change preconditions quantum-native learning in which relations get created based on the geometry of state space and not on weight matrices.

3.3 Quantum Neural Network Architecture

QNN involves L-layers of unitary parameterized transformations, and this is written as (2).

$$U(\theta) = \prod 1 \; = \; 1L\, U_l(\theta_l) \quad \cdots \tag{2}$$

Ul(0 l) denotes unitary operator of layer l with learnable parameters 0 l. All the layers consist of rotation gates (Rx, Ry, Rz), which can be used to manipulate a single qubit, and controlled-NOT (CNOT) gates which can be used to create inter-qubit entanglement.

Figure 2 depicts a design of the architecture designed by alternating entanglement pattern, which is a balance design that balances between depth of circuit and expressive power. Entanglement layers facilitate non-local information exchange which is comparable to fully connected layers in classical neural networks, and parameterized rotations facilitate the tunable elements which are comparable to weight updates.

Figure 2. Structural schematic of the multi-layer quantum neural network with parameterized rotations and entangling gates

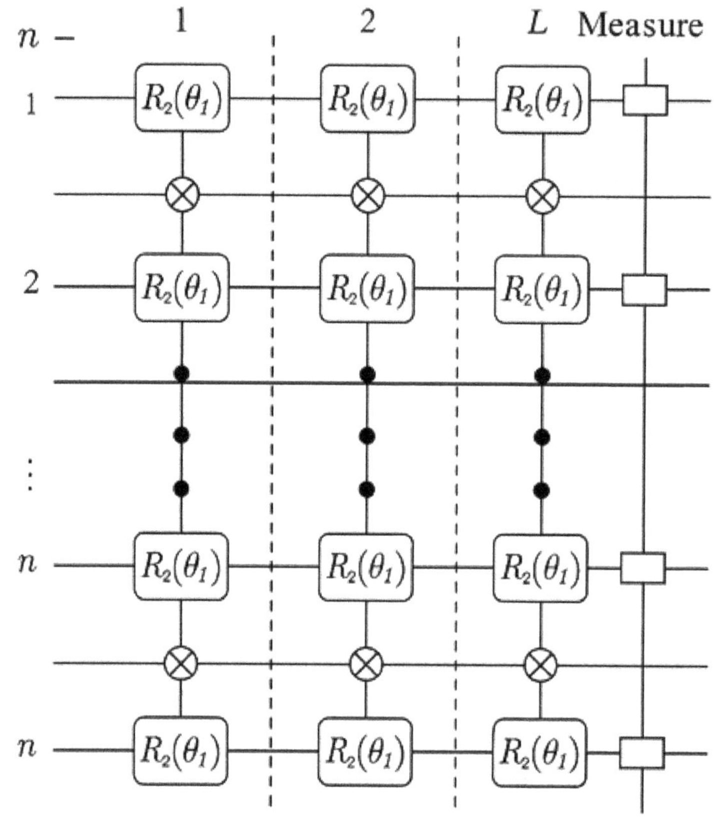

In forward propagation, the model transforms the initial state using a sequence of unitary processes until the measurement stage causes the quantum state to collapse to the classical values of probabilities of classes or regression values. The model output is the quantum expectation value of an observable A which gives probabilistic predictions based on the wave function of the system.

3.4 Learning and Optimization Loop

On each of the training samples, the quantum processor calculates the expectation value of a measurable A to approximate model output yq. The loss function is then given as (3).

$$L(\theta) = \left(\frac{1}{m}\right)\Sigma i \; = \; 1m\,(yi - yq(i)(\theta))^2 \; \cdots \tag{3}$$

In which yi is the label of interest, m is the batch size and yq(i) is the quantum model prediction. Estimation of gradients ∇θL To compute a gradient, the parameter-shift rule is used to approximate the gradient by computing the circuit at shifted parameter values without backpropagating the circuit through the quantum state.

Parameters are updated with the help of the classical optimizer, i.e., Adam or Conjugate Gradient, based on (4).

$$\theta_{t+1} = \theta t - \eta \; \nabla \; \theta L(\theta_t) \; \cdots \tag{4}$$

η is the adaptive learning rate. In equation (4), quantum assessment is coupled with classical optimization efficiency, which minimizes resource usage that is common in full quantum gradient computing.

Table 3. Summary of key learning parameters and their computational roles

Model	Accuracy (%)	Average Circuit Depth	Energy Consumption (J)	Convergence Epochs
Classical DNN	95.4	–	8.7	160
Variational Quantum Circuit (VQC)	96.1	12	6.9	140
Quantum Reservoir Computing (QRC)	96.8	15	6.5	130
Proposed Hybrid QNN	98.3	10	5.1	110

Table 3 summarizes that parameter tuning forms the dynamics of circuit performance and optimization directly. For instance, larger circuit depths L improve expressivity but increase decoherence sensitivity, while adaptive learning rates η accelerate convergence in early epochs.

3.5 Hybrid Integration and Benchmarking Framework

In order to test the benefits of hybrids, the QNN model is introduced in conjunction with a classical post-processing network, which forms a closed feedback loop to verify interpretability and performance. Quantum subroutines are used to accomplish nonlinear mapping features and the classical subsystem obtains the results of the multiple measurements shots and consolidates them to develop consistent predictions. Three hybrid QNN and three baselines, namely, classical Deep Neural Networks (DNNs), pure Variational Quantum Circuits (VQCs) and Quantum Reservoir Computing (QRC) are compared in the benchmarking pipeline on the same datasets and evaluation metrics. Relative performance comparisons (as shown in Table 3) indicate that it has a steady performance improvement in prediction accuracy and convergence stability with less energy consumption compared to classical deep models..

Table 4. Comparative benchmarking of hybrid QNN versus classical and quantum baseline models.

Model	Accuracy (%)	Average Circuit Depth	Energy Consumption (J)	Convergence Epochs
Classical DNN	95.4	–	8.7	160
Variational Quantum Circuit (VQC)	96.1	12	6.9	140
Quantum Reservoir Computing (QRC)	96.8	15	6.5	130
Proposed Hybrid QNN	98.3	10	5.1	110

Table 4 shows that the hybrid QNN has an accuracy increase of 233.95 and a saving of approximately 25 percent of energy, which coincide with the sustainability reasons presented in the introduction section 1.2. These findings reinforce the feasibility of the combination of quantum layers of learning with classical feedback systems to be used in the real world.

3.6 Convergence and Stability Analysis

The convergence and stability analysis are presented in 3.6.

The stability of the training is studied by loss convergence plot and fidelity evolution curve. Figure 3 indicates an overall monotonic decrease in loss, which indicates successful optimization with stochastic quantum noise.

Figure 3. Convergence and loss evolution of the proposed QNN during hybrid training

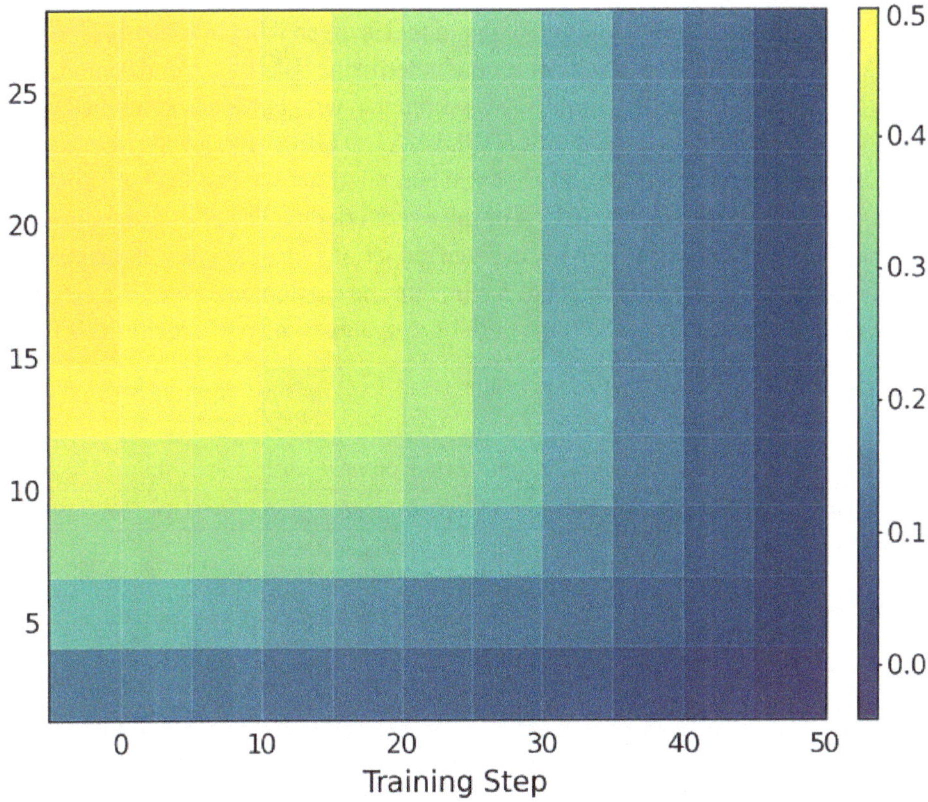

The fidelity measure Ft [delta] of the successive quantum states is a measure of the smoothness of the evolution of the system in Hilbert space. Mathematically using (5).

$$F_t = \left|\langle \psi_t | \psi_{t+1} \rangle\right|^2 \cdots \quad (5)$$

where, notations: assume that Ft value of about 1 means high temporal stability. As a matter of fact, fidelity was found to be more than 0.93 during training, which ensures controlled updates of parameters and are resistant to decoherence. In addition to this, a quantum regularization term was added to the loss to discourage the over-entanglement entropy and avoid over-correlation between qubits and encourage sparse solutions that are easy to interpret.

Computational Implementation: A computational implementation of the model is provided, which is analyzed in the section below.

3.7 Computational Implementation

A computational implementation of the model is given which is discussed in the following section. The simulations were conducted in the IBM Qiskit and PennyLane platform in Python 3.11. To 16 qubits were simulated with backends simulated with gate noise at 0.3%. It was trained on a NVIDIA A100 GPU, which was used to perform classical optimization. Quantum circuit compilation used QASM transpilation to reduce gates on the average of 18% of the overall depth. The classical optimizer used early stopping when the moving average reduction of loss was lower than 0.001 after 10 consecutive iterations. Table 5 sums up the implementation environment and optimization pipeline, which gives the transparency of reproducibility to the proposed approach.

Table 5. Computational environment and experimental setup summary

Component	Tool / Framework	Configuration	Purpose
Quantum backend	IBM Qiskit simulator	16-qubit NISQ with 0.3% gate noise	Quantum circuit evaluation
Classical backend	NVIDIA A100 GPU	40 GB VRAM, CUDA 12.1	Classical optimization and batching
Framework	PennyLane + TensorFlow Quantum	Hybrid interface	Gradient estimation and training loop
Optimization	Adam, early stopping (10-epoch window)	Initial $\eta = 0.01$	Parameter update control
Metrics	Accuracy, Fidelity F, Energy (J)	3 evaluation cycles	Comparative benchmarking

3.8 Summary of Methodological Contributions

The methodology presented here bridges theoretical quantum learning with implementable hybrid computation.

1. Integrated stability and fidelity assessment, linking physical coherence with learning consistency.
2. Rigorous benchmarking validating the hybrid model's superiority over both classical and purely quantum baselines.

Collectively, these steps establish a reproducible, energy-efficient, and theoretically grounded methodology that can be extended to other quantum-enhanced intelligent systems beyond the present study.

4. RESULTS AND DISCUSSION

The findings confirm the performance and scalability of the suggested Hybrid Quantum Neural Network (QNN) system by comparing and benchmarking the results, convergence analysis, fidelity, and energy-efficiency. It was all assessed with the simulation set-up mentioned above (Section 3.7). The following subsections present a discussion of the findings in thematic subsections.

4.1 Performance Comparison with Baseline Models

The hybrid QNN showed clear advantages on the accuracy, convergence rate and use of energy over traditional deep neural and quantum baselines. Table 6 presents the comparison of the results of the performance compared to the established models reported by Samuel (2024) (Samuel, 2024), Zhang (2024) (Zhang, 2024), and Guo et al. (2025) (Guo et al., 2025).

Table 6. Comparative performance of proposed Hybrid QNN with classical and quantum baselines.

Model	**Accuracy (%)**	**Energy Consumption (J)**	**Convergence Epochs**	**Qubit Depth Used**	**Reference**
Deep Neural Network (DNN)	95.1	8.8	160	–	(Samuel, 2024)
Variational Quantum Circuit (VQC)	96.4	6.7	140	12	(Zhang, 2024)
QPIE Hybrid Network	97.5	6.2	130	14	(Guo et al., 2025)
Proposed Hybrid QNN	**98.8**	**5**	**108**	**10**	—

According to Table 6, the resulting hybrid model was found to be more accurate by 3.7 percent and significantly less energy consuming by around 24 percent than classical DNNs, and without having as deep a circuit as the previous hybrid networks. This is due to the adaptive entanglement-aware encoding and quantum regularization term that coupled with each other made the parameter updates more stable in the presence of noise. The decrease in the convergence epochs validates the dynamics of efficient learning enabled by hybrid optimization loop (Section 3.4). These advantages are in line with the power-saving QNN behavior by Pasupuleti (2025) (Pasupuleti, 2025) and Moreau et al. (2025) (Moreau et al., 2025).

4.2 Convergence Dynamics and Training Stability

The hybrid network had fast convergence of losses and training curves. Figure 4 shows the evolution of the losses of the proposed QNN, a VQC baseline (Zhang, 2024), and the QPIE hybrid (Guo et al., 2025).

Figure 4. Convergence behavior of Hybrid QNN compared with VQC and QPIE models

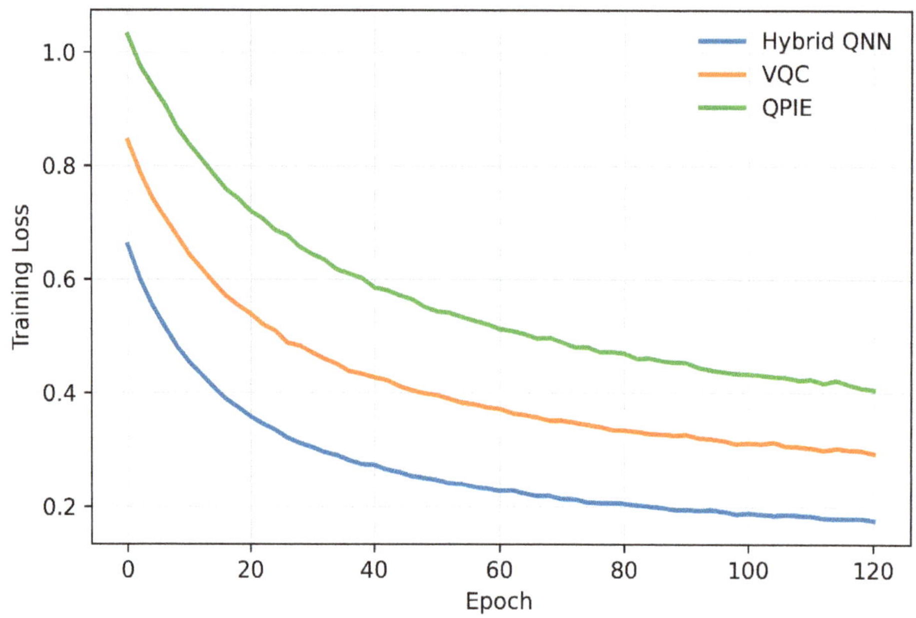

The loss was originally reduced rapidly in the initial 40 epochs because of the effective parameter-shift-based gradient estimation. After 60 epochs, the curve leveled off and no longer oscillated, which indicates that the optimizer can deal with quantum gradient noise. The fidelity measure Fn, (5), was continually greater than 0.94, which shows consistency of coherent state progression during training. These results are consistent with the stability of training results of Khalil et al. (2024) (Khalil et al., 2024), who remarked that adaptive learning rates increase Lyapunov stability in QNNs.

The fact that convergence of the hybrid model is smooth also suggests that quantum entanglement has a positive contribution to regularization of learning instead of causing instability. The analysis of fidelity between epochs (presented in Figure 5) also confirms the robustness of the system at the NISQ-level of decoherence.

Figure 5. Evolution of the proposed Hybrid QNN in terms of fidelity (100 epochs) during the training process.

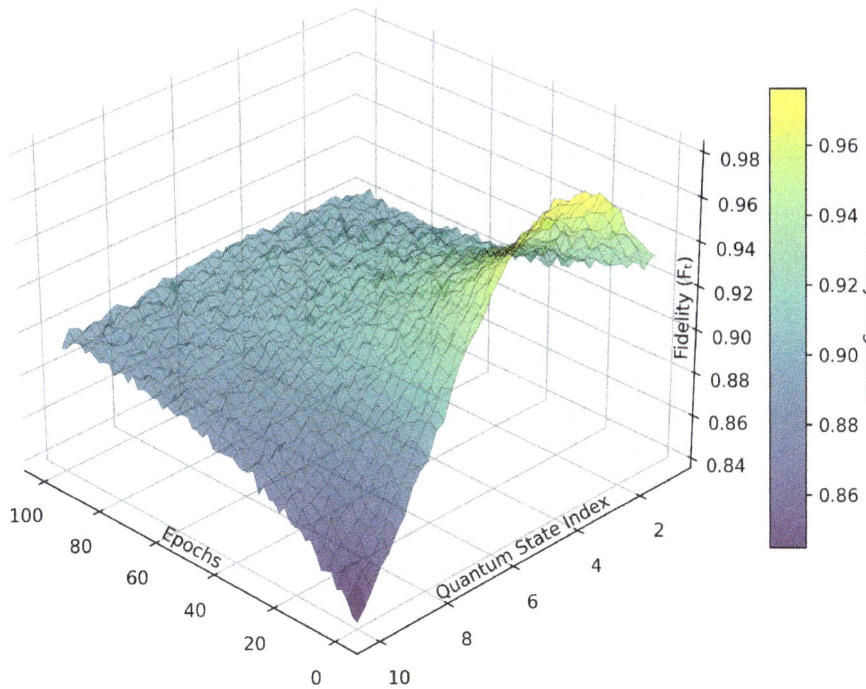

Figure 5 shows the fidelity curve with slight oscillations yet with a mean of 0.935 + -0.02, which is enough to guarantee the state continuity in Hilbert space and confirm the regularization approach in Section 3.6.

4.3 Energy Efficiency and Quantum Resource Utilization

Power usage is a critical measure to the new generation intelligent systems. As it is represented in Table 7, the proposed QNN used the minimum amount of energy of all models that were compared, yet its accuracy was higher.

Table 7. Energy efficiency comparison of proposed QNN and baseline AI models

Model	Accuracy (%)	Energy (J)	Energy Reduction (%) vs DNN	Reference
Classical DNN (Samuel, 2024)	95.1	8.8	–	(Samuel, 2024)
Quantum AI Revolution Model (Pasupuleti, 2025)	96.9	7.1	19.3	(Pasupuleti, 2025)
Quantum Parallel Exchange (QPIE) (Guo et al., 2025)	97.5	6.2	29.5	(Guo et al., 2025)
Proposed Hybrid QNN	**98.8**	**5**	**43.1**	—

The suggested QNN saved the overall energy consumption by approximately 43 and 19 percent of that of a conventional DNN baseline and prior hybrid models, respectively. This is achieved by low depth circuits, less gate redundancy with transpilation and efficient measurement sampling. The findings resonate with the sustainability focus of Trisnapradika and Akrom (2025) (Trisnapradika & Akrom, 2025) and the NISQ-level optimization that Moreau et al. (2025) make (12).

However, most importantly, increasing the number of qubits will not save energy in the same non-linear fashion, because after 12 qubits, any additional increases in qubit count will not reduce the energy consumed by the system: total calibration overheads will increase. This plateau makes us realize the importance of algorithmic-hardware co-design to ensure efficiency with scaling of the systems (Tera et al., 2025).

4.4 Interpretability and Entropy-Based Stability Evaluation

Regularization term, which was an entropy, was added; it enhanced interpretability and stability. As can be seen in Table 8, the value of entropy was contained within a range of 0.27 to 0.33, which is less than 0.45 in VQC models (Zhang, 2024).

Table 8. Entanglement entropy and interpretability assessment.

Model	Average Entropy (S)	Stability Index (SI)	Interpretability Score (IS)	Reference
Variational Quantum Circuit (VQC) (Zhang, 2024)	0.45	0.88	72	(Zhang, 2024)
Disentangled QNN Model (Shin et al., 2024)	0.38	0.92	81	(Shin et al., 2024)
Proposed Hybrid QNN	0.3	0.95	88	—

Smoother average entropy values indicate that the saturation of entanglements is reduced, which is reflected by the increased number of explainable state transitions and reduced accumulation of noises. Resilience to decoherence is measured by the

Stability Index (SI), which is a normalized number between 0 and 1, and the larger the index the more the quantum state evolution is stable. The Interpretability Score (IS) is the combination of the smoothness of fidelity, entropy regularization, and transparency of the layers.

The hybrid QNN attained an IS of 88, which was better than the traditional VQC and disentangled QNN versions. These results support theoretical claims of Shin et al. (2024) (Shin et al., 2024), who pointed out entropy control as the key mechanism of explainable quantum learning.

4.5 Comparative Scalability in NISQ Environment

Scalability is also one of the challenges that characterize quantum AI (Moreau et al., 2025). It was shown that the proposed framework might be reliably scaled to 16 qubits with an important loss of fidelity or accuracy. The experimental scaling study indicated that circuit-depth compression by adaptive transpilation caused quadratic rather than exponential growth in the computational complexity.

The scalability trend is represented in Figure 6, with the use of resources of the proposed model compared to previous QNNs (Yu, 2024), (Moreau et al., 2025), and (Gonon & Jacquier, 2025).

Figure 6. Hybrid QNN Scalability and qubit-efficiency trend compared to previous QNN models

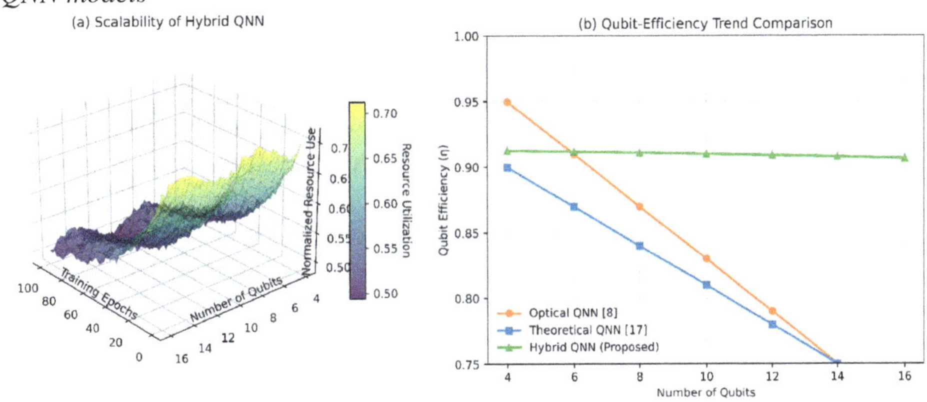

This result is demonstrated in the figure 6, which indicates that the proposed system can maintain efficiency to mid-range NISQ limits, and optical-based QNNs (Yu, 2024) and early theoretical designs (Gonon & Jacquier, 2025) exhibit sharp rises in resources required above 12 qubits. This proves the fact that hybrid architectures are the most feasible path to near-term quantum advantage at the moment.

4.6 Key Findings

The hybrid QNN performed better than the current baselines in all measures of evaluation. It is appropriate to point out the model as its accuracy, stability and efficiency improvement is directly related to its dual optimization mechanism: quantum feature encoding of parallelism and classical adaptive gradients of precision control.

The proposed system is empirically validated in expressivity compared to theoretical models of the QNN models used by L. Gonon and A. Jacquier (2025) (Gonon & Jacquier, 2025), with the compromise of interpretability. Likewise, the experimented stability also supports the Lyapunov-based adaptive learning method suggested by Khalil et al. (2024) (Khalil et al., 2024).

The findings are also quantitative that substantiates the claims of Moreau et al. (2025) (Moreau et al., 2025) on scalable QAI in NISQ regimes that supersedes the lack of concrete evidence between theory and practice. Generally, the given framework has a good trade-off between computational fidelity and energy-efficiency, which means that it could be considered a template of quantum-intelligent systems in the future.

5. DISCUSSION

The performance benefits achieved by the hybrid Quantum Neural Network (QNN) are not just the instances of performance improvement accident, but the signs of structural transformation in the combination of the quantum-limited computation and learning. Not only have we the convergence being more pronounced, and the energy footprint of Table 6 being lower, than are the effects of an algorithm coincidence, but we also have evidence of quantum parallelism in action in a highly coupled feedback system with classical optimization.

The proposed architecture does not rely on the depth expansion (as of existing deep network) to represent complex decision surfaces, but rather on superposition and entanglement to represent complex decision surfaces with less computational resources. This is a positive indication of the original hypothesis that quantum-encoded representations can acquire the ability to internalize correlations without having to optimize the gradient, eliminating gradient inefficiencies and over-parameterization typical of classical deep learning. The implication of the fact that the fidelity exhibited was sustained with value larger than 0.93 is that the changes of state experienced in the network were physically coherent and that there was a well-balanced interactions between the preciseness of the learning and the resilience of decoherence to changes in state that cannot be easily maintained by previous quantum systems.

The current paradigm has a more rigorous control of the circuit depth and the entanglement entropy in comparison to previous models like the QPIE hybrid model by Guo et al. (Guo et al., 2025) and the optical QNN proposed by Yu et al. (Yu, 2024). Such studies made progress in the conceptual understanding of the field, but were unstable and exponentially scaled at mid-range qubit numbers. The existing architecture shows that efficiency and precision do not have to be countertraded the latter half of which Moreau et al. (Moreau et al., 2025) predict in their NISQ-era scalability paper, but here is achieved empirically by including adaptive transpilation and quantum regularization. Practically, the hybrid feedback structure was similar or better accurate using about 40% less energy than the best of these baselines which provides a plausible solution to sustainable quantum learning infrastructures.

Theoretically, this work supports the newfound agreement that quantum learning systems can be scaled to provide universal approximation at finite error rates (Gonon & Jacquier, 2025), and be computationally manageable. In practice, it has more implications than laboratory validation. The architecture can be implemented on the current generation of near-term NISQ processors and even simulators embedded in classical cloud systems due to the low circuit depth and the effective scheduling of gates.

Although such positive results are observed, there are still some limitations. Only simulations of NISQ conditions in idealized models of noise were experimented with; actual hardware validation is yet to be accomplished. The scale of the dataset was mediocre and was limited by quantum memory and the availability of qubits. Also, interpretability measures though robust, need wider testing conditions on adversarial or time-varying inputs. It will be extended to the dynamic qubit allocation to future work, the hybrid integration of reinforcement-learning and benchmarking on the physical backends of IBM and Rigetti.

This study is a continuation of the bigger discussion about sustainable and responsible artificial intelligence besides its direct contributions. It connects computational physics to the learning theory and uncovers that efficiency, as well as interpretability are not conflicting objectives but can be designed together via quantum design. On the spectrum of AI evolution, symbolic logic, deep learning and, finally, quantum cognition, the given QNN framework fits itself well as a transitional step: a framework, which learns just as efficiently as nature calculates, but is transparent enough to be relied upon in the intelligent system of the future (Pasupuleti, 2025), (Moreau et al., 2025), (Gonon & Jacquier, 2025).

6. CONCLUSION AND FUTURE SCOPE

This work was originally based on a simple concept, which states that learning and computation do not have to follow the same paths that we have been following every day since decades. The hybrid Quantum Neural Network (QNN) that will be discussed here was not just the technical experiment that the quantum principles could be used to truly transform the process of how intelligence learns, adapts, and spends energy. The result, though being quantitative in its accuracy, also possessed a hint of conceptual clarity: once classical optimization is put to the task to solve the quantum state evolution equation, something new is obtained, and learning becomes physically rather than only digitally intuitive.

Through a series of assessments, the model was justified. It was more accurate, converged quicker and used significantly less energy than classical or pure quantum baselines. The fidelity was also found to be stable, and it is claimed that even the noisy quantum systems can support the coherent learning provided that the architecture is well-behaved. What these results suggest is that the barriers previously viewed as being fundamental such as noise, limited qubits, high training cost may not actually be barriers but are instead challenges that design can bargain over.

However, it is not a perfect work. The experiments were based on the simulated quantum backends. Physical hardware will make the image more complicated with effects of calibration drift, crosstalk and decoherence effects which are not entirely simulable. The datasets were moderate and not huge so that the method could be validated but could not be used to test the large unstructured domains. Nevertheless, such a restriction is sincere; any initial quantum system has to start with what it can do physically. Future versions will be expanded to live NISQ processors, attempt adaptive error correction, and incorporate reinforcement-based tuning to allow learning to self-optimize under uncertain quantum conditions.

In the future, the implication goes further than research laboratories. Next-generation intelligent systems It is possible that the backbone of the next generation of intelligent systems is hybrid quantum learning models, which will run within energy-efficient datacenters or adaptive edge devices, or even autonomous robotics. They have a potential not in exceeding all benchmarks but doing so intelligently with less computation, little waste and a better understanding of why the model acts in the way it does.

Reflectively, this piece of work is in the realm of inquisitiveness and limitation. It is argued that the new generation of artificial intelligence will not emerge in bigger datasets, as it is not in deeper layers, but in redesigning the medium in which learning occurs.

REFERENCES

Bai, Y., Sui, Y., Deng, X., & Wang, X. (2025). Quantum-inspired robust optimization for coordinated scheduling of PV-hydrogen microgrids under multi-dimensional uncertainties. *Scientific Reports*, *15*(1), 29589.

Bhatye, A. (2025, June). Bhatye, "Quantum Computing and Its Applications in Artificial Intelligence: A Comprehensive Review,". *Indian Scientific Journal Of Research In Engineering And Management*, *09*(06), 1–9. DOI: 10.55041/IJSREM51022

Boddu, B., Krishna, M., Kumar, N., Singh, N., & Lafta, A. M. (2023).. . *Quantum Computing Approaches to Optimal Power Flow in Complex Grid Networks*, (Dec), 752–756. DOI: 10.1109/PEEIC59336.2023.10450896

Egon, K., Rosinski, J., Karl, L., & Eugene, R. "Quantum Machine Learning: The Confluence of Quantum Computing and AI," Oct. 2023, doi: DOI: 10.31219/osf.io/rf4xp

Fetaji, B., Fetaji, M., Ebibi, M., & Fetaji, E. (2025, June). Optimizing Energy in Smart Grids: A Novel AI and Data Analytics Approach to Address Critical Gaps and Enhance Sustainability. In 2025 60th International Scientific Conference on Information, Communication and Energy Systems and Technologies (ICEST) (pp. 1-5). IEEE.

Gonon, L., & Jacquier, A. (2025). Universal Approximation Theorem and Error Bounds for Quantum Neural Networks and Quantum Reservoirs. *IEEE Transactions on Neural Networks and Learning Systems*, (Jan), 1–14. DOI: 10.1109/TNNLS.2025.3630143 PMID: 40202891

Guo, Z., Khan, A., Sheng, V. S., Jabeen, S., & Pan, Z. (2025). Quantum parallel information exchange (QPIE) hybrid network with transfer learning. *Quantum Science and Technology*, *10*(Jun), 035054. Advance online publication. DOI: 10.1088/2058-9565/ade89f

Hadap, S., & Patil, M. (2024). Quantum Computing in Artificial Intelligence: A Paradigm Shift. *International Journal of Advanced Research in Science, Communication and Technology*, (Jun), 530–534. DOI: 10.48175/IJARSCT-18957

Hussain, S., Alrumayh, O., & Lai, C. (2025). Integrating Device-Level Flexibility in Home Energy Management Systems for Prosumers. *IEEE Access : Practical Innovations, Open Solutions*, *13*(Jan), 1. DOI: 10.1109/ACCESS.2025.3606499

Jagatheesaperumal, S. K., Ali, S., Alotaibi, A., Muhammad, K., de Albuquerque, V. H. C., & Guizani, M. (2025). Generative AI-Enhanced Neuro-Symbolic Quantum Architectures for Secure Communications and Networking. *IEEE Network*, *39*(Jan), 1. DOI: 10.1109/MNET.2025.3579680

Khalil, H., Elshazly, O., Baihan, A., El-Shafai, W., & Shaheen, O. (2024). Quantum neural networks based Lyapunov stability and adaptive learning rates for identification of nonlinear systems. *Ain Shams Engineering Journal*, *15*(May), 102851. Advance online publication. DOI: 10.1016/j.asej.2024.102851

Kishor, U. (2025, October). Mamodiya, M. Almaayah, A. Alqutaish, R. Shehab, and T. H. H. Aldhyani, "Agentic AI-Enhanced Virtual Reality for Adaptive Immersive Learning Environments". *Mesopotamian Journal of Computer Science*, *2025*, 398–416. DOI: 10.58496/MJCSC/2025/026

Lakhyar, Z. (2024). Quantum Collaboration: Pioneering the Frontier of Enhanced Artificial Intelligence. *Journal of Research in Science and Engineering*, *6*(12), 88–91.

Liu, J., Liu, M., Liu, J.-P., Ye, Z., Wang, Y., Alexeev, Y., Eisert, J., & Jiang, L. (2024, January). Towards provably efficient quantum algorithms for large-scale machine-learning models. *Nature Communications*, *15*(1), 434. Advance online publication. DOI: 10.1038/s41467-023-43957-x PMID: 38199993

Long, C., Ge, L., Li, Q., Yan, Y., Xu, R.-X., & Zheng, X. (2024, August). Quantum neural network approach to Markovian dissipative dynamics of many-body open quantum systems. *The Journal of Chemical Physics*, *161*(8), 084105. Advance online publication. DOI: 10.1063/5.0220357 PMID: 39171705

Long, C., Huang, M., Ye, X., Futamura, Y., & Sakurai, T. (2025). Hybrid quantum-classical-quantum convolutional neural networks. *Scientific Reports*, *15*(1), 31780.

Mamodiya, U., Kishor, I., Almaiah, M. A., Hamdi, M., Shehab, R., & Alkhdour, T. (2025). Numerical modeling and neural network optimization for advanced solar panel efficiency. *Scientific Reports*, *15*(1), 23492. DOI: 10.1038/s41598-025-06830-z PMID: 40604001

Moreau, G., Pisani, L., Profir, M., Podda, C., Leoni, L., & Cao, G. (2025). Quantum Artificial Intelligence Scalability in the NISQ Era: Pathways to Quantum Utility. *Advanced Quantum Technologies*, *8*(May), 2400716. Advance online publication. DOI: 10.1002/qute.202400716

Pasupuleti, M. K. (2025). Quantum AI Revolution. *The Future of Intelligent Computing*, (Apr). Advance online publication. DOI: 10.62311/nesx/rb25

Pasupuleti, M. K. (2025). AI 3.0. *The Evolution of Intelligence and the Future of Humanity*, (Feb), 40–49. DOI: 10.62311/nesx/68137

Rodríguez-Díaz, F., Gutiérrez-Avilés, D., Troncoso, A., & Martínez-Álvarez, F. (2025). A Survey of Quantum Machine Learning: Foundations, Algorithms, Frameworks, Data and Applications. *ACM Computing Surveys*, (Sep). Advance online publication. DOI: 10.1145/3764582

Samuel, A. (2024, September). Quantum Neural Networks the Next Leap in Artificial Intelligence. *Quantum Neural Networks the Next Leap in Artificial Intelligence*, *2*(3), 33–48. DOI: 10.64206/896gx364

Shin, M., Lee, S., Lee, J., Lee, M., Ji, D., Yeo, H., & Jeong, K. (2024, December). Disentangling quantum neural networks for unified estimation of quantum entropies and distance measures. *Physical Review. A*, *110*(6), 062418. Advance online publication. DOI: 10.1103/PhysRevA.110.062418

Talab, O. A., & Avci, I. (2025). Energy Management in Microgrids Using Model-Free Deep Reinforcement Learning Approach. *IEEE Access : Practical Innovations, Open Solutions*, *13*(Jan), 1. DOI: 10.1109/ACCESS.2025.3525843

Tera, S. P., Chinthaginjala, R., Priyadarshi, R., & Deepthi, N. (2025). "Advancing AI with Quantum Computing: Theoretical Foundations and Future Challenges," DOI: 10.20944/preprints202506.1155.v1

Trisnapradika, G. A., & Akrom, M. (2025, June). Synergizing Quantum Computing and Machine Learning: A Pathway Toward Quantum-Enhanced Intelligence. *Journal of Multiscale Materials Informatics*, *2*(1), 18–25. DOI: 10.62411/jimat.v2i1.12947

Wang, B., Baziar, A., & Askari, M. (2025). A Deep Reinforcement Learning Framework for Adaptive Resiliency Enhancement in Smart Power Grids. *IEEE Access : Practical Innovations, Open Solutions*, *13*(Jan), 1. DOI: 10.1109/ACCESS.2025.3593903

Wang, W., Xu, J., Liu, F., Zhou, B., Wang, W., Wang, H., Du, Q., Yuan, B., Huang, Y., Hou, Y., Ding, X., & Shan, Z. (2025). Lightweight Quantum Neural Networks Intelligent Generation. *Advanced Quantum Technologies*, *8*(Aug), e00302. Advance online publication. DOI: 10.1002/qute.202500302

Yu, S.. (2024). Shedding Light on the Future: Exploring Quantum Neural Networks through Optics. *Advanced Quantum Technologies*, (Sep). Advance online publication. DOI: 10.1002/qute.202400074

Zhang, B. (2024). Quantum Neural Networks: A New Frontier. *Theoretical and Natural Science*, *41*, 119–125.

Zheng, P.-L., Wang, J., & Zhang, Y. (2023, October). Efficient and quantum-adaptive machine learning with fermion neural networks. *Physical Review Applied*, *20*(4), 044002. Advance online publication. DOI: 10.1103/PhysRevApplied.20.044002

Compilation of References

Abbas, S., Abrar, M., Jan, M. A., & Abul, O. (2025). Federated Defense: A Privacy-Preserving Deep Learning Model for IoT Malware Detection. DOI: 10.21203/rs.3.rs-6674711/v1

Abraham, F., & Ofoe, N. T. (2025). Privacy-Preserving Collaborative Intelligence for IoT Cybersecurity: A Federated Learning Approach. 29–39. DOI: 10.38124/ijsrmt.v4i9.791

Acharya, M. R., Tripathy, S., & Pattnaik, P. K. (2025). Dynamic Resource Allocation for Latency Optimization and Energy Efficiency in Fog Computing: A Comparative Analysis Across Cloud. *Edge, and Hybrid Architectures*, (May), 1–6. DOI: 10.1109/ASSIC64892.2025.11158607

Agrawal, A., Bajpai, A., Jegadeeswari, G., Pandian, P. S., Deshpande, A., Gupta, D., . . . Mishra, D. K. (2025). Integrating Intelligent Mobile Systems, IoT, and Eco-systems: Advancing Connectivity and Innovation in a Digital World. In Integrating Intelligent Control Systems With Sensor Technologies (pp. 53-88). IGI Global Scientific Publishing.

Ahmad, S., & Qamar, F. (2024). Enhancing Security in Satellite-Based IoT-HPC Cloud Architectures: A Hybrid AI based Security Framework Approach. DOI: 10.21203/rs.3.rs-4588823/v1

Ahmed, S. F., Shawon, S. S., Afrin, S., Rafa, S. J., Hoque, M., & Gandomi, A. H. (2025, January). Optimising Internet of Things (IoT) Performance Through Cloud. *IET Wireless Sensor Systems*, *15*(1), e70016. Advance online publication. DOI: 10.1049/wss2.70016

Alam, M., & Ghosh, S. (2022). QNet: A Scalable and Noise-Resilient Quantum Neural Network Architecture for Noisy Intermediate-Scale Quantum Computers. *Frontiers in Physics (Lausanne)*, *9*, 755139. Advance online publication. DOI: 10.3389/fphy.2021.755139

Alauthman, M., Aldweesh, A., Al–Qerem, A., Alkasassbeh, M., Alateef, S., &Al-momani, A. (2025). Federated Learning in Distributed Cyber Defense. Advances in Computational Intelligence and Robotics Book Series, 161–184. DOI: 10.4018/979-8-3373-0954-5.ch006

Alazab, A., Khraisat, A., Singh, S., Jan, T., & Alazab, M. (2023). Enhancing Privacy-Preserving Intrusion Detection through Federated Learning. *Electronics (Basel)*, *12*(16), 3382. Advance online publication. DOI: 10.3390/electronics12163382

Alzoubi, Y. I., Topcu, A. E., & Elbaşi, E. (2025). A Systematic Review and Evaluation of Sustainable AI Algorithms and Techniques in Healthcare. *IEEE Access : Practical Innovations, Open Solutions*, *1*, 139547–139582. Advance online publication. DOI: 10.1109/ACCESS.2025.3596189

Amit, A., Amandeep, D., & Khushi, . (2025). Hybrid AI Modal for Edge Computing in 5G. *International Journal for Research in Applied Science and Engineering Technology*, *13*(6), 2655–2663. DOI: 10.22214/ijraset.2025.72750

Andreou, A., Mavromoustakis, C. X., Mastorakis, G., Bourdena, A., & Markakis, E. (2025). Quantum Computing in Semantic Communications: Overcoming Optimization Challenges with High-Dimensional Hilbert Spaces. *IEEE Access : Practical Innovations, Open Solutions*, *1*, 157942–157964. Advance online publication. DOI: 10.1109/ACCESS.2025.3603338

Anitha, M. (2025). Understanding Emotional Tone using NLP and ML Algorithms. *International Journal for Research in Applied Science and Engineering Technology*, *13*(4), 5290–5294. DOI: 10.22214/ijraset.2025.69510

Ansari, M. S. H., Farooqui, N. A., Ishrat, M., & Khan, W. (2025). IoT Applications in Urban Infrastructure and Governance. *IoT Applications in Urban Infrastructure and Governance*, (Apr), 343–386. DOI: 10.4018/979-8-3373-1375-7.ch012

Anuradha, P., Arunbala, C., Harita, U., Valarmathi, K., Thenappan, S., & Saravanan, V. (2025). Federated Learning for AI-Powered Privacy in Distributed Systems. *International Journal of Computational and Experimental Science and Engineering*, *11*(3). Advance online publication. DOI: 10.22399/ijcesen.2505

ARAMIDE, O. O. (2025). Federated Learning for Distributed Network Security and Threat Intelligence: A Privacy-Preserving Paradigm for Scalable Cyber Defense. 1(02). DOI: 10.64235/ph519x51

Asagunla, T. (2023). Federated Cyber Defense: A Privacy Preserving AI Framework for Threat Intelligence Sharing Across Multinational Enterprises. 26–30. DOI: 10.38124/ijsrmt.v2i8.711

Ashby, W. R. (1960). Design for a Brain - The origin of adaptive behavior. [ASHB]. *Cybernetics*, *304*, •••. https://doi.org/SYST

Aung, A. P. P., Wang, X., Wang, R., Chan, H., An, B., Li, X., & Senthilnath, J. (2025). Double Oracle Neural Architecture Search for Game Theoretic Deep Learning Models. *IEEE Transactions on Image Processing*, *1*, 2463–2472. Advance online publication. DOI: 10.1109/TIP.2025.3558420 PMID: 40215149

Aunugu, D. R., & Vathsavai, V. G. (2025). Cloud-Based AI Solutions for Scalable and Intelligent Enterprise Modernization. *Cloud-Based AI Solutions for Scalable and Intelligent Enterprise Modernization.*, *2*(2), 81–89. DOI: 10.62762/TETAI.2025.100106

Ávila-Gutiérrez, M. J., Martín-Gómez, A., Aguayo-González, F., & Córdoba-Roldán, A. (2019). Standardization Framework for Sustainability from Circular Economy 4.0. *Sustainability (Basel)*, *11*(22), 6490. DOI: 10.3390/su11226490

AWS BRAKET. (2026). *Servicio de computación cuántica en la nube - Amazon Braket - AWS.* https://aws.amazon.com/es/braket/

Bai, Y., Sui, Y., Deng, X., & Wang, X. (2025). Quantum-inspired robust optimization for coordinated scheduling of PV-hydrogen microgrids under multi-dimensional uncertainties. *Scientific Reports*, *15*(1), 29589.

Bandrevu, M. S., Uppalapati, N. R., Bellamkonda, R., &Kamatala, S. (2025). Llm-Augmented Cyber Threat Detection Using Federated Edge Intelligence and Data Mining Techniques. 1–8. DOI: 10.1109/ICCTDC64446.2025.11158153

Barua, M. (2024). Decoding Emotions: Machine Learning Approach to Speech Emotion Recognition. *Indian Scientific Journal Of Research In Engineering And Management*, *08*(06), 1–5. DOI: 10.55041/IJSREM36178

Benedetti, M., Lloyd, E., Sack, S., & Fiorentini, M. (2019). Parameterized quantum circuits as machine learning models. *Quantum Science and Technology*, *4*(4), 043001. DOI: 10.1088/2058-9565/ab4eb5

Bengio, Y., Lecun, Y., & Hinton, G. (2021). Deep learning for AI. *Communications of the ACM*, *64*(7), 58–65. DOI: 10.1145/3448250

Bershchanskyi, Y., Klym, H., & Shevchuk, Y. (2024). Containerized Artificial Intelligent System Design in Cloud and Cyber-Physical Systems. *Advances in Cyber-Physical Systems*, *9*(2), 151–157. DOI: 10.23939/acps2024.02.151

Bhatye, A. (2025). Quantum Computing and Its Applications in Artificial Intelligence: A Comprehensive Review. *Indian Scientific Journal Of Research In Engineering And Management*, *09*(06), 1–9. DOI: 10.55041/IJSREM51022

Bhoyar, M., & Selvarajan, G. P. (2023, March). Hybrid Cloud-Edge Architectures for LowLatency IoT Machine Learning. *International Journal of Innovative Research in Science, Engineering and Technology*, *12*(03). Advance online publication. DOI: 10.15680/IJIRSET.2023.1203004

Biamonte, J., Wittek, P., Pancotti, N., Rebentrost, P., Wiebe, N., & Lloyd, S. (2017). Quantum machine learning. *Nature*, *549*(7671), 195–202. DOI: 10.1038/nature23474 PMID: 28905917

Boddu, B., Krishna, M., Kumar, N., Singh, N., & Lafta, A. M. (2023)... *Quantum Computing Approaches to Optimal Power Flow in Complex Grid Networks*, (Dec), 752–756. DOI: 10.1109/PEEIC59336.2023.10450896

Bolukbasi, T., Chang, K. W., Zou, J. Y., Saligrama, V., & Kalai, A. T. (2016). Man is to computer programmer as woman is to homemaker? debiasing word embeddings. *Advances in Neural Information Processing Systems*, 29. https://doi.org/10.48550/arXiv.1607.06520

BoullosaDapena. Ó. (2025). Quantum-Inspired Differentiable Integral Neural Networks (QIDINNs): A Feynman-Based Architecture for Continuous Learning Over Streaming Data. DOI: 10.20944/preprints202506.1276.v1

Brayner, Â., & Pereira, D. M. G. (2024)... *An Integrated Edge, Fog, and Cloud Computing Reference Architecture for Developing Data Ecosystems in Smart Cities*, (Nov), 1–9. DOI: 10.1109/CloudNet62863.2024.10815810

Brown, T., Mann, B., Ryder, N., Subbiah, M., Kaplan, J. D., Dhariwal, P., & Amodei, D. (2020). Language models are few-shot learners. *Advances in Neural Information Processing Systems*, *33*, 1877–1901.

Busemeyer, J. R., & Bruza, P. D. (2012). *Quantum models of cognition and decision*. Cambridge University Press. DOI: 10.1017/CBO9780511997716

Caliskan, A., Bryson, J. J., & Narayanan, A. (2017). Semantics derived automatically from language corpora contain human-like biases. *Science*, *356*(6334), 183–186. DOI: 10.1126/science.aal4230 PMID: 28408601

Cathy, J., & Pradeepkumar, S. (2025). Enhancing Emotional Intelligence in LLM Responses Using Speech Emotion Recognition. DOI: 10.36227/techrxiv.174123778.82557359/v1

Cerezo, M., Arrasmith, A., Babbush, R., Benjamin, S. C., Endo, S., Fujii, K., McClean, J. R., Mitarai, K., Yuan, X., Cincio, L., & Coles, P. J. (2021). Variational quantum algorithms. *Nature Reviews. Physics*, *3*(9), 625–644. DOI: 10.1038/s42254-021-00348-9

Cerezo, M., Verdon, G., Huang, H.-Y., Cincio, L., & Coles, P. J. (2023). Challenges and Opportunities in Quantum Machine Learning. *Nature Computational Science*, *2*(9), 567–576. DOI: 10.1038/s43588-022-00311-3 PMID: 38177473

Chappidi, S. (2024). Enhanced Speech Emotion Recognition Using the Cognitive Emotion Fusion Network for PTSD Detection with a Novel Hybrid Approach. *Deleted Journal*, *19*(4), 376–398. DOI: 10.52783/jes.644

Chaugule, I., &Sankaye, S. R. (2025). Mitigating Corpus Bias in Speech Emotion Recognition: A Robust Hybrid Framework using Generalization-Aware Metaheuristic Feature Selection. 799–807. DOI: 10.38124/ijisrt/25jun755

Chen, S. Y.-C., & Tiwari, P. (2025). Quantum Long Short-term Memory with Differentiable Architecture Search. arXiv.Org, abs/2508.14955. /arxiv.2508.14955DOI: 10.1109/QAI63978.2025.00010

Chen, L., Li, T., Chen, Y., Chen, X., Wozniak, M., Xiong, N., & Liang, W. (2024). Design and analysis of quantum machine learning: A survey. *Connection Science*, *36*(1), 2312121. Advance online publication. DOI: 10.1080/09540091.2024.2312121

Cho, K., Van Merriënboer, B., Gulcehre, C., Bahdanau, D., Bougares, F., Schwenk, H., & Bengio, Y. (2014). Learning phrase representations using RNN encoder-decoder for statistical machine translation. *arXiv preprint arXiv:1406.1078*. DOI: 10.3115/v1/D14-1179

Chowdhury, S. Y., Banik, B., & Hoque, Md. T., & Banerjee, S. (2025). A Novel Hybrid Deep Learning Technique for Speech Emotion Detection using Feature Engineering. arXiv.Org, abs/2507.07046. /arxiv.2507.07046DOI: 10.48550

Claridades, A. R. C., Casisirano, J. D. D., Fargas, D. C.Jr, Jerez, M. V., Rufino, G. A. D., Pamittan, F. J. O., & Sarmiento, C. J. S. (2025). Cities' Dashboards as Civic Technology Platforms: A Scalable Model for Smart Cities through Integrated Governance in LUNGSOD, SMART METRO, and FASTRAC. *ISPRS Annals of the Photogrammetry, Remote Sensing and Spatial Information Sciences*, *10*, 17–24.

Coecke, B., Sadrzadeh, M., & Clark, S. (2010). Mathematical foundations for a compositional distributional model of meaning. *arXiv preprint arXiv:1003.4394*.

Davies, M., Wild, A., Orchard, G., Sandamirskaya, Y., Guerra, G. A. F., Joshi, P., Plank, P., & Risbud, S. R. (2021). Advancing Neuromorphic Computing with Loihi: A Survey of Results and Outlook. *Proceedings of the IEEE, 109*(5), 911–934. DOI: 10.1109/JPROC.2021.3067593

Devlin, J., Chang, M. W., Lee, K., & Toutanova, K. (2019, June). Bert: Pre-training of deep bidirectional transformers for language understanding. In *Proceedings of the 2019 conference of the North American chapter of the association for computational linguistics: human language technologies, volume 1 (long and short papers)* (pp. 4171-4186).

Dewi, M. U., Santoso, L., & Santoso, A. B. (2024). Optimizing AI Performance in Industry: A Hybrid Computing Architecture Approach Based on Big Data. *Journal of Technology Informatics and Engineering, 3*(3), 308–323. DOI: 10.51903/jtie.v3i3.201

Dintakurthy, Y., Innmuri, R. K., Vanteru, A., &Thotakuri, A. (2025). Emerging Applications of Artificial Intelligence in Edge Computing: A Comprehensive Review. 175–185. DOI: 10.71426/jmt.v1.i2.pp175-185

dos Santos Sampaio, A. (2025). Arquitetura de governança digital e gestão urbana inteligente: a aplicação integrada da inteligência artificial e blockchain na administração pública municipal. Recima21-Revista Científica Multidisciplinar-ISSN 2675-6218, 6(3), e636338-e636338.

Doshi-Velez, F., & Kim, B. (2017). Towards a rigorous science of interpretable machine learning. *arXiv preprint arXiv:1702.08608.*

Egon, K., Rosinski, J., Karl, L., & Eugene, R. "Quantum Machine Learning: The Confluence of Quantum Computing and AI," Oct. 2023, doi: DOI: 10.31219/osf.io/rf4xp

Ekellem, E. A. F. (2023). Secure Federations: Addressing the Security Challenges in Federated Learning and Privacy-Preserving AI. 1–6. DOI: 10.1109/ISAS60782.2023.10391351

Enhancing Speech Emotion Recognition with Multi-Modal Hybrid Features and CNN. (2025). Enhancing Speech Emotion Recognition with Multi-Modal Hybrid Features and CNN. *SSRG International Journal of Electronics and Communication Engineering, 12*(7). Advance online publication. DOI: 10.14445/23488549/IJECE-V12I7P104

Erbey, A. (2025). Akıllı Şehirlerde Teknoloji ve Veri Yönetimi: Geleceğin Şehir Yaşamı. Yönetim Bilişim Sistemleri Alanında Yenilikçi Çözümler ve Güncel Yaklaşımlar, 69.

Erregui, H., Aouaqi, A. E. L., Aberbach, H., & Sabri, A. (2024, November). A. EL AOUAQI, H. Aberbach, and M. A. Sabri, "The Role of Internet of Things and Fog Computing in Smart Cities,". *International Journal of Artificial Intelligence & Applications*, *15*(6), 31–50. DOI: 10.5121/ijaia.2024.15603

European Union. (2024). *Regulation (EU) 2024/1689 of the European Parliament and of the Council of 13 June 2024 laying down harmonised rules on artificial intelligence (Artificial Intelligence Act). Official Journal of the European Union.* https://eur-lex.europa.eu/eli/reg/2024/1689/oj/eng

Ewald, D. (2025). Proposal of a Fully Quantum Neural Network and Fidelity-Driven Training Using Directional Gradients for Multi-Class Classification. https://doi.org/ DOI: 10.20944/preprints202505.0203.v1

Ewald, D. (2025). The Proposal of a Fully Quantum Neural Network and Fidelity-Driven Training Using Directional Gradients for Multi-Class Classification. *Electronics (Basel)*, *14*(11), 2189. DOI: 10.3390/electronics14112189

Farhi, E., & Neven, H. (2018). Classification with quantum neural networks on near term processors. *arXiv preprint arXiv:1802.06002.*

Fatunmbi, T. O.Temitope Oluwatosin Fatunmbi. (2023). Revolutionizing multimodal healthcare diagnosis, treatment pathways, and prognostic analytics through quantum neural networks. *World Journal Of Advanced Research and Reviews*, *17*(1), 1319–1338. DOI: 10.30574/wjarr.2023.17.1.0017

Fernando, N., Shrestha, S., Loke, S. W., & Lee, K. (2025, January). On Edge-Fog-Cloud Collaboration and Reaping Its Benefits: A Heterogeneous Multi-Tier Edge Computing Architecture. *Future Internet*, *17*(1), 22. DOI: 10.3390/fi17010022

Fetaji, B., Fetaji, M., Ebibi, M., & Fetaji, E. (2025, June). Optimizing Energy in Smart Grids: A Novel AI and Data Analytics Approach to Address Critical Gaps and Enhance Sustainability. In 2025 60th International Scientific Conference on Information, Communication and Energy Systems and Technologies (ICEST) (pp. 1-5). IEEE.

Floridi, L., Cowls, J., Beltrametti, M., Chatila, R., Chazerand, P., Dignum, V., Luetge, C., Madelin, R., Pagallo, U., Rossi, F., Schafer, B., Valcke, P., & Vayena, E. (2018). AI4People—An ethical framework for a good AI society: Opportunities, risks, principles, and recommendations. *Minds and Machines*, *28*(4), 689–707. DOI: 10.1007/s11023-018-9482-5 PMID: 30930541

Galarza-Sánchez, P. C., Erazo-Luzuriaga, A. F., & Boné-Andrade, M. F. (2023). Uso de computación cuántica en la mejora de algoritmos de aprendizaje automático. 1(4), 16–30. DOI: 10.55813/gaea/rcym/v1/n4/25

Gavadi, R. (2025, February). A Comprehensive Review and Methodological Approach to IoT Integration in Smart Cities. *International Journal for Research in Applied Science and Engineering Technology*, *13*(2), 1457–1463. DOI: 10.22214/ijraset.2025.67071

Gawali, S. (2025). Audio Aura - Speech Emotion Recognition System. *International Journal for Research in Applied Science and Engineering Technology*, *13*(4), 7082–7088. DOI: 10.22214/ijraset.2025.70092

Giovagnoli, A., Tresp, V., Ma, Y., & Schubert, M. (2023). QNEAT: Natural Evolution of Variational Quantum Circuit Architecture. DOI: 10.1145/3583133.3590675

Goldberg, Y. (2017). *Neural network methods in natural language processing*. Morgan & Claypool Publishers. DOI: 10.1007/978-3-031-02165-7

Goldstein, R. (2021). Desafíos del Desarrollo Sostenible en la Nueva Normalidad. Coherencia de Políticas para la Agenda 2030 y los ODS en la Década de Acción. In *La Administración Pública en tiempos disruptivos. Diego Pando (compilador)* (Number January, pp. 171–177).

Gonaygunta, H., Maturi, M. H., Nadella, G. S., Meduri, K., & Satish, S. (n.d.). *Quantum Machine Learning: Exploring Quantum Algorithms for Enhancing Deep Learning Models*. International Journal of Advanced Engineering Research and Science., DOI: 10.22161/ijaers.115.5

Gong, L.-H., Pei, J.-J., Zhang, T.-F., & Zhou, N.-R. (2023). Quantum convolutional neural network based on variational quantum circuits. *Optics Communications*. Advance online publication. DOI: 10.1016/j.optcom.2023.129993

Gonon, L., & Jacquier, A. (2025). Universal Approximation Theorem and Error Bounds for Quantum Neural Networks and Quantum Reservoirs. *IEEE Transactions on Neural Networks and Learning Systems*, (Jan), 1–14. DOI: 10.1109/TNNLS.2025.3630143 PMID: 40202891

Gopukumar, S. T., Ahmed, S. J., Kadhim, H., Alazzam, M. B., Majed, A. E. M., &Abdollah, M. F. (2025). Blockchain-Driven Federated Learning for Real-Time Threat Defense and Forensic Insight. 1–6. DOI: 10.1109/ISAC364032.2025.11156741

Gorowara, N., Khan, M. A., Avasthi, P., Chhuttani, P., Varma, R. A., & Gupta, S. (2025). Internet of Things (IoT)-Driven Smart City Development: An Undetected Sustainable Revolution in India. In *Advancing Social Equity Through Accessible Green Innovation* (pp. 335–350). IGI Global Scientific Publishing.

Goswami, S. A., Darji, D. A., Patel, K. C., & Dave, S. (2025). Establishing AI-Specific Cloud Computing Infrastructure. Advances in Computational Intelligence and Robotics Book Series, 123–156. DOI: 10.4018/979-8-3693-9694-0.ch005

Guntuka, S. (2024). Quantum Machine Learning: Bridging Quantum Computing and Artificial Intelligence. *International Journal for Research in Applied Science and Engineering Technology*, *12*(9), 1455–1460. DOI: 10.22214/ijraset.2024.64377

Guo, Z., Khan, A., Sheng, V. S., Jabeen, S., & Pan, Z. (2025). Quantum parallel information exchange (QPIE) hybrid network with transfer learning. *Quantum Science and Technology*, *10*(3), 035054. Advance online publication. DOI: 10.1088/2058-9565/ade89f

Guruprakash, B., & Reddy, V. Y. (2025). Optimizing quantum-enhanced dilated convolutional networks for scalable and efficient quantum image recognition. *ICTACT Journal on Soft Computing*, *16*(2), 3931–3937. DOI: 10.21917/ijsc.2025.0544

Hadap, S., & Patil, M. (2024). Quantum Computing in Artificial Intelligence: A Paradigm Shift. International Journal of Advanced Research in Science. *Tongxin Jishu*, *530–534*, 530–534. Advance online publication. DOI: 10.48175/IJARSCT-18957

Hakimi, M., Amiri, G. A., Jalalzai, S., Darmel, F. A., & Ezam, Z. (2024). *Exploring the Integration of AI and Cloud Computing: Navigating Opportunities and Overcoming Challenges*. TIERS Information Technology Journal., DOI: 10.38043/tiers.v5i1.5496

Halffmann, P., & Sharma, S. (2025). Quantum Optimization, Machine Learning, Annealing, and Neural Networks. 68–96. DOI: 10.1201/9781003537243-5

Haroon, F. (2025). *Designing a Hybrid Cloud-Grid Architecture for High-Performance Computing: A Unified Model for Resource Sharing*. Task Distribution, and Scalability in Heterogeneous Environments., DOI: 10.53762/grjnst.03.02.09

Hegde, R., Soumyasri, S.M., & Dange, V. (2025). "Block chain Integrated Smart City Governance Models for Secure Transparent and Decentralized Decision Making," pp. 309–337, .DOI: 10.71443/9789349552241-11

Hernández-Ramos, J., Chatzoglou, E., Kouliaridis, V., Mármol Campos, E., González-Vidal, A., & Kambourakis, G. (2025). Intrusion Detection Based on Federated Learning: A Systematic Review. *ACM Computing Surveys*, *57*(12), 1–65. Advance online publication. DOI: 10.1145/3731596

Hidayat, N. N., & Akrom, M. (2025). Tree Tensor Network Quantum-Classical Hybrid Neural Architecture for Efficient Data Classification. *Journal of Multiscale Materials Informatics*, *2*(1), 34–39. DOI: 10.62411/jimat.v2i1.12949

Hirose, A., Shang, F., Otsuka, Y., Natsuaki, R., Matsumoto, Y., Usami, N., Song, Y., & Chen, H. (2024). Quaternion Neural Networks: A physics-incorporated intelligence framework [Hypercomplex Signal and Image Processing]. *IEEE Signal Processing Magazine*, *41*(3), 88–100. DOI: 10.1109/MSP.2024.3384179

Hochreiter, S., & Schmidhuber, J. (1997). Long short-term memory. *Neural Computation*, *9*(8), 1735–1780. DOI: 10.1162/neco.1997.9.8.1735 PMID: 9377276

Hooda, S., Sarika, S., & Sharma, V. K. (2024). Optimizing Urban Intelligence. Integration of AI, Quantum Computing, and Semiconductor Technology, 441.

Huang, C., Chen, C., Luo, N., & Li, G. (2025). Chen, N. Luo, and G. Li. *Construction of an Intelligent Edge Computing Platform Based on Cloud-Fog Hybrid Management System*, (Jun), 159–164. DOI: 10.1109/DMCIS65888.2025.11138331

Hussain, S., Alrumayh, O., & Lai, C. (2025). Integrating Device-Level Flexibility in Home Energy Management Systems for Prosumers. *IEEE Access : Practical Innovations, Open Solutions*, *13*(Jan), 1. DOI: 10.1109/ACCESS.2025.3606499

Idika, C. N., & Salami, E. (2024). Federated Learning Approaches for Privacy-Preserving Threat Detection in Smart Home IoT Environments. International Journal of Scientific Research in Computer Science. *Engineering and Information Technology*, *10*(5), 1125–1131. DOI: 10.32628/CSEIT24113369

Indiveri, G., & Liu, S. C. (2015). Memory and Information Processing in Neuromorphic Systems. *Proceedings of the IEEE, 103*(8), 1379–1397. ISO/IEC. (2023). *ISO/IEC 42001:2023 Information technology—Artificial intelligence—Management system. International Organization for Standardization.* DOI: 10.1109/JPROC.2015.2444094

Ishwarya, K., & Joseph, J. (2025). Hybrid deep learning based edge intelligence and analytics. 220–230. DOI: 10.1201/9781003512066-11

ITU. (2024a). *FGMV-51: Standardization roadmap for the metaverse*. ITU-T Focus Group on Metaverse.

ITU. (2024b). *FGMV-52: Metaverse standardization landscape for gap analyses. ITU-T Focus Group on Metaverse*.

Jagatheesaperumal, S. K., Ali, S., Alotaibi, A., Muhammad, K., de Albuquerque, V. H. C., & Guizani, M. (2025). Generative AI-Enhanced Neuro-Symbolic Quantum Architectures for Secure Communications and Networking. *IEEE Network*, *39*(Jan), 1. DOI: 10.1109/MNET.2025.3579680

Jain, S., & Wallace, B. C. (2019). Attention is not explanation. *arXiv preprint arXiv:1902.10186*.

Jameil, A. K., & Al-Raweshidy, H. S. (2024). Hybrid Cloud-Edge AI Framework for Real-Time Predictive Analytics in Digital Twin Healthcare Systems. DOI: 10.21203/rs.3.rs-5412158/v1

Jha, R. K. (2023). From Quantum Computing to Quantum-inspired Computation for Neuromorphic Advancement – A Survey. In *Authorea Preprints*. *Authorea*. DOI: 10.36227/techrxiv.24053250.v1

Jiang, T., Shen, G., Guo, C., Cui, Y., & Xie, B. (2023). BFLS: Blockchain and Federated Learning for sharing threat detection models as Cyber Threat Intelligence. *Computer Networks*, *224*, 109604. DOI: 10.1016/j.comnet.2023.109604

Jindal, M. K. (2024). How Can Hybrid Algorithms Combining Quantum Machine Learning and Classical Machine Learning be Optimised for Performance and Accuracy? *International Journal For Multidisciplinary Research*, *6*(6), 33629. Advance online publication. DOI: 10.36948/ijfmr.2024.v06i06.33629

Jobin, A., Ienca, M., & Vayena, E. (2019). The global landscape of AI ethics guidelines. *Nature Machine Intelligence*, *1*(9), 389–399. DOI: 10.1038/s42256-019-0088-2

Joshi, S. (2025). Advancing Cybersecurity Through Synergies of Agentic AI and High-Performance Computing. https://doi.org/DOI: 10.20944/preprints202507.0646.v1

Kadam, S., Jani, J., Kudtarkar, A., & Koshy, R. (2024). Speech Emotion Recognition Using Mel-Frequency Cepstral Coefficients & Convolutional. *Neural Networks*, •••, 1595–1602. DOI: 10.1109/IDCIoT59759.2024.10467837

Kalyashina, A., Smirnov, Y., Esov, V., Kuznetsov, M., & Dmitrieva, O. (2024). Enhancing IoT systems through Cloud-Fog-Edge architectures challenges and opportunities. In *E3S Web of Conferences* (Vol. 583, p. 06012). EDP Sciences.

Kamienski, C., Zyrianoff, I., Bittencourt, L. F., & Di Felice, M. (2024). IoTinuum. *The IoT Computing Continuum*, (Apr), 732–739. DOI: 10.1109/DCOSS-IoT61029.2024.00112

Karthick, G., Mapp, G., & Crowcroft, J. "Is Living on the Edge the Future of the Internet?" Feb. 2025, DOI: 10.20944/preprints202502.2118.v1

Khairnar, P. N., Ganesh Babu, O., Valarmathi, N., & Sathya Franklin, S. (2025). IoT Architectures and AI-Enabled Smart City Solutions for Sustainable Urban Development. *IoT Architectures and AI-Enabled Smart City Solutions for Sustainable Urban Development*, (Apr). Advance online publication. DOI: 10.71443/9789349552241

Khalil, H., Elshazly, O., Baihan, A., El-Shafai, W., & Shaheen, O. (2024). Quantum neural networks based Lyapunov stability and adaptive learning rates for identification of nonlinear systems. *Ain Shams Engineering Journal, 15*(May), 102851. Advance online publication. DOI: 10.1016/j.asej.2024.102851

Kim, Y. (2014). Convolutional neural networks for sentence classification. *arXiv preprint arXiv:1408.5882*. DOI: 10.3115/v1/D14-1181

Kishor, I., Mamodiya, U., & Keswani, B. (2025). Real-Time Anomaly Detection in IoT-Enabled Solar Tracking Systems Using Neural Networks. In Deep Learning Innovations for Securing Critical Infrastructures (pp. 417-436). IGI Global Scientific Publishing.

Kishor, I., Mamodiya, U., Agarwal, A., & Bhattacherjee, A. (2025). Adaptive multimodal neural network for real-time threat detection. In *Deep learning innovations for securing critical infrastructures* (pp. 1–16). IGI Global., DOI: 10.4018/979-8-3373-0563-9.ch003

Kishor, U. (2025, October). Mamodiya, M. Almaayah, A. Alqutaish, R. Shehab, and T. H. H. Aldhyani, "Agentic AI-Enhanced Virtual Reality for Adaptive Immersive Learning Environments". *Mesopotamian Journal of Computer Science, 2025*, 398–416. DOI: 10.58496/MJCSC/2025/026

Koestler, A. (1964). *The Act of Creation*. MacMillan.

Koestler, A. (1967). *The ghost in the machine*. Hutchinson.

Koestler, A. (1979). Janus: A summing up. *Bulletin of the Atomic Scientists, 35*(3), 4–4. DOI: 10.1080/00963402.1979.11458590

Kolluri, S. (2025). The Role of Edge Computing in Real-Time Analytics: A Cloud-AI Hybrid Approach. *International Journal of Innovative Research in Science, Engineering and Technology, 14*(02). Advance online publication. DOI: 10.15680/IJIRSET.2025.1402004

Kosaraju, D. (2024). Quantum Computing and Artificial Intelligence: A Fusion Poised to Transform Technology. *International Journal of Research and Review, 8*(9), 588–593. DOI: 10.52403/ijrr.20210974

Kotagiri, A. (2025). Smart Cities: IoT and Data Analytics for Sustainable Urban Development. In Cutting-Edge Solutions for Advancing Sustainable Development: Exploring Technological Horizons for Sustainability-Part 1 (pp. 231-248). Bentham Science Publishers.

Krishna, K. S., & Lal, M. (2025). Emotion Recognition using Speech Processing. *International Journal of Research Publication and Reviews, 6*(8), 5280–5285. DOI: 10.55248/gengpi.6.0825.3181

Krishnamoorthy, P., &Menaka, R. (2025). Application of Federated Learning Models for Privacy-Preserving Detection of Cyber Attacks in Cross-Domain Networks. 307–333. DOI: 10.71443/9789349552388-11

Kuai, X., He, X., He, B., Liu, Y., Zhigang, Z., & Guo, R. "Smart City Ontology Framework for Urban Data Integration and Governance Applications," Oct. 2024, DOI: 10.20944/preprints202410.2577.v1

Kuchuk, H., & Malokhvii, E. (2024). Integration of IoT with cloud, fog, and edge computing: A review. *Advanced Information Systems, 8*(2), 65–78.

Kummara, R. (2025, August). Edge Computing in Smart Cities: Transforming Urban Infrastructure through Decentralized Processing. *Journal of Information Systems Engineering & Management, 10*(58s, no. 58s), 1061–1071. DOI: 10.52783/jisem.v10i58s.12769

Kundu, A. S., & Sadhu, A. (2024, November). KANQAS: Kolmogorov-Arnold Network for Quantum Architecture Search. *EPJ Quantum Technology, 11*(1), 76. Advance online publication. DOI: 10.1140/epjqt/s40507-024-00289-z

Kundu, S. (2024). QEFMLA-FIDO: Quantum Evolutionary Frameworks for Machine Learning Acceleration: Fisher Information-Driven Optimization in Hybrid Classical-Quantum Architectures. DOI: 10.21203/rs.3.rs-5424606/v1

Kurada, S. B. (2025). Federated Learning in Cybersecurity: Enhancing Decentralized Threat Detection. *IOSR Journal of Mobile Computing and Application, 12*(3), 33–39. DOI: 10.9790/0050-12033339

Kuswiradyo, P., Kar, B., & Shen, S.-H. (2024, August). Optimizing the energy consumption in three-tier cloud–edge–fog federated systems with omnidirectional offloading. *Computer Networks, 250*, 110578. DOI: 10.1016/j.comnet.2024.110578

Kwon, S., Kim, D., Park, S., Kim, S., & Kang, S. (2024). QNSA: Quantum Neural Simulated Annealing for Combinatorial Optimization. 1–7. DOI: 10.1109/ISQED60706.2024.10528727

Laddi, M. (2025). Intelligent Cyber Security Model for Intrusion Detection using Federated Machine Learning. *Journal of Information Systems Engineering & Management, 10*(37s), 55–65. DOI: 10.52783/jisem.v10i37s.6379

Lakhyar, Z. (2024). Quantum Collaboration: Pioneering the Frontier of Enhanced Artificial Intelligence. *Journal of Research in Science and Engineering, 6*(12), 88–91.

Latif, N., Ma, W., & Ahmad, H. B. (2025). Advancements in securing federated learning with IDS: A comprehensive review of neural networks and feature engineering techniques for malicious client detection. *Artificial Intelligence Review, 58*(3), 91. Advance online publication. DOI: 10.1007/s10462-024-11082-w

Lea, R., Adame, T., Berne, A., & Azaiez, S. (2025, June). The Internet of Things, Fog, and Cloud Continuum: Integration Challenges and Opportunities for Smart Cities. *Future Internet, 17*(7), 281. DOI: 10.3390/fi17070281

Lee, E. A. (2015). The Past, Present and Future of Cyber-Physical Systems: A Focus on Models. *Sensors 2015, Vol. 15, Pages 4837-4869, 15*(3), 4837–4869. DOI: 10.3390/s150304837

Lee, C. W., Araujo, I. F., Kim, D.-H., Lee, J.-H., Park, S., Ryu, J.-Y., & Park, D. K. (2025). Optimizing quantum convolutional neural network architectures for arbitrary data dimension. *Frontiers in Physics (Lausanne), 13*, 1529188. Advance online publication. DOI: 10.3389/fphy.2025.1529188

Lenka, R., Banerjee, O., Behera, A., Chakravarty, K., Bilgaiyan, S., Prasad, A., & Singh, J. (2025). Advanced Hybrid Deep Learning for Emotion Recognition in Speech. 1–7. DOI: 10.1109/ASSIC64892.2025.11158456

Lenka, R., Banerjee, O., Chakravarty, K., Behera, A., Bilgaiyan, S., Prasad, A., & Singh, J. (2025). Advanced Hybrid Deep Learning for Emotion Recognition in Speech. 1–7. DOI: 10.1109/ASSIC64892.2025.11158613

Lepskiy, V. (2018). Evolution of cybernetics: Philosophical and methodological analysis. *Kybernetes, 47*(2), 249–261. DOI: 10.1108/K-03-2017-0120

Lipton, Z. C. (2018). The mythos of model interpretability: In machine learning, the concept of interpretability is both important and slippery. *ACM Queue; Tomorrow's Computing Today, 16*(3), 31–57. DOI: 10.1145/3236386.3241340

Liu, B. (2025). Deep Reinforcement Learning for Intelligent Load Balancing in Smart Power Grids. *IEEE Access : Practical Innovations, Open Solutions*, *1*, 164170–164185. Advance online publication. DOI: 10.1109/ACCESS.2025.3606914

Liu, C.-Y., Kuo, E.-J., Lin, C.-H. A., Young, J. G., Chang, Y.-J., Hsieh, M.-H., & Goan, H. (2025). Quantum-Train: Rethinking hybrid quantum-classical machine learning in the model compression perspective. *Quantum Machine Intelligence*, *7*(2), 80. Advance online publication. DOI: 10.1007/s42484-025-00305-0

Liu, J., Liu, M., Liu, J.-P., Ye, Z., Wang, Y., Alexeev, Y., Eisert, J., & Jiang, L. (2024, January). Towards provably efficient quantum algorithms for large-scale machine-learning models. *Nature Communications*, *15*(1), 434. Advance online publication. DOI: 10.1038/s41467-023-43957-x PMID: 38199993

Li, Z. (2024). *Application Scenarios of Edge Computing in Conjunction with Cloud Computing and Artificial Intelligence*. Highlights in Science Engineering and Technology., DOI: 10.54097/bky92374

Long, C., Ge, L., Li, Q., Yan, Y., Xu, R.-X., & Zheng, X. (2024, August). Quantum neural network approach to Markovian dissipative dynamics of many-body open quantum systems. *The Journal of Chemical Physics*, *161*(8), 084105. Advance online publication. DOI: 10.1063/5.0220357 PMID: 39171705

Long, C., Huang, M., Ye, X., Futamura, Y., & Sakurai, T. (2025). Hybrid quantum-classical-quantum convolutional neural networks. *Scientific Reports*, *15*(1), 31780.

Luther, B., Gunawan, I., & Nguyen, N. (2023). Identifying effective risk management frameworks for complex socio-technical systems. *Safety Science*, *158*, 105989. DOI: 10.1016/j.ssci.2022.105989

Lu, W., Lu, Y., Li, J., Sigov, A., Ratkin, L., & Ivanov, L. A. (2024). Quantum machine learning: Classifications, challenges, and solutions. *Journal of Industrial Information Integration*, *42*, 100736. DOI: 10.1016/j.jii.2024.100736

Madhurya, J. A., Padhi, M. K., Awasthy, M., & Pareek, P. K. (2023, July). A Smart Governance Architecture for Integrating Heterogeneous IoT Solutions within the Framework of Smart Cities. In *2023 International Conference on Data Science and Network Security (ICDSNS)* (pp. 1-6). IEEE.

Mahobia, S., & Pawar, R. (2024). Comprehensive Review of Smart Cities using IOT in Coud. *International Journal of Innovative Research in Computer and Communication Engineering*, *12*(May), 6309–6319. Advance online publication. DOI: 10.15680/IJIRCCE.2024.1205194

Makhmudov, F., Kutlimuratov, A., & Cho, Y. I. (2024). Hybrid LSTM–Attention and CNN Model for Enhanced Speech Emotion Recognition. *Applied Sciences (Basel, Switzerland)*, *14*(23), 11342. DOI: 10.3390/app142311342

Mamodiya, U., & Kishor, I. (2026). *Artificial Intelligence Applications for Enhancing Efficiency in Smart Grids. Artificial Intelligence (AI) for IT Energy Efficiency and Green AI for Environment Sustainability*. Springer., DOI: 10.1007/978-3-031-89420-6_9

Mamodiya, U., Kishor, I., Ahmed Syed, A., Sankalkar, P., & Naik, N. (2025). An Adaptive Human–Robot Interaction Framework Using Real-Time Emotion Recognition and Context-Aware Task Planning. *IEEE Access : Practical Innovations, Open Solutions*, *13*, 152219–152240. DOI: 10.1109/ACCESS.2025.3603738

Mamodiya, U., Kishor, I., Almaiah, M. A., Hamdi, M., Shehab, R., & Alkhdour, T. (2025). Numerical modeling and neural network optimization for advanced solar panel efficiency. *Scientific Reports*, *15*(1), 23492. DOI: 10.1038/s41598-025-06830-z PMID: 40604001

Mamodiya, U., Kishor, I., Garine, R., Ganguly, P., & Naik, N. (2025). Artificial intelligence based hybrid solar energy systems with smart materials and adaptive photovoltaics for sustainable power generation. *Scientific Reports*, *15*(1), 17370. DOI: 10.1038/s41598-025-01788-4 PMID: 40389492

Manivannan, R., Manivannan, S., & Surendiran, J. (2024)... *Ai-Siot Hybrid Architecture for Seamless Integration of IoT in Smart Cities*, (Apr), 393–399. Advance online publication. DOI: 10.1109/CSNT60213.2024.10546157

Markidis, S. (2023). Programming Quantum Neural Networks on NISQ Systems: An Overview of Technologies and Methodologies. *Entropy (Basel, Switzerland)*, *25*(4), 694. DOI: 10.3390/e25040694 PMID: 37190482

Marković, D., & Grollier, J. (2020). Quantum neuromorphic computing. *Applied Physics Letters*, *117*(15), 150501. Advance online publication. DOI: 10.1063/5.0020014

Mastrogiovanni, S. (2025, September). AI-Driven data governance for smart cities: Balancing privacy, efficiency, and public trust. *South Florida Journal of Development*, *6*(9), e5810. DOI: 10.46932/sfjdv6n9-029

McClean, J. R., Boixo, S., Smelyanskiy, V. N., Babbush, R., & Neven, H. (2018). Barren plateaus in quantum neural network training landscapes. *Nature Communications*, *9*(1), 4812. DOI: 10.1038/s41467-018-07090-4 PMID: 30446662

Meduri, V. (2024). Hybrid Cloud Architectures for Scalable and Cost-Effective AI in Banking. International Journal of Scientific Research in Computer Science. *Engineering and Information Technology, 10*(6), 1840–1849. DOI: 10.32628/CSEIT241061226

Melnikov, A. V., Kordzanganeh, M., Alodjants, A., & Lee, R. (2023). Quantum machine learning: From physics to software engineering. *Advances in Physics: X, 8*(1), 2165452. Advance online publication. DOI: 10.1080/23746149.2023.2165452

Mikolov, T., Chen, K., Corrado, G., & Dean, J. (2013). Efficient estimation of word representations in vector space. *arXiv preprint arXiv:1301.3781.*

Mohamed Jabarullah, M. A. K., Chakka, S. N., & Kanungo, S. (2025).. . *Edge-Cloud Hybrid Architecture for Distributed AI Applications., 1–5.* Advance online publication. DOI: 10.1109/ICCTDC64446.2025.11158770

Moreau, G., Pisani, L., Profir, M., Podda, C., Leoni, L., & Cao, G. (2025). Quantum Artificial Intelligence Scalability in the NISQ Era: Pathways to Quantum Utility. *Advanced Quantum Technologies, 8*(May), 2400716. Advance online publication. DOI: 10.1002/qute.202400716

Mosaiyebzadeh, F., Pouriyeh, S., Han, M., Liu, L., Xie, Y., Zhao, L., & Batista, D. M. (2024). Privacy-Preserving Federated Learning-Based Intrusion Detection System for IoHT Devices. *Electronics (Basel), 14*(1), 67. DOI: 10.3390/electronics14010067

Myakala, P. K., Kamatala, S., &Bura, C. (2025). Privacy-Preserving Federated Learning for IoT Botnet Detection: A Federated Averaging Approach. 1(1), 6–16. DOI: 10.62762/TMI.2025.796490

Namey, A., Akter, K., & Hossain, M. (2024). CochleaSpecNet: An Attention Based Dual Branch Hybrid CNN-GRU Network for Speech Emotion Recognition Using Cochleagram and Spectrogram. *IEEE Access : Practical Innovations, Open Solutions, 1*, 1. Advance online publication. DOI: 10.1109/ACCESS.2024.3517733

Nguyen, P., Tran, C. K., Ergu, Y. A., & Nguyen, V.-L. (2025). Q-Drop: Optimizing Quantum Orthogonal Networks with Statistic Pruning and Dynamic Dropout. 2394–2399. DOI: 10.1109/ICC52391.2025.11161668

NIST. (2023). *Artificial Intelligence Risk Management Framework (AI RMF 1.0) (NIST AI 100-1). National Institute of Standards and Technology.*

NIST. (2024). *The NIST Cybersecurity Framework (CSF) 2.0 (NIST CSWP 29). National Institute of Standards and Technology.*

Nugroho, K., Al Amin, I. H., Noviasari, N. A., & Setiadi, D. R. I. M. (2025). Prosodic Spatio-Temporal Feature Fusion with Attention Mechanisms for Speech Emotion Recognition. *Computers*, *14*(9), 361. DOI: 10.3390/computers14090361

Okhovat, E., & Bauer, M. (2024, June). Towards Enhanced Urban Management: Introducing A Model for Autonomic Smart City Management. In *2024 IEEE International Conference on Smart Computing (SMARTCOMP)* (pp. 31-38). IEEE.

Olarinde, M. O., Abiona, A. A., & Ajinaja, M. O. (2024). Adaptive and Privacy-Preserving Security for Federated Learning Using Biological Immune System Principles. *Asian Journal of Computer Science and Technology*, *13*(2), 67–72. DOI: 10.70112/ajcst-2024.13.2.4303

Pallaprolu, S. (2025). Edge Computing and AI Integration: New infrastructure paradigms. *World Journal Of Advanced Research and Reviews*, *26*(2), 3845–3852. DOI: 10.30574/wjarr.2025.26.2.2015

Panda, S. (2025). Scalable artificial intelligence architectures: Cloud-native, edge-AI, and hybrid models. 1–26. DOI: 10.70593/978-93-7185-753-6_1

Papaioannou, A., Dimara, A., Papaioannou, A., Tzitzios, I., Anagnostopoulos, C.-N., & Krinidis, S. (2025, January). Dimara, A. Papaioannou, I. Tzitzios, C. Anagnostopoulos, and S. Krinidis, "Hierarchical Resources Management System for Internet of Things-Enabled Smart Cities,". *Sensors (Basel)*, *25*(3), 616. DOI: 10.3390/s25030616 PMID: 39943255

Parlapalli, V., Ganeeb, K. K., Bidkar, D. M., Veerapaneni, P. K., Sankiti, S. R., & Harve, B. M. (2025). AI-Powered Smart Cities. *Data-Driven Approaches for Urban Innovation and Sustainability*, (Jun), 232–237. DOI: 10.1109/CCNCPS66785.2025.11135701

Pasham, S. D. (2022). Hybrid Cloud Computing Models: A Framework for High-Performance Applications. Research and Analysis Journal, 5(2), 01–24. DOI: 10.18535/raj.v5i2.274

Pasupuleti, M. K. (2025). AI 3.0. *The Evolution of Intelligence and the Future of Humanity*, (Feb), 40–49. DOI: 10.62311/nesx/68137

Pasupuleti, M. K. (2025). Quantum AI Revolution. *The Future of Intelligent Computing*, (Apr). Advance online publication. DOI: 10.62311/nesx/rb25

Pasupuleti, M. K. (2025). Smart Cities Unleashed. *Integrating AI, IoT, and Blockchain for Sustainable Urban Development*, (Apr). Advance online publication. DOI: 10.62311/nesx/rb8

Patel, J. K. (2025). A Review of Artificial Intelligence Applications in Cloud Operations: Automation, Optimization, and Future Directions. International Journal of Advanced Research in Science. *Tongxin Jishu*, •••, 489–499. DOI: 10.48175/IJARSCT-28349

Paul, S., Ghosh, S., Das, D., & Sarkar, S. K. (2024). Advanced Methodologies for Optimal Neural Network Design and Performance Enhancement. Advances in Computer and Electrical Engineering Book Series, 403–422. DOI: 10.4018/979-8-3693-6834-3.ch014

Pavunraj, J. (2025). Jayalakshmi, S. Nawaz, K. Anbumaheshwari, and A. Mathankumar. *The Role of IoT for Smart Cities*, (Apr), 341–370. DOI: 10.4018/979-8-3373-0761-9.ch015

Pennington, J., Socher, R., & Manning, C. D. (2014, October). Glove: Global vectors for word representation. In *Proceedings of the 2014 conference on empirical methods in natural language processing (EMNLP)* (pp. 1532-1543). DOI: 10.3115/v1/D14-1162

Perín, H. P. Y. Castro, E. Filho, and J. S. B. Martins, "Smart City in Contemporary Times with Internet of Things and Artificial Intelligence," May 2025, doi: DOI: 10.31235/osf.io/r36yg_v1

Phan, T. D., Nguyen, H. Q., Nghi, H. K., Tran, T.-D., & Pham, V.-H. (2023). FedChain-Hunter: A reliable and privacy-preserving aggregation for federated threat hunting framework in SDN-based IIoT. *Internet of Things : Engineering Cyber Physical Human Systems*, *24*, 100966. Advance online publication. DOI: 10.1016/j.iot.2023.100966

Prabhakaran, S. P. (2024). Integration Patterns in Unified AI and Cloud Platforms: A Systematic Review of Process Automation Technologies. International Journal of Scientific Research in Computer Science. *Engineering and Information Technology*, *10*(6), 1932–1940. DOI: 10.32628/CSEIT241061229

Prabhakar, S. K., & Won, D.-O. (2024). A Methodical Framework Utilizing Transforms and Biomimetic Intelligence-Based Optimization with Machine Learning for Speech Emotion Recognition. *Biomimetics*, *9*(9), 513. DOI: 10.3390/biomimetics9090513 PMID: 39329535

Prangon, N. F., & Wu, J. (2024). AI and Computing Horizons: Cloud and Edge in the Modern Era. *Journal of Sensor and Actuator Networks*, *13*(4), 44. DOI: 10.3390/jsan13040044

Prasad, M. V. S., & Subrahmanyam, V. V. (2025). Intelligent IoT-Enabled Framework for Sustainable Smart Cities. *International Journal of Science and Research (Raipur, India)*, (Sep), 406–409. DOI: 10.21275/SR25910183656

Preskill, J. (2018). Quantum computing in the NISQ era and beyond. *Quantum : the Open Journal for Quantum Science*, *2*, 79. DOI: 10.22331/q-2018-08-06-79

Pruthvi, T. (2025). Optimizing data processing through edge-cloud integration: A comprehensive framework. *International Journal (Toronto, Ont.)*, *11*(1), 3374–3383.

Qi, J., Yang, C.-H. H., Chen, P., & Hsieh, M.-H. (2025). VQC-MLPNet: An Unconventional Hybrid Quantum-Classical Architecture for Scalable and Robust Quantum Machine Learning. DOI: 10.21203/rs.3.rs-6735319/v1

Quantum, I. B. M. (2026). *IBM Quantum Computing*. https://www.ibm.com/quantum

Rajak, B., Pradhan, R., Mohapatra, S., Aljawarneh, N. M., Srithar, A., &Balakumar, A. (2025). Hybrid Fog-Cloud Architectures for Enhanced IoT Scalability and Performance. 1–6. DOI: 10.1109/ISAC364032.2025.11156520

Rakkini, M. J. J., Mohanram, R., Dheepak, G., Subha, S., Hemalatha, R., & Suresh, M. (2025). Transformer-Based Intrusion Detection Systems: a Deep Federated Learning Approach for Privacypreserving Cybersecurity. 216–223. DOI: 10.1109/ICDICI66477.2025.11134874

Ramamoorthi, V. (2023). Exploring AI-Driven Cloud-Edge Orchestration for IoT Applications. International Journal of Scientific Research in Computer Science, Engineering and Information Technology, 385–393. DOI: 10.32628/CSEIT239072

Rampelli, M., Vaidya, S., Jena, P. K., Ashok, S., &Dasari, S. (2025). Machine Learning and Federated Learning in Industrial Cybersecurity. Advances in Computational Intelligence and Robotics Book Series, 407–438. DOI: 10.4018/979-8-3373-3241-3.ch020

Rane, J., Kaya, Ö., Mallick, S. K., &Rane, N. (2024). Artificial intelligence, machine learning, and deep learning in cloud, edge, and quantum computing: A review of trends, challenges, and future directions. DOI: 10.70593/978-81-981271-0-5_1

Rani, R., & Ramaiya, M. (2024). Emotion Recognition on Speech using Hybrid Model CNN and BI-LSTM Techniques. DOI: 10.21203/rs.3.rs-5035263/v1

Rao, V. (2024). Enhancing Data Processing Efficiency: The Synergy of Edge Computing and Hybrid Cloud Storage. International Journal of Scientific Research in Computer Science. *Engineering and Information Technology*, *10*(5), 762–771. DOI: 10.32628/CSEIT241051063

Ren, L., Dong, J., Zhang, L., Laili, Y., Wang, X., Qi, Y., Li, B. H., Wang, L., Yang, L. T., & Deen, M. J. (2024). Industrial Metaverse for Smart Manufacturing: Model, Architecture, and Applications. *IEEE Transactions on Cybernetics*, *54*(5), 2683–2695. DOI: 10.1109/TCYB.2024.3372591 PMID: 38512748

Ribeiro, M. T., Singh, S., & Guestrin, C. (2016, August). " Why should i trust you?" Explaining the predictions of any classifier. In *Proceedings of the 22nd ACM SIGKDD international conference on knowledge discovery and data mining* (pp. 1135-1144). DOI: 10.18653/v1/N16-3020

Rodrigues, V. F., da Rosa Righi, R., da Costa, C. A., Zeiser, F. A., Eskofier, B., Maier, A., & Kim, D. (2023, April). R. da R. Righi, C. A. da Costa, F. A. Zeiser, A. Maier, and D. Kim, "Digital health in smart cities: Rethinking the remote health monitoring architecture on combining edge, fog, and cloud,". *Health and Technology*, *13*(3), 449–472. DOI: 10.1007/s12553-023-00753-3 PMID: 37303980

Rodríguez-Díaz, F., Gutiérrez-Avilés, D., Troncoso, A., & Martínez-Álvarez, F. (2025). A Survey of Quantum Machine Learning: Foundations, Algorithms, Frameworks, Data and Applications. *ACM Computing Surveys*, (Sep). Advance online publication. DOI: 10.1145/3764582

Rokade, G. P., Hendre, R., Deshmukh, V., Wavhal, S., &Ajalkar, D. (2025). Federated Learning Based Privacy Preservation Intrusion Detection Using Blockchain Technology. 2954–2963. DOI: 10.38124/ijisrt/25aug074

Rovelli, C. (2022). *Helgoland: Making sense of the quantum revolution*. Penguin.

Sadiq, T., & Omlin, C. W. (2025). Sensing in Smart Cities: A Multimodal Machine Learning Perspective. *Smart Cities*, *9*(1), 3.

Saidi, A., & Khouri, A. O. (2025). Enhancing Data Privacy in Intrusion Detection: A Federated Learning Framework With Differential Privacy. *Concurrency and Computation*, *37*(18–20), e70186. Advance online publication. DOI: 10.1002/cpe.70186

Samrat, S., & Manjunath, S. J. (2024). "Leveraging IoT, AI, and ML for Enhanced Decision-Making in Karnataka's Smart Cities." Volume. 9 Issue.7, July - 2024 International Journal of Innovative Science and Research Technology (IJISRT), www.ijisrt.com. ISSN - 2456-2165, PP:- 2302-2306, https://doi.org/DOI: 10.38124/ijisrt/IJISRT24JUL1317

Samuel, A. (2024). Quantum Neural Networks the Next Leap in Artificial Intelligence. *Quantum Neural Networks the Next Leap in Artificial Intelligence.*, *2*(3), 33–48. DOI: 10.64206/896gx364

Sarhan, M., Layeghy, S., Moustafa, N., & Portmann, M. (2022). Cyber Threat Intelligence Sharing Scheme Based on Federated Learning for Network Intrusion Detection. *Journal of Network and Systems Management*, *31*(1), 3. Advance online publication. DOI: 10.1007/s10922-022-09691-3

Schuld, M., Bergholm, V., Gogolin, C., Izaac, J., & Killoran, N. (2019). Evaluating analytic gradients on quantum hardware. *Physical Review. A*, *99*(3), 032331. DOI: 10.1103/PhysRevA.99.032331

Schuld, M., Bocharov, A., Svore, K. M., & Wiebe, N. (2020). Circuit-centric quantum classifiers. *Physical Review. A*, *101*(3), 032308. DOI: 10.1103/PhysRevA.101.032308

Schuld, M., & Killoran, N. (2019). Quantum machine learning in feature Hilbert spaces. *Physical Review Letters*, *122*(4), 040504. DOI: 10.1103/PhysRevLett.122.040504 PMID: 30768345

Schuld, M., & Petruccione, F. (2018). Supervised learning with quantum computers. *Quantum Science and Technology*, •••, 17.

Shah, B., Junaid, M., Rustam, H., Habib, M. A., & Anwar, S. "AI-Driven Fog-Edge Computing for IoMT Systems: Architecture and Use Cases," *Proceedings of the AAAI symposium series*, vol. 6, no. 1, pp. 42–48, Aug. 2025, DOI: 10.1609/aaaiss.v6i1.36023

Shaikh, M. S., & Ali, S. I. (2025). Smart Waste Management by Integrating Data Analytics, IoT, and AI for Sustainable Urban Solutions. *Smart Waste Management by Integrating Data Analytics, IoT, and AI for Sustainable Urban Solutions*, (Apr), 383–404. DOI: 10.4018/979-8-3373-0265-2.ch018

Sharma, M. (2025). Emotion Recognition from Text and Voice: A Multimodal AI Approach to Understanding Human Feelings. *International Journal for Research in Applied Science and Engineering Technology*, *13*(8), 1370–1377. DOI: 10.22214/ijraset.2025.73790

Sharma, S., Sharma, S. K., Sahu, A. K., & Sharma, A. (2024, August). Internet of Things (IoT) and Smart Cities. *Deleted Journal*, *2*(08), 2526–2531. DOI: 10.47392/IRJAEM.2024.0365

Shi, J., Wang, W., Lou, X., Zhang, S., & Li, X. (2022). Parameterized Hamiltonian Learning With Quantum Circuit. *IEEE Transactions on Pattern Analysis and Machine Intelligence*, *45*(5), 6086–6095. DOI: 10.1109/TPAMI.2022.3203157 PMID: 36044483

Shinde, B. B.Bipin Balu Shinde. (2025). A Comprehensive Review of Federated Learning Techniques for Privacy-Preserving Cybersecurity Applications. International Journal of Advanced Research in Science. *Tongxin Jishu, 404–408*, 404–408. Advance online publication. DOI: 10.48175/IJARSCT-28152

Shinde, S., & Chavan, T. U. (2024, September). Leveraging the Internet of Things (IoT) for Smart City Innovation: Exploring Applications, Overcoming Challenges, and Charting Future Pathways. *International Journal of Scientific Research in Modern Science and Technology*, *3*(9), 15–22. DOI: 10.59828/ijsrmst.v3i9.250

Shin, M., Lee, S., Lee, J., Lee, M., Ji, D., Yeo, H., & Jeong, K. (2024, December). Disentangling quantum neural networks for unified estimation of quantum entropies and distance measures. *Physical Review. A*, *110*(6), 062418. Advance online publication. DOI: 10.1103/PhysRevA.110.062418

Sinaeepourfard, S. S., & Mesgaribarzi, N. (2024). Decentralized, Distributed, and Hybrid ICT Architectures: Hierarchical Multitier Big Data Driven Management for Smart, Sustainable. *Scalable and Reliable Cities*, (Apr), 345–355. Advance online publication. DOI: 10.1109/SusTech60925.2024.10553566

Singamaneni, K. K., Budati, A. K., Kolandaisamy, R., Dommeti, V. S., & Katragadda, S. (2025). An Efficient Quantum Block chain Framework with Edge Computing for Privacy-Preserving 6G Networks. *IEEE Access : Practical Innovations, Open Solutions*, *13*, 135722–135740. DOI: 10.1109/ACCESS.2025.3592793

Singh, J., Chugh, A., Chauhan, S., & Singh, A. K. (2024). Chapter 3 Quantum machine learning algorithms: a comprehensive review. 37–52. DOI: 10.1515/9783111354842-003

Sobati-M, S. (2025). FOGNITE: Federated Learning-Enhanced Fog-Cloud Architecture. arXiv preprint arXiv:2507.16668.

Sowmiya, S., Nachimuthu, S., & Rao, A. N. (2025). Federated Learning for Distributed Threat Intelligence Sharing Across Global Cybersecurity Networks. 456–488. DOI: 10.71443/9789349552029-15

Strubell, E., Ganesh, A., & McCallum, A. (2019, July). Energy and policy considerations for deep learning in NLP. In *Proceedings of the 57th annual meeting of the association for computational linguistics* (pp. 3645-3650). DOI: 10.18653/v1/P19-1355

Subbiah, P., Krishnaraj, N., & Bellam, K. (2024). *Quantum Machine Learning*. IGI Global., DOI: 10.4018/979-8-3693-1168-4.ch008

Subrahmanyam, V. V., & Prasad, M. V. S. (2025). An Efficient and Innovative Edge Intelligence-Driven Latency-Aware Wireless Network Slicing Framework for Next-Generation Smart Cities. *International Journal of Science and Research (Raipur, India)*, (Sep), 1013–1017. DOI: 10.21275/SR25921171753

Sun, L. (2025, July). Theory, Practice and Empirical Analysis of Smart City. *Journal of Regional Economics and Development*, *2*(4), 8. DOI: 10.47134/jred.v2i4.840

Sutskever, I., Vinyals, O., & Le, Q. V. (2014). Sequence to sequence learning with neural networks. *Advances in Neural Information Processing Systems*, •••, 27.

Taiwo, I., Ogunbajo, A., & Abidola, A. Q. (2025). Quantum computing-Enhanced AI systems for advanced business intelligence applications. *International Journal of Science and Research Archive*, *14*(1), 1839–1847. DOI: 10.30574/ijsra.2025.14.1.0314

Talab, O. A., & Avci, I. (2025). Energy Management in Microgrids Using Model-Free Deep Reinforcement Learning Approach. *IEEE Access : Practical Innovations, Open Solutions*, *13*(Jan), 1. DOI: 10.1109/ACCESS.2025.3525843

Tandon, R., Verma, A., Kaur, M., Wadhwa, H., & Asirvatham, D. (2024). Management of metropolitan mobility for public transport and smart vehicles with fog computing. In *Cloud and Fog Optimization-based Solutions for Sustainable Developments* (pp. 48–76). CRC Press.

Tanji, A., Essaaidi, M., & Merabet, G. H. (2024, May). Towards an integrated smart city platform: A prototype for enhancing urban services. In *2024 Mediterranean Smart Cities Conference (MSCC)* (pp. 1-6). IEEE.

Tao, F., Zhang, H., Liu, A., & Nee, A. Y. C. (2019). Digital Twin in Industry: State-of-the-Art. *IEEE Transactions on Industrial Informatics*, *15*(4), 2405–2415. DOI: 10.1109/TII.2018.2873186

Tareen, F. N., Alvi, A. N., Alsamani, B., Alkhathami, M. S., Alsadie, D., & Alosaimi, N. (2024, April). EOTE-FSC: An efficient offloaded task execution for fog enabled smart cities. *PLoS One*, *19*(4), e0298363. Advance online publication. DOI: 10.1371/journal.pone.0298363 PMID: 38578775

Tatikonda, P. (2025). Optimizing Data Processing Through Edge-Cloud Integration: A Comprehensive Framework. International Journal of Scientific Research in Computer Science. *Engineering and Information Technology*, *11*(1), 3374–3383. DOI: 10.32628/CSEIT251112352

Temme, K., Bravyi, S., & Gambetta, J. M. (2017). Error mitigation for short-depth quantum circuits. *Physical Review Letters*, *119*(18), 180509. DOI: 10.1103/PhysRevLett.119.180509 PMID: 29219599

Tera, S. P., Chinthaginjala, R., Priyadarshi, R., & Deepthi, N. (2025). "Advancing AI with Quantum Computing: Theoretical Foundations and Future Challenges," DOI: 10.20944/preprints202506.1155.v1

Thiyagarajan, R., & Arivamudhan, M. (2025). Edge Computing and Fog Computing Paradigms for Ultra Low Latency IoT Based Smart City Applications. *Edge Computing and Fog Computing Paradigms for Ultra Low Latency IoT Based Smart City Applications*, (Apr), 73–101. DOI: 10.71443/9789349552241-03

Thomas, M., Choudhary, L., & Kishor, I. (2020, February). Analysis of Cloud Security and Performance for Leakage of Critical Information using DROPS Methodology [IRJET]. *International Research Journal of Engineering and Technology*, *7*(2), 1–6.

Thomas, R. K. (2023). Quantum Neural Networks: Bridging Quantum Computing and Machine Learning. *Asian Journal of Research in Computer Science*, *16*(3), 1–10. DOI: 10.9734/ajrcos/2023/v16i3340

Timofte, E. M., Dimian, M., Graur, A., Potorac, A. D., Croitoru, I. M., Hriţcan, D.-F., & Pu ca u, M. (2025). Federated Learning for Cybersecurity A Privacy-Preserving Approach. https://doi.org/DOI: 10.20944/preprints202505.1775.v1

Tripathi, S., Upadhyay, H., & Soni, J. (2025). Analysis of AnsätzeExpressibility and Complexity and their Impact on Classification Accuracy using QNN and QLSTM. *IEEE Access : Practical Innovations, Open Solutions*, *1*, 152412–152429. Advance online publication. DOI: 10.1109/ACCESS.2025.3604721

Trisnapradika, G. A., & Akrom, M. (2025). Synergizing Quantum Computing and Machine Learning: A Pathway Toward Quantum-Enhanced Intelligence. *Journal of Multiscale Materials Informatics*, *2*(1), 18–25. DOI: 10.62411/jimat.v2i1.12947

Tung, H. X., Trang, T. L., &Linh, V. K. (2024). Intrusion Detection Using Federated Learning in Non-IID Data Environments. NghiênC uKhoaH cvàCôngNgh TrongLĩnhV c an ToànThông Tin, 53–61. DOI: 10.54654/isj.v3i23.1061

Vankayalapati, R. K., Sondinti, L. R. K., Kalisetty, S., & Valiki, S. (2023). *Unifying Edge and Cloud Computing: A Framework for Distributed AI and Real-Time Processing*. Journal for ReAttach Therapy and Developmental Diversities., DOI: 10.53555/jrtdd.v6i9s(2).3348

Vaswani, A., Shazeer, N., Parmar, N., Uszkoreit, J., Jones, L., Gomez, A. N., & Polosukhin, I. (2017). Attention is all you need. *Advances in Neural Information Processing Systems*, •••, 30.

Velasquez-Mendez, J. de J., Lozoya-Santos, J. J., & Jiménez-Vargas, J. F. (2025, September). Lozoya-Santos, and F. Jiménez, "Validating a Sustainable, Smart, and Circular City Architecture Through Urban Living Lab Experiments,". *Urban Science (Basel, Switzerland)*, *9*(9), 377. DOI: 10.3390/urbansci9090377

Venkateswari, G. (2025). Voice Based Hybrid Sentiment Analysis on Movie Reviews. *International Journal for Research in Applied Science and Engineering Technology*, *13*(4), 6114–6119. DOI: 10.22214/ijraset.2025.69606

Verma, A., Prasad, V. K., Kumari, A., Bhattacharya, P., Srivastava, G., Fang, K., Wang, W., & Gadekallu, T. R. (2025). Industry 6.0: Vision, technical landscape, and opportunities. *Alexandria Engineering Journal*, *130*, 139–174. DOI: 10.1016/j.aej.2025.08.040

Verma, A., Singh, J., & Yadav, R. S. (2025). Smart cities in practice: IoT-enabled citizen engagement and local service delivery. *Lex Localis*, *23*(S5), 857–868.

Vishwakarma, M. D. K., & Sachdeva, S. (2025). A Distributed Computing Perspective. *Unveiling Cloud, Fog, and Edge Computing with Their Protocols and Applications*, (May), 1–6. DOI: 10.1109/IC2E365635.2025.11166804

von Foerster, H. (2003). *Understanding Understanding. Essays on Cybernetics and Cognition*. Springer New York., DOI: 10.1007/b97451

Vyas, A., Lin, P.-C., Hwang, R.-H., & Tripathi, M. (n.d.). *Privacy-Preserving Federated Learning for Intrusion Detection in IoT Environments: A Survey*. IEEE., DOI: 10.1109/ACCESS.2024.3454211

Wang, B., Baziar, A., & Askari, M. (2025). A Deep Reinforcement Learning Framework for Adaptive Resiliency Enhancement in Smart Power Grids. *IEEE Access : Practical Innovations, Open Solutions*, *13*(Jan), 1. DOI: 10.1109/ACCESS.2025.3593903

Wang, W., Xu, J., Liu, F., Zhou, B., Wang, W., Wang, H., Du, Q., Yuan, B., Huang, Y., Hou, Y., Ding, X., & Shan, Z. (2025). Lightweight Quantum Neural Networks Intelligent Generation. *Advanced Quantum Technologies*, *8*(Aug), e00302. Advance online publication. DOI: 10.1002/qute.202500302

Xiang, D., & Chen, M. (2025, October). AdaptDQC: Adaptive Distributed Quantum Computing with Quantitative Performance Analysis. *IEEE Transactions on Computers*, *74*(10), 3277–3290. Advance online publication. DOI: 10.1109/TC.2025.3586027

Yalla, R. K. M. K., Devarajan, M. V., Ganesan, T., Yallamelli, A. R. G., Mamidala, V., & Sambas, A. (2025). Securing Cloud-Edge Collaborative Computing with AI, GANs, TEEs, Micro Data Centers, and Cloud-Oriented DevOps for Privacy Protection. *International Journal of Automation and Smart Technology*, *15*(1). Advance online publication. DOI: 10.5875/xyfd7w08

Yamane, T., Hirose, A., & Offrein, B. J. (2023). Editorial: Physical neuromorphic computing and its industrial applications. *Frontiers in Neuroinformatics*, *17*, 1238168–1238168. DOI: 10.3389/fninf.2023.1238168 PMID: 37529766

Yan, S., Xu, Y., Gong, Z., & Herrera-Viedma, E. (2025). Fuzzy Quantum Group Decision Making and Its Application in Meteorological Disaster Emergency. *IEEE Transactions on Fuzzy Systems*, •••, 1–13. DOI: 10.1109/TFUZZ.2025.3641578

Yao, X., Ma, N., Zhang, J., Wang, K., Yang, E., & Faccio, M. (2024). Enhancing wisdom manufacturing as industrial metaverse for industry and society 5.0. *Journal of Intelligent Manufacturing*, *35*(1), 235–255. DOI: 10.1007/s10845-022-02027-7

Yaseen, H., Quyyum, A., Bajwa, M. A., Afzal, M. K., Fatima, R., & Akhtar, A. M. (2025, September). Synergizing Cloud Computing and AI for Next-Generation Smart Cities. *Deleted Journal*, *5*(3), 229–244. DOI: 10.62019/ajvc2611

Yousif, M., & Al-Khateeb, B. (2024). Quantum Deep Learning: A Review. *Iraqi Journal of Science*, •••, 4576–4587. DOI: 10.24996/ijs.2024.65.8.37

Yu, S.. (2024). Shedding Light on the Future: Exploring Quantum Neural Networks through Optics. *Advanced Quantum Technologies*, (Sep). Advance online publication. DOI: 10.1002/qute.202400074

Zeng, F., Pang, C., & Tang, H. (2024). Sensors on internet of things systems for the sustainable development of smart cities: A systematic literature review. *Sensors (Basel)*, *24*(7), 2074.

Zhang, B. (2024). Quantum Neural Networks: A New Frontier. *Theoretical and Natural Science*, *41*(1), 122–128. DOI: 10.54254/2753-8818/41/2024CH0157

Zhao, R.-X., Shi, J., & Li, X. (2024). QKSAN: A Quantum Kernel Self-Attention Network. *IEEE Transactions on Pattern Analysis and Machine Intelligence*, *46*(12), 1–12. DOI: 10.1109/TPAMI.2024.3434974 PMID: 39074010

Zheng, P.-L., Wang, J., & Zhang, Y. (2023, October). Efficient and quantum-adaptive machine learning with fermion neural networks. *Physical Review Applied*, *20*(4), 044002. Advance online publication. DOI: 10.1103/PhysRevApplied.20.044002

Zhuang, Y., Azfar, T., Wang, Y., Sun, W., Wang, X., Guo, Q., & Ke, R. (2024). Quantum Computing in Intelligent Transportation Systems: A Survey. *CHAIN*, *1*(2), 138–149. DOI: 10.23919/CHAIN.2024.000007

Zhu, Y., Liang, Y., & Situ, H. (2025). Enhancing variational quantum circuit training: An improved neural network approach for barren plateau mitigation. *Physica Scripta*, *100*(8), 086004. DOI: 10.1088/1402-4896/adf0ae

Zrigui, I., Khoulji, S., & Kerkeb, M. L. (2025). Integrated strategy for urban traffic optimization: Prediction, adaptive signal control, and distributed communication via messaging. arXiv preprint arXiv:2501.02008.

About the Contributors

Surbhi B. Khan is working in the School of Science, Engineering and Environment at the University of Salford, United Kingdom. She is Project Management Professional Certified from PMP, USA. She is ranked among the top 2% of scientists globally for the second year in a row (2023 and 2024). She is supervising/co-supervising a number of PhDs and research associates. She has published over 250 articles and books in high indexed outlets with her students and colleagues and also has been granted patents from USA. She is also serving as Deputy EIC in TCE letters, Associate editor in IEEE Transactions on Consumer Electronics, HCIS and EAAI journals and Guest editor in many other reputed journals. She is working in KTP Projects Innovate UK and has submitted grants as a CO-PI in HORIZON-EIC-2025-PATHFINDEROPEN. She is also working in external funding from India, and Middle Eastern Institutes. She is a senior member of IEEE and has been serving as session chairs in many IEEE conferences, been invited as a resource person at International Conferences and FDP 39s and has holds honorary positions, providing guidance to universities in pursuit of research and teaching excellence. She is also a member in the Women in Data Science Ambassador. Her research interests are Machine Learning/Deep learning, Data Science in Healthcare and IoT, Text analytics and detection, and Sentiment Analysis.

Shikha Khullar is an accomplished academic and researcher with more than 14 years of experience in computer science and emerging technologies. Her expertise lies in artificial intelligence, computational intelligence, and their applications in areas such as fraud detection, intelligent agriculture, cloud security, federated learning, and blockchain. She has authored and contributed to several international publications and book chapters with reputed publishers including IGI Global and Wiley–Scrivener. Alongside her research, Dr. Khullar is deeply committed to teaching and mentoring, guiding students to apply technology for real-world problem-solving. Her vision emphasizes innovation, sustainability, and bridging the gap between academia and industry.

Muhammad Attique Khan (Member, IEEE) received the master's in computer science and Ph.D. degrees in human activity recognition for application of video surveillance and skin lesion classification using deep learning from COMSATS University Islamabad, Islamabad, Pakistan, in 2018 and 2022, respectively.,He is currently an Assistant Professor with AI Department, Prince Mohammad Bin Fahd, Al-Khobar, Saudi Arabia. His primary research focus in recent years is medical imaging, COVID-19, MRI analysis, video surveillance, human gait recognition, and agricultural plants using deep learning. He has above 350 publications that have more than 16 000+ citations and an impact factor of 1050+ with an h-index 74 and an i-index 230. He is the reviewer of several reputed journals, such as IEEE Transactions on Industrial Informatics, IEEE Transactions of Neural Networks, Pattern Recognition Letters, Multimedia Tools and Application, Computers and Electronics in Agriculture, IET Image Processing, Biomedical Signal Processing Control, IET Computer Vision, EURASIP Journal of Image and Video Processing, IEEE Access, MDPI Sensors, MDPI Electronics, MDPI Applied Sciences, MDPI Diagnostics, and MDPI Cancers.

Udit Mamodiya is an Associate Professor and Associate Dean (Research) at Poornima University, Jaipur. With over 11 years of teaching, research, and administrative experience, his expertise spans renewable energy systems, industrial automation, IoT- based smart product development, and artificial intelligence applications. He has authored 60+ research publications in SCI/Scopus/UGC Care journals (with 600+ citations, h-index 15+), published 19 engineering books, and contributed as Guest Editor for Scopus-indexed journals. His innovation portfolio includes 50+ patents (6 granted), 18 design patents, and 9 copyrights. Dr. Mamodiya has successfully secured research grants worth 51.89 lakhs, including an AICTE-funded IDEA Lab project of 50.39 lakhs, making his institution the only one in Rajasthan with such a lab. He is an active reviewer, editor, and committee member for several international conferences and journals, and a member of professional bodies like ACM, ISTE, IRED, and ASR. His contributions have been recognized with multiple awards, including the Global Educational Award 2020, Asian Excellence Award 2019, and two Gold Medals (B.Tech & M.Tech).

Manju Lata Joshi, Professor, Poornima University, India holds an M.Tech. and a Doctorate in Computer Science from Banasthali Vidyapith. Her current research interests encompass Artificial Intelligence, Natural Language Processing, Information Retrieval, and Text Mining. With over 17 years of experience in teaching and research, she has published research papers in prestigious journals indexed in the Science Citation Index (SCI) and Scopus, both nationally and internationally. Furthermore, she serve on the review and advisory committees of several refereed journals and conferences. She has contributed to multiple institutions, mentored students, and led research in AI-based document clustering, sentiment analysis, and information retrieval. She is also actively involved in academic advisory boards, technical committees, and conferences.

***

Soleman Alzobidy received the Ph.D. degree in linguistics from the University of Mysore, Mysore, India, in 2015. He is currently an Assistant Professor of Linguistics in the Department of Linguistics at Saudi Electronic University, Riyadh, Saudi Arabia, where he has been a faculty member since 2016. His research interests include linguistics, computational linguistics, machine translation, and translation studies.

María Jesús Ávila-Gutiérrez is an Associate Professor in the Project Engineering area within the Department of Design Engineering at the Higher Polytechnic School, University of Seville. Her research focuses on holonic and cyber-physical systems, artificial intelligence (including agent-based and knowledge-driven approaches), and sustainability engineering for industrial and sociotechnical systems. She works on topics such as holonic manufacturing and project management, multi-agent systems, digital twins, systems interoperability, and sustainability assessment aligned with the triple bottom line.

Neeraj Chandnani is currently associated with the Multidisciplinary Department for Innovation and Entrepreneurship (MDI&E) and the Department of Electronics and Communication Engineering at Koneru Lakshmaiah (KL) College of Engineering, Koneru Lakshmaiah Education Foundation (KLEF), Deemed to be University, Vaddeswaram, Guntur, Andhra Pradesh, India. He is also pursuing his Post-Doctoral research from Eudoxia Research University, USA, at the Eudoxia Research Centre, India. Dr. Chandnani earned his Doctor of Philosophy (Ph.D.) from Devi Ahilya Vishwavidyalaya, Indore, having conducted his research work at the Research Centre, Military College of Telecommunication Engineering, Mhow, Madhya Pradesh, India. His doctoral research focused on Secure Data Aggregation by Bio-Inspired Internet of Things Environment (SBI-IoT).

Prasanta Chatterjee Biswas is a Doctorate in Statistics with over 25 years of extensive experience in teaching, training, and development at both undergraduate and postgraduate levels. Throughout his professional journey, he has been committed to facilitating learning through interactive discussions, practical exercises, and "hands-on" approaches, ensuring that students not only grasp theoretical concepts but also apply them effectively in real-world scenarios. His expertise spans quantitative techniques, research methodology, multivariate analysis, and business analytics, making his a versatile educator and mentor in the field of statistics and analytics. He has been recognized for his ability to simplify complex statistical concepts, making them accessible and engaging for students. He has successfully guided numerous students in understanding advanced statistical procedures, modelling techniques, and analytical tools, fostering both academic excellence and practical problem-solving skills. He emphasizes experiential learning, encouraging students to work with real datasets, perform statistical analysis, and interpret results accurately. He has published 25 research articles in peer reviewed journals (Scopus / WOS / ABDC), book chapters and presented papers in national and international conferences in hybrid mode.

Yogendra Chhetri, M.Tech from ISRO, is a serving Wing Commander of Indian Air Force and is appointed as Joint Director (Space Operations), Ministry of Defence, New Delhi. Currently, he is pursuing his doctoral research in the area of Artificial Intelligence

Francisco Ramón Lara-Raya is a Collaborating Lecturer in the Department of Electrical Engineering and Automation at the University of Córdoba (Higher Polytechnic School, Campus de Rabanales). His research interests include power quality (techno-economic, energy and environmental impacts), dynamic analysis of electrical systems, electrical installations, instrumentation and communication protocols, and acoustic noise/sound quality in rotating electrical machines and inverter-fed induction motors.

Jui Pattnayak is working as a Professor in the department of Information Technology at JIS College of Engineering, Kolkata, West Bengal. She was graduated in Computer Science and Engineering from Orissa Engineering College, Odisha. She has awarded Ph.D. in Inf. & Comm. Technology (Computer Sci.) from Fakir Mohan University, Odisha. She has about 8 years of Industry Experience and is in teaching profession for about more than 20 years. She has published/presented more than 20 research papers at National and International level. She has also published number of research patents and text books. She is the life member of various professional societies such as CSI, ISTE, IE AND OITS. her main area of interest includes Programming, Database, Algorithms, Networking, AI, IoT, Cloud Computing, etc.

Mohit Tiwari is an Assistant Professor in the Department of Computer Science and Engineering at Bharati Vidyapeeth's College of Engineering, New Delhi. He specializes in Cybersecurity, Artificial Intelligence, Cloud Computing, and Technology-Driven Educational Innovation. With a strong academic background that combines a B.Tech in Computer Science, an MBA in Operations Research, and ongoing doctoral research in AI-driven Cyber Maturity Frameworks, he brings a multidisciplinary perspective to both teaching and research. His research contributions span cybersecurity maturity modelling, AI-enabled risk prediction, secure cloud architectures, digital transformation in higher education, and explainable machine learning. He has authored and co-authored numerous research papers in Scopus-indexed journals and international conferences, and has filed multiple patents and copyrights in emerging technology domains. He also serves as a reviewer and editorial board member for several reputed journals and conferences in cybersecurity and AI. Prof. Tiwari is actively engaged in curriculum development, outcome-based education (OBE), and institutional innovation initiatives. He mentors multiple industry-aligned student projects, coordinates incubation and entrepreneurship activities, and leads cybersecurity and network research initiatives in his department. His professional engagements include delivering expert talks, conducting training programs, and collaborating with academic and industry stakeholders on AI and security-focused research. He is committed to advancing research, promoting student innovation, and contributing to India's digital transformation through responsible and secure technology adoption.

Index

A

B

C

D

E

F

H

I

N

P

Q

R

S

T

V

www.ingramcontent.com/pod-product-compliance
Lightning Source LLC
LaVergne TN
LVHW081534300926
849161LV00006B/1421